RICK J

MW00529786

READER:

'Tin Cans, Squeems & Thudpies'

Edited by Bill Knight

Mayfly Productions
Elmwood, Ill.

Published by BookSurge, LLC

First U.S. edition

Grateful acknowledgment is made to the following for permission to reprint previously published material:

"Sin City Social," "Rot your teeth, not your mind," " I call on Hoot 'n' Annie," "Loverboy: because they're there," and "Duets from hell!" first appeared in *CREEM* magazine, and the video-game material in "More fun than a bakeoff and a bloodbath combined" first appeared in *VIDIOT*, all used with permission of CREEM Media, Inc. Thanks to Robert Matheu, Brian J. Bowe and Dave DiMartino.

Introduction reprinted in part from the *Chicago Sun-Times* by permission of the author.

Westside Crop Circles review reprinted by permission of Steve Kilpatrick.

Eminem *Curtain Call* and the Rolling Stones *A Bigger Bang* reviews reprinted by permission of Robert Rowe.

"Mondo, modo, dodo & doo-doo" is excerpted from an interview that originally appeared on Scott Woods' rockcritics.com web site.

Special thanks to Louise Fleishman, Jeff Dunn, George Guzzardo, WIU journalism students Rob Arroyo, Amber Chibucos, Chris Rogers, Kevin Warzala and Tiffany Zack, and Knox College student Rusty Baker.

Rick Johnson Reader: 'Tin Cans, Squeems & Thudpies'
ISBN 978-0-9789156-0-5

Edited by Bill Knight
Designed by Bob Johnson

Printed in the United States of America

Cover photo: Joan Jett and the Blackhearts threaten Rick Johnson and his trademark ponytail with a pair of scissors, circa 1985.
Clockwise from left: Gary Ryan, Lee Crystal, Ricky Byrd, Joan Jett and Rick Johnson.

Contents

Preface 4

Foreword 6

Introduction 8

"Bloato hype, gerbiltones & smellbags" -
MUSIC 11

"Norelco fear" -
TV 161

"A lot about nothing" -
SLEAZEDOWN STORIES 179

"Bambam" -
SPORTS 202

"Weenie Earthlings, cranium pivots & the U.S. of Rick" -
BOOKS 218

"More fun than a bakeoff and a bloodbath combined" -
VIDEO GAMES 224

"A peek at Reek" -
RANGER PROFILE 232

"This is my room" -
LYRICS 233

"Mondo, modo, dodo & doo-doo" -
Q&A 240

"Ranger Rick's Final Ride" -
LAST REVIEWS 242

About those who helped out 247

Preface

By Bill Knight

This anthology is more than a collection of decades-old writing, good deed or act of closure. The *Rick Johnson Reader* is a tribute to a talent who earned respect from old fans who'll enjoy a one-stop jolt of Johnson and from new readers who'll discover a zany genius.

When Rick died unexpectedly in the spring of 2006, shock echoed from his friends through his one-time colleagues to his readers. During his life, Rick made a lot of fans since he was first paid to write a review in 1972 for the Boston-based *Fusion* magazine. After his death, some said it was too bad that there was little of Johnson's unique writing available, particularly his early work. So 24 of his former co-conspirators at *SunRise* magazine and the *Prairie SUN* weekly newspaper– some he'd never met, or run into only as volleyball teammates on *Prairie SUN* "writers retreats"– volunteered to type thousands of words from his reviews and other stories from 1972-1984, which are supplemented here with a handful of *CREEM* pieces and a couple of reviews done in the 21st century.

(You'll find Rick's writings here organized roughly chronologically, then by artist.)

Any profits from this project will be donated to a journalism scholarship fund at Western Illinois University, where Rick went to school and began to write in a style that set him apart from the pack.

"I regard Rick Johnson as Lester Bangs' and Richard Meltzer's equal as a rock writer," says fellow critic Richard Riegel, a Johnson pal who helped with this anthology, "even though his style was very different (actually more 'postmodern,' for whatever that's worth) from theirs, especially in the way he constantly satirized the ever-encroaching corporate culture by 'sampling' TV-commercial catchphrases into his rockwriting and showing how media-saturated we were all becoming."

Such culture commentary extended from rock to TV, another ex-colleague recalls.

"Rick Johnson wrote like we thought – or wanted to think," says Steve Tarter, a media critic and reporter for the Peoria (Ill.) *Journal Star.* "His prose was both lively and outrageous, but – above all – he made you smile as he lowered the boom.

"Writing about television – a time-honored venue for the ambitious critic (go back and read TV reviews by the likes of Harlan Ellison and the *Village Voice's* James Wolcott) – gave Rick the opportunity to train his sights on U.S. society at its most expressive and excessive," Tarter adds.

"You have to be inventive: 'Joe Don Baker plays a cop who's tougher than landlady sweat,' Johnson wrote. He described the cast of some short-lived TV show as having 'the collective personality of a silent alarm.'

"He moved us all and we need to be moved."

CREEM associate Dave DiMartino agrees. Johnson was "one of the finest writers in *CREEM* magazine's history, and by far one of the most inventive.

"Rick was a warm, very sincere, very talented person whose writing influenced an entire generation of music and humor fans," DiMartino continues. "No one has ever successfully imitated his writing style, and no one ever will. He deserved every accolade accorded him and more."

Besides his contemporaries, people who observed Johnson him from different ends of the creative spectrum praise him: publishers and musicians.

"Rick Johnson was the greatest rock critic ever," says Robert Rowe, who hired Rick to write a couple of reviews for Rowe's music news web site Musicblat. "He was simply more concise, more humorous, and more imaginative than any other music writer.

"He was one of the greatest nonfiction writers of the 20th century," Rowe continues, "and there will never be another like him."

Rich Stim of the band MX-80 was reviewed by Johnson, who later struck up a friendship with Stim and his wife Angel.

"If you've ever sat in front of a keyboard and tried to write a review, an article or fiction, then you can admire the freedom (and fearlessness) with which Rick Johnson approached his typewriter," Stim recalls.

"Rick was a graduate of the Lester Bangs/Richard Meltzer school of free-associative rock criticism. If Bangs was the Jackson Pollock of rock criticism, then Rick was more of a Warhol. He had no detectable sense of self-importance, he was fascinated by pop culture, and he was nonjudg-mental about its superficiality," he continues. "Rick approached the developing world of TV celebrity worship and crap-marketing synergy with archaeological glee. For Rick, it was all equal in importance.

"A letter from Rick once ended, 'You never know how boring you really are 'til you type it up.'

"Not true, Rick."

We all were lucky to know Rick in some way. Now more are lucky to read him.

As Johnson might write, That's no bloato-hype.

Foreword:

Dear SOOOOOOO ... Best, REEEEEEEK

By Susan Whitall
Detroit News

I don't remember exactly when I lucked out and became Rick Johnson's editor at *CREEM*, but his postcards and the letters soon became such a tonic in my frantic life that I saved many of them, not to mention all the Detroit Tigers baseball cards he tucked in.

He wrote endlessly, frequently, just as he couldn't stop writing stories and reviews, and I couldn't imagine a time when he would stop.

The notes start off *Dear Sooooooooooooo* or *Essence of Creamcheez*, or *My Dearest Louise* (my middle name) or *Hey Bob-a-Lou, Hey Lulu, Hey Loopy Lou, Hi you animal, Scotty snoot* or *Hey babydoll.*

He would then proceed to list the "Beat Goes On" stories or CREEMedia reviews he was enclosing. Then came the story pitches, written in classic Reeek style:

- *TERRIBLE SECRETS OF BLUE OYSTER CULT. Feat like Queen but with more text. This is one band I've got down plus there's a pile of press upstairs ...It'll be 92% favorable coz I would ignore their last 2 or 3.*

- *THE RICHARD SIMMONS SHOW – I dunno if you've seen this on dee-troit tv, but it's getting popular fast. He's this creepy little jagbag ala Vidal, with tubs of fake sincerity and...HE JUST MAKES ME SICK!!! Did I mention it's an exercise show? Fish in the barrel.*

- *You DID want 18,000 words on my reaction to Ocean Spray's new cran-grape drink, didn't you?*

- *THE RICK JOHNSON STORY – 200,000 wds (serialized to take up about four years of Creemedia) (all leads, of course) about how a mentally disabled but plucky young writer burst out of Chicago's South Side to become one of the national's leading experts on raccoon psychology. Hey, when I was in Chi over xmas, my dad took me by our old apt at 69th & Stony Island and we discovered it's been torn down to build a big garage for garbage trucks. Talk about fate!*

I rarely changed his copy, which he loved, muttering darkly about how others tampered with his sterling prose. I did turn down a few Rick ideas – well maybe one or two. He tweaked me: *"At this rate I'm going to be able to put out Rick's Rejects every week."*

Rick had his magnificent obsessions. We talked a lot about baseball, and he taunted me when Ron LeFlore was traded by the Tigers and ended up with the White Sox. For several letters he ranted about wanting to review some Vidal Sassoon TV show, until the fresh outrage of the Richard Simmons show diverted his attention.

Once he conceded that he'd been wrong about Elvis Costello.

PS You were RIGHT about Elvis C!!! I admit it!!! Ever since what you wrote about him, something clicked in my "ears" and now I'm playing all his LPs to death! Now – to be fair – you have to start watching BRADY BUNCH.

I apparently told Rick about how we could buy legal 222s (half codeine, half aspirin pills) across the river in Windsor, because there are innumerable references to his dear editor "Whiteside" or "All-Wheat" or "Soozie-Q" stumbling around in a "codeine trance" or crawling in the gutter looking for a codeine script.

Then there were the personal updates.

I have to move again in 2 1/2 weeks to a WORSE DUMP, can you believe it? And it's on the 3rd floor – FOUR ENTIRE STAIRWAYS from Earth. Why don't you guys start paying $1,000 for BGOs?

There were no health benefits for freelancers, so when Rick, on a self-described bender, fell down not only his stairs but his neighbors' stairs as well, the neighbors took him to the hospital. Of course he couldn't pay for his treatment.

Miraculously, he hadn't broken anything, telling me that was probably because his body was "a basket of Crisco from all the booze," but he suffered extensive cuts and bruises. Although his letter is full of the usual frantic, hilarious description, I picked up on a serious tone that worried me.

I told *CREEM* publisher Barry Kramer that we had to help, and he quickly wrote out a check for Rick for a couple hundred in "just because" money. He was worth it to the magazine 10 times over, and I was grateful Barry realized that.

In person, Rick was a tall, enigmatic Swede; the opposite of his hyperkinetic writing persona. He wrote hilariously about a visit Richard Riegel and his wife made to sleepy Macomb, Ill., to visit.

"Quiet Rich" and "Bashful Rick," the best of friends long distance, didn't say much when they were face to face.

But Rick had a rich inner life that we could enjoy thanks to all that bashing away on his benighted, ribbon-challenged typewriter.

Dear Rick (pronounced "REEEK"), we loved you then and we love you still.

Introduction

By Jim DeRogatis

Pop music critic
Chicago Sun-Times

Rick Johnson was a rock writer whose work should be much better known, and few who read him from 1975 through '88, the years in which he succeeded Lester Bangs as the funniest and most incisive wisecracking bad boy at the late, lamented *CREEM* magazine, will ever forget him. His fans included Bangs himself (who died in 1982) and Dave Barry, the syndicated columnist who cites Johnson as an influence on his own irreverent sense of humor.

Johnson was found dead in his apartment in Macomb last April. He was 55, the victim of what an autopsy showed was a series of heart attacks over years – despite clichéd suspicions otherwise. (Johnson lived for a time as hard and fast as the rock stars he wrote about, but he had been sober for more than a decade.)

Born and raised in the Chicago suburb of Dolton, Richard E. Johnson lived in Detroit for a few years in the early '80s while working at the offices of *CREEM*. But the tall, quiet, pony-tailed Swede spent most of his life in downstate Macomb, where he moved to attend Western Illinois University, and stayed to freelance in between managing Cady's Smoke House, a local institution where he spent hours thumbing through the extensive stock of magazines, including a lot of glossy publications with writers who weren't nearly as good, but which wouldn't deign to publish his work.

"The stuff I write just wouldn't fit in anywhere anymore, plus I don't want anything to do with the music business," Johnson told me in early 1998, when I interviewed him for *Let It Blurt*, my biography of Bangs, the legendary rock critic.

"I got out at a good time, when *CREEM* folded," he continued. "Unfortunately, I had all my eggs in that basket, and I didn't really want to start from scratch, [though] I see magazines that might publish my kind of stuff sometimes, like *Details* and *Spy*.

Johnson's "stuff" was wry, acerbic and often hysterically funny, and it was well-suited to the dire years in the '80s after punk and before alternative, when the rock scene was dominated by hair metal and soulless corporate pop creations that had far less flair and personality than the reviews, features and news stories in which he deconstructed them. Witness the master weighing in on the Doobie Brothers' ill-fated and quickly forgotten attempt at a hard-rock reinvention circa 1977:

There are no fast songs to speak of, a major disappointment, considering the Brothers' hammerhead rep. If they really plan to dump their booger image for the teddy-bear waters of Dinah Shore, they're going to have to make this new stuff work, not just stare at itself. It looks promising, but until they get decided, it's strictly reruns on the Doob tube.

Or this about the ascendance of a new teen heartthrob:

Meet Shaun Cassidy, fast-rising star of tube and groove and latest idol of rube pubes. Already a star in Europe, Cassidy has parlayed his co-starring role on 'The Hardy Boys' into American shake appeal, as well. Following his smash remake of 'Da Do Run Run,' Shaun the Maun promises to be the biggest thing since the training bra.

And how about Johnson's glossary of "New Musical Instruments of the '80s," which included "the Tenor Breen" ("a plastic replica of Doug [the Knack] Fieger's smile that, when twanged, goes, 'Breeennn!!!'"), "amplified cheese," "fusion scissors" and "electric soap." (The writer also once defined the word "riff" as "the sound made by a very thin dog.")

Johnson always said the biggest influence on his writing was J.D. Salinger's *The Catcher in the Rye*, though he also cited rock writers Bangs and Richard Meltzer. But if those greats read like Beat heroes Jack Kerouac or William S. Burroughs reinvented as punk rockers, Johnson wrote like a snotty 13-year-old overdosing on sugary cereal while watching Saturday morning cartoons. I mean that as a compliment, and his writing perfectly conveyed the spirit of – and, as I said earlier, often stood as better art than – the music he wrote about.

Yes, there are still plenty of wiseass comedians in rock journalism. But few have the heart or the intellect of Johnson.

"The first time I talked to Lester [Bangs], he told me he liked me because I was the only one who knew who [the French existentialist philosopher Louis-Ferdinand] Celine was, as well as Carlos the Jackal," Johnson told me. "I dug terrorists, so we grooved on that."

Rock writing's equivalent of a terrorist tossing well-deserved bombs at over-inflated hypes, Johnson not only deserves to be remembered and read, we should hope that his work will be rediscovered by a new generation of bedroom critics who are sorely needed to tackle the omnipresent pop cons of the moment with the style and flair that stand as his legacy.

Bloato hype, gerbiltones & smellbags: MUSIC

MOVE
Split Ends
(United Artists)

ELECTRIC LIGHT ORCHESTRA
E.L.O. II
(United Artists)

ROY WOOD'S WIZZARD
Wizzard's Brew
(United Artists)

The odds are 99 percent that any magazine you pick up these days will have an article on the demise of Move, usually with a real sharp title like "On the Move" (*Woman's Day, 3-73*), "Move Over" (*Dairy Products Annual, fall '72*), "Groove With The Move" (*Arizona Highways, 4-73*), or "Moved To Tears" (*Rona Barrett's Hollywood, 11-72*). Every last one of 'em goes into resentful details on how Move were the latest greatest group since the International Submarine Band, yet they were brutally ignored by crass American record buyers who never read reviews. Seeing this as the Last of Move reviews, let's get just two things straight: (1) you didn't miss much, and (2) I'M GLAD THEY'RE GONE.

The main face behind Move was Roy Wood, a progressive fatling who ran out of ideas during the recording of their first album but successfully faked it through a ton of singles and three more albums. He received a lot of help on the later stuff from Jeff Lynne, who joined up on the third album (*Looking On*) and wrote all of the more interesting material from then on. That Wood wrote all of their 200 consecutive European hit singles (all of which bombed here) only attests to the fact that he's a master of repetition.

He's not master enough to bust the U.S. charts, however. What he failed to realize was that his winning formula in England was a losing formula where the big money is. That left it to Jeff to come up with their near-miss, "Do Ya," a classic stomp wad that sounds like an obscure Shadows of Knight killer. The success of "Do Ya" is the basis for *Split Ends*, a representative collection of late Move that will save you the trouble of wading through their sea of singles and lesser album cuts.

Move's well-publicized switcheroo into the Electric Light Orchestra is already frightfully documented, so let's just say that after the first ELO album (*No Answer*), Roy realized he was hopefully out-classed by Lynne and split to form Wizzard. The Wizz aren't terribly interesting unless your piece of toast is tinny rock revival with interminable sax-cello workouts. There are a couple of beautifully forgettable short rockers on one side, but Brew on the whole is a pretty bland dish.

The real action is on *ELO II.* Although they've picked up three guys from the London Symphony Orchestra, there's nothing scarier here than the soundtracks to old WB cartoons about performing penguins and rabbits in blackface. With Lynne in control, any classical pretensions are forced to exist within rock sensibilities, so while they're not as ostentatious as ELP, ELO are firmly dedicated to fun and games. "Roll Over Beethoven" is the neatest conceptual trick this side of "A Lover's Concerto," and the other tracks – Lynne compositions all – are packed with his crystal ear for melody and engrossing, quirky arrangements.

So here's the very last Primer & Guide to Move. Don't play it safe with *Split Ends* unless you enjoy kicking dead horses around. Don't bother with Wizzard unless your best friends are sequined corpses. ELO's the hottest thing since the cap snaffler, and they're the only ones doing anything on the charts so you may as well fall in with the majority because sooner or later you're going to have to anyway.

May 1973

ROY WOOD
Boulders
(United Artists)

Roy Wood likes to impress people with the fact that he played about 30 instruments on this album, including guitar, cello, drums, oboe, bonzo-phone, handclaps, etc., to name just a few, while also composing, arranging and producing all the songs, painting the front cover and conceptualizing the back. In the midst of all this credential flashing, one fact tends to get looked over: There is one instrument on this album he did not play! It even says so on the cover, only in microscopic letters squeezed in beneath his 50-line list of credits. Sure enough, you get down to the bottom of the column and there in parentheses (and following an asterisk no less) are these words: "except harmonium on "Songs of Praise": Surfin' John Kurlander."

Just who is this Kurlander character and what strange hold does he have on Mr. Wood that he should get his name on the cover? Are the rumors of a long-lost and presumed-dead twin brother perhaps true? Does the presumed fact that Roy's father drove his business partner, "Curly" Ned Kurlander, into ruin hold any water? Or is it that Roy Wood, master of musical instruments and studio knobs too numerous to mention, CANNOT PLAY HARMONIUM?!

The implications are frightening.

December 1973

ELECTRIC LIGHT ORCHESTRA
Discovery
(Jet)

Jeff Lynne, chief cook and viola tamer with the Ethiopian Lapdog Orchestra, is one of those people who like to complicate things. He scrambles his eggs with an undersea oil-drilling platform. Ask him what it's like outside and he'll explain the psychological pressures that led John Coleman to dedicate his life to a 50-percent chance of precipitation. I will refrain from describing what he does in bed, even though he uses up a kilowatt eon of electricity nightly.

Give Jeff and his Effervescent Lichen Orchestra a simple, hummable tune and they're bound to wreck it. "Confusion" begins with a likeable, Beach Boyish melody, only to be buried in a synth-string slime that coats it like semi-frozen tomato sauce. Ditto with "Last Train to London," an unfortunately logical antecedent to "Last Train to Clarksville" that shows up pop history as the laughing whore that it really is. Even the hit "Shine A Little Love" nearly gets lost in the full Endocrine Legionnaires Orchestra treatment of knob-molasses and little stringed birds snipping telephone lines with tiny electric scissors.

Who wiped their shoes on Jeff's ears anyway?

"Now, when this here Eleganza Lulu Orchestra sets out to be serious, all mung breaks loose. *Discovery*'s two official ballads, "Midnight Blue" and "Need Her Love," are ideal if you want to just maybe sit back, languish and defer to the unspeakable, and with "The Diary of Horace Wimp," the Elevated Lucite Orchestra sets – *oh, excuse me a minute.* There's a man at my door with a barrel of fish. Now where's my bazooka?

Initially, Lynn's ambition for his Entrenched Lanolin Orchestra was to take up where the Beatles left off with *Magical Mystery Tour.* Obviously, they've succeeded beyond his accountants' wildest dreams. Now, if they'd just keep following the Beatles' lead and *break up* ...
June 1979

SPLIT ENZ
True Colors
(A&M)

Nobody knows exactly what Split Enz is: some weird group from some two-bit country, frequently confused with Skyhooks, ticket splitters and tight ends. With the single exception of Krokus, everything that's someplace other than the U.S. or U.K. stinks anyway, so who cares

The real action on this LP is the holographically-imprinted laser design on the record itself. Viewed in plain, old-fashioned daylight, all you can really see is a bunch of flat colors and funny shapes. That's because it's supposed to be viewed under "certain types of lighting" to get the true effect. Otherwise, it looks pretty *stooooopid*.

Only trouble is, they don't *tell* you what kind of light. I checked the cover, sleeve and disc for a clue, but no dice. They give you the name of the assistant engineer and all the management, publishing and company stats, but not one word about producing the pretty colors.

You know what that means: They want us to use our imaginations. Well, shit. I already used mine on the Chicago Bears opener, and it's tired. What d'ya want, this ain't PBS or anything! We want colors and we want 'em now! I could see that, once again, I would have to resort to Science!

First, I dug my emergency flashlight from under a heap of empty sugar-free Dr. Pepper cans and old copies of *Chinook News* and tried it on the record. No go. I held it up to peach, cherry and underpants-scented candles to no avail – although it smelled better. The refrigerator light seemed promising, but I couldn't tell if it worked with the door closed.

Stepping outside, I hopped down the block to a huge spotlight that was publicizing the grand opening of another combination miniature golf course and nuclear waste dump, but that didn't work either. Auto taillights failed as well, and then the driver backed over the first three cuts on side two. Big deal.

Dribbling the album like a two-dimensional basketball, I headed back home and tried every light in the house. Yellow anti-bug lights … Sid Vicious nightlight … snail farm aquarium globe … Popeil scuba baton … even my genuine souvenir *Mr. Novak* hi-intensity study lamp. Duds all. Not even flashbulbs could help me get the picture.

After striking out with the phosphorescent slugs in my "basement" (whose only interest was in *eating* "Double Happy" – I hoped *they* liked it), I started to get a little … well, we're all grownups here, I guess I can say it … a little *ticked off*. I momentarily removed my blowtorch from the chamber where I had Melissa Manchester hanging by her toes over it, but succeeded only in burning a big hole in "Shark Attack." No great loss. I held I up to the TV during a Bonjour jeans commercial and even stooped to shutting it in the closet with my Post Cereal glow-in-the-dark hooter tooter, but no luck. What do they want? *Children of The Damned* eyeballs? Comet tails? Blast furnace reflections? Damn! The neighborhood steel mill just shut down last week.

Then an idea seized me — as they were wont to do. I wedged the LP cover into my grill, liberally applied some charcoal starter and then set it off. Talk about colors! The shiny crud they use on album covers burns like crazy and smells better than a bag full of glue!

It made me almost wish I hadn't sold my record collection down the river, because this was *a lot of fun*.

Then I noticed. The entire porch, even the caved-in part, was bathed in dazzling psychedelic colors and bizarre geometric shapes not unlike a magnification of *Romper Room*'s magic mirror. I was as hypnotized as a wired moth over Hiroshima, digging them DayGlo colors, man, when … oops!, I got it a little too close and scorched the rest of side two. No matter. I know my priorities.

Also included are two instrumentals.

September 1980

HELP YOURSELF
Help Yourself
(United Artists)

Here's an amiable, meandering collection of outdated old styles and out-dated newer ones that's got a little something to please anybody who's pur-chased an LP in the past five years. That's why the group is called Help Yourself – they throw a friendly musical game of 52 Card Pickup at you and you're supposed to help yourself to whatever you like. And if you don't like any of it, you can always eat the Hippy Nouveau package it all comes in, it sure is sweet enough.

Let's allow the absurdity of an obscure English band doing a tune called "American Mother" to slide and get into the real irrelevance at hand. Just about every style that's ever been in vogue (and on the charts) can be found lurking within the grooves of this album. You want teetering guitar lines somewhere in between Superfly and CCR? Then just give a listen to "Alabama Lady" and stand back before it stomps you into a little fleshy ash-tray, that's how commercial it is. If that's too AM for anyone, they can check out "She's My Girl," which has absolutely nothing to do with the Turtles' chartbuster of the same name, and includes the most downhome pronunciation of the word "girl" (something like "geeuurrll") since Clarence White himself crawled out of the steaming swamps of Los Angeles, his man-dolin dripping with hogtoads and chitlins.

There are lots of other tweeter twisters to play around with here, but if you're pressed for time, HY had the courtesy and forethought to include "Reaffirmation," which crams the highlights of the past decade or so into only 12:34. It starts out in the self-righteous Mellotron-thumping style that's been so popular these last couple of years, then clambers into an instrumental portion that covers everything from Garcia-Cipollina acid shards to that long Latin thing Poco did so badly on their second album, plus all the essential developments between.

Wait a minute! It was just revealed to me by an unimpeachable source that Help Yourself isn't really an obscure English band at all, but in reality the latest secret supersession to leak from the vaults of a Major Record Company! Well what do you know, all those fake names sure fooled me. Malcolm Morley turns out to be Norman Greenbaum! Paul Burton is actual-ly none other than Paul Revere! Guitarist Richard Treece is better known as George Harrison, drummer Dave Charles is in reality the long lost Dewey Martin, and The Shadow . . . well, I'm not even gonna tell you who he is. It's so shamefully obvious that you'll have to figure that one out for yourself.
May 1973

STRAWBS
Bursting At The Seams
(A&M)

The last thing you ever want to ask somebody who records for A&M is whether or not they've met the Big A himself, good old Herb Alpert. They might not want to admit it, because friends of Herb tend to get excluded from the real *hepster* circles. Take Quincy Jones. He knows Herb and what should happen but he ends up dating Peggy Lipton and looking forward to an 11-day tour of Japan. One of Peggy's *Mod Squad* pals, Pete, knows Herb, too. He once brought his scratchy, fingerprinted copy of "The Lonely Bull" to a catnip party some friends of his were having. They thought it was a big, black potato chip. Pete received no more invitations after that. Friends of Herb also have to contend with the rumor that he refused to sign Joan Baez until she got a haircut.

About the closest the Strawbs ever come to Herb Alpert is the brass in the orchestra that backs them up on one cut this time out, so it's pretty safe to say they don't help Herb polish his trumpet. Just who they do pal around with is anybody's guess, although I'd turn to the Moody Blues as likely prospects, sharing as they do that older uncle-with-greasy-bellbottoms look. And if their music isn't related, it's at least friends.

If the Moodies had started out as a folk group, they'd probably sound like the Strawbs by now. The Strawbs did start out as folkies, and it took about five years to develop from the Strawberry Hill Boys into the mighty Mellotron squeezers they are today. Throughout their conversion into a commercial-progressive outfit, they held on to their fine sense of traditional English melody while their instrumentation and production were expanding, resulting in a sound not unlike an updated version of the early Byrds. "Lay Down" in particular bends the folky air into high pop, with a repetitiously catchy melody that leans toward anthem proportions while remaining thoroughly entertaining.

Despite several high points like "Lay Down," the Fairport Conventional rocker "Stormy Down," and the cod-blimey pub singalong "Part Of The Union," the material on *Seams* is a bit weaker than their previous outing, *Grave New World*. It could be that big cheese Dave Cousins was saving his best stuff for his recently released solo disc, *Two Weeks Last Summer*. Now that that's out of the way, the Strawbs ought to be ready to come across with the real cow-catcher of British pop-folk.

It could be the best since *Bob Dylan Sings The Hollies*.
May 1973

EAGLES
Desperado
(Asylum)

STEPHEN STILLS & MANASSAS
Down the Road
(Atlantic)

The super concert refuses to die. In fact, it won't even fade away. If the Beatles had only known what a mammoth shitfall they were going to let loose with *Sgt. Pepper*, they undoubtably would have gone ahead and done it anyway, but maybe if the rest of us unpsychedelic peons had been warned in time, there would have been a lot less gnashing of cutout mustachios. What a prodigal chain of events might have ensued with the absence of that one fateful record—the Stones might have gone on to release *Flowers II, Tommy* would have met massive consumer feh, Flaming Youth (and scores of Little Leaguers like them) could never have even conceived of their 1969 space-rock epic *Ark 2*, and where would that have left Jefferson Starship? Hopefully lost in the slug of leftover acid fatigue that spawned *Desperado*.

This hotdog cowboy crud has been driven so far into the ground that it's not surprising we're starting to get Oriental buckaroos like Kung Fu hip-pity-hopping their way across the lone prairie, six-shooter in one hand and hot judo in another. No matter what Robert Hunter and Nils Lofgren might say, the last justifiable piece of cowboy-pop was "The Man Who Shot Liberty Valance," and every last chaps-slapper since then has been strictly extraneous, leaving the Eagles with an album full of conceptual burlesquery. Not only are their lonesome-outlaw lyrics about as poignant as plugging your speakers into a roll of pastel toilet paper, but the music which showed signs of life on their first album has coalesced into a tiresome heap of mandolin pedantry and pathetic stabs at hard rock. There's no way they're gonna milk this baby for three hit singles like they did the last one, and though it's reasonable to expect nothing of "Take it Easy" caliber, it's the realization that there's nothing here which even threatens "Peaceful Easy Feeling" that sets off the uncontrollable giggling.

Leave it to the old washed-out polo player himself, Stephen Stills, to come through with a tenable, easy-going job within somewhat similar musical boundaries. Stills has the brains to realize that you don't have to indulge in tedium media to give an LP some unity. A record album can't help but be heard as a concept anyway, at least within the context of the artist, and Stills has formulized his image through hard-core repetition of everything from cover art to placement of songs. Steve ain't exactly inventive, but he sure is dependable. You can always count on him for a strictly adhere-to mixture of CSN&Y ionized harmony numbers, alternately fancy and lazy picking, a Spanish title or two, and maybe a Chris Hillman composition to round things out. You get all this plus his inimitable brand of front polemics, dressed up in the latest clunky lingo. Steve tends to come off as the sort of guy who spends his spare time sitting around trying to think up new peace signs, especially when he insists on throwing around song titles like

"Business On The Street," "City Junkies," and the priceless "Do You Remember The Americans?" Sometimes he even stoops to disguising the lyrics in Spanish, but don't worry about getting a translation because they're just as dumb either way.

Listen, a great idea just came to me in a blinding flash of caffeine. Maybe Stills could fire what's left of Manassas these days (they all look alike anway) and hook up with the Eagles for the super concept album of all times, sort of a cross between *Blows Against The Empire* and *Bonanza*. A gang of rabid outlaws (played by the Eagles, unless it's a low-budget production, in which case Mason Proffitt will have to do) hijack the first Conestoga wagon to pass through the Cumberland Gap and proceed to drive it directly into Monterey Bay, thus inventing the houseboat. That's where David Crosby comes in.

July 1973

EAGLES
Eagles Live
(Asylum)

"Double Live Album" is one of those red-flag phrases that anyone sensible doesn't want to hear. Those three little words carry a Nuisance Potential comparable to such winners as "consecutive life sentences," "minimal brain damage," or was that red car yours?" and rival the infamous "Dear Tenant," for provoking a fear of upcoming events so anxiety-provoking that many sufferers are forced to medicate themselves with alcohol and illegal drugs. As Jack Brickhouse says, "HEY HEY!"

However, if you're an Eagles fan pre-disposed to enjoying live LPs, this is a good one. What you're getting upfront are excellent—if slightly protracted—versions of their hits that truly sound "Just Like The Record." Even the vocals—where most groups come unglued live—are remarkably well performed and recorded.

A partially successful attempt has been made to lower crowd noise, a major irritant of live recordings. One group, the Santa Monica audience of July 29, deserves to be awarded special five-pound bags of Mandolin Chow for—as we in the Biz say—*shutting the hell up!* Too bad the fans present on the 27th and 28th didn't get the idea too. The nearly obligatory wrong-beat clapping and yak mating whoops make quieter songs like "I Can't Tell You Why" sound like they're being served up at pancake time in the Buzzard House.

With its full-color poster of a stadium full of Eagles fans squinting to see the tiny moving bugs onstage three miles away and a heavy-duty embossed cover easily identifiable to tequila-blinded listeners, This Package Will Make a Delightful Xmas Gift Item. You know, the kind where it looks like you spent enough money to keep the recipient off your back for another year. Who cares if they *like* the Eagles or not? It's pretty and it goes around, which is more than you can say about hankies or after-shave.

November 1980

TEMPEST

Tempest
(Warner Bros.)

You may as well face it, these guys are pretty mean. They want to sleep with you in your deathbed. They'll take the pennies out of your loafers and press them on your eyelids. Cops get raped at their concerts. They make *A Clockwork Orange* look like the time of day.

Got some big names here. The rhythm section of Jon Hiseman and Mark Clarke is straight out of the ruins of Coliseum, one of the earlier jazz-rock mixers. Paul Williams is a name almost everyone has heard somewhere, only this is the wrong one. Not the ex-Tempt, not the ex-rock critic, and not the soapy composer, but the ex-singer with Juicy Lucy, and he even doubles on keyboards. Guitarist Alan Holldsworth isn't particularly famous right now but soon will be.

Just like the Lone Ranger made his mask out of his murdered brothers' bloody duds, Tempest have ripped the innards out of the jazzy-heavy ranks and put them through a meat grinder formerly used for cleaning the library breath out of old Unipaks, giving them a sound that's familiar in its speed and power but somewhat inventive in the way they put it to work in the pursuit of infamy. Take "Brothers," for example – while Williams is raving about how "ancestors' mistakes/ casts ingots in death/ and you die forever," Holldsworth is spewing out fractions, semi-random chords that sound like somebody trying to pull their leg out of a moving elevator. They even manage to sound exactly like the idiot savant of all time, Arthur Lee, on "Gorgon," right down to the torn-nasal yelps and doomsday bass line that glows greasily within its own crass little aura. Tempest just aren't about to be legible for anybody, they're not gonna give you any words to hang on your wall unless maybe you want to spray "If yer stuck on some one she'll melt the glue" all over your ceiling in yellow fluorescent paint. They'd probably like that.

They know a lot of good riffs, too, and once they've got one going, they don't beat it to death, they beat you to death with it. "Foyers Of Fun" is a nice one, twisted off the "Born Under A Bad Sign" motif and refueled with a pre-exhaustion blast that's got "Here today – gone today" written all over it. "Strangeher" is another golden piece of shit, building on a headlong riff that rolls over itself at times, only to be split wide by a Holldsworth solo that could only have been conceived in a state of total amphetamine dry-drool.

No matter how you try to deal with it, these guys will make you feel like you're in an iron ant farm if you sit too close to the speakers. It's not surprising that POWER is the word most frequently chosen to describe their music and it's one tag they'll never need to deny. Tempest have enough of the stuff to crisp every last prisoner now awaiting the big shock on Death Rows everywhere (a pet project of theirs, by the way). And if I ever go to the chair, my last request is to be listening to "Strangeher" on headphones when they pull the switch.

July 1973

GEORGE HARRISON
Living In The Material World
(Apple)

I remember George Harrison. He used to dream of becoming a stockbroker someday, but instead ended up as one of the Beatles, which was lucky for him because it pays a whole lot better. He was the madcap moptop who went around saying rude things about Cathy McGowan while penning the whole pile of mid-'60s gems like "Don't Bother Me," "If I Needed Someone," and "Taxman." Then the *Sgt. Pepper* era came along and all of a sudden George was some kind of a tinkle-tail, parading around in shiny white suits and turning out drone like "Within You, Without You" and "Blue Jay Way" along with readymade Hollyridge Strings gushers like "Something" and "Here Comes The Sun." His seeming inability to compose music with any sort of bite since then could be chalked up to any number of reasons: psychedelic fascism (his favorite painter is Hitler), religious overindulgence, self-conscience musical maturity (pronounced ma-tour-ity) or even chronic vegetarian constipation, but I think it's just the real stockbroker in him finally coming out of the closet.

Not that there's anything wrong with wimpy rock 'n' roll. Krishna knows that George has come across with some deadly radio melodies combined with a mastery of AM repetition modes that belongs at the top of the charts. In fact, if Stockbroker Lib would excuse me again, I'd go as far as to say that the entire album is perfectly programmed for casual listening in windowless rooms where people add up numbers. The really catchy stuff in "My Sweet Lord" vein like "Give Me Love" and "Don't Let Me Wait Too Long" is all well-cushioned by monotonous post-raga phonothons designed as rest areas where the listener can hum the pretty ones to himself while the current cut painlessly erases the hook from his memory.

Unfortunately, while this may stretch your coffee break, it's not easy to just sit and listen to without wanting to turn on the TV, read the funnies, or go make crank calls to your little sister's girl friends. About half of *Material World* could easily be classified as pleasant filler, and the real meaty parts— woops, sorry George—the really ricy parts of the album are so scattered as to lack any consistant impact. The big single, "Give Me Love," the title tune, and "Don't Let Me Wait," which is the sharpest melody he's come up with since "While My Guitar Gently Weeps," give side one the edge as far as durability goes, but also makes it the more disappointing. With the proof that he can still write superb teen love songs like "Don't Let Me Wait" staring you in the ear, it's heard to compensate for the mysterio godhead goo he chooses to spend most of his time with.

Occasional self-righteous pomposity is easy enough for anyone who's been exposed to the pop protest of the past few years to deal with, but Harrison insists on preaching every chance he gets, running everything through his humorless Sunday School wringer until nearly all of this lyrics, especially those on side two, ready like some fakir's version of *Senior Hi Challenge*. Just a minute! Did I hear somebody say humorless? Not George

"Caprice" Harrison! Why, that little joker tossed in the "Sue Me, Sue You Blues," a positively waggish commentary on Apple's legal problems—"you serve me-and I'll serve you- swing your partners- all get screwed." Yuk! Yuk! But let's not get carried away, like the man says in "Be Here Now": "A mind that wants to wander 'round a corner is an un-wise mind."

Well, he won't catch my mind hanging around any street corners. George Harrison is exceedingly competent at what he's doing, and if you like his previous solo efforts, you'll probably luv this one because it's the same deal, only more so. Back in 1965, a reporter for *Rave* asked George what he would most like to be and, josher that he is, he told her he'd like to be a cornflake. It looks like he finally made it.

August 1973

WINGS
At The Speed Of Sound
(Capitol)

One expects a lot of padding from a Wings album and, consummate knob-turners that they are, even their filler is usually interesting, if sometimes on the level of aquarium ornaments. In the past, their albums were cushioned with minor McCartney compositions, tunes that were pleasant though unmemorable, but now he's come up with a better idea. Paul's decided to let the rest of the band provide the filler, while only his best tunes find their way to vinyl, and in so doing, he's come up with an album that not only works, but contains an ideal blend of the merely consistent and the frequently inspired.

McCartney's first move was to hang up the new car smell of the *Venus & Mars* LP. That record was "nice," but you kept expecting Mrs. Olsen to totter out between cuts and mumble something about mountains. Having grafted a more low-key antiseptic sound on to the usual suntan blanket production, he's given the tunes a bit more room to move it, so they're not necessarily like watching a *Dick Van Dyke* rerun for the sixteenth time.

The songs themselves are some of McCartney's best in a long time. "Silly Love Songs" is one of his better radio-begging melodies, and the Beach Boys vocal arrangement gives it a gorgeous shampoo séance quality. "Beware My Love" contains more of the superb lo-cal harmonies, and finally snowballs into a near-epic production reminiscent of the Four Tops Greatest Hits. All of his tunes on *Speed* are magnetic, even in low profile. While most songwriters begin to sound like mechanical Paul Simons after a while, McCartney's melodies always have a fresh feeling despite the frequently dumb and/or hieroglyphic lyrics.

As for the Other Songs, they're all very harmless, if not exactly ear bruisers. Denny Laine's cuts ain't no "Go Now"– in fact, "The Not You Never Wrote" is so slow you can almost hear bread turning into penicillin in the background– but he is basically inarguable. The same goes for McCulloch and English's token tunes. Enjoyable, but nothing to write home

21

about. Linda's song, "Cook of the House," is a greasebait Fats Domino soundalike, in mono no less, and spiff despite the leaden vocal.

The real action is in the McCartney songs though, even if the filler is splashier than usual. It may make you want to paint your walls the color of old soap at times, but this is easily Wings' best album.

July 1976

WINGS
Back To The Egg
(Columbia)

Paul McCartney is well on his way to becoming the next Rod Stewart. Not his image—it's a little hard to picture Paulie running around in see-thru Danskins, wagging his weenie at the front row and whispering "D'ya think I'm sexless?" But it's not difficult in the least to imagine an infinite string of formulized Wings albums stretching into that dreaded future time where people have forgotten how to say, "Who cares?"

There's a lot to be said for the formulaic approach to record making— like "So what?", "I could give a shit" and "Oh, no, not another one!" It only makes sense to repeat what's been successful for you (the author's ex-girl-friends being comparing notes) when stagnation set in like yogurt mites running wild in a dying fridge.

And it looks like it's about the end of the we'll-swallow-anything road for Wings. Not even Paul's incredible ear for melody or his Sunshine Girls production skills can obscure the fact that *Egg* sounds exactly like his last three or four LPs, right down to petty things like the running order of the cuts (a Stewart specialty) and where to unleash Linda. This is great for hardcore Wingies but Z-city for the rest of us dummies.

To coin a phrase, If You Like The Last 82 Wings Albums, You'll Probably Like This One Too. Predictability is its own reward.

Just like boredom.

July 1979

RINGO STARR
Stop and Smell The Roses
(Boardwalk)

A new novelty record from Ringo is out! Highlights include:
* no spitting in the river
* six different producers, including Ringo himself
* two songs written by Paul, one of which is real good!
* one song each by George and Stephen Stills
* half a song by Ron Wood
* three by Nilsson, extending his consecutive lame composition

streak to 23 tunes!

    * remake of "Back Off Boogaloo"
    * three cuts that would sound a little like the Kinks if they were dead
    * token C & W remake, "Sure To Fall"
    * token reggae cut
    * cryptic dedication reference to "My Three Brothers"
    * no matter where I put the cover, little Meowface wants to sit on his nose
    * Ringo in cop gear on back with hand over eyes
    * lyrics included!
    * special appearance by Lawrence Tuber
    * the Harrison cut, "Wrack My Brain," is likeable!
    * backing vocals by Linda M.
    * Boardwalk Records' address
    * pointlessness for the sake of pointlessness
    * some arrangement by Van Dyke Parks
    * the perfect Xmas gift for that special someone you're totally indifferent to.

November 1981

PAUL KANTNER, GRACE SLICK & DAVID FREIBERG
Baron Von Tollbooth & the Chrome Nun
(Grunt)

Scandal Randall, a local punk of renown who bears a frightening resemblance to Paul Kantner, has a theory about the decline of this former fave raves, Jefferson Airplane. He figures that the frequency of appearances of the word "sun" is directly related to their general drift toward shittyness. It starts out with a few vague references to the old orb in *After Bathing at Baxter's*, then grows somewhat more apparent in *Crown of Creation* with the repeated yelping of SUNSUNSUNSUNNNNNNN at the very end of the record. By the time *Blows Against The Empire* and *Bark* rolled around, the airplace had gone into total dog-faced hysteria, coming up with sunguns, sunstorms, sunsnorts, sunmung, and the immortal subwit lyrics from "Hijack"—"only the sun knows what we really need to know-only the sun holds the secret." That wasn't the end of it, though. The final bunco came, in Scandal's own words, "when me and my buddy Spokes went into this record store. Up on the new shit shelf was this hideous mind-rot of an album, all creepy orange with a defective baby face gaping out at ya. And the title … the title was *Sunfigher!* Heeheeheehee…" At this, he passed into a catatonic state from which he recovered days later, claiming to know nothing concerning starships, Paul Kantner, or the sun.

If I know where Scandal was being kept now, I'd head right over and play *Baron von Tollbooth & The Chrome Nun* for him; it might provide the shock needed to set him on the road to recovery (he still refuses to go out until after dark). Maybe it's David Freiberg (an ex-Quicksilver for all you ex-Quicksilver fans) on vocals and keyboards, or perhaps the relative lack of Kantner materia. Whatever it is, this is the strongest thing to come out of the Slickantner nexus since Marty Balin hightailed it into obscurity. Or to put it another way, any LP with three lusty numbers by Grace Slick can't help but be likable in a morbid sort of way.

Where JA's old strength was in their intelligence, KS&F are masters at celebrating their own rock 'n' roll dumbness. They throw together a bunch of blatant Airplane readymades, add in their demented worldview, and mix it up when their cheesiest production since *Volunteers* to deliver a thoroughly mindless fun job highly conducive to reading the skull palace ads in the back pages of the *LA Free Press*. You can drop five tabs and lose it to "Your Mind Has Left Your Body," smash the state to "Flowers Of The Night," get horny to the suggestions of Pauly's seven-inch psychedelic pud in "Across The Board," or just plain vomit on the sleazy anatomy text cover, and I'll betcha every steaming chunk comes out on the downbeat. That's what a brain-bludgeon this record is! Only a couple slow ones, and they've either got trendy mellotron howl to play with or else their fairy tales about mainland China, so you still can't go wrong. And superstars! David Crosby ditdoots on the title cut (it would make a great single), Robert Hunter wrote the lyrics to another (it would make a perfect obscure B-side), and Jerry Garcia actually stoops to play a hard-rock lead that, while not going anywhere, is kinda nice right where it is. Take it from me, there's enough diversion in this package, not even counting the lyric sheet and handy useless info enclosed, to keep anybody with higher metabolism than a Focus nut on a spiritual plane that's the closest thing to free jazz since record prices went up. Kantner, Slick & Freiberg have invented color radio!
August 1973

JEFFERSON STARSHIP
Red Octopus
(Grunt)

After any number of psychedelic washouts, dizzy business delusions, a Nazi streak that made Blue Oyster Cult look like the Jewish Defense League, and the departure of half the original lineup at raygun-point, Jefferson Starship are still a viable outfit. In their past few releases, they've been increasingly able to tie up their loose ends and present meaningful variety instead of t   throw-the-dogfood-at-the-ceiling-and-see-if-it-sticks approach.

With *Red Octopus*, they sound more like a cohesive band than ever before, due to a promising—if tentative—compromise between founder Marty Balin's renewed dedication and the gradual curbing of Paul Kantner's Hawkwind excesses. They still have some problems coming up with solid material despite (or because of) having seven writers in residence, but then seven of these burnouts is equal to about one-half a Neil Sedaka so you can't expect miracles. At least the concept of Starship-as-alien-slaves of Slick &

Kantner has been hung out to dry for a while.

There's no way to talk about the new JS without resorting to the standard testimonials about Balin. Tuff trunks, punks—the reason all this legendary snore got rolling in the first place is because he's the man who *put* the Jefferson in the Starship back in the stupid '60s, and his absence was like the Jimi Hendrix Experience without Jimi (currently billed as Mahogany Rush). Now that he's back singing those inimitable weave jobs with Grace, things seem more in place. All of the album's high spots occur with Balin at the controls—the two eloquently drippy ballads, "Tumblin' " and "Miracles," and the stinging "Sweeter Than Honey," a thudfest of minimal lyrics and maximum bump appeal.

Vocals are really the main hook with JS, and the harmony work between Balin, Slick and Kantner is better than ever. "There Will Be Love" is the pick here, an anthemic number not unlike the Airplane of old. They never really used to write these monolith lovejags until some cigar type like the belatedly late Ralph J. Gleason told them to, but nobody else could pull it off except The Who and Slade, which puts our dupes in good company.

Just to water down the meat some, there's two useless instrumentals, "Git Fiddler," a crypto-hoedown designed to make Papa Joke – er, John – feel like he's more than some charming derelict Grace picked up on an off day, and "Sandalphon," which is fairly OK although it starts to sound like musty old drapes after a few listenings. Then of course, there's Kantner, an angry man with a Frisbee on his shoulder. "I Want To See Another World" does not refer to the NBC soap of the same name. It's unfortunately another one of Paul's UFO-D.'s. Really, this guy belongs in a drool ward. If he wasn't such a great rhythm guitarist and voice-horse, it would be a treat to see one of his hovering plates take a squat on him while he gaped helplessly in glazed post-coke sincerity. Maybe the whole outer-space chauvinism that almost sunk the Starship once would disappear with him in a dry little cupcake tin of burnt grass and mirrored-out sand.

But it's a pretty solid record on the whole. Grace's songs, two standard JS rockers and a rather sticky ballad with strings, as usual as usual and Sears, Chaquico and Freiberg are writing better than ever and very much in the Starship mold. *Red Octopus* is easily the best package ever released under the Starship logo, and with Marty back on the tracks and Paul crouched under a rusting missile silo somewhere in the Southwest desert, things have never looked more promising.

August 1975

STARSHIP
Earth
(Grunt)

Earth is the lamest slice of mung that any of the various crews of journeyman heads laboring under the name of Starship has ever come up with. And that includes some pretty questionable product, too, since their entire recorded output adds up to a handful of good cuts surrounded by innumerable unconvincing arguments for the long-playing record.

The absence of solid material is the major problem Slick, Kantner and Balin – the core holdovers that make up Jefferson Starship's feeble reason for being – have apparently completed the drying-up process began many puddles ago. Mostly, they're reduced to scribbling lyrics for the likes of Pete Sears and Craig Chaquico, whose songwriting abilities rank right up there with Ringo Starr and Billy Wyman. Grace does contribute a pustule-pleasing protest-ballad called "Show Yourself," but you could find a better melody if you stuck your ear in a cake.

The band's performance equals the excitement level of the material. Lacking even one standout cut to shine on, they've opted for the fishheads-in-the-blender approach. The prime example of this multiple-shotgun technique is "All Nite Long," a six-minute keynote address that's so overblown you need machete-phones to even get near the tune. What with Sears' Moog tribulations, Chaquico's overview of Jerry Garcia's career and Freiberg's ongoing salute to Al Kooper: A Man And His Organ, you'd hardly even notice there was a song there if it didn't finally end. You wonder where all the silence came from.

Other sitting ducks include "Fire," where the Craig Chaquico Experience causes an otherwise tolerable cut to vanish in a chord of guitar excess, "Skateboard," a trivial synthesizer error that's unlikely to make anyone forget Jan & Dean, and the aforementioned Pillsbury emanations of "Show Yourself." "Love Too Good," the tune currently receiving maximum bloato hype, is one of those rare tunes that are slow enough to make the hands of the clock appear as blurs while you wait for it to end. Slick, Kantner and friends have been sleazing on their reputations for years now, cranking out half-realized LPs that only their artifact-addled fans find any merit in. *Earth* should be an insult even to the most sentimental Slicklicks, as well as the final proof that Starship is one of the most overrated outfits in pop history. At least since Jefferson Airplane.
March, 1978

JEFFERSON STARSHIP
Freedom At Point Zero
(Grunt)

The latest new-look Jefferson Starship has arrived on the scene like a block pieplate, and guess what? Yep, they sound a lot like the last few editions, despite another drastic personnel shuffle leaving Paul Kantner as the only remaining original member. Kantner and the gang have done a remarkable repair job, however, turning in a set so daringly formulated that Starship could well be on their way to becoming the next Uriah Heep.

The important new face here is Mickey Thomas, the former voice with Elvin Bishop who wisely extricated himself from a solo career nearly as successful as Farrah Fawcett, Wayne Rogers and Greg Sierra. Mickey's quite a find, too, having altered his voice in such a manner that he can replace both Marty Balin *and* Grace Slick in the gang-of-four harmonies that are the Starship trademark. Thomas for Balin and Slick is the kind of move you'd expect from the Cubs, although any smart remarks from the Mick and he goes to Foreigner for Ed Gagliardi and a percussionist to be named later.

The music's a bit harder this time out, sounding not unlike late-period Grand Funk tackling John Philip Sousa. Mighty anthems of splat. No rewrite of "Miracles" this time—the melody having been licensed to Vicks for an opening snot-relief ad campaign—but the band has courteously provided a pair of ballads that enable reviewers and listeners alike to get up and fetch another cup of coffee. Or in the case of "Awakening," a cut consisting of seven long minutes of Angel-like keyboard washes and decorator murmurings, it almost seems like you have enough time to buzz out to Frisco and shake Joe DiMaggio's hand.

In a conscientious move to support young songwriters, Paul asked his little girl China to write some of the lyrics on Zero, but it didn't help. It's the same old falling walls, fields of rapture, here comes the saucers, blah, blah, etc. Maybe this stuff sounds so stupid to me because I'm embarrassed that I used to fall for it years ago. Nah, I'm not embarrassed. I'm *appalled.*

Can we just forget about these guys now? Please?
December 1979

HARRY LUBIN
Music From One Step Beyond
(Decca)

TV's *One Step Beyond* was a real spooker. This was back in the days of *Science Fiction Theater,* long before *Twilight Zone, Thriller, Outer Limits,* or *Alfred Hitchcock,* in the days when television could really scare you juiceless without beating you over the head with gothic shadowgraphs and lame monsters, when you and your little brother could crouch motionless in the dull Sony glow, waiting for the secret eyeball that would shock you into little puddles of giggling pee. Instead of using the obvious bugaboos like invaders from outer space, the writers of *One Step Beyond* relied on more insidious fear inducers, like a grandmother who dies in her favorite easy chair and leaves her silhouette on the wall, a shadow that doesn't go away when the horrified family moves the body. They try all the usual stuff, like painting the wall and moving the lamps around, but the shadow stays until finally the father admits he poisoned her and then proceeds to kill himself in a guilt-stricken panic. The moment after he blows his brains out, the shadow vanishes. Then the creepy music comes in.

And Harry Lubin sure can compose a creepy tune when it's needed. It's the kind of music that people on TV psychodramas listen to while they slowly waste away over the mysterious death of their hubby, all twisty, suggestive strings with a lead instrument like an oboe that grabs on to one sinister note when the climactic evidence is uncovered and then drills it into your steadily liquefying brain. So you see, Mrs. Lewis, it must have been this ancient Aztec sacrificial blade that killed your husband. But how could it have gotten into the library...? Nrrr-nrrrrrrrrrrrrrrrrr!

The big number here is "Fear," the theme song from *Beyond*, which features a grisly electronic instrument called the Trautonium that sounds suspiciously like a Theremin. The melody alone is just downright scary, but when it's associated in the back of your skull with all those skittish evenings before the television, you have to fight an urge to yank the needle off and play something cheerful like Hawkwind or Van Der Graaf Generator. Outside of the theme song and "Weird," which was the music they played in the background of all the ghastliest scenes, the rest is pretty tame stuff, mostly haunted-house Muzak with a couple upbeat numbers tossed in to ward off hypnotism.

At no extra cost, you get superb liner notes by *Beyond*'s host John Newland that hint darkly at plots that go along with the tracks, like "the 'Jungle Aire' from 'Echo,' the story of a guilty man's conscience-ridden vision of his own terrible fate – a fate he cannot evade as he is driven to run even faster toward self-destruction to the accompaniment of an irresistible Afro-Cuban beat..."

If you can picture yourself being driven to self-destruction to the accompaniment of an irresistible Afro-Cuban beat, this is your kind of record.
August 1973

ROLLING STONES
Goat's Head Soup
(Rolling Stones Records)

RASPBERRIES
Side 3
(Capitol)

Who needs the Rolling Stones anyway? Rolling Stones Records does, or else there wouldn't be anybody on their label. *Rolling Stone* magazine does, or else they wouldn't have anybody to fill out their gossip column with. Jehovah's Witnesses do, or else it would blow their whole theory on the imminent end of the world. Truman Capote does, or else it would blow his whole theory on the imminent end of chic.

But who *really* needs the Stones, huh? Efrem Zimbalist Jr. doesn't, Tom Poston doesn't. Neither does Jane Fonda, Peggy Cass, Lassie, Paul Lynde, Nora Ephron, Gay Talese, Faron Nuff, Tom Eagleton, H.R. Haldeman, King Feisal, Queen Elizabeth, Faye Dunaway, Melvin Laird, Clifford Irving, Goldie Hawn, Kitty Carlisle, M.T. Box, Perry Mason, Jim Backus, Larry Csonka, Johnny Carson, and neither do you.

The Raspberries are the hottest shit in town these days and if you don't believe me, look at the evidence: The Stones are loaded up with dreadful competence. The Raspberries are still learning how to play their instruments. The Stones wear matching smirks. The Raspberries wear matching suits. The Stones look like rock stars. The Raspberries smell like rock stars. The Stones' lyrics sound like a semi-classy $1.95 paperback novel. The Raspberries' lyrics sound like a greeting card. The Stones used to steal a lot. The Raspberries still steal a lot. The Stones do slowed-down fast songs. The Raspberries do speeded-up slow songs. The Stones use a horn section. The Raspberries are horny. The Stones think like professional killers. The Raspberries think like juvenile delinquents. The Stones' favorite TV show is *Mannix*. The Raspberries favorite TV show is *Dow Finsterwald's Golf Tip of the Day*.

Goat's Head Soup is a sure bet to become Marianne Faithful's favorite Stones album. The only way they could make a record any drudgier would be to record 10 new versions of "As Tears Go By." They could even toss in 10 new versions of "Sister Morphine" and make it a double set. It would be more fun than dragging a river, wouldn't it?

Raspberries, on the other hand, are more fun than a good hanging. Make that 10 good hangings – they're that much fun. They're still unconscious enough of their own image to deal in the subleties that the Stones miss while going through the motions. Little things like losing their breath, barely missing the upper registers, stupid beach sound effects, and not spending all their time recording musical mirrors to check out their wilting Sinestro postures. They'd even sound good with pineapple chip dip spilled on both sides, so they're safe for spicing up Tupperware parties. If you spilled chip dip on the Stones LP, it would steal the show.

To get down to particulars, 60 percent of *Goat's* (I forget the titles) is spent warming up. That covers all of the first side and a bit of the second. If you remember "Sway" you've heard all of these. Twenty percent more is a dress rehearsal for the biggies, so that leaves two songs, "Silver Train" and "Star Star" (formerly "Starfucker") to spend your money on. It would be easier to buy a single, but they had to go and put "Angie" and some other nonentity on this year's 45. Even the two tracks that manage to transcend a vague loiter lack the punch of a goodly portion of *Exile*. I'd call them a slap.

Raspberries don't fart around. They always put a hit single on side 1, and *Side 3* ain't about to chuck a winning system. You wouldn't either if you could be tried for statutory rape in 37 states like Raspberries' lead singer Eric Carmen could. "Tonight" has at least the heat of "I Wanna Be with You" and more of those shocking chords. They don't even sound so much like the Beatles – or, indirectly, Badfinger as they used to, although it's close. The Beach Boys influence that was seeping in on their last album is starting to spread. So when they so "On the Beach," you could just about surf across the Mersey on the harmonies.

There are six more indelible melodies on *3* and a lot of swell lyrics about premarital sex, premarital babies, and premarital dancing. The only stinker is a "blues" cut called "Money Down," but it's the last track on side 2 and thus an easy must to avoid. So that's 8 outta 9 for Raspberries while the Stones go about 2 for 10, which is pretty shitting batting even in 1973. Some kinder sportscasters might give them another single or two, but I'd say they are errors.

But none of this answers the question of who the world's greatest rock 'n' roll band is. It's Slade, of course. What a stupid question.

November 1973

RASPBERRIES
Starting Over
(Capitol)

If yer one of the few dupes dumb enough to have been reading reviews over the past 12 months, you might recall bout his time last year the Raspberries and the Stones had themselves a battle of the bands right here. *Goat's Head Soup* vs. *Side 3*. The results of the knockout, rocks-off, drag-jock showdown are plain enough to see: The Stones are TOO WUSSY to try it again after the way they got their puds whipped last time. Oh, yeah, Mick's still mixing it down in L.A. and trout have eyelids too – probably they'll sneak it out on the eve of the deadline to try and look good but don't be fooled!

The Razz has this end of the game all wrapped up and the Stones are just a bunch of sniveling nurds on the run.

Anyway, here it is, the first LP by the "new" Raspberries, their former rhythm section having dropped out to do cowboy-hat imitations in Cleveland bars. Good riddance, too, 'coz the new combination of Scott McCarl on bass and Mike McBride on drums has given the band a quantum power squat that makes even Kleenex ballads like "Rose Coloured Glasses" shake and bake. McBride, in particular, shines, from his Dennis Wilson fill-outs on "Overnight Sensation" to Keith Moon bambam acrobatics in "I Don't Know What I Want," and McCarl – outside of being a forceful and ever-vigilant bassist – also writes some inescapably catchy rhythm ballads like the aforementioned "Glasses" and "I Can Hardly Believe You're Mine," which is guaranteed to attach itself to your brain crabgrass-like until you have to sit and play it a few times just for mercy.

Now hits aside, Eric Carmen is the real heart and twat of the Razz. His string of great hits keep rolling, with the magnificent "Overnight Sensation (Hit Record)," a production triumph that takes up where "Band On the Run" petered out and builds sequentially into the most impressive record to grace AM record since "Good Vibrations." Eric ain't just a brainsuck tho. In fact, it looks like he could do just about anything he feels like. His rock 'n' roll epic this time – way ahead of even his earlier smashes like "I Wanna Be with You" and "Tonight" – is "I Don't Know What I Want," a murderizing tribute to the early Who that puts everything on *Odds & Sods* to shame with the sheer power of the Razz' presentation. Bashing in Townsend-esque bender guitar and Moon rimjobs left and right, Carmen steers into the picture with a vocal sneer that would make James Dean look like Eddie Haskel:

My old man says success is the measure.
Maybe so but I don't need the pressure,
not right now,
coz I got enough.
Teachers tell me I don't lack for brains;
ask me if I'm under some kinda strain.
Well, that's too much
and I really can't take it.
They all say that I'm not getting' younger
& I better make up my mind.
Man you'd think I was committin'
some kinda crime.
COZ I DON'T KNOW WHAT I WANT
BUT I WANT IT NOW

Simply one the greatest rock'n'roll songs ever vinylized, right down to
the hesitation-stomp at the end. Meher Baba should have it so good.

There's lots more – hard stuff from lead guitarist Wally Bryson ("Party's
Over"), hot dog car songs ("Cruisin' Music"), and even a mind-in-the-gutter
"Yellow Submarine" soundalike called "Hand's On You." One of the best LPs
of '74, it has some of the best cuts ever. Miss this and you deserve John Denver.
November 1974

ROLLING STONES
It's Only Rock 'n' Roll
(Rolling Stones Records)

It' s been an awful long time since the Stones put out an LP that anyone could agree on. After the universal anathema that greeted *Satanic
Majesties* and dog-face adoration that *Let It Bleed* inspired, the reaction to
their last three efforts has been a bit mixed, to say the least. While *Sticky
Fingers* introduced the "Brown Sugar" chords that currently enjoy more
teenage mileage than anything since "Louie Louie," it also set loose the suf-
focating mug-aura of Marianne Faithful morbidity that Mick and Keith so
love lurking in, leaving the album something of an airball.

The unguent genius flaw of *Exiles* further served to disperse response; the
true believers hated it and the non-believers didn't believe it so they loved it.
By the time *Goat's Head Soup* came out, everybody was so busy either reading
a book or learning to differentiate between themselves and the upholstery
that they just bought it and told it to shut up. But as steeped in dormosnooze
as it was, *Soup* allowed the Stones to blowtorch a goodly hunk of the *Mondo
Depravo* glacier that was squatting on their cribs. After "Dancing With Mr.
D.," there's no way that these wailing commercials for tooth decay could
mutter about what a pain pleasure is without at least cracking a smirk.

So now it's only supposed to be rock 'n' roll or something like it – a

31

spontaneously contrived mixture of outdated styles new and old housed in Peellaert painting that leaves one somewhere between puke and sarcasm. As usual, the "Glimmer Twins," producers and Jagger-Richard androids, have demixed the sound into an uncluttered mass of muddle that's guaranteed not to insult anybody's sense of mono.

Richard's guitar still sounds like its being played by a rat and the vocals are as precisely incomprehensible as ever. A case in point is the title track and juke fave of the season, the tune everybody OD'ed on before they even heard it. Kicking in with the famous tickly acoustic and Mick Taylor's deceptively unfocused slide, "It's Only R'n'R" gives subwit repetitiousness the honored non-rep it deserves. In terms of consummate redundance, this one's got to rival "96 Tears," "Wipe Out," "Satisfaction" and the Bo Diddley songbook for its crafty wallowing in rote honk. Great song, real uselessness spit in the face of boredom and a perfect mull testament to the monolith tedium that makes rock music such trash.

Replicas abound, with the Chuck Berry-primed "Dance Little Sister," the Exiles soundalike "If You Can't Rock Me," and the token Twat Fear number, "Short and Curlies" (it's too bad she's got you by the balls) leading the pack in therapeutic noise. In the minority – abuse and general-racial-slur dept., there's another out take from the ill-fated *Rolling Stones Abort Motown* LP, "Ain't Too Proud To Beg," that scores points for kicking a dead horse and not being the least big respectful about it either, plus a paranoid R&B hoke-up called "Fingerprint File," complete with pre-inaudible wah-wah and Mick creaking in his best lynching drawl "these days it's all secrecy and no privacy." There's also "Luxury," a reggae-tainted insult to everything Jamaican.

The vacant-cared Stones' ballads are around, too, scattered throughout the program like a fistful of Sleepeaze at a somnabulist's slumber party. They're not quite as dunced-out as, say, Mott The Hoople or David Bowie ballads, and there must be somebody somewhere who like these things. But as far as I'm concerned they're solid coma food.

"Time Waits For No One" is pretty close to "You Can't Always Get What You Want" attitudinally, but not near as catchy (although it does display an epic crystal-cold guitar solo). Same goes for "'Til The Next Goodbye" and "If You Really Want to Be My Friend," the latter which guest stars Blue Magic on some background fills that are designed to be decidedly unmagical and blue only in the grayest sort of way. It does make Mick sound better though, just like the strings on "As Tears Go By."

Of course, none of this lethargy interferes in the least with the basic non-manipulation that makes the album work like a finely honed soporific, taking full control of the listener's boredom threshold and twisting it all out of shape. The Stones can make you listen like no other band around, and whether you decide to like it or not is really beside the point. Gross effect is all rock 'n' roll is meant to be anyway, and the Stones are masters at exploiting any available feeling or lack thereof. It's only teenage despotism, but I like it.

November 1974

ROLLING STONES

Love You Live

(Rolling Stones Records)

The Stones suck. Everybody knows it, but nobody wants to admit it. After all, if the world's greatest rock 'n' roll band is exposed as the overpaid rag-runners that they really are, where will that leave the sucker establishment the band has courted so carefully all these years?

Scraping out buckets of ear sludge is where they belong, that's where.

With *Love You Live,* the big, bad Rolling Stones have finally laid it flat on the line: They can't play, write or sing anymore, and their live performances – once their saving grace – have passed from mere rote to lifeless imitation. These duds are over the hill and the jury has had it.

Tracing their deterioration is more effort than it's worth. Better you should do something worthwhile like watch *Operation Petticoat* or chat with a plant. It should suffice to say that *Let It Bleed* was their last solid LP, and everything since then has been image-filler or worse. The chicken-shit critical doubletake that hot-aired *Exile* into backward classic status was nostalgic kindness at best, and they haven't faked anybody out since then except lip worshippers.

Point out what's wrong with the Stones these days is like shooting Corvairs in a junkyard.

Hmm, let's try this canary yellow number over here with the big floppy grill. Mick Jagger's voice has joined fellow relics like Daltrey, Lennon and Harrison in the throat detention pen. Not only have the notes deserted him, but his famous brat-fear phrasing has ducked out as well, leaving Mick hurling squirrel grunts into the void.

Most of old innertube-mouth's Sybil-like personalities are present on *LYL*, but they just make for an overcrowded nod-party. There's MJ as the guy with a fire dept. snorkel unit for a prick in Muddy Water's "Mannish Boy," but it sounds like he's sticking to the lower registers to avoid voicecicles. There's MJ starring in *The Three Faces of Eve* on "You Can't Always Get What You Want," but who could resist some unfocused noodling on such a bloated epic? You can also catch wild, wild hoarseness in his abominable performance of "Happy," wobbly knees of sleaze on "Little Red Rooster," or even Mick as a quaint white reggae booster on "Crackin Up."

"Quite a performance," Sally Fields was heard to comment, "but what's he choking on?"

His voice, that's what. Jagger not only can't get his nodes where he wants them anymore, but he's usually so far ahead of the band that any attempted phrasing wouldn't help anyway.

Another problem area is Ron Wood and Keith Richard's apparent incompatibility on stage. Whether they're just not listening to each other or they just can't play well together is hard to tell, particularly with the haphazard mixing job that probably used up all the paper cups and string in the studio. Wyman and Watts try valiantly to keep the guitarists on base, but the band falls apart on side 4, fumbling the vital beginning of "Brown Sugar" and consistently getting lost in "Jumpin' Jack Flash." Sloppiness can be a virtue when it's the result of over-enthusiasm, but with the Stones, it's just plain messiness edged with contempt.

The selection of material is none too great either, plugged as it is with tune flakes like "Hot Stuff," and "Fingerprint File," and inferior versions of songs that weren't great shakes to start with, such as "Gotta Move" – which sounds like a box of hungry puppies doing imitations of Rita Coolidge, and the aforementioned reggae throwaway of Bo Diddley's "Crackin' Up." Even the cover looks like a George Gross book run through a body scrambling device. Can't these dummies do anything right?

At least one. Their new approach to "Tumblin' Dice" is a surprise. They've slowed it down and added a swelling Kooper/Dylan organ that brings out previously undisclosed twists in the melody. Jagger is in beautiful form, teasing and bouncing syllables off the rhythm guitar like Jamaican Silly Putty. The guitars team up as the cut builds to a climax, and Mick gets into moangear and starts humping and sighing until he's screwing the daylights out of some nightmare taste-treat until you half expect the song to come.

It's that one superb effort that shows the Stones could still be great if they tried. It's that same high point that shows up the rest of this record as off-hand bullshitting. If you buy this loser, I hope Andy Warhol does the cover for your live album.
October 1977

Rolling Stones Mossed

Lotsa people have had lotsa stuff to say about the Rolling Stones since the band's origin sometime around the dawn of the Industrial Devolution. Teen magazine alternately flash-drool and cross their legs over them, while teen mags for big kids, one of which is even maned after the band (*Bait & Tackle*) examine their every twitch and sniffle for evidence of rumors. Even Sunday Supplements run stories like "Mick and Bianca – the New Ernest and Ethel?" and it's whispered in publishing circles that Anwar Sadat barely nosed out Charlie Watts as *Time* magazine's Man of The Year. Even Ed Sullivan once called Mick "handsome" on the air. (Of course ol' Ed like to flash aquariums, too).

Outside of the media, the loudest trombone of Stones blab has come form the Fans Themselves. Now, the number of hard-core, dyed-in-the-rags Stones fans who spend all their time trying to figure out that one line in "Satisfaction" is actually about the same as card-carrying members of the Red Brigade. But like those wild-and-crazy terrorists, all they have to do is make a lot of bambam and everybody else falls into line, or falls period. Come fall, it'll be "which one did you say has the funny teeth?" time all over again.

Ask Dummies

The big question, after all the hype and hormones have blown over is: Do the Rolling Stones have any legitimate reason to exist at this late date other than pure dollarslobber? While this useless query has been charco-broiled by the press until it's about as inviting as a virgin in Jello, nobody's ever asked the non-Stone-fanatical man/woman on the street what they think. Not that anybody gives a shit, but who's left to ask?

So with the same scientific sampling techniques used by the Neilsen company to select *Mass For the Criminally Insane* as the nation's most watched television show, our panel of experts (an ant psychologist, an anthropologist and an accordionist) went out and asked people just like you (Heaven forbid) the burning question that's on every informed American's mind:

If you were a veterinarian with a needle full of sodium cyanide, would you put the Rolling Stones to sleep?

Hank B. (lawnmower customizer) "Shit, yeah! These turkey assholes have been putting out shitty records for so long that people are gonna forget how good their old stuff was. It disgusts me, it makes me physically ill (pukes on arm to demonstrate) that all these young Stones fans are going around singing "Angie" totally ignorant of Stones classics like "Gomper," "In Another Land," and "Pass That Joint, Matey.""

Jane J. (battered wife) "Oh no, they're the only band around with any sex appeal. I hear that Mick's so big that he needs a bladder ladder just to go to the bathroom. They're not all that great though. On my personal sex-preference chart, Wyman and Watts occupy the two places above "dead clam" and Keith came in behind microwave oven."

Amanda J. (housewife/brain surgeon) "Yes, they deserve to die because they'll never be any good on TV. I mean, you can see them on *Alice*, or maybe starring in a new MTM production? I can see it now: Ron Wood gets a job at a South Dakota radio station, where he's always getting hassled by the gruff-but-lovable station manager (Keith) and the obnoxious anchorman (Mick, of course). You can see right off it wouldn't work. All five of them would wanna be Phyllis."

Rick J. (writer) "Are you kidding? The Stones are the best press there is. If they weren't around, hacks like me wouldn't be able to earn our pinball money cranking out stupid Watts-is-the-Walrus stories. Get this, next week I'm going on a junket to England to check out the rumors about Margaret Trudeau digging up Brian Jones' grave and ...""

Gary B. (occupation unknown) "Naah, I don't think so. At least they've got personalities, repulsive as they may be. The way I see it, Jagger's the weiner-wagger, Watts is the bashful stockbrocker type, Wyman sells angora-scented luv dolls, Richard is a cadaver at a Dental College and Wood's the Beaver."

Mary S. (correspondent) "I'd wanna kill 'em only if I could jump on 'em afterward. Shit, I don't care what I say, you're making up these quotes anyway."

Franky F. (character from author's past) "No, if there were no Rolling Stones, then Rolling Stones Records would go out of business and who else would there be to release Bill Wyman solo albums? I always play *Monkey Grip* before bedtime to get my pet chimp in the mood!"

Keith R. (rock musician) "You got what? Sodium cyanide? Hey man, you got any of that stuff on you now? Yeah? Is it good shit? Listen man, c'mon back to the hotel. I've got some buddies there that'll try anything!" *July 1978*

ROLLING STONES
A Bigger Bang
(EMI)

A Bigger Bang is a truly disgusting dish, something that even a dog would rather roll in than eat.

Considering that this is the Stones' first all-new episode in eight years, you'd think they'd show up with a whole lot more quality material. I mean, what've they been up to since the last century, other than playing endless games of spin-the-rehab?

Apparently not much. Well, you've probably heard about Keith Richards' upcoming E! Network reality show *My So-Called Death* by now, as well as Charlie Watts' new side-career as a forensic beautician model. The grapevine tells me Ron Wood's been doing sound for Amish TV. Did they ever get another bass player? Beats me!

As for frontman Sir Mick, it looks like he spent most of his time scouring the world for manufacturers of idiotic ladies' hats he could prance around in onstage for this season's salary drive. And to think we scoffed when we were warned years ago of the Millinery-Industrial Complex.

Seriously though – the guy's been on a collision course with Earth for so long he had to crash eventually. Once a bold, black-hearted lyricist who could come up with stuff about crossfire hurricanes and not getting any girl reaction, now he's just a drivel-spouting canal of Rubicon-crossing and – oh no – politics! Dude, they have a Visine for that.

It's not like there's *nothing* worth hearing on this disc, however. The opening track, "Rough Justice," deftly rocks that smoky corner of your brain where the pinball machines are. Keith's big, nasty chords – cooked up in the same taxidermy oven as "Start Me Up" - totally kick tutu and Mick cries out like a man whose toupee tape's been stolen.

That song, along with rockers like "Driving Too Fast" and "Look What the Cat Dragged In," even recall the post-magical Rubbermaid-recommended sound spectrum of *Exile on Main Street* (1972). It's just an ear-thing, though, a taunting echo of two minds that would rather be in Switzerland trading emissions than merely penning classic songs.

When the Stones slow down the tempo, they're usually in trouble, and this disc is no exception. The one song getting the most press coverage is "Sweet Neo Con," a monumentally lame protest-bleat that appears to imply our Commander-in-Chief is a "hypocrite." During wartime, no less! Come on, you guys, when Jagger tries to reset himself as head devil sympathizer again, he comes across as Tootie Incarnate.

If you think that poop stinks, check out "Laugh, I Nearly Died," a pallid ballad where Sir M. insists he's "been to Africa looking for my soul." O.K., class, what's wrong with that statement? Right, he didn't lose it there to begin with. When he whimpers he's so "sick and tired" (well, sick anyway) of being sick 'n' tired, you just want to grab the remote and hit Language Select instead. Laugh? I nearly ran around freaking out like an angry coyote in a Hello Kitty boutique.

Not to just drone, fellow consumers, but on a CD that's more than 62.4 percent ballads or mid-tempo piddling, you have to address the putty or just run a tab, right? So check out the penalty phase of the album, "This Place is Empty." Letting Keith sing is never a good idea, but supporting his ghastly croaking with an ersatz mix of tinkly-dink piano and bottle-throttlin' guitar scraps borders on what detective mags call a crime against nature. Not to mention a leading cause of preventable metaphors.

There is one non-rocker that stands out. "Biggest Mistake" flutters in on a perfectly formed falsetto and sports an unmistakably true melody that's a throwback to great tunes like "Ruby Tuesday" and "As Tears Go By." Despite the fact that this heavenly cooing is employed by Satan, it's just plain lovable. *Ich bin ein* Lou Christie.

As for the rest of the product, most of these songs should be reported immediately to PETSD (People for the Ethical Treatment of Shifting Demographics). The once-great Rolling Stones – having no concept whatsoever of their ever-aging fan base–are now nothing more than a tribute band to their bad selves. I say we honor them with a mock standing ovation tonight! *July 2005*

BEE GEES
Best of BeeGees Vol. 2
(RSO)

Fuck the BeeGees. What really matters is the Model of The Year Pageant, held a couple weeks ago in some Miami hotel where people were tuxes and clap a lot. If we had a TV column this would be in it but we're too cheap, so all you BeeGees fan(s) out there are gonna have to pay for it.

This rag doesn't even have a TV, not even a black & white one, and if they did it woulda been turned to the educational channel that night anyway coz B.B. King was on there giving his opinions on the economy, etc. And I know there's some wise guy saying, "Oh, man, but dat's da real blues" and I say fuck ya: THIS IS THE REAL BLUES!!!

Now let's get down to some fluff. Model of The Year was on the same night as *Miss Teenage America* but it had the upper hand since it followed *Bob Newhart* and also had better hosts. Rona Barrett and Hugh O'Brian to be exact, new faces on the beauty circuit and, judging by the way they continually messed up, that's how they'll stay. Plus there was a panel of ex-runners up who, along with Rona, were supposed to predict which toots would take the crown. The way I see it, if they were so smart, howcum they were runners-up?

Choreography was handled by the same guy who used to do the Mouseketeers marches, and the music, played by a New York lounge super-group, was strictly from the back pages of *Downbeat*. Also three low-cal female voices behind the curtain somewhere piping "model udda year model udda year who willll it beeeeeee?" Not enough to stomp yer TV over, but sappy nonetheless.

In case yer wondering when I'm gonna get to the women-as-fleshy-hangers syndrome that lurks around these pageants like the ghost of Susan B. Anthony, you can forget it. If you wanna hear about that yer gonna have to go read *Orgasms for Industry* 'cos I sure don't give a shit. Oppression ain't half the mind-rot that TV is.

Anyway, MOTY featured 34 women walking around in various states of smile, all with colorful past occupations like stamp collector, catnip inventor, combine driver and gas station attendant. That last one allowed Handsome Hugh his only chance for a sex yuk all evening when he quipped, "How would ya like to pull into *her* gas station and say FILL 'ER UP?" Face it, Hugh. Yer no Tom Poston. So after they cut the 34 down to 13 semi-finalists, 9 finalists, 5 lightweight contenders and 2 or 3 packages of individually wrapped ground-beef patties, Cybill Shepherd – wearing her usual wiseass smirk – came out to crown the champ. For the winner, it was a guarantee of seeing her face in a few thousand dollars worth of cosmetics ads in the next year. For Cybill it was just a *cinema verite* scene for her next movie, *Hot Tiaras over Miami.*

And now a word from our sponsor. BeeGees (or B.G.s) is Australian for Buncha Gimps if you really wanna know. As for *Best Of BeeGees Vol. 2*, it's the long awaited follow-up to *Best Of BeeGees Vol. 1.*

Barbara Walters would like it. Pat Loud would say, "It's nice."
November 1973

BLUE ASH
No More No Less
(Mercury)

What with everybody going back to the '50s and '60s for inspiration these days, it was inevitable that somebody would rediscover folk rock and do an update on it. And not the cufflink box tinkle slime that passed for "rock-folk" in the *Time* and *Life* articles on the Youthquake, but the Merseybeat-influenced hard stuff that the Byrds, Turtles, Beau Brummels and Love (who also borrowed heavily from the Stones) used to serve up at every Sunset Strip truncheon luncheon worth attending. The bard corps watered it down into country-rock in no time at all, but now Blue Ash are on the scene, there's gonna be some changes made. Heads will roll. Mandolins will be buttered and eaten. Steel guitars will be traded in for hair spray. Iridescent sharkskin hiphuggers will come back into style.

Blue Ash know what they're doing. *They took The Byrds' Greatest Hits and*

38

mated them with *The Turtles' Golden Hits* (Volume One in both cases since the followup collections are fakeouts), filtered them through just about every mid-'60s bargain-bin group they could find (including Autosalvage, Baroques, Blond, Bubble Puppy, Buffalo Springfield, Candymen, Cherokee, Children of Paradise, Circus Maximus, Colours, Country Funk, Crabby Appleton, Cryin' Shames, Fifth Avenue Band, Flame, Golden Dawn, Glad, Hackamore Bruck, Herd, International Submarine Band, Jake & Family Jewels, Kangaroo, Kensington Market, Keith, Left Banke, Lothar & The Hand People, Merry Go-Round, Montage, Moon, Nazz, Oxpetals, Passing Clouds, Paupers, Pinkiny Canandy, Puff, Redwing, Remains, Robbs, Rockin' Food, Rose Garden, Sopwith Camel, Southwind, Sunrays, Tremeloes, Tradewinds, Troll, Unspoken Word, Wackers, and the Yellow Payges), listened to a lot of Beatles and Slade, and added variations gained from playing their originals interspersed among Top 40 sweeties and oldies on the Ohio club circuit for the past five years to come up with all these high, hard harmonies and some of the meanest Bosstown fuzz guitar ever scraped.

And you know their lyrics are OK because they sing the word "time" like it was spelled tie-yeem.

So you get everything they're good at on this first album. All originals except for Dylan's "Dusty Old Fairgrounds," which sounds like it was written around the time of "Subterranean Homesick Blues," and the Beatles' "Anytime at All" done up in a lurid Slade rollover style. The stuff they write themselves is all pretty familiar sounding and highly accessible. "Plain To See" sounds like a tuff version of the Hollies' "Just One Look" and "What Can I Do For You?" is "For What It's Worth" for all practical purposes. The rest is mostly splendid harmonic rockers, the biggie being "Here We Go Again." Just that one song is better than 75 percent of the first three Byrds LPs and twice as good as America's entire *Homecoming* album.

So stay away from the bargain bins for a while and pick up Blue Ash. After all, the average 1968 MGM cutout contains 1.7 good songs and costs 67.43 cents. Blue Ash has at least 10 out of 12 killers and goes for around four bucks, so it's a bargain anyway you look at it.
November 1973

SLADE
Sladest
(Reprise)

"The beat is the main thing with us. We like to hit their guts with the beat and get some feeling going through their bloodstream into their hands. If you want to come and sit down and delve into the music, it's no good coming to see us. We get our kicks from pulsating music." — Noddy Holder

So do the teenage hoards of Great Britain. They've got the pop perspective to make every Slade single Top 10 on the day of its release. They know what they're doing, too, coz if it says Slade on the cover, you can be sure the heavy buzz formula has been followed precisely, with a fanatical post-technocratic fervor.

The Americans, however, allow no rites without obligations. We live in such a consistently mindless state that we can rarely appreciate simple mindlessness for the sake of mindlessness. Whew. The British don't have this problem, though, because England is really truly shitty; it's always cloudy and your father probably died in a coal mine.

The band's earlier labels – Polydor and Atlantic – couldn't get Slade singles on the radio where they belong, leaving their albums to die slow, morbid deaths. Polydor's best idea was to drag the Dunce of American Rock Critix, Lester Bangs, over to London for a Slade concert. He liked it. He wrote about it. Slade continued to bomb.

Now Warners has the band, and they have the necessary pull with radio programmers (a pull in the general direction of the bank) to get Slade on the airwaves and into the racks of every supermarket in America, where they belong. *Sladest* is the perfect record to do it with, a collection of their smash English singles with a new track or two, all bearing the humanistic heavy metal of primal Slade. And the Slade Sound? It consists of equal amounts of piercing, tweeter-twisting lead guitar from Dave Hill, bruiser rhythm guitar and paralingual vocals by Noddy Holder, the mechanical men in the rhythm section, and a live ambience not unlike a Mellotron fitted with applause tapes.

With at least half the cuts good enough to be the national anthem after *Wild In The Streets, Sladest* is one solid album. Every track has the total concentration of a monster single, thanks to ex-Animal Chas Chandler's (the Jimi Hendrix merchandiser) calculated production and the band's single-minded determination to stomp babies. "Mama Weer All Crazee Now," "Gudbuy T'Jane," and "Cum On Feel The Noize" have all gotten some airplay here and might be familiar.

If you like those, you'll like the rest because everything they do sounds pretty much the same, even when they substitute keyboard for guitar. But what do you want, blood? Slade is the first dependable name since Beatles, and that's enough for me. If you know what's good for you, it'll be enough for you, too, and *Sladest* is the right introduction. Buy it now because today might be the last day of the rest of your life.

December 1973

BARNABY BYE
Room To Grow
(Atlantic)

10cc
10cc
(UK Records)

When you feel like turning off the sound on *Mannix* and replacing their cocktail suspicion music with some really blatant ear thugs, there's never any problem. Grand Funk, N.Y. Dolls, Black Sabbath, Copperhead, Stooges ... everyone's got their own heroes when it comes to supplying the necessary adrenalin to truly appreciate the dynamics of stomp. But what if the sound you wanna blot is *Room 222* or the *Miss Teenage Librarian Pageant*? Unless you're one of those boring ironists, the *Look at that! Karen Valentine singing a drum* solo types, you'll probably want something a bit more compatible to the wimp zone on the screen. You just *don't* play *Slade Alive* over the *Mary Tyler Moore Show*. It ain't etiquette.

So what ya gonna do, turn off the TV? Hell, no – I'm here to tell you that there's two brand-new lightweights that can solve your viewing problems without crossing the wimp line into Twerp Heaven – the place where people automatically stack up their Partridge Family discs right before David, Shirley and Frogface and the rest hit the screen. Or if they feel really incestuous, they play 'em during *Brady Bunch*.

Not too long ago, Todd Rundgren was the king of the creampuff. But then he decided to go nuts at the knobs and produce himself into a corner, building a massive wall of studio sound behind which he could hide his serious shortage of decent material. Well, no sooner does he phase out (to the rerereleased tune of "Hello It's Me") than his parking place gets snapped up by a N.Y. band with the unlikely name of Barnaby Bye, whose members include an ex-Blues Magoo (!) and a pair of identical twin brothers cute enough to be both halves of a Popsicle.

Barnaby must have been listening real close to Todd's earlier stuff, because they have this true romance pop sound memorized down to the last stifled whimper. The lead vocals especially (and most of the gobs of feathery background vocals) often duplicate his horny-lonely inflections, and the highly domesticated instrumentation could have been played by the same friendly robots who backed Rundgren up on *Something-Anything*. Each song has an intensely persevering melody, so that even after MTM is over you'll find yourself singing along right through *Bob Newhart*.

And speaking of situation comedy, 10cc – the group with the most drug-oriented name since The Reefers – has already reached the pinnacle of storytelling pop ditties on this first album of theirs, and they won't be satisfied until they've stretched the form out enough to keep other artists busy catching up for the next few years. What we've got here is nothing less than the biggest development since the Beach Boys, and I ain't just blowin' farts.

If you enjoyed their single hit, "Rubber Bullets," you're only getting a small part of the picture. The album version is a bit longer, incorporating a neato dream sequence and a whole extra verse that includes the lines of the year: "We all got balls and brains/ but some's got balls and chains." Beats the Dr. Pepper prison break any day.

One look at the components of 10cc explains why they're so good at what they do: Graham Gouldman, composer of "Bus Stop," "For Your Love," "Look Through Any Window," "There's A Kind Of Hush," and 10 million others, Eric Stewart of "Groovy Kind of Love" Mindbenders fame, plus Kevin Godly and Lol Crème of Hotlegs, who had a hit with "Neanderthal Man," and an album cover that was directly lifted for Alice Cooper's *School's Out* extravaganza.

With people like that, you can't very well miss, and 10cc doesn't. Their songs, though fairly complex, are made up of deceptively simple parts that fit together perfectly. They can do quick little rockers reminiscent of the Small Faces and the middle (post-*Generation*, pre-*Tommy*) Who, full-blown Beach Boys production numbers, or finely crafted pop contrivances like "The Dean and I" (which really should be the theme for a TV show, possibly a follow-up to *Nanny and The Professor*), all with equal confidence. Plus, they're second to none in the clever twist of cliché that makes lyrics memorable.

Here's how to do it then – 10cc is for the high-class visual stuff like *Adam's Rib* or *Marcus Welby* (funniest show on TV). For uncomplicated sillies like *Calucci's Dept.* and *Lotsa Luck,* it's best to stick with Barnaby Bye. TV ain't half bad so long as you don't bother to listen. That's why none of the good shows are on radio anymore.
January 1974

PETER PETER IVERS BAND
Terminal Love
(Warner Brothers)

10cc
Sheet Music
(UK)

SPARKS
Kimono My House
(Island)

The commercial viability of *mondo progresso* pop music is generally slim at best, but every now and again it slips out of the Number 276-with-a-bubble chart netherworld into the big money. It's like, say, Focus, who are weird if nothing else, going over like a cupcake at a pedarists' convention all because they lucked out and yodeled in the right places, providing the essential popularity hook for the can't-understand-it-therefore-it's-great-crowd to latch onto. The *real* advance threat to pop-as-we-know-it, though, is in artists you can sorta appear to deal with when all the time they're really *dealing with you*, playing up to your nice-guy side while they lounge snidely in wimp cynicism – bands like the three ear-sneaks above, swell creepy crawlies at best and pushy seatsniffs on their off-tracks.

Peter Peter Ivers is the one you've really gotta watch out for. Right off he's peeling brain gum for you with his name. Why couldn't one Peter suffice? Why the gory cover from a Bob Weir lookalike? Why the presence of not only a former Fanny in his band, but an ex-Fraternity of Man who helped write their famous busted-in-Denver showstopper, "Fuck Her?" Peter's just *bent*, that's all. His songs are terribly catchy in a twisted way, not necessarily in a pretty-melodies or nice-riffs sorta style, but a wormy, covert approach to trapping the back of your ear and tickling it. His music has a very loose base in some semi-secret blues idiom somewhat similar to the place Captain Beefheart used to draw his inspiration from. It might take a few listenings, but eventually you can't resist something like "Alpha Centauri" or "Sweet Enemy" when it comes back days later and squats a trance on your memory. Great lyrics too, like "Since you been out of town, the machines broke down" from "AC" or the snide request in "Felladaddio": "I threw the blues in her face/ I told her take 'em from me honey but/ don't spend 'em all in one place."

Peter's a real star of mad science and you oughtta take it upon yourself to look into him before he looks into you.

10cc aren't really all that strange, tho they do hint at the fun of camel-humping in one song and have invented a dance fad, "The Sacro'Iliac," which consists of doing nothing. Their first album was much more presentable, what with goodies like "Rubber Bullets" and "The Dean and I" showing off the commercial dittydom of their all-star members. This time they've chosen to stretch out a bit more and skip the numerous-potential-hit-singles approach that was the joy of their first LP and start taking things a bit *seriously*. No need for that if you ask me, but you still get a few nice radio pieces like the McCartneyish "Wall Street Shuffle" and pseudo-heavy "Silly Love," along with the dragged-out tickets to snoozedom such as "Somewhere In Hollywood" ("Norman Mailer wants to nail her" – bit the bitter Sunday Supplement, Limey Legend snuffers) and "Old Wild Men," which is a dull attempt at doing an arty version of "Rock and Roll Heaven." There were at least four or five songs on the first album that accomplished a lot more by being likeable while still pushing the borders around, and unless 10cc is planning to become a wimpy Vanilla Fudge, I suggest they cool the concepts next time and get down to business.

Sparks are another case of hit-and-miss trendyness. When they hit, like with their brilliant English smasheroo, "This Town Ain't Big Enough for Both of Us," they're truly superb: guitar on the verge of short-out, bruiser drums, skillfully hot teen lyrics, ("census, the latest census/ there'll be more girls who live in town though not enough to go around") delivered with Russell Mael's precise, permanent-wave vocals. Most of their material is in this mode, although generally less frantic, more dependent on keyboards, and certainly less focused than the single. Sometimes they slip into bitch-boy cloy ("Equater," "Talent Is An Asset"), but they're usually sneaky enough to walk the line between comic-book opera and candy underground without getting too cute, resulting in tight little vignettes not unlike the Who's *Happy Jack* period. There are real neat lyrics throughout, too, penned mostly by Ben Turpin lookalike Ron Meal, little Russ's big brother and father figure. A studied threat to anybody's clear edge on reality, they're a fun rock 'n' pop band to boot. Pick up on some of this engaging weirdness before you find yourself left out in the cheese.

October 1974

10cc
Deceptive Bends
(Mercury)

Another 50-50 from 10cc, the band with the love/hate relationship with itself.

These guys, let me tell ya. Coming up through the UK minors in the '60s as they did, they're masters of radio flypaper. Every now and then their survivor mentality gets in the way, casting a screen of contempt that turns their more commercial efforts into razor blade popsicles. But it's no big deal.

You'd never even know that half the band is missing. Sure enough, Lol Crème and Kevin Godley have taken off for bigger and better things. Ha ha, the illusions of obscurity. Graham Gouldman and Eric Stewart carry on with true studio vanity though nothing's wrong with this picture.

If they could only stick with low-key stuff like the taste treats on side one, 10cc could emerge as a ABBA without tits. While "The Things We Do For Love" sounded a lot better on the radio, it's still a chrome Sweet Tart, and the rest of the side is so likeable you could almost believe this band isn't a poor man's Wings. The new single, "People In Love," is soft enough to pass for flu soup, and "Marriage Bureau" gives Stewart a chance to nearly top the lyrical taffy of his guitar lines on the old "Headline Hustler," still their most thoroughly realized cut.

Boredom sets in on most of the second side. You want to take songs like "I Bought A Flat Guitar Tutor" and rub their nose in it until they stop trying to be so oppressively cute. "You've Got a Cold" is equally irritating, but the real Vitamin Duh is "Feel The Benefit," a three-part bloatothon that drags on the rest of the record like a fresh tinkle tail.

Deceptive Bends is at least less eccentric than the last couple of 10cc offerings, if somewhat less inspired. If you're a fan of their pop poop, the first side should be enough to keep you out of the dark alleys where the little kids play. But if you're one of those poor unfortunate ear cases in it for their candy experiments and Tinker Toy confrontations, DB is just more of the same.

Bring back ugly radio!

May 1977

SPARKS
The No. 1 Song In Heaven
(Elektra)

I'm not a real big disco fan.

I hate Sparks. They should be sent to Iran.

I detest Elektra/Asylum Records and everything they stand for.

So you can see why I was asked to review this record, even though it didn't have any television sets on the cover. Little did we know it would change my life.

You see, I never really did "fit in" with the disco scene. My clothes are all borrowed from Junior High School exhibits of Unsuitable Attire. I have difficulty remaining "animated" during pointless pick-up conversations. And when I try to dance, I look like a demonstration of rubber farm implements.

Then *No. 1 Song in Heaven* came into my life. "Hmmm," I said to myself, "a disco Sparks album; just what I need first thing in the morning." Well, *second*.

Way back when, I used to "love" Sparks (he confessed) even though Russ Mael's voice sounds like a ground squirrel's last thoughts as it makes an unsuccessful attempt to escape the wheels of a speeding fire engine. Tweet, smoosh.

But then my friends started to like Sparks, so I had to quit. I didn't think it was "cool" (note bad attitude) and besides, if you say you don't like anything your friends like, people will think you're "ahead of your time." What a fairy tale *that* idea is.

Anyway, Bill sent me the record. (He's still mad at me for the time I got loaded to "the max" and tried to drink his entire house. I didn't know, I thought it tasted good.)

Hands *still* aquiver, I scraped the dried clay off of my "turntable" and plunked down the record. As the first whines split the morning air like wiener-knife lightning, an amazing transformation came over me. I made my bed.

Later that day, I *tucked in* my "Tramps Like Us" T-shirt. I washed my lunch *before* I killed it. I watched *Bozo* and identified with Frazier Thomas instead of Garfield Goose. I took out the garbage and *threw it away*.

Then, that evening, I asked a "woman friend" of mine over for dinner, drugs 'n' disco. Pretty cute, huh? I even went so far as to suggest that maybe she could teach me "a few new steps."

"WHAT DO YOU THINK I AM, YOUR FUCKING MOTHER?" she replied.

See?
May 1979

CAPITAL CITY ROCKETS
Capital City Rockets
(Elektra)

Wotta cover – a pink, yellow, green and orange phallic stencil job that looks like a bad day at an alternative newspaper's printer and the whole skweegee is embossed so even Stevie Wonder fans can read it. The back side is the ugliest bunch of subhuman lip suckers ever to grace an Elektra cover. It makes the Stooges look like Bread, primped up as a counterfeit roller derby team no less, all shiners and TV blood. There ain't a jammer in the bunch, though. They're the kinda guys who get caught beating off behind the bowling alley on rainy Tuesday nights. That's coz lead singer Jamie Lyons used to be the main man in the Music Explosion and by now has to be too burned out by one-night stands in sleaze havens like Macomb, Ill., to be roller-derby tuff, but soon as one of those goons tossed a bench in front of him at 60 mph he'd be hanging up his skates and starting a stamp collection.

CCR (did they pay big bucks to John Fogerty for the initials?) are trying out as the punkiest of the new punk-rockers and anyone who wants to top them is gonna have to go pretty far, like maybe playing completely out of tune or recording at a gas station. Their occasionally forced lameness, particularly the tin-toned rhythm guitarist, is refreshing as an Audie Murphy flick at 4 a.m. and the lyrics are way better – like "Come back baby, I know your head's in outer space" or "I'd make my will out to ya but I'm too tired to write," or even "You might find my orange tie wrapped around your NECK." That sure beats the juice outta "Gimme peace on Earth," don't it?

Of the 10 songs included, any one could've been the second best cut on the Music Explosion's first album, right after "Little Bit O'Soul." They all take the crispy Bacon Bits approach that's been the key to many of AM radio's (c.1966) greatest moments, with the kind of riffs that drive people shitty when it comes on the car radio because if they have the slightest little crack in their speaker the guitar will just buzz the crap out of it. "Breakfast In Bed" should be a great single, but it looks like a stiff, so your radio's safe for the time being. "Ten Hole Dollars" would make a good follow-up bomb since it concerns the price of Capital City snatch, as would "Grab Your Honey" – which is my candidate for the most mindless refrain noise of the year. Once you've heard it, you'll never get rid of it – not even when you're sicker than snot with it.

Whether or not this punkier-than-thou stuff is gonna sell remains to be seen, but it sure is nice to have some more killer trash for after the grooves on N.Y. Dolls start to go. It's the kinda music that would make a perfect soundtrack for two bowling balls and five babies going around in a dryer, and you can't ask for much more than that. Get it now and stomp on down to the laundromat.

January 1974

JO JO GUNNE

Jumpin' the Gunne
(Asylum)

Total bloato excess is what pop music is all about. Just let somebody find one good movie, even a single indisputable deathblow riff, and they'll keep glutting it out onto eternity, running it into the ground until not even a dead horse can hear it without puking pus, then revive it 10 years later and call it nostalgia. Tons of people have done this, from big boys like the Byrds and Steve Stills down to unabashed redundos like the Seeds with their 40 recorded versions of "Pushin' Too Hard," and entire genres have been based on it, with the Lobo-Bread-wimp-into-twerp sector being the most popular lately (although the glitter goons are crawling in fast). Just carve out that niche in the Pop Zone and sit in there holding your breath 'til the money bags come hopping, begging for mercy.

And if there's anybody who appreciates excess for the true conceptual Winnebago camper it is, Jay Ferguson is the man. You'd think he'd have soaked up enough of it with Spirit when he was mainman with them, since they never were exactly applauded for their good taste. They sure were a great band, too, piling Jay's bizzaro flagellation numbers on top of Randy California's comatose it's-not-nice-to-fool-Mother-Nature eco-rants in top of Lou Adler's Mantovanoid-creamed string readymades on top of Moog instrumental fakeouts that might have sounded futuristic in the '50s (when sludged-out American record buyers made a gold LP out of a ping-pong match recorded in then-novelty stereo) but finally came across like one of those Vanguard techno-yukyuks like *The In Sound From Way Out.*

No doubt about it, Spirit had what it takes. If any particular excess of theirs wasn't up your alley, you could be sure they'd eventually hit your own personal dimwit heaven and you'd sop it up like the cretinous sponge farm everybody really wants to be.

It wasn't enough for Jay, though. He wanted to indulge *his* private scum dream of nonstop boogie coupled with the friendly masochism of rock stars gone to seed, scrounging for more degenerate yummies they can reject *just for the fun of it*! He really knows how to have a good time! This is Jo Jo's third album now, so if you figure about 10 songs per, that's 30 songs dealing entirely with what a sordid bummer it is to be a hotshot pop fave who looks just like the Winchester Man and have all these drained-out lovelies crawling all over your keyboards with beg in their eyes but you'd really rather tell 'em how much sleep you didn't get in the past *X* years and all the cosmosis complexities involved and besides, eating raw meat is way more fun anyway. Is it the decadence, or just Dorian Gray beating off in front of a mirror?

But bad taste is its own reward – as all of us hopheads who've been gobbling up this fiendishly contrived shit the past 20 years oughtta know by now – and Jo Jo flings it out faster and with more banal exactness than I'd care to throw a stack of Gary Lewis & The Playboys records at. It's the final triumph of utterly mindless nullity that you can toss on this album and sapout in ultimo passivity at the brilliance with which these guys manipulate the noise we love to hear. That's nothing to say about the music, except it's a consummate whiz — always fast, generally bulbous, and packed solid with the heavy jagoff hooks and habitual riffing that lets you put yer brain in yer boots and stomp the sentience out of it. This is no mere beer-and-hankies hype either: JO JO GUNNE IS THE AMERICAN LED ZEP, only more so.

So let's get down to the important stuff like song titles — "High School

47

Drool," "Monkey Island," "Neon City," "Turn The Boy Loose," "I Wanna Love You," "Getaway," and the primal sleaze-monger of 'em all, "Red Meat":

I want that red meat
Laid out on the table
Want dat red meat
You don't need no label
Want some red meat
I'll be sure to bring it
Got dat red meat
now everybody sing it:
BIG MAMA! BIG MAMA!
BIG MAMA! BIG MAMA!

Other important factors: Ferguson's publishing company is called Bulge Music, fatso bass player Jimmie Randall (who replaced ex-Spirit pretty face Mark Andes a while back) is really starting to hum it coz he plays it fat instead of pretty; there's a piss blitzing powerhouse called "To The Island" on which Jay has a minimum of five Howling Wolf-organ cum-squats; the lead guitarist still makes more amped-up speed noise that a deaf-mute convention in a firecracker factory; the jumbo pig-kisser on the cover looks up for bring a butt-buddy; and the label is Asylum, so if ya buy lots of these Jay might still get to screw Joni Mitchell.

After that she'd slit her wrists for sure!

February 1974

JO JO GUNNE
So...Where's the Show?
(Asylum)

Not too many bands get uglier and greater at the same time, but Jo Jo Gunne shows that it can be done. Matt Andes, the last threat to Jay Ferguson's Winchester Man supremacy, is now out, as his unrecorded replacement, Star Donaldson, who was probably too cute. Al Staehely, formerly of the fake verson of Spirit, is on guitar now and take it from me—if these guys get any uglier they're gonna have to be made into dogfood.

Jo Jo is still the fine metallic rockers they've always been, thanks mainly to Jay's hot vocals and keyboards, Al's powersaw guitar, and the enormously fat playing of Jimmie Randall. Talk about gruesome — this guy looks like a 17-year-old David Clayton Thomas trying to imitate a shovel.

But his mean detective movie bass lines make two of the best songs, "I'm Your Shoe" and "Around The World," roll like hardcore cave music.

Toxic riff numbers predominate, as usual, with "Big Busted Bombshell From Bermuda" and "S&M Blvd" leading the pack, while the transcendental redundancy of "She Said Allright" wraps things up with a classic tube solo from Al. This is something you gotta see live to appreciate: it looks like he's making pigeon mouth to a cellophane snake, playing sticky lead guitar, and trying not to pee his sneaks all at the same time.

To show he's not totally antihuman, Jay throws in a couple of his icepick ballads with spiraling keyboards and knockout choruses. Also, an embossed cover for fans who've been blinded by cherry bombs at Jo Jo concerts. See? Liking Jo Jo Gunne isn't a matter of taste, it's a matter of *class*.
January 1975

SPIRIT
Spirit of '76
(Mercury)

Since the original Spirit broke up a few years back, we've seen more fake Spirits than you'd care to shake a snooze at. John Lock had one, Ed Cassidy had one, Randy California had a handful, and a couple of Greg Allman look-alikes named the Stachly Brothers even had one for a while. Sometimes two or more of these bands would find themselves on the same bill, which created all sorts of amusement for the promoters involved. Better yet, all these bands sucked.

Spirit ceased being any sort of a reality when Jay Ferguson left to rev up Jo Jo Gunne, one of the great ignored flash outfits. Without Jay's composing and vocal talents, the future of Spirit became strictly academic.

So now we're being asked to buy the '76 model of Spirit, with Randy, Ed and a bassist named Barry Keene. They're surprisingly listenable, considering. Although nowhere near the old band in style or power, they at least display a sense of humor, an ingredient which was sorely lacking in the last 20 regroupings. At least I guess it's a sense of humor, because with retread versions of everything from "Walkin' the Dog" to "The Star Spangled Banner," there's yuks a-plenty, intentional or otherwise. Randy's penchant for reworking pointless old songs, as on his *Captain Kopter* LP, always suggested terminal flakiness (he did have a serious accident that cracked his nut a while back), but he's developed such a low-profile attack that you hardly even notice anymore. "Hey Joe" sounds almost exactly like Hendrix, the Stones' "Happy" is so anemic it sounds like they plugged into a space heater, and "Like A Rolling Stone" is nothing to shit yer sox over, Rangers. Boys will be boys, and burnouts will be burnouts.

California's originals come across a lot better when they come across at all. While possessing a disturbing ozone-alert haziness, several of the tunes sound like they were written around the time of *Dr. Sardonicus*, with those light, dry vocals and acoustic guitar inlays. Of course, without the punch of Ferguson tracks like "Mr. Skin" and "Animal Zoo," Randy's material tends to run together, eventually dissolving in dummy sound effects.

The only thing really exciting here is the rumor that Ferguson, fed up with the lack of bucks Jo Jo has been ringing up lately, is considering teaming up with California again in a real version of Spirit. As for the '76 gang, only fanatics need apply.
June 1975

GONG
(BYG)

MAGMA
(Seventh Records)

KOMINTERN
(Harvest)

ARTHUR BROWN'S KINGDOM COME
(Polydor)

Now that the Mothers have become "just another band from L.A.," the lover of the bizarre in music finds an emptiness in his life, something missing. Or does he? The really discerning album freak can find music just as twisted as Zappa's ever was by searching through those elusive-import stores. Yes, friends, Europe has become the center of the bizarre.

Perhaps the leading contender for the throne vacated by Zappa is Daevid Allen and his band Gong. This ridiculous band based in France could quite easily replace the Mothers as the world's leading absurd band. Allen – or, as he is elsewhere known, Bert Camembert, Dingo Virgin and Captain Capricorn, to name but three – has produced the story of the Pot Head Pixies from the planet Gong and created a whole musical scene around them centered on Radio Gnome Invisible, a radio station broadcasting from a flying teapot directly to the brain.

I was fortunate enough to witness Gong on their second British tour in the space of a few months just the other night and I can safely say that I came away distinctly impressed. The virtuosity of the individual members of the band equals and at times exceeds that of former Mothers. The full lineup of the band is difficult to determine but the following Gongpeoples are easily recognized: ex-Soft Machiner Daevid Allen and Steve Hillage on guitars; Didier Malherbe, reeds; Christian Tritsch, bass; Gilli Smyth, voice; and Francis Bacon, synthesizer.

Gong's continuous, two-hour set opens in darkness with the entrance of Allen carrying a glittering candle. Liberal application of Dayglo paint adds to his bizarre appearance in a 13-inch-high green hat with a nylon propeller on the top. Dingo announces the arrival of Gong in ceremonial and ritualistic terms while Gilli enters with a large witch's hat and flaming crimson zodiacal gown and launches into wailing and heavy breathing in a most stimulating fashion. A crescendo is reached with all members of the band on stage, at which point the set effectively begins.

From this moment on, the music takes over and guides the audience through the void to the accompaniment of further theatrical cuts from the four Gong albums, all played with startling competence. As Hillage plays straight guitar, Dingo wrestles weird sounds from his instrument that would make David Gilmour envious.

Surely fame and riches will come Gong's way soon. Their exposure in the States has been minimal, with their first three albums appearing on the French BYG label. In order of appearance, *Majick Brother, Banana Moon* and *Camembert Electrique*. This last album easily qualifies for my Top-10 albums of all-time. It a really good-timey record loaded with humor and damn good playing, with cuts like "Squeezing Sponges Over Policemen's Heads," "I've Been Stoned Before" and "Dynamite: I Am Your Animal."

Their latest album, *Radio Gnome Invisible*, is perhaps more widely available in the U.S. on the Virgin label. *Radio Gnome* is a kind of telepathic pirate radio which transmits from a flying teapot coming from the planet Gong. In the words of Capt. Capricorn, "Radio Gnome comes to you direct, brain to brain."

But Gong are not the only ones on the bizarre scene. There's Magma from France, for instance – perhaps not as openly bent as Gong but making up in music what they lack in showmanship. As far as I know, there are two Magma albums, but even here in England they are so hard to obtain that I've only seen one, *1001° Centigrades* by name. The music has a strong Uncle Meat/King Kong feel to it, with strong blowing and subtle arrangements. Komintern, however, is much more blatantly humorous, and their own album, *Le Bal du Rat Mort* (Dance of the Dead Rat), would have become a classic if it had had wider distribution. As it is, the band and the album have vanished into obscurity, totally ignored in their native France.

But France can't claim all the credit. Here in the U.K., home of the Bonzo Dog Band, we have Arthur Brown's Kingdom Come. Arthur "I Am The God of Hell Fire" Brown has had it together for a couple of years and has produced three outstanding albums on Polydor: *Galactic Zoo Dossier, Kingdom Come* and *Journey*. The first and third albums stand out with some scorching guitar from Andy Dalby in particular. Arthur uses no drummer on *Journey* but relies on a Bently Drum machine, which suits his music. *Zoo* even includes a very small excerpt from Vivian Stanshall's "Brain Opera," which was never really heard except on a radio show once. The tapes have since been erased.

Well, that's just a small sample of what's to be found if one really looks hard enough. In the words of Bert Camembert:

"Hare Krishna
"Hare Supermarket."
February 1974

TODD RUNDGREN
Todd Rundgren
(Bearsville)

Todd Rundgren has gone so far into himself that I can't understand him anymore. Past a certain interior point, you know, nobody can vicariously participate in the fantasy-illusion-distortion and therefore cannot comprehend what yer talking about, Charlie. And this identification, of course – along with a certain generalized catchiness – was once the redoubtable Rundgren's forte. This disc ain't exactly catchy either. A frequently unreliable but always resourceful source told me that this album represents Todd's commercial suicide.

Anyway, in a situational development such as this, every facet of the product is drastically affected. And I don't think I like this record because, although there are some very refreshing oases – i.e., those cuts that bear more than a dysfunctional relationship to, say, the material on *Something-Anything*—much of this deluxe two-record set is, shall we say, "accessible" only in what has come to be known as a "total bloato excess" context. In other words, you can really only listen to it while approaching the anti-structural elysia of oblivion. And after you reach that point there's no reason to listen to it because that's where it was all created from. Re-read the first sentence. If you still don't understand, you shouldn't even be reading this review, much less be contemplating buying this journal of psychic masturbatory techniques.

What it amounts to, attitudinally speaking, is summed up pretty well (as it is obviously supposed to be) in the lyrics to "An Elpee's Worth of Toons": "Who's that on the racks again? A portrait of a crazy man/Trying to make a living off an LP's worth of toons/A picture of a soul in pain/Trying to change the world with an LP's worth of toons."

I guess Todd, in his introvertedly abused state, is moving on to higher ground. No, lissen up, I really think the man is more than a minor songwriter with major woman problems, as some pimply critick once called him. Take f r instance "Number 1 Lowest Common Denominator," a bit of mathematico-public esoterica, that's something Todd the Bod would never have thought of doing prior to his current madhouse zombie manifestatory state. Who can know? Who do you trust? Or "Heavy Metal Kids" (trendy title) in which he (embarrassingly enough) tells of his new cynicism when we all know that if he has to tell us about it he's really only whimpering over his wounded pantywaist idealistic moralism.

Cold boredom is the label for too much of this album, with machine-made non-entities like "The Spark of Life," "Drunken Blue Rooster" and "Shaft Goes to Outer Space" leading the list of mechanical atrocities that waste a big chunk of time for such an expensive piece of merchandise. It's even more infuriating in the face of a handful of superb Rundgren pop ditties like "Izzat Love," "Useless Begging" or the best Rundgren tune of the decade, "A Dream Goes On Forever." When you know he can come across with such moving, emotionally *real* human songs more or less when he sets his mind to it, it makes you want to grab him by the false eyelash, twirl him around a few times and say DO THIS STUFF, YOU IDIOT, not the dial-twiddling tape twists he's grown so jadedly fond of.

Until the boy shapes up – and I really think he will sooner or later – Todd's albums are going to be pretty much restricted to the few who actually *like* his more bizarre bends, and to those who are willing to tolerate his excesses in order to get thru to the real meat and kissy-face he's so frustratingly capable of. I certainly don't like the former shit, and as for the second alternative, I think it's a BIG PAIN IN THE ASS.

March 1974
[Kim Urban also contributed to this review]

THUNDERPUSSY
Documents of Captivity
(MRT)

We all know that Illinois ain't such hot shit, right? There ain't no museums of shiny corridors bleeding mercury vapor at night 'cept for Chicago, and it sure don't glow banshee if ya hit yer map with a flashlight. In fact, about all the Land of Lincoln *does* have going for it is its all-star dirt, squoozed out of the bedrock by some heebie Mesolithic eon drizzle and laying there a few million years waiting for the first soybean seed.

So it's not too surprising that Illini bands tend to sound like a cow in the last stages of Bang's Disease squatting on a steel guitar, play 'bout as fast as a drugged leech on a sticky driveway, and record their albums in greenhouses. There was even some scam called "River Music" bouncing around here for a while, no doubt referring to the tendency of the thick-witted Big Miss to clog-out into total scum-bottomed anti-motion, leaving everything within 50 miles smelling like a damp basement in July.

Then along comes Thunderpussy like a beer fart in Sunday School, really cleaning the air. There's a lotta slice guitar topped with high, lean harmonies, sorta like taking the upper two vocals off an early Byrds *harmonikschwelle* and amping 'em up a ways. Basically metallic in approach, they range all over (standard h. metal concept, really) from bat bleep guitaro attacks (lotsa those) to a couple acoustic moments and even a jazzbo or two.

Since it's a kinda concept album, it's fair enough to deal with one side at a time, which is great cuz side two is where the real action is. "To Be Real" leads off in fine side-opener form, building up to a monster chorus, taking time off for a quirky instrumental that makes so little sense it fits exactly, then revs up into that chorus again, giving ya bed spins every time. "Moonlite Ladies" is another stalker, not resisting the chorus or the air of apprehension the lyrics give, kicking in with, "And finally we are like the times" and getting more hopeless all along. "In The Forest" leads out the side nicely, capped with a trembling instrumental, "The Then."

Side two is so neat it's better not to dig into the flip too much, cuz that's where T-pussy's excesses get the upper hand. "Observations Of Us" is the main offender, the music sounding like a bad excuse for putting across the fine lyrics, all about June boxes, lust pits and a "Fear of his mother's brass iron bed." There are a lotta swell, pre-paranoid lyrics throughout, actually – hinting at the presence of silent accidents and edgy bunco squads, when the balance of error goes bad. You get a lyric sheet, too (mine's pink), so don't hesitate to scarf up on the numero-uno monster band in the state. Quick like, before some smart-ass plays 'em a Merle Haggard record and aims 'em at the cowboy-hat store.
April 1974

KISS
Kiss
(Casablanca)

No weak sisters here, no posed heavy smellbags either and for sure no gay chauvinism (gays are just the new hippies anyway, so who cares?) – just a bunch of sleazed-out, small-time punks who know that the only good slow song is a dead one and might just bleed yer face to prove it. Kiss are the same guys who used to beat up the New York Dolls after school and ain't about to let up now.

It's really too bad that they're getting tossed in the New York City glitter scumbag right away, cuz that whole scene has a shit commercial fad image, even if a lot of the bands are real cool monsters, cuz Kiss are all about hard rock 'n' roll: Chuck Berry amped into power chords and a bass player who's walked on Black Sabath's grave and lived to tell. They've smartly stayed away from the Dolls and Blue Oyster Cult's limited – though brilliant – approach to pop gimmickry, recognizing the limits and preferring to keep business simple and deadly.

With the superb production team of Kenny Kerner and Richie Wise (Dust, Stories, et al) Kiss has laid down some of the most on-target, concise hard rock to grace the treadmill since the Stones farted off into Troubledome Heaven. The main feature in their attack is the one-two onslaught of lead guitarist Ace Frehley and rhythm man Paul Stanley. Stanley is constantly on top of things with his two-chord whiplash reverb attack, while Ace alternates between that and mean lines that lead back into the rhythm and then come slithering out in nympho-heat flashburns. Gene Simmons plays a staggering low bass that keeps the guitars from sailing off into Quicksilver-twirling dog-suck, and drummer Peter Criss stays in between, thudding throughout.

But most important of all is the fact that Kiss can write actual songs that don't wander off or droop into virtuoso coma cuz there's no place else to go. Nope, they keep 'em short, mostly in the neighborhood of three-anna-half minutes, and above all harder than even Dillinger's legendary boner. The majority ("Strutter," "Firehouse," "Deuce," "Nothin' To Lose," buncha others) stick with the nasty two-chord bite and vocal pain yuks that makes ya wanna kick dead animals or give your little sister's telephone number to perverts. Even when they dip into the sleaze pit, they ain't no fluffs, as the slimy "Cold Gin" ("the cheapest stuff is all I need") or dumbo break song "Love Theme From Kiss" will testify.

Creeps and stooges everywhere, wise up. Kiss is our band, and I ain't just blowin' monkey breeze, so forget the twaddle pusses on the cover and crawl on down to the nearest liquor store that sells discs. Half pint of cold gin'll run ya under a buck fifty, *Kiss* even less if ya swipe it. And remember: "It's cold gin time again – you know it'll always win." My ass goes out to Kiss.

April 1974

KISS
Hotter Than Hell
(Casablanca)

Although their last LP was kinda on the fast side, Kiss picked up on the BOC snooze transistion, whipped a swept-back oldie "("Kissin' Time") onto the charts to keep everybody drowsy, and have now de-surfaced with this new nod that sets death to music pretty damn well. It's still got an awful good beat compared to sensory deprivation, but not enough to rile anyone's finely constructed sense of depression. When it comes to the cagey elucidation of gloom, they have no real competition, whether it's Black Sabbath, Alice, the Stones or even Harry Chapin. Cupcakes they ain't.

The fast cuts still have the edge numerically, but lack the hope-deadening power drool of the others. Like Jim Morrison once said, "They got the guns but we've got the downers." The Number-1 wrist-slitter is "Goin' Blind," a cute little treadmill about a 93-year-old geeze trying to make it with a tweeter of 16, featuring some fine jr. high gluehead buzz forms from guitarists Ace Frehley and Paul Stanley. The second-place bottle of pills goes to "Strange Ways," a gothic blitz that out-Blacks Black Sabbath at drawing fear lines and then smudging them.

"Parasite," "Comin' Home," "Mainline," and other fast tracks cover all the fave topics like parasite eyes, scuddy hotels, and animal sex, respectively. All their sex songs are great really, existing in that pumped-up zero zone between despising the opposite sex and wanting to screw. Superb loser sentiments whiz throughout this vinyl suicide note, so don't pass it by if you want to give up living to a fine heavy background. Kiss are even better than Blue Oyster Cult now, and that's saying a lot about nothing.
December 1974

KISS
Dressed to Kill
(Casablanca)

DAVE CLARK FIVE
Glad Over Again
(Epic)

NAZARETH
Hair of the Dog
(A&M)

I don't mean to brag, but I personally rubbed suede shoulders with Dave Clark himself in a Hammond, Ind., parking lot the same afternoon he and the boys suffered collective broken ribs while being nearly swallowed by thousands of fans at the theater where their *Having a Wild Weekend* flick was playing. Even then he looked like a midget. But for a bunch of Limey runts with thick eyebrows, the DC5 did ok in their time. What other band can lay claim to: 1) almost bringing back the Dr. Kildare shirt, 2) being to the stacked Cuban heel what the Beach Boys were to striped shirts and 3) practically inventing heavy metal? It was the TV close-ups of those stomping heels that made "Bits and Pieces," even if those dorky shirts made their heads look like doorknobs, and when you add the bruiser sax (since replaced by fuzztone) and wall-of-earache sound all their best records have, you've got Led Zep c. 1965. If they'd just have recorded one chrome riff like "Ticket to Ride" (they nearly did in "19 Days" but copied the wrong part) with the powersaw attack of theirs, developments like the Stooges and Deep Purple would have occurred three or four years earlier and where would we all be today? Listening to this DC5 album, that's where, coz it's 100 percent great.

Kiss wears dumb makeup and platforms instead of Cuban doctor drag but they still get your ears by the throat. For their third album they've parted with old producers Kerner & Wise and stripped down their sound from the fluorescent buzztones of *Hotter than Hell* to something more like the basic bones of the first album. But don't sweat yer scales, Kiss fans, it's still the same suburban flash tonnage, with doomsday bass lines, decibel harmonies and hard stalking lines like "Yer good lookin' and yer lookin' like you should be good." Although the lyrics aren't as exquisitely hateful toward women as usual, there's still plenty of collective neuroses for all.

Nazareth is another hard case, and they're definitely back in the game after that dud they called their last album. It appears that dumping producer Roger Glover was a great move, since his quick-draw glad-handing at the knobs was one of the major scabs on the machinery last time. Bullish on thud & whine once again, Naz do an amazing version of the Everly's "Love Hurts," forcing out into the open all the pissy cynicism of lines like "Love is just a lie made to make you blue." Solid version of N. Lofgren's "Beggars Day," too – in fact, Nazareth are one of those super rare bands who do great covers as well as excellent original stuff. They may never be stars in Hammond, Indiana, but then who would want to?
May, 1975

KISS

Kiss Alive

(Casablanca)

Ace and the gang have been hot on the trail for a couple of years now on a search-and-record mission bent on turning their three cutthroat studiotech albums into the ultimate bleeding crayon of live iron and rainbow sludge that turns normally solid-state audiences into deprived artifacts of deep creeping abandon. And here it is, Halloween every day, the fatal sandwich. You can't help but bite it.

Described by various genius dupes as everything from "wrist-slitting junior-high glue-head buzz forms" to "sleazed-out small time punks who know that the only good slow song is a dead one," Kiss have overpowered the heavy metal live LP format by the sheer rabid bite of their own lethal dumb-animal heat.

Scope the scorebox: BOC did their live set with crystalline curb-snore and steaming trench giveaways, and burrowed into the chart slums to stay. Grand Funk unplugged all their producers and faced the thud only to discover that there was a medical possibility that they could actually *play* together, thus outliving themselves. Aerosmith are due for a live rumble – but how do you translate cock lips to vinyl? Nope, as undeniably Godzilla as these other guys are, Kiss have the minefield all to themselves, where they can stomp newly impure alloys at will 'til *Zero*, like a clone of platformed robots in heat. No more competition because these hoods burned down the Chuck Berry factory.

Behind all the glitter Clearasil, Kiss is basically two alternatively rival and incestuous tag-teams: Paul Stanley and Ace Frehley (shiner star and silver goggs, respectively) are the guitarists – singers whose whiplash lines and cruel vocals are the cold heart of the group. Along with bass throbbist Gene Simmons, they're hot writers, too, staking out the cathode palsy of the '70s where dogpack aggression and dunce sex are the two-chord reality of daily nullness. Rhythm jockeys Simmons and Criss (ash-tongue and drum claw) keep the downer foundation staggering and ready to collapse in a grimy piss cascade of radio fragments.

The old "they're great live but their records suck the rug" theory does not apply here, either. Plenty of munglobes – 90 percent of whom have never seen the band play – will tell you that Kiss is just cartoons and smoke bombs, that the levitating drums, dry-ce microphones, and rocket-launching guitars don't carry over to records. They'll give Alice Cooper as an example, poor duds. Many of these subwits suffer from spine-sprain as a result of too much autosuck also.

Anyway, great as the boys are live, their records have all the sticky-seated excitement of their concerts, and anyone who tells you different is either a Joni Mitchell fan or your mother. *Alive* contains the very fastest of Kiss ground into one killer disc of mass-nympho proportions. Play this loud and you *deserve* to get the heat called on you, it's that great.
November 1975

KISS
Destroyer
(Casablanca)

Kiss finally blew it.

After three genius moron studio albums and a live LP that could make toe-victims cast off their roller skates, it looked like they had the hierarchy of scum all stitched up, besides running the inside track in the Great American Rock Band of the '70s sleazedown. After all, they've got the fluid, reds emptiness that Aerosmith (I.Q. 78) are slightly too smart for, the autistic insight into the slag realities of the '70s that peace sign fans like Grand Funk will never pick up on, and a futuristic Chuck Berry vision of everyday punkism that has expanded their following from a cult of hard-core alky misogynists into the National Ked power base that made their live album a platinum seller.

Destroyer was to be the next step in their Master Plan to make the world a dimmer place to live in, but this time they spread the darkness a little too thin. The biggest mistake was hiring on Alice Cooper's producer, Bob Ezrin, who – after lucking off to success with the cartoon menace of Alice – has no idea what he's dealing with here. Kiss may be being *marketed* as the next Billion Dollar Babies, but their music has a genuine creep appeal that is only burlesqued by Ezrin's headless babies of sound. While he *has* added some definition (you can't really call it depth) to their sound, his main effect has been a thinning-out of the band's monumental rabies heat. Where once you always heard the rusty power saws plugged into Silvertone speakers, now you get garage George Harrison lines not unlike the decline of Slade.

The new Kiss do have their good points – "Detroit, Rock City," with the skating fear of the rhythm section, the chorus blaze on the great single "Shout It Out Loud," and the dump-truck drums that collapse into Kim Fowley's excellent "Do You Love Me," a regular Kubrick Dave Clark 5 Shiner. Now for the pus-test results: two absolutely irredeemable ballads, "Beth" and "Great Expectations." If you've ever wanted to hear Kiss simper like all the Laurel Canyon singer-songwriters at a PTA pot party, here it is. Scalded muskrat vocals. Pillowy banks of M.O.R. strings. Tenderly weeping piano. Flutes. Tubular bells. Worse yet, they put one of these Kleenex sobs on each side, effectively ruining the flow of boot holes in the shag forever.

It's easy to blame producer Ezrin, who gets all the orchestration as well as multiple writing credits, for this clean-up-after-puppy wimplash. Unfortunately, every Stones has an "As Tears Go By" side and Kiss is no exception. But if they choose to sissy-out and extend the diaper service to their next album, I have the perfect title: *Kiss It Off.*
July 1976

KISS
Love Gun
(Casablanca)

Every time a new Kiss LP comes out, all the washed-up typewriter-faces come stumbling out of the dusty corners waving old copies of *Fisherman's Digest* and screaming "Hype, I tell you – hype!" like senile slugs on a milk buzz. So let's just get the lecture over with early so we can get on to the cake and candy.

Sure, the Kiss Phenom is a P.R. dream, feeding on itself and growing new bank-robbing tentacles daily. But the band, at its most basic level of crinoid appeal, is more. Kiss earned their rodent credentials *before* their hype – which may well be an after-the-fact lightbulb – took off. One listen to their first album will show you these guys were high-steppin' scum that had more to do with the Dolls than Alice before Dollar Drool set in, and anybody who says they're all hype has no ears, and, more importantly, no brain. Okay now, Gramps, down off that cantalope crate and over to the stereo before you hurt yourself.

Love Gun is the best album of Kiss' second phase. It's got filler, sure. What do you expect from a 10-album-a-year schedule? What's more important is that the boys are getting their groove back, only this time with tighter reins on the willing suspension of you-know-what.

The title cut is truly a masterpiece of domesticated drool. Everything good about new Kiss is in it: Meow Mix Criss drums his way in totally unlike the guy who started out as though the entire weight of Black Sabbath was on his shoulders. Then Simmons rumbles in, running bass slaves on his underground railroad direct to the Low Blow Zone. Suddenly – crackle, pow, guitar-friction bolts, fast stabs of cranky lightning and then brick-wall curtains of rhythm guitar, some tommy-gun drums, and we're off. Bat Lizard's singing slits the aural zip-locks better than ever, and when the backing vocals start dripping aureole like Mammoth Cave melting, you know they're gonna drip all over *you*. Not a bad song, actually.

That's not all. "Love For Sale" had all the ants on my floor running around in circles with its neat buzz riff, "Hooligan" is tsk-tsk bad fun ("Dropped out of school when I was 22/what can I do to satisfy you"), and "I Stole Your Love" has a catch-on melody in addition to its velocity.

Stinkers: "Almost Human" (as scary as watching *13 Ghosts* without 3-D specs), the token anthem "Tomorrow and Tonight" (falling asleep at step one), and a couple of other smellers, too (sound of reeking in the background caused by "Plaster Caster").

Kiss is once again on the verge of becoming immorally acceptable. It's mostly done with animation, but the good kind, not that Yogi Bear crap where only the lips move. Buy it or grow up.

July 1977

KISS

Alive II

(Casablanca)

If you've still got a puss spot in your heart for Kiss after their last few humdrum efforts, *Alive II* is for you. There's none of the farting around of their recent studio LPs, just straight-ahead patho crunch followed by screams – as it should be.

Alive II solves the problem of getting the new Kiss tunes of the last couple of years into one place. All of their best recent material is here – "Detroit Rock City," "Shout It Oud Loud," "Makin' Love," etc – and much hotter versions as well. Kiss is still great when they really get into it, and if they put half the energy into their studio albums that they display live, it would be possible to sit through hot/cold LPs like *Destroyer* without constantly fighting your groan threshold. Even dreck canisters like "Christine Sixteen" sound good here, and a guaranteed winner like "I Stole Your Love" almost makes "Beth" tolerable.

With such strong live stuff, you have to wonder why they included an entire side of new material recorded in their Drab City studio. The four originals are typical of recent Kiss – fast and noisy, but rather uninspired. It's hard to tell whether they're actual new tunes or just left-overs from previous albums, though I suspect the latter. "All American Man" and "Rocket Ride" go over pretty well, but live they'd have sounded a lot better. The other two newies are strictly styro. The surprise number is the Dave Clark 5's "Any Way You Want It," and Kiss' version is faithful down to the cheesy echoes and one-armed drumming. These guys are too smart to mess with classic Hefty fodder.

Extra toys this time include an "Evolution of Kiss" booklet (which proves once and for all that these dupes didn't really descend from iguanas), some instant Kiss tattoos that you'll want to display prominently on the soles of your feet, and, of course, a handy Kiss Special Merchandise catalog so that you can send away for Kiss posters, patches, hats, gloves, artificial hearts, jumpsuit maintenance kits, and little viles of genuine Gene Simmons muke. The only thing missing is the long-awaited life-size poster of Gene's tongue. It seems the U.S. Conservation Service objected to their chopping down the state of Oregon for the paper.

If you've been disappointed by Kiss' output since the first live album, don't let it keep you away from *Alive II*. It makes thinned-out slush like *Love You Live* sound like the nap crap it is.
November 1977

GENE SIMMONS
PAUL STANLEY
ACE FREHLEY
PETER CRISS

(Casablanca)

Many bands have dreamed of simultaneously releasing solo albums by each of their members. The Monkees were once well on their way to such a feat until they got to Mickey Dolenz. He wanted to call his *Circus Man*, with Noah Beery, Jr., producing. Goodbye, Mickey! The Beach Boys at one time had several individual efforts in the can, but before Al Jardine could complete his LP, David Seville died, leaving the project bereft of chipmunks at a crucial point. And John "Mr. Team" Fogerty tried to whip Creedence Clearwater into line way back when, but Doug – the-sincere-if-dodo-like-drummer – could only come up with three songs, two of which ("Lord of The Skins" and "Beats Me") were about how boring it is to be a drummer.

So Kiss is the first, another high spot on the band's career treadmill. Dealing with their solo works individually is kind of like interviewing a juggler's bean bags, but lumping these diverse songbirds together would not be fair to either of their many fans. And fairness is our most important babyfood, or however that goes. Still, if Kiss had *really* wanted to be ratjags, they could've put these out as a four-record set. Wouldn't have sold shit, but what an attitude!

Gene Simmons' wryly titled *Gene Simmons* is far and away the most interesting of the four. Old bat spit has a smartly sick sense of humor typified by "Living In Sin," where moronic Blue Swede ugga-uggas give way to a breather-appeal spoken part: "I know… (slobber, drool)… you write me… (lick, snort) … SEXY LETTERS!" Weird production touches, like the sudden appearance of the Church of The Living Dead choir on "True Confessions" or the random oriental hosannas, also help keep Gene's tongue above water.

Simmons is a pretty fair songwriter as well. His Kiss-formula tunes are generally superior to recent group efforts, and he displays a pederast's fondness for '60s English pop, an interest he shares with Paul Stanley.

Stanley, who would have you believe that he was once punched in the eye by a starfish, is the other obvious talent in the band. His enigmatically named *Paul Stanley* LP contains the most highly developed production and performance tits of all. Rockers predominate, ranging from K-form crankers to beefier tunes with less stereotyped chord changes. There are a couple of ulcer-icepick ballads, but these can be easily slipped past by the timely spilling of blood. That brings us to the Doug and Al of the group, Ace and Peter. Guitarist Frehley's album is a thin sketchbag of heavy moves topped by his vaguely audible vocals. Peter's beater, produced by Vini "I Stoop to Ringo" Poncia, has more variety, but then so does hamster food. With a voice that sounds like it was hung out to dry in a BB-storm, Criss could do as well tweeting these ballads through a Junior Mints box. And let me be one of the first to point out his bizarre resemblance to WGN's Cookie The Clown moments after discovering that Bozo swiped his jellybeans again. Awww.

Also included in each LP is one-fourth of an ingenius tape-together poster designed by the same whiz who draws the pubic hair on luv dolls. It's hard to imagine anybody buying all four records just to complete the poster, but you never know. As Gene Simmons drools on his album: "Sometimes…(dribble, hock)…my love goes TOO FAR!"
November 1978

NAZARETH
Rampant
(A&M)

URIAH HEEP
Wonderworld
(Warner Brothers)

All quiet on the heavy metal front. A major lack of any sense of direction, not unlike the mess following the demise of the Beatles, has set in and the stink's starting to hit the fan. It's not necessarily that the form has exhausted itself, but rather that the major smell bags who once set the style are showing obvious signs of metalflake. The big boys like Led Zep, Black Sabbath, Deep Purple, Ten Years After, and the Heep are either settled into a profitable snooze or else becoming increasingly incompetent in their search for the big noise, while the 2nd and 3rd generation pre-influential snipers like the Blue Oyster Cult, Hawkwind and Thunderpussy haven't yet made much of an impact, leaving the middle bands like Nazareth, Queen, Status Quo and Montrose looking about anywhere for clues as to what their next move might be.

As it turns out, they're all too often looking in the wrong places, clutching at airballs that are already covered with the robotic fingerprints of previous feedback strike-outs. Which brings us to the new Nazareth album, a solid disappointment from a band that looked like they were headed for international whizdom and the quaalude seal of approval. Two albums ago they made a bit of noise over here with a near-hit single, "Broken Down Angel," quite an accomplishment for an essentially unknown metal outfit. The album from which "Angel" came, *Razamanaz*, was a solid effort and a flying squat above their earlier LPs. *Loud 'N' Proud*, the next LP, was even better, with one faultless side of high-speed thrashers that combined the Neanderthalic intensity of Slade with the transonic futurosity of Deep Purp, and one side of Z-wad dormosnooze for slow learners.

Then along comes *Rampant* and blows the whole progression. Working off an ill-advised notion of stretching out from their previously swept-back approach into a more lyrically and instrumentally oriented one, all they've succeeded in doing is stretching their material out of focus. After the dynamic opener, "Silver Dollar Forger," side one bites the chrome with alarming willingness. "Glad When You're Gone" is a pointless exercise in the unexceptional, complete with gospel girls, and "Loved & Lost" drags things down even lower, a cretin blues with innovative lyrics like "bad luck is doggin me around." "Shanghai'd in Shanghai" nearly redeems things with the return of the old Naz thump, but even that's sluggish and marred with more ultra-typical backing vocals. Side two bogs into the fart vacuum even deeper, despite a nice try at "Shapes of Things" that unfortunately drifts into instrumental limbo. "I'll use anything I think's gonna help" is an OK motto for Dinah Shore, but Nazareth had better cool the conceptual diddleyshit and start crunching turf again unless they want to become the Happy Homemakers of Heavy Metal.

As for the Heep, they're becoming increasingly difficult to judge in any sort of metal context. A Moody Blues context, or maybe even the Strawbs, but what the present Heep has to do with the old obnoxious incoherents who put cardboard mirrors on their covers and garnered more bad reviews than five Grand Funks is beyond me. Their new philosophy is succinctly delineated in "Something or Nothing": "We'll find the line that's in the middle and roll." And roll they do, like a bunch of donuts on the verge of sentience. That might be smart pastry to you, but I keep remembering the band that did Demons and Wizards and wondering who put the Sominex in their yogurt. Like Dave Byron sings in "So Tired," "I'm so tired and uninspired –I need some help."

July 1974

NAZARETH
Expect No Mercy
(A&M)

Nazareth has had a hard time coming up with consistently strong material ever since they first applied their aural burp-guns to vinyl. While they've shown occasional flashes of song-writing excellence and they've always played like they had a hungry garbage truck on their tails, their overall track record is pretty spotty. One big song is usually diluted to three or four weak sisters that mung up the total effect.

Expect No Mercy is the final result of this compositional bankruptcy. Only a handful of cuts rise above the interest level of a motel vacancy sign, and they're not exactly history-changers either. "Revenge Is Sweet," an ill-tempered rocker with a nasty performance from singer Dan McCafferty, and the barreling aphid train riff of the title cut keep side one afloat, but just barely. Neither tune is exceptional, but they sound extra good when surrounded by duds like their dried-up, de-sleazed version of the Crazy Horse classic, "Gone Dead Train," and the lumpy "Shot Me Down," a duh-provoking ballad that sounds like a deservedly obscure Dylan tune.

If you're at all familiar with Nazareth, you already know not to bother with side two, as these guys are the al-time champeens of one-sided albums. Too bad their records don't list for half price. One solid cut, a belt-buckle slugger called "Kentucky Fried Blues," leads into a series of clinkers, from the trademark monotony of "New York Broken Toy" to "Place in Your Heart," yet another Dylan-for-beginners effort.

For a band that's capable of a great LP like *Loud 'N' Proud*, Nazareth are starting to get that over-the-hill feel to their music. If they continue to crank out lifeless albums like *Expect No Mercy*, that's exactly the response they can expect from their fans.
November 1977

URIAH HEEP
Firefly
(Warner Brothers)

Firefly introduces the new Heep lineup and the first question has to be: Are they as good as the old guys? After all, they've changed bass players every couple albums (an English tradition) but a new lead singer is something else again.

Unless you're a real David Byron stooge, new screamer John Lawton fits in just fine. Having perfected tonsil-death with triple-A group Lucifer's Friend, he has his death moans and deviate sexual assault mannerisms down tight. The only thing lacking is Byron's gum-wrapper vibrato, and that's about as bad as losing a lingering disease. New bass player Trevor Bolder replaces John Wetton's unobtrusiveness with some fairly threatening stuff, giving Heep that old undercurrent of soft menace.

The tunes are as solid as ever. In fact, it sounds like Ken Hensley was cracking the whip to give the new lineup a strong debut. Even Gerry Bron, the group's

Godfather, was brought in to produce. He's trimmed things a bit, and supplies occasional gooses when called for. George Martin with a whoopee cushion.

Classic dub/Mellotron-soaked epics tend to predominate, though the rockers are given equal time. It must be the melodramatic arrangements, sounding as they do like an attempt to orchestrate the melting of the polar ice caps or something of equal jaw-dropping import. These slow-pokes aren't altogether unattractive however, as the title track demonstrates. Starting out as another catchy-but-draggy Hensleytoon, it puts on sneakers halfway through and ends up as flashy as the cover, a *Demons & Wizards* throwback if there ever was one. This band's covers look like a half-cooked tamale TV dinner that was run over by a steamroller.

Drummer Lee Kerslake contributes a surprisingly melodic radio speeder containing a truly historic kitchen appliance distorto guitar solo by Mick Box (is that a name or what?), and even boss Hensley comes through with "Do You Know," a candidate for the "Easy Livin'" school of transistor cheese food. *Firefly* is never less than acceptable and usually a lot more interesting than the last few Heep efforts. Forget Angel and get the real thing.

May 1977

URIAH HEEP
Innocent Victim
(Warner Brothers)

Uriah Heep albums are like Girl Scout Cookies: They come out right on schedule every year and you can always be sure of a certain consistent quality (unless some itchy-membraned Brownie squatted on 'em while listening to a Shaun Cassidy album). That sounds kind of yummy actually (wonder if it costs extra), but as long as Ken Hensley is running the show, you can count on their LPs being absolutely Heep-like to the point of Xerox.

Innocent Victim sticks precisely to the U.H. formula, with the majority of cuts being highly acceptable keyboard-tipped guitar rockers and the rest hovering in the gauze-dotted Mellotron flatlands. Vocalist John Lawton, who joined up last album after spending several seasons in the West German Industrial League with the Berlin Padres and the Düsseldorf Orioles, has settled in nicely, as has much-traveled bass pounder Trevor Bolder. The rest of the crew is still hanging tough, especially the redoubtable Mick Box, guitar skinner extraordinaire and owner of one of rock's great names, right up there with Mick Can, Mick Carton and Mick Tote-bag, lead singer with Chicago punkers There Goes the Shutout.

As can be expected, the fast songs are the winners, with mainstream Heep issue like "Flyin' High" and "Free & Easy" leading the pack. Ken's gonna have to start coming up with some new lyric moves, though. Haven't they already got a half dozen songs called "Free & Easy," or even an album or two? Hensley's such a freedom fascist that he can't seem to write about anything else, even in his drama-drenched ballads. Speaking of which, "Choices," an actual non-Hensley tune (not that you'd know it) is possibly the most overblown aural tissuethon in Uriah Heep's long parade of doiliedom. The gloom-laden air of soap-opera doom is so convincing that you expect a phone to ring in the middle of the cut with a fateful message for Ken. "Mr. Hensley? This is Sgt. Fosdick of the State Police. I'm afraid I have some bad news for you…"

But sitting through a stinker or two is part of the Heep experience, so you can't really complain. If you want to hear their always top-drawer rockers, you have to go along with Hensley's love of drag. That's the heartbreak of Uriah, sis. *March 1978*

BLUE OYSTER CULT
Secret Treaties
(Columbia)

A truly epic album here from the most fear-provoking band presently stalking rock music. Makes all the other collective-neuroses stuff that's kicking around today like Cooper, Sabbath and the Stooges look like so much fluff, and renders past attempts like the Doors or the Stones laughable. Sure, this might all be "intellectual slumming," "soulless diabolism," and "fashionable quasi-fascism," as one British reviewer took it, but then you have to look at people like metal cretin Ace French, who calls *Secret Treaties* 'the *Exorcist* of Rock," or even wimp kingpin Elly Bea, who insists "these guys should be put away for singing like that." It takes all kinds.

Treaties is very loosely based (mostly not at all) on this brief pseudo-quote which appears on the inner sleeve: "Rossignol's curious, albeit simply titled book, *Origins of a World War*, spoke in terms of *Secret Treaties*, drawn up between the Ambassadors from Plutonia and Desdinova the foreign minister. These treaties founded a secret science from the stars. Astronomy. The career of evil." Real heavy stuff there, 'bout as scary as a lizard scene on *Cisco Kid*. But that's the whole fear angle that Blue Oyster Cult exists on: the old double fake-out, or — it's so scary it's dumb and thus doubly scary. If you try and take this stuff too seriously you're bound to crack up unless you're a Satan loony. It's better to just let their anxiety-impressionism seep in cipher by cipher while you're being flattened by their deathblow metal sounds because, as usual, the real action is in the music.

As far as foreshadowing and coloring the lyric goes, the Cult's music succeeds admirably, but it's a lot more fun to listen to it as the stunning rock 'n' roll it's above all meant to be. They've taken the deadening Sabbath z-wads of the first album and the manic Purple speed runs of *Tyranny and Mutation* and packed them into a much tighter framework for *Treaties*, giving them a futuristic punk-rock edge that far exceeds their past records both in listen ability and accessibility. It's still mostly fast, riff-oriented stuff but there's much more concentration on vocals, keyboards, and general beat-mongering, as well as an air of old Seeds albums on a sticky afternoon.

There's eight big songs just like the last LP, but this time they're of more equal length and there aren't exercises in futility like "7 Screaming Dizbusters" to weigh things down. Side one kicks in with Patti Smith's "Career of Evil,," a chunky guitar and keyboard riffer that sounds a bit like "Talk Talk" (remember the black-gloved Music Machine?) properly amped-down to '70s retardosleeze, "Subhuman" is next burying the pace a bit with buzzing Sabbathisms about "oyster poison" and "deathlike creatures" and an inventive, precise guitar solo from Buck Dharma. Then up comes the highlight of the album, "Dominance and Submission," to show you what BOC are all about. Now, we've had the entire music staff, their friends, relatives, and casual acquaintances at work trying to figure out the lyrics to this one, but it's so slurred and loaded with oblique obscurities that it's impossible to follow but scarier than shit with its pre-subliminal hinting and symbol-begging imagery. It's maybe a radio song or a sex song or a history-of-pop-culture song or just a whip song, but whatever it is, it runs through a couple master verse refrain jobs that build into a vocal tradeoff between the group (who scream "DOMINANCE"), and a bizarre bass voice that comes out of nowhere and croaks "radios appear." It's deadly catchy, extremely powerful, and bound to leave you in such a contemplative stupor that you miss most of the next number, "ME 262," a fine Nazi song and death to Chuck Berry to boot.

Side two carries the disease exceptionally, with a pair of outstanding R. Meltzer numbers, "Cagey Cretins" and "Harvester of Eyes," and a pair of mysterious Sandy Pearlman (the Cult's manager-producer-guiding paw) creations, "Flaming Telepaths" and "Astronomy." These final two are pure Blue Oyster Cult, shot through with descending keyboard waves, rancorous guitar lines and snotty fatalistic lyrics, including the line of the decade, "I'll settle for lies." Both pairs succeed together as a cohesive side, and the record bulldozes out on "the nexus of the crisis" behind more screaming Dharma guitar shards and some North Pole wind effects.

So there you have it, what'll probably go down as the Number-1 fast album of the year. It sure runs circles around everything else that's come down the tube so far, *Burn, Sabbath Bloody Sabbath, Montrose, Shinin' On, Rock & Roll Animal,* etc., all turn turtle when BOC's in town. And just one word about the cover: Yuk.

May 1974

BLUE OYSTER CULT

Spectres

(Columbia)

The Blue Oyster Cult are America's Number One Rock Band, outdistancing all the other leaden fists by a least two Aerosmiths. And *Spectres*, while not quite their "best" album to date, is surely their most complete. All of the expected spooky stuff is here – death, destruction, vampires, wallet-sized snaps of Michael Landon's family – as well as some incriminating evidence of actual human feelings lurking in the depths of their sneer-filled hearts. Greasy feelings, to be sure, but enough to flesh out these mahonies into more than Dorian Gray's bowling buddies.

While their trademark doom throttle sound still predominates, the Cult is toying with it more than ever. Their true genius is that they can do this silly stuff with a straight face. "Godzilla," for example, with its Black Sabbath thunder tunnel riff, is only as scary as its subject. And when was the last time you were frightened by a guy in a plastic lizard suit, throwing model trains at superimposed mobs of terror-stricken Japanese? At any rate, they give themselves away with a good-timey chorus of "Oh no! There goes Tokyo! /Go go Godzilla!"

Or how about "Nosferatu," which is truly a beautiful song above and beyond the pulp intimations. As the keyboards melt into gothic guitar mumbles, The Listener is transported to "the heart of Germany," where bad guy vampire Nosferatu is causing all kinds of unpleasantness. Dying crops, babies with two noses, all that stuff. And wouldn't you know it, "only a woman can break his spell," or so says the Cult with stunning harmonies. After a brief interlude of switchblade syrup from Buck Dharma's guitar, The Woman (played by Andrea Marcovici) gives herself to the vampire, and he's "BLINDED BY LOVE" as waves of Harlequin Romance background vocals throb in the distance. Meanwhile, the sun sneaks up, the vamp's turned to dust, and for the first time in BOC history, the bad guy loses!

But take themselves seriously or not, BOC's sixth album is full of tunes that will tickle the ectoplasm. The Cult have really put some work into the vocals this time, from the majestic comball of "Celestial the Queen," a synth-slider that sums up and surpasses the entire career of Styx in 3:24, to the petrified folk-rock of "Fireworks," a follow-up to "Reaper" if ever there was one. There's plenty of power rock too, including R. Meltzer's latest, "Death Valley Nights," with its deceptive piano-bar verse that sounds like a doddering Tony Bennett after some failed longevity experiment, and "R.U. Ready 2 Rock," an ostensibly normal boogie that the Cult bends into one of their fiendish doubt-doses ("Who will rock with you?") before speeding to a powerhouse ending featuring Eric Bloom screaming "yeah, yeah, yeah." I'm sure they had a riot recording that one.

The only sour note is that when you send away for Cult lyrics, you now have to enclose 50 cents, for "postage and handling." Maybe it's worth it though, if only for the idea of a roomful of characters from BOC songs gleefully handling lyrics. With lead gloves on no doubt.
November 1977

BLUE OYSTER CULT
Some Enchanted Evening
(Columbia)

Just another live album here folks. Nothing to get too excited over, so don't get all drastic and marry a Cowboy or something. Beating the Xmas rush, keeping the fans awake 'til next year and the name on the charts: all the good stuff live albums are made of.

And more! What looks like a throwaway stocking filler turns out to be an industrial-strength set recorded in a burning stable as the last flaming embers hit the bitter horse. "Dad! Come quick," Packey cried. "Fury's writing F-I-R-E on my Etch-a sketch with her hoofs! Do you think she's trying to tell us something?"

BOC have countered the usual album-retread blues with a pair of excellent non-Cult picks. Despite an opening lifted intact from the deservedly-rare Santana/Eric Burdon collaboration, *Brown Man's Burdon*, "We Gotta Get Outta this Place" is pure slum-envy. And their million-BTU version of the MC5's ultimo "Kick Out the Jams" is not only a Stunning Tribute to the greatest live rock 'n' roll album in the history of hyena-torture, but a furious armed invader of the ears as well.

The Cult faves are delivered in a hopped-up but sensible fashion, solid instrumentally (and no solothons) if a bit lackadaisical at times vocally. "Godzilla" and "R.U. Ready 2 Rock" aren't as funny or heavy as the dead versions, but now they shake and gurgle like the floor drain at a disco slaughterhouse. "Astronomy" is still a spooker, quite an accomplishment onstage, while the sly villainy of "Don't Fear the Gipper" has been replaced with a threatening viciousness. OK, OK, guys, I'll hurry up and kill myself right now! SOR-REE!

By turning what could have been a gift-suggestion quickie into a highly respectable two-night stand, BOC have once again proven they've got class out the ass and then some. One thing though, if any of you moms and dads out there are planning on dishing out this LP for trick or treat this year don't try it on Buck Dharma's block. Either he gets his fair share of Reggie bars, or he'll vandalize your daughter.

October 1978

MOTT THE HOOPLE
The Hoople
(Columbia)

There's a bunch of new faces here, but it still sounds like old Mott face overall. Lead guitarist Micky Ralphs has departed and signed on with Paul Rodgers' Bad Company, along with some randomly selected King Crimson execs, but his place has been filled nicely by Ariel Bender, nee Luther James Grosvenor, former Spooky Tooth and the David Palmer of Stealers Wheel. Mainman Ian Hunter has decided to stick with rhythm guitar so he can run around more on stage, leaving the keyboard chores to Morgan Fisher. And drummer Buffin has finally admitted that his real name is Dale Griffin.

Anyway, Mott still sounds like Mott. The bizarre blend of British AM radio, Stones flash, and mid-Dylanisms that constitutes their style is very much under Hunter's control and he's really a decent tyrant. The Bowie influence that made the band a commercial entity again with *All the Young Dudes* is still in evidence, mainly in the vocal arrangements and Mod Lang lyrics, but Mott has such a tight squeeze on it now that it's become a basic part of the sound. Same goes for the *Sticky Fingers* rhythm guitar and occasional *Blonde on Blonde* keyboards — Mott just wouldn't be The Hoople if they didn't sound like that, and the originals are starting to sound more like each other all the time anyway, so it's good to hear that somebody can still do it right.

Hoople is basically a lot tighter and much faster-paced than their previous LP, *Mott*. The ballads, "Trudi's Song" and "Through The Looking Glass," don't both sound like the same song, thus finally beating the Mott Standard Ballad curse, which marred some of their previous albums. "Trudi" is actually a pretty catchy number, with one of the most believable vocals Hunter has ever put down, along with some nice changes and a thin Dylan harp. "Looking Glass' is a massive production number, a good rock melodrama with strings and a tubular bell or two.

But like most every other rock band in the world, they're way better when they stuff the strings and put on the crunch. They've included their two latest English singles here, "Roll Away the Stone" and "Golden Age of Rock 'n' Roll," and they're masterpieces of intelligent BBC accessibility. All the elements of British radio gold are included, from Wizzard bruiser horns to intricately tacky backing vocals to the attractively wide-ranging Hunter vocals – all of which combine to knock you dead in under four minutes. Of course, that's not always enough time for Mott to get all their kicks in, and they're equally brilliant when they stretch it out. "Marionette" comes from the Bowie side with plenty "voix grotesques a la Quasimodo," some strange dialogues between Marionette and Teacher's Pet, and the usual slam guitar carrying it all along potently. "Alice" is almost early Mott, with Hunter going Dylan ape on the lyrics while Fisher alternately pounds a sure-fire piano riff and drifts linear organ fills over the chorus.

Saving the best 'til last, there's "Crash Street Kidds," the most monstrously calculated rock nihilism set loose on an unsuspecting world since "My Generation." Based on a nearly post-musical riff that sounds like Ariel Bender shoving the neck of his guitar up Pete Townshend's ass with all the knobs turned to 10, Hunter screams bloody sarcasm and lobar violence until the song destroys itself in monolith guitar suicide, leaving a mooged-up Ian shrieking "now yer dead, now yer dead, now yer dead!" while the drummer tries to get back into the song, fails, and kicks it in.

So there you have it, Mott's best yet, nearly overloaded with intelligent delinquence and power-hungry music that only lets up to sneak behind you, so watch out you don't bend over near this album. Coming up soon is a live set that may or may not include the time Ian leaped off the stage and kicked the shit out of a bottle-thrower who nearly offed his lead guitarist. The man's an animal.
May 1974

NEW YORK DOLLS
Too Much Too Soon
(Mercury)

Great second effort from the Dolls, and a spit to those who hoped they might be just another flash-in-the-mascara gutter squat band that got accidentally famous coz they happened to be in NYC at the right time. Sorry turds, but it looks like the Dolls are all right: they insult minorities, strike twitchy poses, puke in Paris, violate oldies and play some of the most spontaneously contrived hard rock to hit the charts since the Stones grew up. And *they like girls too*, so blow it out yer barracks bag, muscle duds.

New producer this time around, and a superb choice he is – Shadow Morton, the man who put the La in the Shangri-Las and whose motto is, "We're not talking about talent: we're talking about *sound*." Morton has helped clean up the vocals a bit while retaining the fuzzy push factor of the instrumental attack, thus superimposing some differentiation upon the essential sameness which the Dolls' motion thrives on. So we have a somewhat more swept-back sound while still incorporating the coprophilious grit that pleases both the affected art major voice and the mental punk aberrant.

Reducing it all to concrete song-title efficacy, what you get is 10 new Dolls tracks: six fine originals and four pre-obscure outside comps. It's these non-Dolls tunes that give the whole LP an entirely different line of attack from the first: an approach based on flash & grind novelty as opposed to glossy sleaze.

"Stranded in the Jungle" is the prime show-off, an old Cadets silly that has David and the boys doing bloato black-face swipes that are subliminally dumb enough to make them not only TV stars but prime top - 40 candidates as well. "Bad Detective" runs in a similar vein, a maybe Coasters tune with a tinny cast of stupefied chinks and finks. More stereotypes strut out in Gamble-Huff's "Showdown," a dance feud not to be confused with the Electric Light Orchestra's paranoiac hit of the same name. Sonny Boy Williamson's "Don't Start Me Talkin' " is insult number 4, though here it's more in the form than in the content.

As for the Dolls originals, they're as great as ever, flashy and grabby, catchy and sexy, loaded with great lines and pygmy fatalism. "Chatterbox" is a classic Johnny Thunders tune that the Shadow has built into a girl-group revenge song with sneak lines like, "C'mon, gimme some lip." "Puss 'N' Boots" is another one that oughtta be a standard somewhere, mean twat vocal and an inescapable chorus: "Just like puss 'n' boots – I hope ya don't get shot for tryin'." Dunced-out eeriness pervades "Who Are the Mystery Girls," which isn't really mysterious at all and doesn't even try to be.

Lots more good stuff, too – the Dolls have the line on compact throwaways that make no effort at transcending themselves and succeed perfectly in the moment they're created for. Obsolescence is timeless.

June 1974

DAVID JOHANSEN
Here Comes the Night
(Blue Sky)

A lot of people wrote David Johansen off after his last LP, but they shouldn't have been so hasty.

Now that his third solo bomb is out, it's *really* time to write him off. Another collection of half-baked original material supported by sleepwalking backup, *Here Comes* isn't going to receive any comeback-of-the-year awards.

It's about time that DJ realized he can't cut it as a songwriter. His new composing partner, Blondie Chaplin, hasn't really helped anyone to ... *wait a minute, Blondie Chaplin?* Ex-main brain of Flame fame and longtime Beach Boys tour drummer? Seems like he was in another band or two (possibly with East Europeans) but the facts are currently unavailable for recall. That's fine with me – a defective memory not only does away with the fuss and bother of actually *remembering* stuff, but you can forget anxiety-provoking thoughts *in advance!*

A few Johansen facts *you* might want to forget include: his boring tunes, unimaginative arrangements, general coyness and the total breakdown of Blue Sky Records A&R. Seriously, who else is on their roster? Rick Derringer? Edgar Winter? Randy Hobbs and his Bluesbreakers?

Since we're drinking to forget, how about finally letting go of the New York Dolls legend? The prosecution is willing to stipulate that the Dolls were one of *the* great rock 'n' roll bands, but nothing the least bit memorable has filtered out of these guys since the last Dolls album in 1974, whenever *that* was. Scope the stats: Syl Sylvain? Killer Kane? The Dead Murcias? Or how about Johnny Thunders' Heartbreakers, who were so forgettable that Tom Petty stole their name and got away with it?

One last time: dud material, faceless players, Blondie Chaplin. Try and remember, OK?

July 1981

TED NUGENT'S AMBOY DUKES
Tooth Fang & Claw
(DiscReet)

STATUS QUO
Quo
(A&M)

HEAVY METAL KIDS
Heavy Metal Kids
(Afco)

This here is a real daddio season for deep squatting ear thugs, what with brand-new releases from the self-proclaimed world's greatest guitarist, England's numero-fungo boogie band, and the Isles' latest young drod hype circulating in this basket-brains play pile like a twat hungry midget juggling nuns. If it's lobbed-out metal action and the freezing buzz of a numb tele-phone yer after, ya might wanna try some of these vibe jockeys on for size.

Nugent seems to be the man everybody's heard about but never really heard outside of random festival appearances and one-night stands within sniffing range of Detroit. There was that buggy acid song of his on the radio a few years back but that about covers it 'coz he was signed to Mainstream, whose distribution rivals that of the once-and-future-defunct. Ardent in obscurity. Without really going anywhere. Ted's come long way since then, going through more band members than a Savoy Brown reunion, trading flashy white suits for a rancid beaded loincloth, and passing through Polydor on his way to Zappa's DiscReet label. He gets lotsa promo now for his pro-wrestling-level guitar battles with Cactus and his Noble Dunce insistence on killing his own dindin, but that's all meat under the bridge when it comes to his new record.

Surprisingly enough for such a dope, it's really hot stuff, starting out in the Cooper-Wagner-Ezrin manic guitar zone and blasting its way into a new nether hothouse of slice and whine like the cannibalistic instrumental "Hibernation" or the cloned riff numbers like "Lady Luck" and "Free Flight." Nugent's a bunco asshole of Buddy Miles proportions for sure, but he makes punishing monster music of the first order. Pick up Fang if ya want the fastest album this month, and stay outta the woods when Ted's out to lunch.

The Quo's sordid history has been chronicled before so let's skip it except to say, YES, these are the "Pictures of Matchstick Men" guys and NO, they don't sound anything like that anymore except in terms of sweet repetitiousness. For a band so scoped into boogie that they used to make ZZ Top sound acoustic, they've swept things back this time, sometimes going so far as to introduce a fourth chord into their repertoire.

Heavy on percussion and pumped-up Canned Heat progressions, the Quo is totally dependable for producing good party-storming music and driving critical nurds up the wall bitching about unimaginative Limey gopher chokers in a manner not unlike Grand Funk used to. Well, they can bite my snail-imagination is about as relevant to rock as baton twirlers are to football.

Quo provides a good booger beat and even toss in classy instrumental shit (middle of "Slow Train") and robotic Buddy Holly ("Fine Fine Fine") without letting up on the stomp. Playing "Break the Rules" (a Limey chart-topper that even has some harmonica) for your average snot-nosed, Randy-Newman-loving friend is almost as much fun as insulting a member of the Incredible String Band, and you can do it in the privacy of your own dump, so snarf dutifully.

This speedy puke ain't all great shakes, though, as the insultingly named Heavy Metal Kids prove. Maybe this rusty pus goes over big in terms of the ant-like response of English rock pygmies, but put it on vinyl and ship it over the Atlantic and it sucks door knobs. These retards have nothing whatsoever going for them other than a couple pretty faces and typically Rod Stewart-ish singer who used to be in some pud London play 'til he bit the bitter airball and decided to butter his angels with a trendy rock band.

They've got one good song, "Ain't it Hard," but the rest of their shiny original tunes have snoozy non-riffs that couldn't carry a damp Kleenex in a glove compartment, building up to no less than a REPRISE (remember those swinging '60s?) of one of their more innocuous numbers, which fades out side 2 like a blind gimp in a Silly Putty chamber. Avoid these grease-sponges at all costs and point yer peeve at the Dukes and the Quo

.*November 1974*

STATUS QUO
Rockin' All Over The World
(Capitol)

Status Quo is famous for their three-chord wooly mammoth booger beat, so it comes as a surprise to hear them let up on it a bit. Don't expect any headlines like "**QUO FORSAKE BOOGERS**," however, because the understructure is still all in place. It's what's on top that's different.

The addition of an outside producer (Pip "Squeak" Williams) for the first time in several albums has a lot to do with the lighter approach. Williams hasn't tampered with the basic redundo throb and clanging guitars that sound like they're bouncing off a basement mirror, but he's tightened things up considerably and induced the boys to try some overdubbed lines that add depth. "Hard Time" is typical of this slightly altered approach, sliding in with an airy, sparrow-pee opening that threatens to become a leave-the-room ballad until the boogers rip in moments later and things start to move. The vocals and guitars don't sound like they've been buried under concrete biohazard containers, and the rhythm section stays further away from plod town than ever, but it's still pretty much good old Status Quo ape ballet.

While most of the tunes stay close to the Quo mode, there are some entirely new moves. Usually, when hard-rock bands try to expand their territory, the result is stiff, irritating pretend music. Not so here. From the well-done, Kinks-like "Baby Boy" to the mid-tempo *Beatles* '65-outtake "For You," the Quo schmoes refuse to capsize into over-ambition. They even sneak a couple of horns into the irresistible "Too Far Gone," but they're snappy and totally acceptable in a "Got To Get You Into My Life" sort of way. Somebody's really swimming under the barge if they don't put this speedster out as a single.

As hard as this might be to believe in these days of two-songs-plus-filler LPs, there are **NO STINKERS** to be found and that's out of 12 cuts too. I never buy this hype about bands that are supposedly "dedicated" to their fans, but it isn't that hard to believe coming form Status Quo if *Rockin'* is any indication. So now why don't they prove it with a profit-sharing plan?
February 1978

ANDY FAIRWEATHER LOW
Spider Jiving
(A&M)

Andy Fairweather Low started out years ago in a highly successful British teenybop band called Amen Corner whose material developed from screechy soul covers early on into full-blown psychedelic epics like "Scream and Scream Again" toward the end. Due to various business and musical entanglements, Fair dropped out of the scene for several years and has now resurfaced with this highly facile album on A&M.

Despite a solid band (including Henry McCullough, Denny Seiwell and Mick Weaver) behind him and a distinctive vocal style that has been com-

73

pared favorably with Joe Cocker, Fair has been Elliot Mazer-ized by his producer, whose idea of funk is the ominous competence of the Memphis Horns. Mazer is probably also the culprit behind some decidedly incongruous stylistic moves that sometimes work (such as the surprise horns and steel in the middle of the fine Hammond organ-based ballad "Everyday I Die") and sometimes don't (like an ill-advised fiddle and banjo break that kills the pace of the guitar rocker "Drowning on Dry Land").

Andy triumphs over this meddling, however. His credible vocals and basic lead guitar work (something like an imaginative Neil Young with a sense of rhythm) stand up throughout, and his mastery of R&B-based song structures is undeniable. Several of the stronger tracks like "Mellow Down," "Same Old Story" and "I Ain't No Mountain," while definitively done here, are bound to turn up in powerful cover versions by the likes of Cocker, Raitt, Ronstadt and Bramletts.

Capped with the single "Reggae Tune" and a little slice of cabaret called "Dancing In the Dark," this is a solid, entertaining album, not overwhelmingly imaginative but certainly good listening.

December 1974

JONAH
Jonah
(20th Century)

Highlighted by banks of finely layered light vocals, irresistible melodies, easy rhythms and subdued sympathetic arrangements, Jonah's debut album puts them in the ranks of such lightweight greats as Bread, the Carpenters, the Turtles and Curt Boetcher's various permutations. While the band is something of an unknown quantity right now, their trainers have already paid their fluff in full – producer Ron Dante was the lead voice behind epic studio calculations like the Archies and the Rainbow, and executive producers Terry Cashman and Tommy West have been a regular hit factory for some time now.

Jonah's major strength lies in smoothly arranged ballads with the lead singing and exquisitely stratified background vocals such as "The Fool," which builds out of an acoustic guitar cover into a deadly hooked chorus. "Waitin' for The Change" works off a buoyant horn part that's pure MOR folk-rock (great bathing-suit music). The real standout is "It's Always Dark Before the Dawn," a wishy melodrama with predominant ascending vocals and precise orchestration. Definite radio food.

They get into some upbeat goods, displaying crisp guitar and cagey beat, although it's not about to make anyone forget BTO. With any number of potential singles here, Jonah's debut album is quite impressive, and it isn't hard to imagine them settling into a comfortable Lobo-Bread groove with a bit of AM attention.

December 1974

HUDSON-FORD
Free Spirit
(A&M)

When Richard Hudson and John Ford left the Strawbs a while back (taking all the life out of that band) and put out their *Nickelodeon* album, it looked like they had found a comfortable niche as an excellent, if rather Beatle-derived, outfit. But on their second LP, H-F have reached far beyond their influences and blossomed into a straight-ahead working pop-rock band.

Hudson-Ford specializes in wily, well-constructed ear grabbers with their own distinctive close harmonies and ace guitar-keyboard interplay between band members Mickey Keen and Chris Parren. Most of the tracks are brisk melodic numbers with high-powered choruses and exacting arrangements, while also taking time out for an enticing, moderately orchestrated ballad and a couple of British folk-rock-based tunes.

If you enjoyed their first album or some of their fine work with the Strawbs, *Free Spirit* expands that sound and is sure to please. And if you've never listened to them before but are attracted to quick melodic guitar and keyboard productions *a la* Wings, you won't go wrong with Hudson-Ford.
December 1974

JOHN ENTWISTLE'S OX
Mad Dog
(MCA)

Ox is the latest antidote to Who bassist John Entwistle's boredom with being Who bassist John Entwistle. His last one was called Rigor Mortis (he sure names his bands accurately) and before that there were two solo albums. None of this solo output has been better than mediocre, leading one to believe that it's his lack of good material rather than Townshend fascism that holds him to one song per Who album. The old George Harrison syndrome.

As an eight-piece beast with an overweighted horn section, Ox is best at the handful of upbeat blues-flavored numbers they tackle here. Tony Ashton, who tends to dominate every session he works on, is a standout on piano, and several tracks sound like watered down cuts from the fine LP he made with Jon Lord last year. Too bad he doesn't handle the vocals also, because Entwistle's voice is almost completely unsuited for this kind of material, going dry and plain just when it should rock.

The rest of the album is your standard Roy Wood workout, torpid stylistic roulette that never really gets off the ground. If Entwistle is really as big on working in a band context as he comes on, he ought to hire an interesting vocalist, dig up some good material and stick to bass playing. Of course, then he'd be right back where he started at with the Who.

Can't wait for Keith Moon's album.
March 1975

ROGER DALTREY
One of the Boys
(MCA)

Self-consciousness is the doom of rock 'n' rollers. They can shine for years as relative nobodies, but as soon as it dawns on them that everybody *really* is watching or, worse yet, *listening*, they inevitably choke and lose the low spark of spontaneous dumbness that got them there in the first place.

Exhibit no. 1: Roger Daltrey. He started at 18 with consummate nastiness ("My Generation," etc.) and the rare ability to tone it down a shade for the chickenhawk-in-the-boys-chorus slickness of "The Kids Are Alright," jacking out unnerving vocal moves that went from cringe-tailed P.W. to icedog revenge in under five minutes. All downhill from there.

He should've quit while he was ahead. Few singers ever approach their high-water mark once it's passed, and Daltrey's no exception. From *Tommy* to the present, his delivery has become mannered to the point of cartoon. What more can you say about a guy that carries his own picture around in his wallet?

While old incisor-face's first two solo wads were nothing to write home about, *One of the Boys* out-sucks them with ease. The man's been losing his voice for some time now, but it took this record to sink him in the George Harrison School of Croak for good. His vocal chords are too rotted for fast songs (tennis throat) and he goes after ballads with a knuckleball voice that doesn't knuckle. There once was a note, uh huh.

The title cut, an ugly Steve Gibbons tune, is the only rocker on the album, and it comes off surprisingly well. Roger steps back from the mirror a minute and bends that parakeet gravel voice into the vague shadow of a growl. You hear that and you wonder why he doesn't turn this "handicap" into style like Dylan did way back when.

No such luck. Everything else is ballad or pre-ballad. Oatmeal aspiring to be granola. You want facts, we got facts. The Courtney/Daltry compositions are as dull as the ones on the last two albums. "Giddy," an anonymous slice of stop & go that Paul McCartney wrote especially for Roger, just goes to show that Paul saves the good stuff for his own albums. Moving right along, Daltrey neuters Andy Pratt's "Avenging Annie" with the help of Alvin Lee, kills his Zombie connection with a tuneless Colin Blunstone number (no wonder Rod Argent plays keyboards), and – in all fairness – embarrasses the ability of the Goodhand-Tait team equally by soaking a couple of their songs in rancid Mazola. Irony fans will enjoy "Say It Ain't So Joe," written by Murray Head, who played Judas in *J.C. Superstar*. Is this cute or poot?

No member of the Who has ever put out a listenable solo album, and they never will because they're too old and smart to be anything but boring. It may be self-defeating getting on the case of big boys like Daltrey, but all the time and money lavished on greedy millionaires like him just erodes the energy that could be spent on all the deserving young talent currently going to waste. The entire Superstar establishment stinks, and the first crazy Sirhan

Sirhan of rock 'n' roll that takes out one of these fogies deserves a medal. And a contract with MCA.

July 1977

WHO

Who Are You
(MCA)

This new pan of Who Helper isn't nearly as useless as their last couple of records, but it's still nothing to fall down the stairs over. The songwriting has improved slightly, although most of the tunes have slow, serious sections that drag on them like a freshly-applied tinkle-tail. Roger Daltrey's voice is a little stronger and less forced, but it's not hard to spot the places where he's pushing it. And the playing, usually one of the band's strong points, isn't any more lifeless than what has come to be expected.

Before we dismiss these flabby whores as the vinyl dead weight that they've become, let's take a look at *Who Are You*'s high points. Some of the more engaging cuts are slowpokes for a switch. The title cut has a likeable doot-doot CS&N chorus that sweetens up the mundane verse, and "Guitar and Pen" glides on some smooth voice and synth for a while before it degenerates into "Mona" sung by pixies. The ballad "Love Is Coming Down" (and me without my galoshes) almost skates the cake as well until it's sunk by the pigeon-convoy string arrangement.

It's the upbeat stuff that gives these doze-ponds away every time. The opening cut, "New Song," is good, if typical, Who boo until the words dawn lightbulb-like on unsuspecting ears: "I write the same old song with some different lines ... but do you really want to hear it?" While historians can note the "NO" heard 'round the world, the rest of us lemmings have to wonder howcum the boys gave away the punch line so soon. It ruins the whole joke.

Speaking of jokes, how about "Sister Disco," another disco protest rant that features the dumbest chorus since "Boris the Spider." Now the Village People ought to put out a song called "Sister Townshend." Other humor can be found in "Music Must Change," a cool-provoking air-trap with all the charm of smoke-filled kitchenettes and scratchy Teresa Brewer records, "Had Enough," the title of which speaks for itself, and "905," where canoe-voiced John Entwistle delivers a melody-bare "idea" song about test-tube babies. Nice idea, John. Call collect when you get another one.

That's the trouble with the Who anymore. Their butts are where their brains should be and vice versa. Right now they're probably all standing on their heads in a darkened pub, trying to think up new album titles. All the easy ones are used now, so stay tuned for the Who LPs of '79, '80 and '81: *Who Left The Light On In The Bathroom, Who Was That Deaf, Dumb And Blind Boy I Saw You With Last Night,* and three-record set *Who Who Who! Those Wacky Knock-Knock Jokes Just Crack Me Up.*

September 1978

ACE
Five-A-Side
(Anchor ABC)

HUSTLER
High Street
(A&M)

SNAFU
Situation Normal
(Capitol)

Although pub-rock is about to go down the economic drain with the rest of England, there'll be plenty of greasy vinyl artifacts left for late-coming Americans to dig their spindles into. Even though great records by Ducks Deluxe, Brinsley Schwarz and (hopefully not) Kokomo have come and gone, some of the secondary bands are just now getting released, and if any of them can match the success of Ace, you can be sure we'll be seeing a lot more.

As you've probably heard at least 10 times a day for a month, Ace are all over the airwaves with their superb "How Long" single. There's more where that came from, and *Five-A-Side* is definitely worth checking. Sounding not unlike a Motown Moby Grape, Ace run through 10 originals that range from the quick & sneak "Sniffin' About" to the well-settled "23 Hours," all with an ease that gives all their songs a casual lived-in appearance. Although occasionally leaning toward sound-alike complacence, Ace's debut is still full of enjoyable summer music.

Hustler has a much rougher sound than Ace, resembling a less-polished Free at times. That's fine with me coz Free eventually smoothed themselves into the studied hardness of Bad Company, and Hustler seem more the vindictive types. Bullet-domed vocalist Steve Haynes is particularly outstanding, with a nasty attitude that would send hangers-on like Mick Ralphs back to Ian Hunter's knee. The tunes once again range from the slinky to the snotty, and if their material lacks the consistency of Ace, it also lacks the blandness.

Snafu are somewhat more country-oriented than most pubbers and have a lot more variety to offer, from diddling mandolins to a long workout in "Playboy Blues." Possessing neither the bite of Hustler nor the loaded charm of Ace, they have a tendency to throw in everything instead of sticking with the little that matters to a zoned-out pub audience. It remains to be seen whether they can shape up and shake.

May 1975

FLAMIN' GROOVIES
"You Take Me Down" b/w "Him or Me (What's It Gonna Be?)"
(Bomp)

Alive Forever
(Skydog)

Grease
(Skydog)

The Flamin' Groovies story is a classic of being pimped by Da Biz. Starting out as the only hardcore rock 'n' roll band in San Francisco, they ran epic shows at the old Fillmore with the Stooges, MC5 and themselves that are still talked about by the few acid casualties who can still put an entire sentence together. They put out three great LPs on Epic and Kama Sutra that were under-promoted into oblivion, and would have had a hit single on their first attempt if somebody had remembered to print up anything other than DJ copies. Finally, they tried the old trip-to-England-to-sneak-conquer-America trick, accidentally picked up a fanatical French following, and finally wound up back in the States with zero bucks and zero band. Through all this monumental bullshit, they managed to keep their sense of humor and their unbeatable stomp gears, and record a bunch of crazy sides that whip the pulp out of any and all competition. Now we're in the midst of a genuine Groovies revival — something of a replay of an event that never really happened.

Anyway, the Groovies are back together on the coast with a hot local single, "You Tore Me Down," out on Bomp Records, and while it ain't exactly murderizing the charts, it's faster than anything you're likely to hear this year. To keep more of this rude stuff around, Skydog Records has put out two killer EPs of some older Groovies goodies, and you ain't gonna find meat much rawer than this. *Alive Forever* has two monster cuts, a fist of noise called "Blues From Phillys" and a lightning version of "Jumpin' Jack Flash" that makes the Stones sound like BeeGees in a bathtub. *Grease* goes it one better with four power cuts, including the classics "Dog Meat" and "Slow Death," both of which are merciless MC5-like rockers that have been known to turn basket cases into disco queens.

If the present Groovies push doesn't get off the ground, all this stuff might dry up fast, so if you wanna get in on a rock legend guaranteed to leave yer sneakers full of a certain gummy substance, better scarf up now.
June 1975

OZARK MOUNTAIN DEVILS
The Car Over The Lake Album
(A&M)

Like the other country-rock bands (Eagles, Heartsfield, etc.) who belatedly discovered radio pop as the road to Joe Namath mohair carpets on the mountain, the Ozarks are having problems nudging their traditionalist roots and hanging on to their early supporters while at the same time gleefully taking the tickets of their newfound fans. The Eagles have chosen to go for everybody with an ominously professional mixture of fine, memorable tunes and two-LPs-a-year filler, and Heartsfield has adopted the old shotgun approach, but the Daredevils' solution is to book up on the division of songwriting chores that has gotten them this far and to solidify it even more.

This doesn't make for cohesive records, but then oatmeal is cheap.

What we get is four easily identified types: Type A contains all the logical follow-ups to "Jackie Blue." You just look for the "Jackie" writer's name (Larry Lee) and you can't miss. "If I Only Knew" sounds like the late Badfinger's (including dead member) adaptation of "J.B." with some borrowed horns. Anyone who's ever strayed within one basement of a piano has written a song like this. "Mr. Powell" is the next hit as covered by the Association. Very pleasant music to macramé by. Lurking harpsichords. "Time to Time" is America's follow-up to the Association's follow-up *ad bloatum.*

Type B is the three-chord rockers that roll from "If You Want To Get To Heaven." Ozark is especially good at these. "Keep On Churnin'" is the lead cut, with some fine Randle Chowning guitar and good chorus horns. "Thin Ice," the so-far nowhere single (too punk) has a great bar riff and some "Sugar Shack" organ fills. "Southern Cross" brings back the horns and Steve "Johnny" Cash singin' those Folson Prison Blues and practicing his I-Drill-You-Pussies stare from 100 yards.

Type C is a rest station, with the strings and harpsichord-burdened (these guys ain't no Left Bank) "Cobblestone" and a fade track, "Wipporwill," giving everybody a shot to flush those sighs. This puppy needs a home.

Type D is the old Tears-In-the-Truckstop throwback item. Brooding cavemen behind the wheel. "Leatherwood" is a regular Porter "Skull" Wagoner/Gram Parsons adaptation of that "now I lay me down to sleep" prayer you learned when you were still kneeling on Twinkies. "Gypsy" is a first-album hoedown retread with deodorized mountain yelps in the background. *Beverly Hillbillies.* The truly dull "Out On The Sea" is a miscegenated shadow of the above.

Formula aside, this is an enjoyable album, through hardcore Ozark fans tend to bitch about it. I ain't no O.M.D. hardcore, and "Jackie Blue" was one of my favorites this summer. Take it from there. Take it away.
November 1975

STYX
Equinox
(A&M)

ARTFUL DODGER
(Columbia)

This seems to be a big season for English fixations. There's Angel doing their Uriah Heep act, the Mersey surf music of the Hudson brothers, Kansas' recent metal extensions and now Styx and Artful Dodger.

Styx have always maintained a strange balance of Limey derivation and Chicago bar noise, and *Equinox* is their most successful refinement yet. Not only have they directed their electronic augmentations out of the madmen-at-the-knobs mold, but they're letting their hard rock roots show more, too.

The result is their best album in several tries. The opener, "Light Up," sets the tone of the LP, sounding like one of Argent's better songs with pleasant melody traps and the good old "high on love" lyric line that became obsolete with the discovery of amphetamines. Another tuneful radio possibility is "Lorelei," a convincing imitation of the *Who's Next*-period Who doin' the Cryan' Shames. Two fine guitar rockers top the second side, with "Suite Madame Blue" being the only Frankenstein, one of the who-lost-America concepthatons that go over like a lead Buckinghams.

Artful Dodger is a whole different cup of meat. Taking off from the hardcore Small Faces/Troggs school of Limey crime, they've perfected all the moves from gravel harmonies to big skuzzy links hunks of genius **RHYTHM GUITAR** rote honk. You can rarely have a truly great rock 'n' roll band without great rhythm guitar, and the Dodger's Gary Cox has it like a young punk John Lennon. Plus … Aerosmith's producer for proper thud formation.

The majority of songs rock with a straight-ahead scratchiness like a herd of donkeys stampeding on a concrete plain covered with puppy chow, and have deadly catchy choruses to boot. But best of all is their attitude – they used to be called Brat and it shows. Artful Dodger is one of the most exciting hard rock debuts in recent memory, right up there with Trooper and Hammersmith, so don't pass it by.
December 1975

STYX
The Grand Illusion
(A&M)

Styx ain't half bad, but they almost are. If you only heard the first side of *Grand Illusion*, you'd think they were sensational. If you flip it over, you'll experience that helpless sinking sensation peculiar to Cub fans and the disease-prone.

For a band that started with two strikes against them – 1), they're from Chicago and 2), they're all named Panozzo) – Styx has done remarkably well, both commercially and artistically. They've become such big stars in

Canada that even mooses ask for their autographs, and they're getting bigger all the time down here – no small job when you come from the city of big shoulders and small audiences. Better yet, they've thoroughly integrated the mainly British influences that caused so much early awkwardness, into the Midwest power base that's their true strength. These Panozzo-la's got class.

At least on side one they do. The title cut, while perhaps a trifle overblown, gets things off to a good start. Synthesizer flourishes and Townshend-esque guitar smacks give way to a fine melody and well-controlled light/heavy contrasts, while an electrified Anglo folk drone adds a hint of black dog menace. Stonehenge falling domino-like on a surprised tourist's big toe. "Fooling Yourself," penned by the increasingly valuable guitarist Tommy Shaw, features another strong melody, plus Dennis DeYoung's unnerving ability to make his synth sound like a herd of bagpipessurrounded by hungry wolves.

"Superstars" makes it three in a row, with excellent vocals stacked on an odd hump-and-delay beat from the all-Panozzo rhythm section, evidence that brothers make the best bass/drums combinations. Bunk beds of sound. And can this band sing! You don't have to hold a loaded hedge trimmer to their heads to get the high notes. They're just *there*. "Sail Away" wraps up things with a fake-out arrangement that starts slow and then hits you over the head with a deadly refrain.

Grand Illusion has a second side also. It stinks. Why anybody would want to write – much less *record* – an anti-beauty queen number at this late date is beyond me, but here comes James Young's lead-off cut, "Miss America." I mean, "in your cage at the human zoo"? Next album he'll probably come out against Vietnam. Of course, *all* their lyrics sound like a self-help book hosted by the Silver Surfer, so Young's isn't the only red face around.

Styx unfortunate once-is-not-enough complex fills out the rest of the side with two bloato-dramatic slowboats and a "Grand Finale" filler that Sums Things Up for all us dummies in tone-arm land. Eight and a half games in front at the All-Star break and they blow it to the Mets.

Can't really complain much though, a least they had the brains to put all the good stuff in one place, unlike most. Side one is Styx's best work ever and possibly one of those rare cases where it's worth the whole album. It'd make a believer out of door knob. If they ever make an entire record of that caliber, Panozzo will become a household word. It's easier than Yastrzemski.
July 1977

ANGEL
Angel
(Casablanca)

Catholic Rock has been with us for quite a while now, from the earliest meanderings of Manfred Mann and Keith Emerson's Nice (not forgetting our own Association and Electric Prunes) through the acid scares of the amazingly influential Moody Blues and King Crimson, right up to FM '76, where everybody from Argent to Zzebra is sniffering for the Meaning of Life, the Universe, Diet Pepsi, etc. and finding mostly dulling galactic soap operas and enigmatic funny noises. "Progressive Rock" as such has pretty well exhausted its initial inspiration running down blind aluminum alleys, but it's become as legitimate a genre as heavy metal or country-rock, and bands like Yes, ELP and Pink Floyd still sell well into the platinums.

English groups used to have a monopoly in the spaced race, due mainly to a fault in their national character that encourages deep-fruit introspection, Death Delving and the like. But some irrepressible Anglophiles are always thinking that Limeys are real sharp because they have cute accents, wear horn-rimmed glasses, drink their beer warm and make an art out of being depressed. So a few hundred thousand kids did acid, listened to Moody Blues albums, and grew up to be Styx, Kansas, Pavlov's Dog and Angel.

Angel is very serious about, and very good at what they do. They've got everything going for them to be the next Uriah Heep phenomena, especially if the Heep keep cranking out those boring Warner Bros. formula albums while Ken Hensley follows his Rick Wakeman star.

The lead cut, "Tower," is the prototypical Angel song. A massive sound-effect opening that blips like an oscilloscope plugged into a seagull's ass, roaring Amtrak bass lines, deep-sea organ washes, guitar that's sealed in a vacuum-packed feedback container, holy-water Mellotron, and guilt-drenched vocal dramatics that carry muddled lyrics concerning dreams, pain, monasteries, ox-carts lumbering over dung-covered cobblestones in the evening mist, that sort of thing.

While about half the tracks are steeped in this dim, sullen mood, Angel displays a lively, upbeat "Easy Livin'" edge in songs like "Sunday Morning," "On and On," and a genuine straight-ahead killer called "Rock and Rollers" that sounds like a sure-fire encore tune. After that, they probably go into "Johnny B. Goode" with the synthesizer taking all the guitar parts. Applause, more matches.

These guys are gonna hit big.

December 1975

ANGEL
White Hot
(Casablanca)

Angel are the Penthouse Pets of rock. They're always photographed puckering in a gauzy haze like five Dinah Shores lost in a steambath. Their rococo hairdos imply halos and their costumes make them look like tail-less-but-soulful sperms. They probably have little white wings on their dicks, too.

They don't make pouty music though. With a remarkably bottom-heavy rhythm section that out-thuds even Nazareth, they come up with some truly hard stuff. It sounds like they play gigantic instruments that have to be towed in by tugs and held erect by jumbo-jet construction cranes. This is one group that can unhesitatingly be described as *heavy*.

They don't fall into the trap of producing sludge however. Guitarist Punky Meadows, who's often referred to as St. Punk for his extra-angelic appearance, keeps things relatively crisp while keyboard incubus Gregg Guiffria resists the common the tendency to play synthesizer with meat mallets. To top things off, vocalist Frank DiMino generally sings instead of screaming until the melody comes out his ears.

While their material is a little on the plain side, their performance dresses it up considerably. "Under Suspicion" is the top cut, riding a rail-bending riff that shows off St. Punky's exceptional drill abilities. Neat vocal moves, too, especially the Ooo's From Beyond. Other winners include "Hold Me Squeeze Me," ruled by Felix Robinson's outstanding 16 tons of bass, their hovering, choir-proof ballad "Winter Song," and a near note-for-note knock off of "I Ain't Gonna Eat Out My Heart Anymore," a required tune for any group with a member named Felix.

The sole stinker, a tribute to the ponderous Harrison side of the Beatles called "Flying With Broken Wings," doesn't detract from the proceedings all that much, making *White Hot* Angel's most consistently rocking LP. And if you don't like their music, there's always the scratch-and-lick cover.
February 1978

TUFANO & GIAMMARESE BAND
Tufano & Giammarese Band
(Ode Records)

Rock resurrection! If you haunted old teen dance palaces in the mid- to late-'60s, waiting to ask a girl to dance so you could try to pick her up, or strolling nonchalantly past rows of guys so they would dare to talk to you, this band will bring back the good and bittersweet memories of that era.

Tufano & Giammarese is superficially the reformation of the Chicago kings of teen places the Buckinghams, and yet is a strong new act – full of older musical references and newer twists, curls and melodies. This debut album shows off their production capabilities – with smooth orchestrations, tight arrangements and slick vocal harmonies – and teases listeners with things to come.

Side 1 starts off with a defiance that provokes one to remove the Buckinghams connotations and listen to these musicians for themselves. Both "Let in the Light" and "Gone like the Wind" are evocative, pleasant tunes that savor their pop-ness and express a willingness to be naïve, immature and musically less than sophisticated. The remainder of the side flows together well, with "Honest Man" ending the side with an upbeat rhythmic rocker.

Side 2 stirs some romantic recollections quickly with their new version of "Kind of A Drag," then appropriately blends into "Times Change." The side accelerates with non-Neil Sedaka-style pop poop, ending with a wistful song, "Summer Night."

The focus of Tufano & Giammarese, like their famous predecessors, is their choral vocals and velvety harmonies and lead tones. However, the comparison will be forced if drawn too closely, for T & G are in the midst of creating an identity and direction for themselves separate from the good and bad aspects of the Buckinghams' legacy. With some delicately pointed promotion, limited radio airplay and company support, Tufano & Giammarese could quickly grab a foothold in the climb to success.

After all, such Fraternity Rock is nevertheless rock, but we can't deny that we loved the Bucks.

T & G, board that El for an uptown stop; you're going places.
February 1976

SWEET
Give Us A Wink
(Capitol)

The Sweet rule. They can't be denied any longer as one of the great heavy metal kingpins. They've got a fresh approach with their Cool Whip vocals layered over Andy Scott's genius blunt object power chording. They've gained total control over the material and production. They write great songs. And best of all, they're doing it *all over the radio.*

As old as it finally got, "Ballroom Blitz" was still a fine thrasher, and that was over two years old, being the final effort of their long and highly successful collaboration with the domineering writing team of Chinn/Chapman. Sweet came into their own with "Fox On The Run," and then completely wiped that off the waves with the great "Action," the lead cut on the new album. Everything that's right with that song – the snarly, slow-reflex fast-pickup lead vocal, the queerbait backups, Scott's life-on-other-planets guitar, and the overall falling, safe effect of the rhythm section – is built on and thoroughly explored in the rest of the cuts.

Picking highlights ain't that easy, but for starters there's "Lies In Your Eyes," with its "Teenage Wasteland" synthesizing, and brief but hot quotes from "Shapes Of Things," "Satisfaction," and various Sweet tunes, "White Mice," wherein Andy Scott runs Jimmy Page through a riff-shredder and comes out smelling sweet as a slag-heap rose, an excellent, vaguely Bowieish ballad called "Lady Starlight" which shows that slow songs on fast albums do not have to be Turtle Pamprin, and the monumental "Healer," the final product of downer conducivism and seven minutes of total thud reduction.

Wink just about has the competition PW'd already, and if I was Led Zep or even Nazareth, I'd memorize this LP and then do like Jefferson Airplane did when they heard *Sgt. Pepper* (though they heard it wrong) – run back to the studio and do the next album over, only *this time with feeling.*
March 1976

SWEET
Off The Record
(Capitol)

Are the Sweet really the MC5 disguised as Uriah Heep? It could be, because behind that defensive aura of flashy artificiality lies a tough-minded band who can grind out that numbing Detroit rhythm drone with the best of 'em.

What the Sweet need about now is a producer with his sneaks on the ground but a weakness for dramatics, like say Shadow Morton or a less compulsive Terry Knight. As it stands, the band does a pretty good job themselves, but they try so hard that the underlying plug-grit tends to get overlooked for fancy studio effects.

They do have the Sweet Sound down to perfection though. The vocals are a unique mixture of squirrel grunts and tin angel lightness that sounds like a Terrytoon of James Dean's ascension into heaven. The rhythm section is hard to lay a finger on at Tucker and Priest's speed, especially on the turns, and Andy Scott has his trademark guitar hum down to a science, using his secret gadget that makes it sound like six midgets squeezing fuzz-boxes in a handball court.

The showcase cut is "Windy City," a seven-minute cavalcade of thud in flight. Built on a supertanker buzz riff, the tune builds into a remarkable instrumental section that begins like the soundtrack to *Vacuum Cleaners From Hell* and eventually winds into a quirky synthesizer interlude that could easily pass for Country Joe and The Fish tackling the Doors Songbook.

Other big rockers include the torrentially heavy "Hard Times," "She Gimme Lovin'," where the "Ballroom Blitz" drums put in a brief appearance, and "Stairway To The Stars," which has less to do with the Blue Oyster Cult song of the same name than it does Jose Greco doing the tango with Frankenstein.

In the right hands, Sweet could develop into the next Led Zep, so get into 'em now before they get fat and buy castles.
May 1977

THIN LIZZY

Jailbreak

(Mercury)

How'd you like to run into Thin Lizzy in a dark alley? No, thanks, they'd remove your face for future lampshade use. They treat life like a napkin.

No group since the Stooges and – way back – the Stones has so perfectly capitalized on their own elemental meanness. Having "The Boys Are Back In Town" constantly creaming the airwaves this summer is making the entire season habitable. Not only is "The Boys" a great single, but it's the theme song of our entire neighborhood. If you've never heard that tune blasting from three houses on a corner all at once, you probably lead a drab existence.

We're not dealing with a bunch of amateurs here. This is T. Lizzy's fifth album, and behind singer and bassist Phil Lynott they've gotten better every time out. Lynott and drummer Brian Downey lay down the silver wads of rhythm that twin lead guitarists Gorham and Robertson pick up and fly off to the sky zone with. A perfectly constructed band.

Jailbreak is something of a loose concept album. The title cut is T. Lizzy's "Gimme Shelter," fueled by everyday hatred of everything and massive guitar aggression. They shoot their way out of jail, do a couple of near-ballads (too fast to be "slow songs") and wind up with the fear-inspiring "Warriors."

All that needs to be said about the flip side is "The Boys Are Back In Town." Some of the hottest guitar and nasty words to break the AM barrier in years.

This is really one of the greats. I know that's said about a different album every six months, but if you don't like it, you know what you can do? Go kneel on a popsicle, that's what.

October 1976

THIN LIZZY
Bad Reputation
(Mercury)

Thin Lizzy's fear-boss, Phil Lynott, is a classic beautiful loser. Textbook schizonoid, a regular sawed-off moo. Not just an Irishman, but a Black Irishman. Worse than mean, he's unpredictable, like a kitty cat that severs arteries in mid-purr.

He's also a first-degree rocker, and leader of possibly the most underrated band of the last X years. Why? (They asked breathlessly.) Well: A) All Dixie boosterism aside, TL is the only band that knows what to do with dual guitars (hit each other over the head with them), B) More importantly, TL has the rhythm section to end all rhythm sections. Lynott on bass and Brian Downey on drums play right through each other, faking and crunching, slapping and slugging. Even the slowest butts quickly evolve brontosaurus helpers. Most important though, is D. Dee dee dee.

Getting back to Phil's persona, he's a genuine sunset artifact who can't decide whether to throw policemen at rocks, buddy up to the M&M Man or what, and the resultant angry confusion is the stuff from which friction genius is made. Something for anyone, but nothing for everybody.

"Soldier Of Fortune" breaks things right in with a dose of Lynott's Irish-outrage that's kinda Limey-quainty to us but Nam to them. And he doesn't know whether to throw stuff or coo, so he yells. The title cut keeps it going with guitar scrape and bass/drums thump & groan, and "Opium Trail" (title courtesy of *Parade* magazine) ain't a loser either, with tricky vocal moves that thoroughly confuse everyone.

Skip the slow song, flip it over and it's "Dancing In The Moonlight," a nice if ignorable sleazy single effort which doesn't sound like a hit to me, thereby guaranteeing it google platinum status. "Killer Without a Cause" brings on Death Toll USA, and ultimo flash guitarist Brian Robertson dies of terminal ketosis immediately afterward. He's been replaced with a thresher.

There are other pleasantries, including war, Muzak, angel pee, and one total surprise ("That Woman's Gonna Break Your Heart") that the Searchers might have done if they'd all been dying of something. Gibberish aside, try not to miss this band. They bite, but you'll shiver instead of hurt.

September 1977

THIN LIZZY
Live And Dangerous
(Warner Bros.)

Live albums are a great idea, and like most great ideas (the electric backpack, adult-proof bottle caps, any given country's constitution), this animal stands with bovine distraction between the feed trough and its own shit, wondering, "Which one should I eat first?"

Cow puzzlement is a sorry sight, and live albums aren't much of a listen. There have been some great live albums (MC5's *Kick Out The Jams*; I forget the other one) but most of them have an uphill battle to achieve even boredom.

Live And Dangerous isn't really boring for the most part, but it's never much more exciting than franking privileges. As a Liz whiz from way back, I was expecting the songs to sound like answers to the *$20,000 Pyramid* category THINGS HIT BY TRUCKS. Instead, the whole project comes off like that TV commercial where the ape drives the semi over the suitcase, but it never breaks open. Handy if you're expecting any truck-driving primates, but hell – *this* stuff is *supposed* to bust apart all over the place, nailing listeners with 50 MPH socks and ricochet underpants.

Thin Lizzy never do break out here, instead going for consistency and getting all the notes on the right shelves. That's OK – if you're not familiar with most of the material here, it's going to sound just fine. Solid rocking, superb playing, all the good stuff. But you can't fool a Liz fan, and one listen gives it all away: *the boss is asleep!* Phil Lynott, glam-dunk bassist and bronco-throated singer, slept through the entire four sides. It's amazing, because he says stuff and plays & sings and presumably jumps around, but this guy is in Z City all the way. The catalyst has turned to dead milk.

With Phil just going through the motions, not much happens. The strongest material is still strong and the playing is tremendous. Neither guitarist is tired at all, and they let it show. If Lynott had delivered with half the intensity of Gorham and Robertson (and drummer Brian Downey), the audience probably would have run down, seized Argentina's uranium stocks, and blown up the world. Instead, big Phil just slaps at airballs like a mood agent without a mood.

IT PISSES ME OFF, and what pisses me off even *more* is that they fall flat on their faces on "The Boys Are Back In Town," possibly *the* great modosong of our time and the one song you'd think they'd go all out for. But they *blow it completely*, Lynott unable to even draw out all the words. It's worse than the Cubs could ever imagine being in September, lower than a hundred throws into the dugout. Forget the dugout, throw it away.

Thin Lizzy are still a great group and all I suppose, but conditions are now ideal for them to fast become over-the-hill, and only the Stones have any fun at that. Somehow, it's hard to picture Lee R. and Margaret T. rubbing up to Phil, begging for some coke and minilingus. Claudine L. maybe.
July 1978

HEAD EAST
Get Yourself Up
(A&M)

TROOPER
Two For The Show
(Legend-MCA)

Head East is truly a talented band, and we're all rootin' for the home-town boys to make it, so maybe this one'll do it. Trooper's a whole other story, being from the boring wastelands of Canada, you know – that big bathroom of a country across from Detroit? But they're still good anyway.

Midwest and Canadian bands seem to have something in common. What, you ask? How the hell should I know, the author replies. No really, both regions produce bands that have to rock hard for their money, since what else is there to do, pick corn and shoot mooses? They usually feature crashing guitar and drums with hotfoot singers that know how to menace an audience.

Head East has had the edge on commercial success ever since their single "Never Been Any Reason" nearly cracked into the bigtimes. Their second album is more in the flash-hard style of "Reason," with more emphasis on the guitar lines and less keyboard meandering. "Monkey Shine" and "Jailer" are particularly deadly, in the REO-vein but harder, and for a change of pace, "This Woman's in Love" drives and soothes at the same time. (Makes you horny too.)

BTO figurehead Randy Bachman has tightened up the production on Trooper's second album, so you get to hear a bit of their "quieter" side preserved in a tense aura of stomp. The title cut is even medium-slow, opening the possibility that the band may actually possess feelings (God forbid), but they really start to shine on tunes like "The Boys In The Bright White Sportscar" and the precisely unattitudinal "Santa Maria," wherein a bunch of weirdos try to discover America on a moldy sardine boat but get too wasted to care. If that ain't class.

Trooper and Head East are two young bands that are already looking good and have tons of potential. Save up your Sno-cone money for a while and pick up on one of 'em.
October 1976

STARZ
Violation
(Capitol)

Michael Lee Smith, singer/miscreant with Starz, is not your everyday mean. He has this slimy other quality, a real grease spot of a personality. He uses puke-scented mouthwash. His dog's best trick is "grovel."

You put a guy like Smith in front of a band, and you're bound to get some hot results, and *Violation* is a real cellblock of a record. "Pull The Plug," that euthanasia standard from the first album where Smith actually dies onstage, taking the unwary audience with him as the hall erupts in flames a la *Carrie*, was nothing compared to Starz' new mini-series of cartoon paranoia.

Every song has its own sketchy story, and some of them are pretty grim. "S.T.E.A.D.Y." is a tyranny-and-mutation number where The Authorities round up all the punks and make them stand in a corner wearing wet Supertramp t-shirts. With producer Jack Douglas going at the controls like Jorma Kaukonen locked in a wah-wah pedal factory, the cut builds into an epic of Artis Gilmore-like dimensions. The title cut is another fear opera where the Science Police won't let the kids rock 'n' roll, and "Subway Terror" is a fine cop show where uncooperative delinquents carve graffiti in citizens' foreheads while the world ends unobtrusively in the background.

On the lighter side there's "Sing It, Shout It," where an expertly lobotomized Steely Dan verse leads into an unlikely baby-food chorus which only begins to make sense with the inclusion of a strychnine-addled guitar solo imported from 1967. "Cherry Baby" is a genius reworking of Neil Diamond's classic tribute to statutory tail and a prime candidate for the AM Hall of Shame. "Rock Six Times" covers the old WW III angle, with a decrepit survivor discovering a scratchy copy of "Walk This Way" in a heap of radioactive sardines. Starz even had the audacity to include a ballad called "Is That A Street Light Or The Moon," which Michael Lee delivers with the earnestness of a freshly-gelded colt.

Violation is one great record, better than anything Kiss or Aerosmith have been trotting out lately. Besides, if you don't like it, Mr. Smith'll come over and use your face for a nail file. Some sense of humor.

April 1977

STARZ
Coliseum Rock
(Capitol)

Michael Lee Smith is one of the most exciting rock vocalists to squeeze the collective membrane since Stevie Tyler sat on his first ice pick. He has a much stronger voice than most screamers, and the razor timing born of restrained menace. What with Smith's convincing wolf-jammer backed by a pyrotannical guitar band who gives arson investigators constant headaches, Starz should be trop draw in the meat zone.

So howcum Starz *ain't?* Part of the reason is their indecisiveness in choosing a musical direction, or at least a style more consistent than random street crime. They've done Kiss Mart buzzers, show-yer-pink pop, studio epics, and ballads that would sicken a valentine collector, plus seven or eight other styles that beat scientists are still trying to classify.

The other problem is that Starz' execution far exceeds the depth of their material. That these guys can sound so good with such plain tunes demonstrates the truly benign power of sick minds. I bet Starz could even do that disgusting Neil'n'Barbra tune that's laying slug trails on the radio and make it kick ass. Only they'd probably want to call it "You Never Bring Me Hoses."

Enough damning with faint boogie – *Coliseum Rock* isn't bad at all. The band has stripped their style down to a basic, almost-live-in-the-studio sound and it's about time. As great as some of their big productions like *Violation* were, there's nothing like a tough singer and some hot guitars to stick pins in your blood.

Top itch goes to the lead cut and radio hopeful, "So Young, So Bad," another one of Michael Lee's rockers about fake ID's and spreadeagle moppets. (Somebody really should give him a copy of *The Roman Polanski Story*.) Similar winners include the well-matched riff daggers "Take Me" and "No Regrets," and the irresistibly tumescent "Outfit," a '60s-dipped amp-out concerning the heartwarming sight of hardened teenage nips poking through silk like two PT boats breaking the ribbon in a photo finish at the annual Naval Follies. Wouldn't let 'em sink Hawaii this year.

The only duds are the final two cuts, the stilted "Riot" and "Where Will It End," a fumbled attempt at a big number. This excess baggage can easily be avoided by hurling an underage Starz fan at the turntable right after the all-guitars title cut. Watch the little sneak thrash.

Smith's lyrical preoccupation with humping 12 year olds is getting a bit tiresome, however. This man needs a Sharon Tate, and soon.
December 1978

EDDIE AND THE HOT RODS
Teenage Depression
(Island)

Eddie and the Hot Rods are an everyday bar band that's more than an everyday bar band. They're as simple as the Ramones, and almost as fast. Stripped down to the bones as they are, with their tinny guitar, monotone bass and a tape of skittish rats on concrete instead of a drummer, they have to rely more on sudden impact than some. They always come through, too, even though they bitch and moan like all the new bands.

As a product of the latest wave of Limey club acts, the Hot Rods are faithfully predictable, adding grease marks of respectability like "96 Tears" and "Gloria" to their own carefully bleak material. Two-chord speedballs predominate, and Barrie Masters' you-talkin'-to-me-punk voice is displayed as prominently as a lemon yellow '57 Chevy.

The best cuts are the canary metabolism rockers like the title track and "Why Can't It Be," an inspired welfare state groan that sounds like what the guy on the cover is thinking as he blasts his brains to Endust. Even the ready-made remake of "The Kids Are Alright" is delivered with convincing numbness.

The final statement of this thud parade is "On the Run," the closing epic that's enough to make R. Dean Taylor chew his chains with its feedback German Shepherds snapping irritably at the ever-tightening guitar drone. This album looks best from the other end of a choker leash, but that's just part of the grime mechanics. Eddie and the Hot Rods are tuff and cool and deserve a jump at your dirt track.
April 1977

VIBRATORS
Pure Mania
(Columbia)

The Vibrators are about half punk rake-noise and half straight-ahead pub rock in the style of Eddie and the Hot Rods or the late Ducks Deluxe. This makes for a pretty good combination – you get your bearings-rattling rhythm noise as well as a breathless beat to accelerate liver disintegration by. Accessible even to those with no access.

Like most of the other new wavers, guitar rules in the Vibes' sound. Unlike standard punk fare, however, they feature *two* guitarists (John Ellis and Knox "College") whose thought-out crossfire interplay stands out from the usual all-amp blare. This well-etched guitar sound – along with the tinny, double-speed rhythm section and edgily melodic tunes – gives the whole project a scrappy Merseybeat air, like Wayne Fontana and the Mindbenders gobbling odd-lot whites in a deserted sardine-can factory.

Maximum-pleasure shoppers will like the fact that *Pure Mania* contains 15 cuts, some of them too long. Most numbers are so hair-triggered that the entire LP goes by faster than one Led Zep song. Top values are either pure speeders built on lumber jacket chords like "Into The Future" and "Petrol" (a girl's name, naturally) or pure speeders with catchy refrains like "Whips And Furs," which has nothing to do with either item unless it's pussy-whipped and mink sex.

With the exception of a couple misshapen slowish tunes that are easily ignored, the Vibrators' debut is sure to be one of the fastest records of '78. Perfect for timing Cookin' Bags, as long as you throw out the food and eat the plastic.
March 1978

CAPTAIN BEYOND
Dawn Explosion
(Warner Bros)

Fishing from the grainy mists of cosmosis, his streaming locks afire (got too close to the barbecue), his permanent-press cape billowing in the stiff psychic breeze, and tiny bolts of tin lightning shooting from his temples, it's Captain Beyond, hero of fishbowl-heads everywhere and sworn enemy of Japanese disco!

Formed several years ago by rejects from the likes of Iron Butterfly and Deep Purple, CB initially set out to create Latin space-rock. Not exactly what the fans expected from six guys named Rhino, it went over like a lead aphid. Ping. So they broke up for a while and waited for the psychedelic nostalgia movement to pick up steam before they donned their metalflake sweatsuits again.

This time around, Rhino #1 dropped the timbales in favor of cement boxing gloves. Still kind of psychedelic, it sure does weigh a lot. Cuts like "Oblivion" sport trippy effects like half-filled Coke bottles being hit with tuning forks and fat ladies sitting on electric trains, but they're stricken with the crawl of a wounded school bus. "Sweet Dreams" is a mopey old echo of Country Joe and Fish cryo-funk, with underwater guitar figures and sardine isotopes, while "Breath of Fire" lingers like a new disease waiting to be caught.

Since they're currently playing small Midwestern clubs with all the ambience of a Mexican jail, the Beyondies also include a couple of canary-metabolism numbers, the most promising being "Icarus," about the mythical chump who flew too close to the sun and burned his wah-wah pedal. Of course, any song about "getting Mother Nature" can't be all bad.

The real question for all this wiener wrap, however, is: What does the Captain Beyond symbol (two interlocking triangles) really stand for? Is it Pyramid Power? The lost continent of Atlantis? Noah's Ark? The Bermuda Triangle? Or perhaps – and this is just speculation, mind you – *two half-eaten ice-cream cones?*

May 1977

PETER FRAMPTON
I'm in You
(A&M)

Peter Frampton is such a nice guy. He never strikes infants with baseball bats. He always sends his mum a card on Mother's Day even though she's dead. He'd probably stoop over to rescue a worm drying out in the sun. That's not so bad. Ted Nugent would eat it.

It's hard to find something bad to say about such a nice person, but I'll try. His voice whines like an overheated egg. His guitar playing is whiny as well. In fact, when he trades off his vocals with his guitar, it sounds like two extremely tired waitresses discussing a particularly obnoxious customer.

Considering his popularity, Frampton could hardly have played it safer on his first studio LP in years. If you want retreads of the live album (which itself was retread-this guy should be selling tires) you'll find plenty here. All of the first side and half the other are guaranteed to satisfy most Frampton ferns.

Some variety sneaks up in the form of the "Road Runner"/"Signed, Sealed, Delivered" medley. Where this cupcake gets his Stevie Wonder fixation is questionable, because he's got NO GROOVE AT ALL and every Wonder tune he does comes off leaden enough to neutralize 10 tons of Kryptonite. As for " Road Runner," it has all the spirit of a burned-out hot comb. Which is more than you can say for "Rocky's Hot Club," a "Rocky Raccoon" tribute faithful down to the fake tape hiss.

Maybe the key to liking Peter or not is in his material. Like most composers, he keeps writing the same melody over and over again. If you like it, you're home free. It's a great tune to hum while squeezing the day-old Twinkies at the Sunbeam thrift shop. His lyrics have never gotten beyond using the word "feel" for every other line. Lots of great rhyming prospects there though — teal, kneel, congeal, even *deshabille!*

This midget's enormous popularity is truly oversized considering his modest talents. He's definitely nice, but so are thousands of other performers who don't generally sell 7 million albums. If anybody is asking anything more than why he never wore elevator shoes in five years, we can all have a good laugh on ourselves and the recording industry. 'Til then, snickers will suffice.

September 1977

BALCONE'S FAULT

It's All Balcone's Fault

(Cream Records)

Balcone's Fault is where the Gulf Plate rubs noses with the quake-prone Midwest Plate, running through the heart of Texas and generally behaving itself except when it gets the jitters and threatens to throw Galveston in the tub for no good reason.

Balcone's Fault is also a band that never manages to behave itself, and intends to dump the whole world in the soup, ears first.

These guys are something else: Eight Austin-area burnouts direct from outer space. The character you notice straight away is criminally-insane percussionist Steve Blodgett (pronounced Blodgett). He's constructed this Chinese Christmas tree out of old car springs, obscure Ubangi religious medallions and rusted-out Lone Star beer cans that he runs around and beats on so fast that you can never tell what bam effect is coming up next.

The rest of the group has their own ideas of ear-fear as well. Working from a solid base of Texas sleaze-beat, they throw in countless personal touches that give them instant identity. Mustang Ranch piano, premarital sax and guitar lines weighted with buckets of beer all come and go with fascinating irregularity. They write great songs as well, the standouts being "42nd Street," a proto-Dixieland job about the place "where the underworld can meet the elite," and "I Got Fooled," a tale of moving furniture and drinking gin that contains one of the great lines of the 20th Century. "She promised me a jellyroll/and said it would be BIG AND BROWN."

But the real androgens occur on Randy Newman's "Leave Your Hat On," where singer Michael McGeary croaks, "I know what love is." No doubt he's right, but who in their right mind would want to admit it?

Go ahead, get this one – take off your skin and let the wind blow through your bones.

February 1977

JAM

In The City

(Polydor)

STRANGLERS

Rattus Norvegicus

(A&M)

Limeys, beagle-brows one and all, have this thing about calling anything different a "New Wave." They have new-wave TV comedy, new-wave SF, new-wave dentistry, new-wave wavelengths and now new-wave rock. But whether you call this gorgeous crud noise new-wave or punk rock or post-psychedelic root beer damage, there's no getting around it: Hot Shit has moved into the neighborhood – next door in fact – and right now they're pissing on your marigolds.

The Stranglers are a curious foursome of gin-slurping acidheads with a compulsion for rat necrophelia. Jean Jacques Burnel is the main brain. His vocals have a kind of deadened Jim Morrison quality like Lou Reed is sitting on his chest in a bathtub, and his all-star bass is the controlling instrument in the line-up, driving the band like they're trying to force each song through a tiny hole in a passing lava flow. Keyboard wit Dave Greenfield provides another earmark, another Doors/Velvets miscegenation of lyrical off-handedness and goose neuroses.

Their prime effort is "Peaches," with a great talk-talk riff carrying Burnel's tale of beach-grazing, boob-hunger and suntan lotion ("spread it all over my peeling skin baby/ooo, it feels so GOOD"). Definitely a bullseye classic and the kind of summer song that's like diving gleefully into the cool cool water and getting your snorkel stuck in a decaying cement-shoebox victim. Take a deep breath now, J.J., and deliver those famous last lines: "It sure is better than being down in the streets/or down in the sewer/or maybe on the end of a skewer."

If you're ready for degraded "Light My Fire" machinations and the whole school of Doors/Velvets crypto-smear taken to the heights of unapproachably genius fake-stupidity, you'll love the Stranglers.

The Jam are even better. In fact, they're the best English hard rock band to pounce down the shaft since Slade and then some. These guys have gone back to the *early* Who (*My Generation* LP *only*) and *early* Kinks (*Kinks Eat Babies* and *Kinks Kill Honkies*) and crammed these two metal-munching styles together into a stunning blade-focus attack. The friction created when leader Paul Weller's Townshend power chops and drummer Rick Buckler's Keith Moon crash landings meet Kinks broadchords and inner licks zooms their tunes like appliance-loaded shoplifters through a magnetic turnstile.

"Art School," the opening winner, is a pure speed lobe assault featuring robot gravedigger feedback and the Jam motto: "Say what you want coz this is the NEW art school." Suck my plugs, Roxy Music. Stompers abound, from the warily melodic "In The City" and *early*-Stones fade of "I Got By In Time," to their fearless rendition of the Batman theme that actually outdeclasses "Theme From Kiss."

First group that re-does "Peter Gunn" gets to screw Caroline Kennedy.

Other masterpieces include the wrecking-crew blockbuster "Bricks and Mortar," where Weller's vertical guitar crashes take off into a feedback cyclone stop-me-before-I-kill instrumental (this kid's a sensation!) to the nearly-nice tin air of "Away From The Numbers," where "I Can See For Miles" meets "The Kids Are Alright."

Listen, I thought that all this anglo punk shit was just another sick joke from the folks that brought us warm beer and the SST. Wrongo, Bernie — these ferocious debuts from Jam and the Stranglers could make entire landfill housing developments crumble into their component tin cans and greasy pizza cardboards given the chance. Grab 'em now and become your own garbage dump.

August 1977

STRANGLERS
No More Heroes
(A&M)

Here we go with the rats again. Seems like every "new wave" LP you pick up these days has something about our furry little friends on it, and you can blame the Stranglers for starting the whole rodent rah-rah. Rat tail chokers were bad enough, but rat down pillows are just a bit much. Hopefully the Stranglers won't be remembered only for their pet preferences, because they're easily one of this year's best new bands. They should start taking after Ireland's Boomtown Rats and start showing rat eradication films onstage.

The Stranglers' music is deadly basic, based on shattered, angular riffs and melodies you remember like scars. J.J. Burnel's bass is the boss instrument, and the way he goes at it could revolutionize bass playing. His extra loud, high-speed bass lines rumble along like tanks on a treadmill, frequently devouring themselves and taking off on independent missions. The other noise king is organist Dave Greenfield, whose *Addams Family* shadings are reminiscent of Ray Manzerak, former Doors' key squeezer and runner up to Paul Kanter in the Chad Stuart look-alike contest. Best of all, though, is singer High Cornwell, a star student of throat torture and rumoured Black Flag guzzler. His fearsome growl has been known to stampede yogurt at 20 yards.

Their material is your basic hate music, ingeniously repetitious and full of lyrical ice wads like "Bitching" ("Bitching/I'm telling you the gospel truth/Bitching/why don't you all get screwed") and "Bring On The Nubiles," which gets a special subtlety citation for the line "you can turn on my tap – I'll drip!" There are more "serious" moments, like Leon Trotsky's introduction to an ice pick in "No More Heroes," or Cornwell's calculatedly feeble attempt to describe his lack of love for anything in "English Towns," but mostly it's just good old hatred of anything with a pulse. While the songs aren't as varied as the ratcakes on their first album, they're more to the point, the point being to eat some shit.

The highlight of the record and the Stranglers' brief career as well is a masterpiece of landfill proportions called "School Mam." It fades in with a tape of kiddies' voices yelping in a playground, into which Burnel's grisly bass marches like an army of child molesters. As an arrangement of organ slams, firing-squad feedback and incredible bass flights unfolds, Cornwell grunts a churning tale of math, science and sweaty butts heaving on tile floors, inciting the listener to "use your 20th century brain if you have one." Talk about building to a climax, this cut accumulates running feedback lesions for five minutes, gradually destroying itself until nothing remains but puddles of tormented wavelengths begging for release while Hugh babbles on about two plus two, four times four and three into 128 (let me pause for reflection for a moment).

The Stranglers might sound merely simplistic on paper, but they've taken hard rock apart piece by piece and put it back together again all crooked, with the super-structure sticking out and getting knocked around. They're also just plain great, and hands-down the most important of the "new wave" bands. Pull up a rat and give 'em a spin.

October 1977

HIRTH MARTINEZ
Big Bright Street
(Warner Bros)

For over two years now, I've had this enigmatic plaster bust of Hirth Martinez in my Inspiration Room, right by the other vital trash icons like the Paul & Rick Reuschel Big League Brothers baseball card, Crazy Ralph Ginzberg brainstorm pic, Freddie Patek RC Cola can, Sox "We're no. 1" pennant (the Cubs pennant is currently turned to the wall in memorium) and, of course, my prized cassette of ZZ Top's bass player explaining why they don't have glitter bands in El Paso.

Hirth has lasted while lesser toys like Officer Baby have been relegated to the "living" room because of the portentous **HERE COMES A LIGHT-BULB** expression on his flaky little face. This Martinez is something else in real life as well. Using a rundown Hollywood laundromat as his base of operations, he attracts big names like Robbie Robertson and Dr. John to play and record with him – all while doing their wash free of charge. Hirth just sings and grins, his mind permanently set on spin.

His voice is an engagingly grainy croak not unlike Lowell George choking on chicken bones, and his songs are quirky little boppers that walk around like sleepy ducks trying to avoid piles of mallard shit. "Nothin' Iz New" features plenty of backing diddy-bops and actually rhymes *joy-ride* with *genocide*. "Star" is very much in the pre-top hat Leon Russell vein, and if "Driver" – a quaint tune about driving around all night and then screwing all morning ("it was good for his head") – isn't in Little Feat's future, it should be.

There's a couple nice snoozy ballads with fine-tuned orchestration by producer John Simon and a Big Finish, "Only In America, Jim," about the amazing success of a singer reminiscent of Hirth himself. He's so big, "even his publisher lives in a giant mansion overlooking space." See what I mean? This Martinez character is kinda Off Somewhere, but he's fun to listen to, and good front-porch music to manicure your nails by.
August 1977

FOGHAT
Live
(Bearsville)

Live albums are a lot like watching TV with the picture off. You think you're getting the idea, but the audience always gets it twice as hard. They "haw-haw" when you only "hee-hee," and no matter how hard you try, there's no way you can fill in the picture. That is, unless you're one of those repressed goons that use live LPs to recreate Great Concerts of Your Life in the comfort of your very own living room, or cell. You probably stuck you first hanky in a Bible too.

Unfortunately, most groups take this souvenir approach. All the favorites, played as perfectly as passable. Worse yet, they record it extra cleanly, dipping their picks in rubbing alcohol and using a vacuum-packed hall that makes the entire proceedings sound like they're coming from the inside of a huge nurse. This backward-seeming logic is way above my head, teetering on a large mound of dollar bills.

But not Foghat! This is one live album you can sink your choppers into. Not only was it recorded as cleanly as is possible in the basement auditorium of a small elementary school in Tennessee, but they go out and shove aside all the prissy-careful playing and "stomp 'dem babies" regardless. When the rhythm guitarist was thrashing with every bit of equipment burned-out except a tiny Pignose amp buried under a pile of USO tarp, *they feature it!* Have a little trouble getting the vocals together on "Fool for The City?" No problem, we'll make it the first song on the album! And when the drummer and bassist start playing different songs halfway through another cut, they just plow away until it all falls back together. Stick *that* in your Bible, perfection-oids.

But this record isn't a beater because of the screw-ups, it's because of the Fog's fearless boogie double-vision. Guitarists Lonesome Dave Peverett and Rod Price work up a superb chugging density born of L.D.'s bottleneck past, and when that's stacked on Roger Earl's "keep hittin' them cymbals, Steve" drums and Craig MacGregor's bass-of-prey, you've got elemental stomp that'll make your ears get up on a little aluminum folding chairs and throw cherry bombs at your brain.

All the hits are here, top cuts being the fearsomely sloppy "Fool," *Energized*'s "Honey Hush," a full-speed rip-off of every Yardbirds rip-off ever recorded including "Psychotic Reaction" and the inevitable "Slow Ride"— which grabs you by your scrawny neck like a massive mom and shakes all the porn and dope out of your pockets. There's some brief guitar indulgence on "I Just Wanna Make Love To Willie Dixon," but they can make it count. And best of all: NO DRUM SOLO!

Just once through, when the singer yells out, "Is everybody havin' a good time?" on these live records, I wish the audience would sit back quietly and – in unison – reply, "Not particularly!"
September 1977

SAVOY BROWN
Savage Return
(London)

The latest reconstruction of Savoy Brown may not rate as much excitement as say, the upcoming *Rescue From Gilligan's Island* or *Exorcist 6: Linda Sells Bad Dope*, but it's still interesting. To go through more members than the Guess Who multiplied by the Byrds and still sell records says something about the viability of brand names if nothing else. What some smart reviewer-type ought to do is copyright every possible band name (Frontier Ozone, The Pus, Eat On The Run, The Important Fuckers, Wounded Or Maimed) and then license them to new groups. Every time they make a comeback bid or put out a reunion album, this guy would get royalties, which he could invest in something *really* profitable like a Midwest newspaper or a nuclear waste dump.

TRUE FACT: This scheme is how Roger McGuinn pays for the constant expansion of his vast home video system, which is now large enough to broadcast TV's *Midnight Special* to Pluto. He alone owns the name "Byrds."

Speaking of business deals, the new addition of Savoy Brown is all business, down to the last Willie Dixon riff. Their basic sound – big thud in a small place – has remained encouragingly constant throughout the years without getting too terribly watered down in the process. Lots of the hard, choppy guitar work that made Foghat a household noise, funneled down into relatively short, high-speed cuts.

The only interference with this otherwise likeable crunch stuff is singer Ian Ellis, who gets so overly cute with his climax-breath at times that it sounds like he's got a gob of broccoli stuck halfway down his throat. (See what happens when you don't chew your food thoroughly, little Rangers?) Ellis is fine when he doesn't push it, though, and with Kim Simmonds' weighty, six-door garage chords dominating the overall sound anyway, the Browns can hardly miss.

Simmonds is so good, in fact, that the only way to escape his career-long underassessment may be to spin off another band from Savoy Brown. Then they can go through another decade of split-ups, reunions and lucrative world tours as opening act for Donovan. This could go on forever. It probably will.
August 1978

NEKTAR
Magic Is A Child
(Polydor)

European progressive fans have been claiming for years now that Nektar isn't just another set of outer-space fundamentalists like Yes, Floyd or Pluto Doom, but you have to wonder. These very same ether-ears will also tell you that King Crimson was a great singles band and that deadly forces exist in and around the much-vaunted East Peoria Triangle.

This time the fishbowl-heads are right, though. For all their portentous lyrics and occasionally odd production, Nektar are eminently approachable. In fact, at times they're *flagrantly* catchy.

Nektar is composed of three Brits and a Yank who basically met in Germany while stealing secrets for the Baader-Meinhof gang. After a few years of terrifying the continent with psychedelic artifacts like *Journey to The Center of The Eye* and *Tab in the Ocean* (best LP title of '72), they lightened up their sound a bit and began touring the States to great success. They can't even walk down the street in St. Louis without being asked to autograph some windowpane by dedicated fans. Last year, they decided to relocate in the U.S. so that they could watch *Lost In Space* whenever they felt like it and actually witness armadillos.

Magic Is A Child, their eighth album, continues their trend toward likable, radio-aimed songs enhanced by wild-eyed production. Nektar's basic sound is something of a cross between attractive tunes along the lines of less ponderous Moody Blues efforts like "Ride My See-Saw," and hard-to-pinpoint Genesis-styled riffs that slide off the griddle like mercury burgers.

"Away From Asgard" is the snappiest, with speedy harpsichords and inter-mittent bells giving it an air of rotund villagers gaily munching cobble-stones. "Train From Nowhere" is deadly catchy as well, although an Adam's apple instrumental section intrudes occasionally.

Like all prog bands, Nektar also have an overly serious side that comes out in bursts, like the elephant trauma that begins "Midnite Lite" or the deep-sea meanderings of "Listen." Not even Lloyd Bridges could find a melody in that one. Where it really hurts is in the lyrics, which often reek of Alpine horns, chariots of Thor, a Sense of Wonderment, and an unfortunate tendency to rhyme four-syllable words. Edgar Allan Poes they ain't. They almost make up for it with one classic line from the profoundly unsubtle "Spread Your Wings": "She had me screaming at the cellar door." Another case of rusty hinges.

Magic stays on the lighter side for the most part, at least musically, so if you never completely recovered from 1967, pick up on Nektar for further diz contentment.

October 1977

RICK WAKEMAN
Criminal Record
(A&M)

No lyric sheet needed! That's what I've always liked about Rick Wakeman records – no dumb singing. Smart too, because if Rick tried to launch those biplane lips of his into song, it would sound like rubber shut-ters flapping on a stormy night.

Of course, the lack of vocalizing isn't the only reason I hate Wakeman much less than I hate Yes. Old ochre face always adds some *classy touches* to his albums. Like this one is dedicated to Fabio Nicoli, who, judging from my main reference source, never once played Major League Baseball. *Fine* name nonethe-less, and there's more. Every single member of the Ars Laeta choir of charming Lausanne, Switzerland, who back our *generous maestro* on one cut, gets his or her name on the back, including such lowly appointees as the ball boy and the eunuch squeezer. Francoise Cardinaux, Claud "Alain" Favez, Sylviane Savez, et al. No hicks in this group, some celebs in fact: Rene Monachon (father discov-ered Monachonia, a disease peculiar to B&W photographers.) Francoise Emery (aunt invented Emery boards), and, of course, Elizabeth Pahud (the sound of a falling pud when it hits the ground: "pa-HUD!")

Best name of all though is NuNu of the Yes Road Crew. He's the luggage-head who has to carry around all of Rick's *axes*, and he was *pretty busy* for this LP, lugging around pianos, harpsichords, birotrons, tirotrons, clavinets, mini-Moogs, poly-Moogs, muchograndeMoogs, Fender Rhodes, Hammond C3s and numerous beer bottles filled with varying amounts of liquid to *alter the pitch*, for which NuNu had to use a special bottle opener called an *alter top*.

Some of you fascists out there are probably wondering about the songs by now, so here's a quick rundown. "Statue of Justice": a flock of delirious com-puter blackbirds attacking a coven of Swedes. "Crime of Passion": Moog's Moog and Arp's arp. Moooooog. Arp! "Chamber Of Horrors": ricky-tick toy fire engine commercial. "Birdman": "poignant ... *moving*" – Liz Smith. "Breathalyzer": the sound of your brain after losing a tequila duel with Ricky Ricardo. "Judas Iscariot": ghost of a pipe organ hovering over whiffle orchards.

And More! The liner contains several interesting stories about *true-to-life* criminals like wife-killer Dr. Crippin, acid-bather Mr. Haigh and tag-team stranglers Burke and Hare. No doubt about it, the Wakeman character might *look* like Flipper in a Farrah wig, but the guy's got a *soul of pulp*.
(signed: Rick "Fabio" Johnson
December 1977

SEX PISTOLS
Never Mind The Bollocks
(Warner Bros.)

Now's the time to throw out all your old records, kick holes in your speakers and abuse your pone into brainstorm duh-transcendence because *this is the stuff*. The Sex Pistols' album is finally out and it's the hottest thing since they put the belladonna back in Contac.

That the Sex Pistols are a big story now is no surprise because – aside from their everyday headline stunts, this is the most stunning rock 'n' roll LP since the Ramones' '76 debut. It's *better* than that, in fact, climbing up the ant-farm hierarchy past landmark screamers like Slade or early Kiss right up to the first N.Y. Dolls record and then some. They've got everything a Z-ear could ask for: full-speed guitar chop, indecipherably obscene lyrics, a grievous lack of forethought and the crayons-in-the-dark genius of singer/boss Johnny Rotten. Plus they've made CBS News twice now, and if the sight of Roger Mudd's talking head making news noise in front of a Pistols blow-up isn't enough to re-enact *The Tingler* on your spine, then your nodes were probably fed to ferns long ago.

The Sex Pistols' sound is rooted in the paroled-development autistic grab-bag of low-number chords that all the great rockers from Chuck Berry to Iggy have drawn from. Guitarist Steve Jones aims the songs more from a dynamic base than from chord changes, all the while tearing off scrappy inner licks that hang out like weatherbeaten electrical tape. The rhythm section basically grabs and throbs while Rotten dumps lines wherever he sees fit. His mastery of phrasing is such that he can make sound like a throwaway, which most of his lyrics are anyway.

Their material rises to their amazing performance, a rare event in these days of quiz kids with porpoise fingers. "God Save The Queen," their famed British chart-bomber, leads the pack with full-court cement basketballs that'll have you singing the "nooooo future" tagline to yourself day and night. Other epics include "Anarchy in the U.K.," the moron anthem that some red pens have attempted to attribute to politics (**HA HA**), their hilarious farewell to past record labels called "EMI," and the Pistols' theme song, "Pretty Vacant." If you're not buzzing around in a racked-up state of advanced ear-fear muttering "We're so pretty/oh so pretty/**WE'RE VACANT!**" after that one, hang it up and bury it.

Bollocks is simply one of the very few great records to filter through the dozing muck of this decade, a sludge-carved obelisk of unforgettable rock 'n' roll caught at the moment of trashed inspiration. Drop everything, listen to this and don't ever go back.

January 1978

HAWKWIND
Quark Strangeness and Charm
(Sire)

If you like the unremitting throb and drone that makes your eardrums feel like a tomcat's morning mouth, then Hawkwind's your band. This isn't the blaring power hum of outfits like Can or Bottle, however, but rather a sort of weak throb like the last dribble of pulse before slit dispatch. Easy listening drone. Top that with comic-book lyrics delivered in a sing/talk style not unlike Jim Stafford with his hand in a toaster, and you've got the final solution to transistor apprehension and outright Norelco fear.

Various configurations of Hawkwind have been shuffling around the world for several years now, bringing their guardian noddism to every town bigger than Petro Smell, U. K. They were the big blab in England for about two hours one year, inspiring hoards of fans (sometimes referred to as The People) to wander around like dosed-out radiologists muttering things about outer space and the future. Outside of diode fanciers, they appeal mainly to the same murk-minds that can recite *Chariots of the Gods* word-for-word at the drop of a tab, and who are forever staring up at the sky, anticipating flaming saucer turds at any minute. Real dumdums, in short.

You don't have to be a subwit to like Hawkwind, but it helps. Now I like throb crud as any self-respecting rhythm casualty, but these guys are so far gone, they didn't even remember to turn up the bass until halfway through the second side, making for a tinny drone reminiscent of a wet telephone. There are some good cuts, though, like the upbeat (for them) title tune with its miss-half-the-time handclaps and lyrics like "Einstein was not a handsome fellow/nobody ever called him Al." "Spirit of the Age" isn't bad either, a cryophillic moan emulsifier with the boys chanting the title in the background. Lucky they didn't call it "Fist Heart Mighty Dawn Dart" or we'd be here all day.

Outside of that, there's a couple of goony instrumentals, a relatively normal (for them) song that sounds like "Ride My Seesaw" coming out of the speaker of an electric train transformer ("Damnation Alley"); and some timely tunes about petro-dollars and the Class of '67. Don't take no Erik von Daniken to predict this stuff.

But more importantly, do you know what Hawkwind's favorite candy is? Quark Bars!

February 1978

MX-80 SOUND
Hard Attack
(Island Import)

MX-80 Sound is the kind of band you rarely encounter, constantly whirlpooling into fearless inspirational frenzy and generally coming back in one piece. Much of their music includes room for improvisation, but you sure won't find any whipping-the-drippings with these guys. To make a couple of rotten comparisons, they're as unafraid to shoot deadeye for their own inner noise as the Stooges or Velvet Underground were in their respective heydays. And to think this all began on the assembly line of a small Indiana Meow Mix factory, where the boys met while constructing tiny meows. Now ain't that the American Dream?

This Sound's sound is characterized by the seemingly chaotic rhythm of a conveyer belt with a finger stuck in the gears, over which all-star guitarist Bruce Anderson spatters crazily angular riffs that sound like glass eyes in the dishwasher, bouncing and shattering everywhere. The other big sound is vocalist and rhythm guitarist Rich Stim's singing, which tends toward a gripping monotone closer to talk-talk most of the time. Let's put it this way: If you tied him to a log headed for the buzzsaw and told him no deals with Mighty Mouse unless he sings "Don't It Make My Brown Eyes Blue" in a relatively normal voice, he'd probably do it. But he doesn't need to make cupid lips because his delivery is absolutely riveting, even *engaging* in a broken-arm-healed-wrong sort of way.

As for the songs, they're uniformly excellent, and weighted toward great. The most straightforward (as in straitjacket) cut on the album is "Crushed Ice," a heartwarming story of kisses and appliances with an incredible solo from Anderson that sounds like a reversed movie of the attack on Pearl Harbor. Another stupifier, beat of the dead rising pissed-off from their graves, builds on to the key line "**LOOK OUT FOR THE ROADBLOCK OF SOUND**!" A real summer-upper, that. There's short, crazy stuff like the hilarious "Fascination" or the kidnapping tale "Kid Stuff," as well as longer (say 3:59) numbers like "You're Not Alone," which works out from a worm's stepladder riff into a beautiful middle part that's as airy as falling in slow-motion down a Battersea smokestack.

The lyrics are superb, edging in genius too — sometimes funny, sometimes scary, but always slashing at the evidence of essence while still remembering puns. (I bet Stim tells a great knock-knock joke.) Try "Fascination" on for size: "It's not love/it's a fascination/it's not love/over and over.../She comes to him/and then they whisper/and then he kiss her/But it's not love/What's a fascination?"

I'd quote some more, but I don't want to cut into the profits on the *MX-80 Sound Songbook* when it comes out.

Is there *anything* these guys can't do? I doubt it, and I could rave on all day only I must clean up here and go buy some more Children's Sucrets. Let's just say that *Hard Attack* is the only record in the entire history of the world that you can play in place of your TV audio and it

will appear to make sense. Is there any higher compliment?
February 1978

WIRE
Pink Flag
(Harvest)

Wire isn't just another crew of Limey gearhogs dropping empty black paint cans down the trash chute of some hovel skyscraper. Besides reducing punk noise to a drone essence not unlike stripped-down Ramones, they've left incriminating brain marks all over their lyrics, suggesting a deadly I-beam intelligence pure enough to measure red shifts in the reflection off a greasy urinal handle. Late-night TV news captioned for the comprehension-impaired.

Their sound captures not only the electric pencil sharpener amped through T-bird tailpipes guitar churn of most punk outfits, but also the buzz-laden sludge confrontations of the early Stooges (although purposely lacking the unleashed power). B. C. Gilbert's guitar buries the rest of the band, leaving the tap-dance drumming and crossword bass playing lip service to the concept of "band" dynamics. Singer Colin Itess – who was recently voted the rock personality least likely to be asked to join Angel – delivers with a passionate deadpan that sounds like Johnny Rotten and Joey Ramone taking turns dropping rotten fish in a garbage can. Sneer ... plunk.

In a move that should go over big in Japan, *Pink Flag* contains 21 cuts, ranging from a very-concise 26 seconds up to the granddaddy, "Strange," which turtles in at 3:55. If these guys ever put out a three-record set, I quit. This transistorized approach to songwriting does make its point though, and the songs are real good besides. They're about half demonic-fast and half beehive-mung in the cement mixer, except for two tight, melodic cuts that appear back-to-back from nowhere on side two and quickly exit, leaving you wondering. The latter of the pair, "Mannequin," even has stinging back-up vocals, and the overall sound of one of those "pretty" mid-tempo tunes like "Blue Turns to Gray" that the Stones used to try but could never quite pull off. It could be a single, of all things.

Wire spits out some of the best lyrics in a long while too, falling into that echoey missile silo of fleeting anxiety somewhere between G. M. Hopkins and MX-80 Sound. You find instant clichés like "It takes one to catch one" or "You ain't got a number, you just wanna rhumba," as well as brow-bending excursions into prehensile emotion such as "Fragile": "Tears fall in slivers/you broke my shades/the light too bright/let me bury my heart." Who says beatniks are dead?

Pink Flag is so confoundingly simple and direct at times that it appears dense or merely stupid. But Wire has a clear shot at taking all this punk clunk to an entirely different conclusion, one that could easily guide them and their listeners into a blissful state of catatonic puzzlement. At least you don't have to drive.
April 1978

BUDGIE
Impeckable
(A&M)

A budgie is a bird, a parakeet to be exact, and you know what that means. Shit everywhere. Not just in the cage, although there's always plenty stored up there to be safe in case their supply is suddenly cut off by floods or nuclear war. Parakeets have this moral obligation to spread their cute little budgie bombs over as much of the immediate area as possible, thus designating it as their "turf." If every parakeet on Earth zoomed out the window at the same time and began practicing this peculiar method of land acquisition, the entire world would be their turf in less than 10 minutes.

These little blue and green Zionists have two basic methods of making their sticky point of view. First is the old parakeet-in-search-of-hidden-treasure approach. They hop up brightly to their latest pile, painstakingly pick up a sample in their scaly little beaks, examine it at close range and then toss it angrily over their shoulder. You can almost hear them say "I *know* I dropped my car keys in here *somewhere*, but all I can find is this stupid shit!"

This technique starts to aggravate the poor tweeters before too long, and when their locomotive metabolism gets channeled into Bird Anger, look out. That means it's time for their other scheme – the famous parakeet-as-hovering-traffic-helicopter bit. "And now it's over to Officer Budgie. Bud?" "Thanks, Ray. I'm over the Dan Ryan right now and let me tell you, this is the darndest thing I've ever seen, traffic fans. Not only are there no backups or overturned thumbtack trucks to speak of, but everything in sight is covered in shit!" Meanwhile, you can imagine what all this in-cage hovering has done to the local bird-turd situation. Scattered the troops, you might say.

Parakeet, Budgie, beak-face—no matter what you call 'em, there's no interrupting their lifelong romance with their own droppings. They would make excellent politicians or rock critics. The only thing you can be sure of if you let one of these little fece-matics into your home is that sooner or later, when you least expect it, he'll pick up a piece of wet, gummy shit and throw it right in your face.

Smile! You're on Candid Parakeet!
April 1978

GENESIS
...And Then There Were Three...
(Atlantic)

The members of Genesis are three of the sweetest guys you'd ever want to meet. They would never hide behind a rock and show old ladies the bottoms of their feet. None of them ever stand still long for fear some passing housewife will pour gravy over them. And if you put a picture of Genesis next to a carton of Velveeta, people would keep coming up to you and asking "Which came first?"

Such nice folks usually make music that belongs in the dairy morgue, but Genesis is different. While much of their material has an atmosphere enhanced enough to conduct telepathic communications between far-flung members of the Radar Victims Network, they always come down to Earth with their distinctive, keyboard-heavy Atco-beat. Damn! Too many toymakers in the dishwasher again! This intermittent thud, coupled with the band's determination to create all their own noises instead of relying on hoards of string-winkers and anxious glockenspiel attendants, keeps their music from diluting itself into decorator puddles of Bible School Kool-Aid.

The candy heart of Genesis' appeal lies in their charmingly ludicrous juxtaposition of silly songs about cigar-chomping silverware and all-fish bowling teams with chilling, essence-seeking arrangements. Take "Ballad Of Big," a trivially amusing tale of feedbags and Indians. Even a story line cornier than clowns on gumballs sounds spooky when cloaked in a tense production of ulterior harmonies and keyboard attrition. On top of that is Phil Collins' misty/creepy voice, which sounds like it's sneaking through a colander packed in medical snow. He can deliver the words "mother's milk" in a way that makes you think he's singing about iced snot.

Give this guy a split-fingered fastball and he'll probably take over the world.

Collins' ever-steady nerve-saw and a sprinkling of attractive, small-curd ballads make ...*And Then There Were Three* ... another winner in a long line of remarkably disbelief-suspending Genesis albums. Just once, though, I wish they'd get caught doing something really disgusting. Listen, Phil – I hear that if you bait your mousetrap with a used tampon ... ah, forget it. With my luck, he'd probably catch *me*!
April 1978

SEALS & CROFTS
Takin' It Easy
(Warner Bros.)

Really tasty wimpy music is harder to come by these days than a good $10 stick of gum. Facial twats like Shaun Cassidy and Leif Garrett lack the penny-loafer sentiments needed to deliver thoroughly asinine material convincingly, and the true wimps of our time like David Crosby or America soil their otherwise gorgeously spineless work with "meaningful" lyrics and wooden production.

But Dash and Lash are undeniably true-pink, dyed-in-the-pigeon wimpoids. Give 'em a box of newborn kittens and a sledgehammer and they'd probably build the useless meows a tiny railroad. One of the reasons they have jasmine minds might be their devotion to the Baha'i faith, a religion that rates just above coma on the gentleness scale. In the finest George Harrison tradition, our little hummingbirds have decided to shove this hokum down our throats with the charming "Tribute To Abdu L-Baha," a moldy prayer to some bigshot hoodoo squeeze. Now, when these characters get together to pray, it sounds like a bunch of little kids imitating race cars: "EEEEEE-EEEEEE (rummm rummm) EEEEEE!"

It's unlikely that this cut will be chosen for their next single.

Why bother with bug-buzz like that when they've got four or five solid smasheroo radio transparencies here that cannot under any circumstances be unhummed if heard more than once. Dash and Crash, along with some help from a Batteau or two, write some of the most intensely catchy melodies since the lightweight division was inaugurated, and they deliver them with those unmistakable harmonies that sound like two land crabs in peach leisure suits and Panama hats doing the Tiger Rag down a stairway made of fluorescent piano keys. Busby Berkeley for arachnids.

Hum kings include Batteau's "You're The Love," a near-perfect definition of wimp phrasing and desires, the uptempo tribute to cherry popping entitled "Breaking In A Brand New Love," and the enticingly flimsy "Nobody Gets Over Lovin' You," featuring great guest-teen vocals from Tanya Tucker, Shirlie Matthews, Venetta Field and Jimmy Gilstrap. (A gilstrap is a device worn to protect your gil during contact sports.)

Plus, there's a big inside-cover photo that says more about Dash and the Masher than any million words: the guys get settled down for a leisurely afternoon of making up album titles at the ol' fishin' hole when suddenly, all the local vegetation drops dead.

From one true believer to another, b'hoo-b'hoo.
May 1978

DMZ

DMZ

(Sire)

Listening to DMZ's debut is like living next door to the railroad tracks. You're likely to be assaulted at any given moment by loud, unpredictable noises that make the entire house picture itself as rubble. You want to turn your inner TV up full blast to something soothing like *The Price is Right* so you don't worry so much about some skyscraper tank car doing a belly flop into your poppy patch and snuffing you in your sleep with deadly fungo fumes. But when people ask howcum you don't move if all this rumble & toot is too much for your precious little nerve endings, you stop and "think" for a minute and then reply: "I dunno; I guess I kinda *like* it."

These barf pedestals from Boston deliver nothing but fast, loud thudpies that could easily pass for a '65 Stoogemobile (if they made 'em back then): sharp slabs of Johnny Sokko chopping up a flock of Karate instructors. A rhythm section methodically engages in series after series of Pinto rear-end collision tests. And instead of a singer, they've got a mad dog in a straitjacket barking headlines in pidgin German.

DMZ don't just kick ass, they stomp it tin-can flat.

Several heroic cuts emerge here, but the winner has to be "Baby Boom," a great speeder about the generation any sensible parent now regrets having had anything to do with. Top contenders include a pair of two-chord Iggy's piggies, a stunningly bungled rip-off of "Pipeline," and a remake of the Troggs' "From Home" that for once sounds nothing like the original except for the undercurrent of matinee savages dressed up like *Lord of the Flies* cast kids squatting in smoky caves beating on walrus skins.

DMZ have a higher grunge content and a lot more tuffs than most of the new crop of beat cat high-stickers, and as such come recommended for total ear-blot and nostalgic hemorrhaging.

Good BBQ music for cooking the landlord.

June 1978

BAD BOY
Back to Back
(UA)

Bad Boy wants to be Cheap Trick when they grow up. They've got the same diet heaviness that the Tricksters borrowed from the Move, a couple of budding songwriters who like to bite the hook, and plenty of the required guitar buzzwork. Now all they need is for one of the guys to wear a hockey facemask backward or something equally cute and they're all set.

While *Back to Back* won't go down as one of the great debut albums like *Mandrill I* or *Meet Elephant Candy*, there's still plenty of potential to be found here. When they go with the patented big guitars/little voices sound as in "It's All Right" or "Accidental" (which includes the 137th registered appearance of the chords from "Do Ya"), they're as convincing as a tank rolling over half a barbershop quartet. But then they're stricken with the Raspberries Syndrome, a perverse desire to include deadly plain, Berry-form rockers that are almost as exciting as finally discovering that long-misplaced pencil sharpener. Add to that a dirged-down version of "For Your Love" invitingly entitled "Take My Soul" that would have been a smash at Keith Relf's funeral, and you've got a first album that sounds remarkably like a first album. Shooting ants with a shotgun.

But don't count these pie-sucks out just yet. When they start pasting the catchy choruses onto the right songs, they're gonna sound sweeter than a thighful of honey. And you know how easy it is to get your ear stuck on *that!*

June 1978

DERRINGER
If I Weren't So Romantic, I'd Shoot You
(Blue Sky)

If you don't expect a little Fey-faced squeem like Rick Derringer to be much of a rocker, you're absolutely right. As somebody wrote about Paul Kantner way back when, he's a hell of a rhythm guitar player. And that's it. (Not to dump on rhythm guitarists—who are more important to a band than a whole Marineland full of hot-finned lead players.) It's just that Rick doesn't have the presence to give this group anything more than a pretty face.

Derringer's musicians play together well enough, but they have a real problem digging up suitable material. Rick's songs are weak, studiously hard rockers that could have been learned from training films. His collaborators are no better. The title cut, written with Alice Cooper and Bernie Taupin (Arte Johnson and Howie Greenfield being unavailable) sounds like a slow, wandering introduction to a much better song, and "Sleepless," the much-speculated-about team-up with Patti Smith, is nothing more than some mediocre Smith lyrics stuck on the *Peter Gunn* theme. Why stop there, guys? Write one with the *Hazel* theme, or better yet, *Partridge Family*: "Hello world/meat cringe past blood/poets dead in night-ripped alleys/c'mon get happy!"

There is some good stuff on *Romantic*, but it's eat-around-the-bad-spots time, as usual. "It Ain't Funny," the token Chinn/Chapman tune that producer Mike Chapman insists on leading all his knob jobs out with, is a solid C/C rocker with the expected buzzing guitars, straight-ahead multi-vocals and some crisp drumming from good old Myron Grombacher. Some of the other outside comps also shine, particularly Warren Zevon's snappy "Lawyers, Guns & Money." I'd been awful suspicious of This Year's Pen, but with an opener like "I went home with a waitress the way I always do," Warren must be an OK guy. Watch for his upcoming feature film, *Zevon Brides For Zevon Brothers*.

The real winner though—and the direction Derringer ought to head in—is bassist Kenny Aaronson's "Attitude," one of those ton-of-bass crunchers where they spell out the title in the chorus. Only this time, they spell it *wrong*. With a great attitude like that, these guys could dump the paddle-wheels and proceed directly to Bambam.

Solution to the Derringer problem: boot little Nellie-nuts out and change the band's name and sound to "Aaronson." Listen, it's better than Grombacher. *June 1978*

MOODY BLUES
Octave
(London)

Listening to Moody Blues albums is like going to school, only harder. At least in your average classroom predicament, there's an actual answer to the question you slept through, i.e., *Mandingo* really does have an author, whether you know who it is or not.

But these MB questions are tuffies. "Nebulous," I think you might call them, although other, less kind students have described them as "pointless," "meaningless," "circular," and "who gives a shit anyway?" (*Bad* attitude.) I think the least we could do is try to answer a couple. After all, maybe Pinder and friends are asking because *they don't know!*

There's a really E-Z one in "Survival," if you can hear it over the bus-loads of background vocals. This is one band that's never been chintzy on the back-ups. In fact, here come some more now on the train. Hanging out the windows, waving their hairpieces and — Wait a minute! — they're even floating down from the sky in parachutes, hundreds of 'em all groaning out that distinctive Moodies vocal gruel. Before those other guys on the ponies get here, let's ask that question: Q: "If I gave you every dream, would they grow?" A: Nope, not unless they're *dreamlings*. Told you it was E-Z.

While I try and find some towels for these background vocalists that just drifted in on rubber rafts, the rest of you guys can study "One Step Into

The Light." You can tell it's important because some of the lyrics are in Bold Face. **LIFE FORCE, LIVING BREATH, FREE** and of course, **TRUTH.** Now, I realize that commenting on Moodies' lyrics is like trying to judge a Most Pathetic contest with George Harrison as the only entrant, but *still.* The only LIVING BREATH I ever saw was on a TV commercial where these guys with daisies for guns came out of a spray can and turned it into some grotesque mint flavor. "Now all the gals want to bowl with Frank!"

The other question we want to cover before Drug Hall begins is in "Top Rank Suite," if you can locate it in the backwash of shotgun production perks. Talk about overblown, these gasbags should change their name to the Moody Balloons. You can see 'em get one little prick (like Pinder's) and explode into millions of tiny pieces of Moody Mung, flying off into deeper and deeper space, passing the entire history of radio, television and radar along the way. Anyhoo, the question: Q: "Two lonely people/Can mend a broken heart/Love, and you'll never fall apart/But can you tell me why?"

A: Why? Because we *like* you!

Hold on a second, this is a Reunion Album? People will want to know *that*? These guys haven't put out a record together in how long? Well, shit, how was I supposed to know? I haven't listened to a Moody Blues album since they did away with the Draft! I didn't think you *had* to anymore.
July 1978

RADIO BIRDMAN
Radios Appear
(Sire)

Radio Birdman's first album is the No. 1 motivational LP of Summer '78. It can psyche you up to any performance you want, whether it's mere world domination or *important* shit like racking up competition-devastating scores at pinball. It's almost *all* fast, the songs are great, the playing's stupendous and you can hardly hear the words.

Now if they'd just invent the electric brain, we'd be all set.

First consideration with these MODO discs (as in: "I am now MODO-vated to stomp on your reproductive organs, sir.") is fast except for "Man With Golden Helmet," which can be easily skipped over by hurling something cement at the turntable when it comes on.

The number-two thing to check is whether the songs themselves are any more than fleeting stops on the speeding monorail of obsolescence. One listen to "Aloha Steve & Danno" – a kind of MC5-goes-Hawaiian showblower that incorporates the theme from *Hawaii Five-O* into its murderous surf-thunder – should take care of any lingering doubts that a band with such a stupid name has anything less than Tru-Vu into pulp life. If "against one cool guy/the guilty will not go free" isn't one of the greatest lines vinylized this year, then it *has* to be "BOOK HIM DANNO—MURDER ONE!," regardless of one's feelings toward the snivel appliance that remains Jack Lord. This cut is the most logical connection between rock music and TV in

110

the entire history of media squirm. (Sorta makes you want to shake hands with your tube.)

The great playing doesn't jump out and tug your nosebone like the great songs, but it's still there. Lead guitarist boss bird Deniz Tek always makes sure that his sidekick Chris is pumping out a juiced-up rhythm before he takes off on one of his Ted-Nugent-Meets-Dick-Dale runs—which are 100-per-cent short and to the point. The other hero is bassist Warwick Gilbert (a warwick is something you light if you want to start a war), whose mother obviously listened to "Pipeline" too many times while pregnant with him.

So here's the final score. *Radios* contains about half new classics and half merely great cuts, not counting the sole odor. It'll modo your mojo 'til all you can do is go-go, and most importantly, it makes everything in my crummy dump rattle like Doomsday, even the rug.

The ants love it and you will too.

July 1978

CHERYL LADD
Cheryl Ladd
(Capitol)

While the whole world isn't exactly hanging off the side of a mountain with teeth flashing, waiting to hate this album, some people are. Other than malcontents and owners of sour grapes, some legitimate concern has been expressed by "music lovers" (both of them) who suspect that Cheryl Ladd's singing debut trades more on skin than timbre.

Not me. I still have *both* Patty Duke LPs, as well as Peggy Lipton's big move from *Mod Squad* to cod squawk. Her well-tread-on version of "These Boots Are Made For Walking" is sure to make your spine feel like vertebrae. My singles rack contains not only Farrah's biggie, where she repeatedly whispers "hump me" in fractured French, but also the ultra-rare 45 that Suzanne Somers recorded years ago to pay off the massive hospital bills accumulated by her infant son after he had the misfortune to crawl into a crack that had suddenly opened in Earth's surface. All they did was mike-up her Fleshy Extensions while she stomped two carats of army ants to death on a rubber floor. Not much in the lyrical dept., but what a beat!

The only problem with Cheryl Ladd's first album is that she really can *sing*, and this isn't a bad record at all. Cheryl has a surprisingly strong, musky voice in the Dusty Springfield/Jackie DeShannon mode, and a sharp sense of phrasing to boot. A truly engaging singer, she'll make you forget what's on the cover, which isn't all that hard considering that she's packaged about as attractively as Dead Jack's Bacon. You want to turn her over to see if the backside is green.

Top marks go to producer Gary Klein for avoiding the temptation to use Ladd as a knob-turner's plaything *a la* Lisa Burns. He just gave her the ball and told her to throw it past 'em, which she does more consistently than anybody in Chicago, to be sure. They could have gotten together on some better material, however. The lack of disco groan is commendable, but the overabundance of MOR tune drippings slows everything down. While she can sail away on upbeat familiars like "Think It Over" and "The Rose Nobody Knows," she overfocuses on some of the slowpokes, her voice thickening as though she'd just eaten a macaroni dinner without first cooking it.

With her first album now out of the way, Cheryl should be able to apply the smoke in that voice to some more of the hot-to-trot material that best suits her. Forget the star-turned-singer considerations—I think Cheryl Ladd is a budding Jackie DeShannon. And lookit those buds!

August 1978

MOON MARTIN
Shots From A Cold Nightmare
(Capitol)

Moon Martin already has several invisible claims to fame. He was a heavy in Southwind, an excellent band that failed to overwhelm record buyers while accidentally paving the way for Little Feat. He wrote "Cadillac Walk" for Mink Deville and "Victim Of Romance" for Michelle Phillips, of all people. And for *real* stats, he grew up not 15 miles from the town where they filmed *The Last Picture Show*. (Moon had a bit part as a small area of scrubland.)

So maybe he never got to screw Cybill Shepherd, but the Moon's a pretty big deal anyway. His songs are built on a menacing Texas drone-shuffle that sounds like all musicians had to cross the desert in astronaut shoes to get to the recording session. The arrangements are precisely basic, just the Moon Beat, some horizontal guitar, and Martin's resigned-but-needling vocals – which seem to drift at an odd angle out of some heat-induced bird spell. The sound of real, can't-run-fast-enough nightmares, not cartoon exploding stuff.

The Moon's always got an eye on the classics, and several of his own tunes are headed in that direction. "Hot Nite In Dallas" is the best, a heat wave mumble that sounds like night sweats put to music. Other Moon Beat winners include the equally sticky "Bad Case Of Lovin' You," "Paid Killer" – an anonymous droner in the manner of the Stones' old "Play With Fire" – and "She's A Pretender," which is good enough to off-handedly toss in lines like "My baby's got long black hair/she lies about how much she cares."

Martin also throws in a couple of fine pop poopers, particularly dearest Michelle's "Victim," which borrows heavily from "Be My Baby" (or maybe it's "Chapel Of Love"). Either way, when you get to the chorus and hear The Moon chomp down on VIC-DUMB, you'll know you're there.

Moon Martin's songs dig at what hot, slimy, dead-expectations summer nights are all about. Sit yourself down with *Cold Shots* and a cool bottle of Cactus Puke, take off all of your skin and just let the wind blow through your bones.

August 1978

GERTZ MOUNTAIN BUDGUZZLERS
Go Surfin'
(Budguzzlers)

Strange but weird effort by seedy New Jersey mopes who describe their sound as "fungus rock." Recorded using the very latest survival-of-the-fittest studio techniques, *Surfin'* ranges from down-home psychedelic porn to uptown drunken sod corn. Top cuts include "Vacant Lot," a half-eaten tale of guzzling too many a Bud and passing out on the front lawn, only to wake up and find your house torn down. (So what else is new?)

There's also "Uncle Steve's Song," which consists of mainly the line, "I want to quit my job/and move to the country" moaned over fruity bongo emanations that sound like Jimmy Buffet right after puking shrimp all over Stephen Bishop. Wanna be budguzzlers instead of dumb puds? Just find yourself a mung tree and guzzle Buds!
August 1978

BOSTON
Don't Look Back
(Epic)

Let's get this out in the open right away: BOSTON SUCKS. The corrupted simplicity that's the base of the Tom Scholz Big Sound is totally hollow. Their music is so exterior, you shouldn't really listen to it. You should paint your water tower with it. The success of every song depends wholly upon the arrangement that carries it, and the insubstantiality of this pastel heavy metal has an awful funny sound to it, like a big noise in an empty room.

So why are these Cake Commandoes so big? Good question. If Boston can sell a million, think what you could do with a recording of some chipmunks dodging laser beams! Because that's all this band is: a lot of whine and fluff. The one solid cut, "Don't Look Back," makes it only because of a departure into Cheap Trick territory via Jeff Lynne/Move drive. Even though it's based on a desperation chord progression coated with layers of gratuitous production gratoot, there's enough *real song* here to pull it off.

Unfortunately, that still leaves us with lots of album to deal with. Stuff like "Feelin' Satisfied," yet another of those obligatory tributes to how rock 'n' roll will make your shit smell good and fill you with "That Funky Feelin'." You know, like when you hop into your sneaks in the morning only to find that your dog spent the whole night sucking on them. Probably rock 'n' roll *will* Clean Your Soul, too although for those *special situations*, I prefer safe, reliable Soul-O-Dent (now available in grape).

There's no sense looking under the tutu at the rest of these tinkertones. Boston are like a zillion other bands – they can play faster than their kid brothers, but they wouldn't know a good song if it came up and bit Brad

Delp's ambulance. The title cut is the only hit, and the rest will sound real neat on a good stereo, which seems to be the main point of most records these days anyway. And as a bonus, this record is excellent for bringing on that troublesome first heat in young kitty cats.

Boston is Meow Mix for the ears.

September 1978

ELTON JOHN
A Single Man
(MCA)

ELTON JOHN GROWS UP: And it's about time. The guy's already had more second childhoods than an amoeba. The various re-incarnations of "Croc Rock" have been enjoyable, but it's nice to hear Elton take his material a bit less broadly for a change. When the characters on TV's *One Day At A Time* start doing imitations of you, you *know* it's time for a change.

ON SLOWING UP AND THROWING UP: Elton is one of the few pop songwriters around who can turn out a strong ballad and there are four slowpokes on *Single Man*. One of them ("Shine On Through") is a killer of "Your Song" caliber and only one of the others ("Georgia") is a stinker. Plus there are no half-assed Bernie Taupin lyrics to mess things up.

DIRTY, DIRTY: There's still a respectable contingent of trivial tunes as well, particularly "Big Dipper." Ho ho ho, I know what this song is about. I'm no dummy. Those lines about sailors and licking aren't exactly subtle, and the "dicksyland" arrangement gives it away. Can't put one over on this old-timer. Listen, it's really a cute idea, but no more songs about drugs, OK Elton?

TRUE INCIDENT: When the aforementioned song came on, two flies that had been eagerly fighting over a sticky drop of I'm-afraid-to-guess on my little table here stopped trying to de-wing each other and started *fooling around*. What this indicates about the sexual preferences of flies I'm not certain, but they sure are easier to smash that way.

YOU'LL HAVE TO SING LOUDER ON THIS ONE, BOSS: A big surprise here is "Song For Guy," a mildly upbeat instrumental that's very likeable if a bit too kissy-kissy. Tulips, angels, etc. – you get the picture. Is this EJ's first instrumental? I could give a shit, and our Research Dept. is out to Autumn.

A SEVERE CASE OF THE HITS: Among the lighter tunes, "Part Time Love" is an extra catchy sing-along job that has Number-1 encoded in its grooves. "Return To Paradise" is more of a Number 6, slowed down as it is by a Latino-type arrangement suggestive of lonely bulls malingering outside the hovel.

"MADNESS!": is the title of *Single Man*'s one major odor. A pseudo-rocking protest gobble about bombs and bang-bang, the only madness evident was the decision to include this track on the album.

WHAT E.J. FANS EVERYWHERE WANT TO KNOW: Should I put down my hard-earned purse-snatching money for this record? If you like Elton's earlier, more understated material, you'll like this. If not, then blow it out your barracks bag.

November 1978

114

BERNIE TAUPIN
He Who Rides The Tiger
(Asylum)

A lot of heavy thinking goes into picking the best album of the year, but how about the *worst*? It's easy to go down the line, throw your favorite LPs in a pile and then forcibly align them in reference to some imaginary standard. But how do you measure the STINKERS?

Important factors you'll want to weigh into your final decision include: 1) Number of forced exits from room per side, 2) Duration and intensity of said exit urge (i.e., brief feeling of strangulation, uncontrollable sweating of ears and genitals, careful listing of emergency numbers of suicide prevention centers on wall near phone), 3) Ratio of gag-time to total perceived personal degradation (ask yourself, "Was it the day that I played the other side of *Sue Saad and the Next* that everything started to go downhill?"), 4) Total combined weight of objects thrown at turntable, and 5) Number of times record is used as murder weapon.

The cumulative effect you want to look out for is the feeling that any particular record *ruined your life*. I know for a fact what screwed *my* life up. It was the night about four or five years ago that I got drunk-beyond-drunk and voluntarily – if unwittingly – played the Paul Anka album containing "Having My Baby" *twice in succession*. It was one of the first promo records I'd ever seen, and I was impressed as hell by the NOT FOR SALE sticker and the prominent cut-out hole punched through Paul's left ear.

The next day, I noticed that my neighbors were pointing me out to friends of theirs and laughing wildly. Complete strangers, even *incomplete* strangers, would walk along a few steps behind me on the street humming "I'm a woman in love and I love what it's doin' to me" until I ran off in terror. Then a mysterious and probably impotent vandal painted the words NELLIE NUTS above my door in lamb's blood. This is the *real* story of why I changed my name.

At any rate, it took me years to live down that goddam Anka album. Even now, I occasionally receive odd mailings from Right To Life groups, but at least they don't send *promos*. Think what a *big puncher they'd need!*

So, just when it seemed like I had almost everyone convinced that I'd *really* liked Kenny and the Kasuals all along, a local puke uncovered the grisly fact that I had recently special-ordered an Anne Murray single. Not just requested, not just ordered, but *special-ordered*, like a pair of chain-link underpants. Then it all spilled out … "The Yellow Rose Of Texas" … Annette's bumps … *The Gail Storm Show* … "Johnny Angel" … Haley Mills … "MacArthur Park" … Peggy Lipton … *Family Affair … Live Dead* … Freddie Tieken's autograph … Joni Mitchell … The Knack … even Debbie Boone's version of "Girl Don't Come."

…And now, Bernie Taupin has become a tradition in my home, like dead crickets or hair on everything. *But it's not too late for you!*
May 1980

AEROSMITH
Live Bootleg
(Columbia)

Everybody's live album is described as "long-awaited" these days, but Aerosmith's really was. With a string of solid studio Lps and a well-deserved rep for providing the kind of concerts where cherry bombs *throw people* at the stage, the Steve and Joe Show was long overdue in living color.

The big surprise here is that *Live Boot* is great, easily the top live album of '78. And that's taking into consideration some pretty tough competition, too, like Thin Lizzy and BOC. What sets Aerosmith apart from the others — besides the inspired performance throughout — is that this *really sounds* like a live recording. No needle-point perfection, little or no studio sweetening and none of the my-solo's-bigger-than-yours farting around common to live blowouts. Every song here needs a haircut and some clean shorts.

Aerosmith is a guitar band all the way, and the scrappy interplay between Perry and what's-his-name (no damned names on the cover again) is comparable to a charged-up Richards and Wood, if such a thing were possible. They chucka when chucka is called for, and some of Joe's hatefully-timed corona flares have blinded unsuspecting A-bomb pilots overhead. Stephen Tyler is in excellent form throughout, one of the few screaming weenies left who can still cream his sneaks on a dime.

Superior blasts include "Last Child," where the guitarists take turns pulling Tyler's wings off, a take of "Back In The Saddle" that's so ragged it deserves its own Skid Row, and a high-speed demolition course through "Mama Kin/SOS." Even tunes like "Dream On" and "Sick As A Dog" that are difficult to put across in concert come out smelling sweeter than a lizard hole in winter.

Archive nuts should love the 1973 recordings of "I Ain't Got You" and the indescribable "Mother Popcorn," where Tyler bares his soul, howling "POPCORN POPCORN CHEESECAKE CHEESECAKE YEAH YEAH YEAH!" until the audience molds over. There's even a live version of "Come Together" thrown in so that you hardcore insect collectors won't have to shell out for *Sgt. Stigwood*. What more could anyone ask for?

Some *names* on the cover, that's what. Not everyone has 'em tattoed on their no-no, ya know.
November 1978

LOU REED
Take No Prisoners
(Arista)

Lou Reed is the Fonz of rock comedy. Just because you never know what species will appear when Lou snaps his fingers doesn't mean he isn't funny. It just means his Happy Days are on another channel. If it wasn't Boston's hilarious remake of their first album, this would be the comedy record of the year.

Take No Prisoners is one of those rare live LPs where the music is just an annoying diversion from the between-the-songs patter. There's not that much music though, so don't let it scare you away. While there are a handful of legitimate songs – the intense "Pale Blue Eyes," the intenser "Berlin," and the drained-of-intensity "Satellite of Love" that Lou delivers like the Supervisor of Goat Torture telling a young ewe in goat-talk that it really doesn't hurt – none of the actual "tunes" seriously interfere with the fun.

The best monologue comes during "Walk On The Wild Side," where Lou tells the sublime story of how he came to write the song. It seems some hot young producer wanted to make a film of the book of the same name and he wanted Lou to do the songs. He gives Lou a copy of the book and says "make an 'X' where the songs should go." Somehow this rap meanders into a yuk-packed put down of everybody from the Warhol crowd to Robert Christgau and music reviewers in general. Makes me glad I'm just a comedy critic.

The audience is full of comedians too, and Lou frequently plays Dean to their collective Jerry. When he introduces "Waitin' For The Man," he mentions that the guy always shows up late. "So do you, Lou!" cracks one of the many wits gathered there. Some of the other crowd-busters include "Hey, Lou!," "Hey, Louie!," and of course, the many-leveled "LOOOOOOOOO REEEEEEEEEED!"

All laffs aside, this is *not* the record to send Mom this Xmas in place of an explanation. Tell her some other way.
December 1978

NEVILLE BROTHERS
Neville Brothers
(Capitol)

You don't get many of these anymore. A soulful, low-key album distinguished by memorable tunes, restrained playing, vocals smoother than clouds and best of all, NO DISCO! You can play it in the morning without making your head feel like a sponge in a seashell, or better yet, you can play it late at night, when everything's *all right!*

Between the four of them, the Neville Brothers have been around since forever. Individually, they've played with everybody from Ray Charles to The Wild Tchoupitoulas, but they're perhaps best known as the founders of New Orleans' famed Meters. Or, if you've got any class at all (the readers share a hearty chuckle) you'll remember Aaron Neville's indelible 1966 hit, "Tell It Like It Is."

Graced by Jack Nitsche's expertly understated production, the brothers' first LP together is solidly tuneful without the sap, something like Allen Toussaint with more of a pop edge. Some of the cuts – like Leiber-Stoller's great "Dancin' Jones" or the unstoppable "I'll Take My Chances" – actually could be played in a disco without melting anybody's hairdo. But the Nevilles' songs are so *real* that it's hard to act polyester to them. That goes double for ballad picks like "All Night, All Right" or brother Charles' instant imprint, "Vieux Carre Rouge," the addictive melody of which is currently under investigation by the DEA.

The Neville Brothers' "debut" is one of those rare records you can

describe as *mellow* without deserving funny looks. Give it a spin before play-time some night and you too will know the meaning of VOOLAY-VOO.
December 1978

JIM MORRISON & DOORS
An American Prayer
(Elektra)

This entire project gives off a quantum rat odor that reeks from here to Jim's two-tub tombstone. It's nearly always bad news when previously (read: *wisely*) unreleased material hits the racks – particularly when it's been tam-pered with and the best you can hope for is some unrepresentative "represen-tative" music and the taste of fingerprints.

Jim Morrison wasn't exactly a great poet, but he was better than Patti Smith. He had the usual let's-solve-America hangups of his time and a truly annoying fascination with his legendary weiner, but some of his less pretentious imagery isn't half bad. Morrison was a *promising* poet, and these are his sketchbooks.

If Jimbo ever hears what they done to his song, you better watch out for mysterious incidents of beer-scented ground lightning in the immediate vicin-ity of former members of the Doors. The band was never known for their stunning musical invention, and *American Prayer* won't harm that legend any. Some of Robby Kreiger's penlight guitar beams and Ray Manzarek's depressed-insect keyboard trails were once big on the Evocation Circuit, but all they evoke now is the remarkable stupidity of those old bargain instru-mental LPs like *Doors' Music* with the tiny subtitle, "as interpreted by Doug's Bluesbreakers."

The title cut, with its shocking pronouncement "Wow, I'm sick of doubt!," is the mope opus of the LP. While the band blunders from tune-up jams to wooden disco to hunks of "The End," Jim raves in monotone about mutants, pillows and television. TV is a big subject with The Bulge That Talked, no doubt because he was jealous that the tube was subversive and he wasn't. Other bits of verse you'll want to embroider on burlap and hang in your dump include "Curses and Invocations" ("I'll always be a word man/bet-ter than a bird man") (*but not a soul man!*) and the charming "Lament For My Cock," where he describes his little pal as "a tongue of knowledge." Yeah, but can it play "Wipe Out?"

Let's leave the metaphysics of a new "live" recording of a long-dead per-son being drowned out by crowd noise ("Roadhouse Blues") to the experts and take a peek at some of the other dead folks who are putting out new records for Christmas. Don't miss Totie Fields wailing down-to-Earth ver-sions of "Skinny Legs and All" and "Walk This Way," Keith Moon reciting a few of his favorite prescription labels, Gig Young's touching readings from *I Love My Wife* or best of all, the upcoming recording of Sid Vicious' late girl-friend's heart-felt rendition of "His Way." They're all killers.
December 1978

STEVE MARTIN
A Wild And Crazy Guy
(Warner Brothers)

HENNY YOUNGMAN
Take My Album, Please!
(Warehouse)

It's getting harder all the time to tell the comedy records from the serious ones these days, what with Devo and Kansas and jazz (of all things) straining the petty nodes of brain fanciers. One can listen to most anything now and say "I liked it, but you have to laugh."

Both of *these* albums are funny on purpose, though. You can tell because people laugh right on the record! That, and the cuts all have titles like "Drunks and Trains," "A Charitable Kind Of Guy" or "Shopping With Bricks." Could be a smarter-than-me Talking Heads set I suppose, but there you go with that fine-line, Is It Art? business, like the ironic piddlings of a stunned crossing guard freshly hit by a school bus.

Steve Martin is everybody's favorite right now, a distinct disadvantage when you try to put it on record. Almost all of the material on AWACG has been performed on TV in the last five minutes, and Steve's jokes aren't exactly forgettable. Other than the relatively unimportant lack of visual effects, the only difference between tube and disc is that you get to hear him say "shit" and "fuck."

Fuck that shit. (I'll say 'em for free.)

A lot of Henny Youngman's stuff is familiar, too, but with his compulsive, near-vomit delivery of one-liners, there's bound to be a few new ones. Like did you hear the one about the Polish terrorist who went to blow up a car and burned his lips on the tailpipe? Or did you know why the new Italian navy has glass-bottom boats? To see the *old* Italian navy. Not bad for a guy who looks like a sleeping bag for a Volvo.

None of these yuks, except maybe for Martin's "excuuuuuuse me!," is likely to go down in the history of great comedy lines like "I hate them meeces to pieces," "fan mail from some flounder?" or "AR—AR! Earth Humor!" Still, there's a lot of good material here. YOU WILL LAUGH at either record. Once.
December 1978

JAPAN
Obscure Alternatives
(Ariola America)

Japan might look like a bunch of leftovers from the "Let's get some mascara and be the next Dolls" period, but their sound is more like post-war music from a war that hasn't happened.

These guys have got rhythm – but not just your everyday vibrations from an overloaded washing machine. Their superb rhythm section takes the hesitation beat to new heights of nervous anticipation, and second guitarist/big Jap David Sylvian scratches out an unnerving insectile rhythm that sounds vaguely like reggae guitar played through a pachinko machine, etc. You could probably dance to it, but you'd need a extra pair of two legs.

The standout cut here is "Sometimes I Feel So Low," a mid-speed rocker that manages to be chunky and angular at the same time, with sinuous guitars and the drummer pounding on a roll of aluminum rugs. The title cut further defines their starko *futillisimo* guitar sound while Sylvian delivers the key lines "we are dying of admiration here/mastering obscure alternatives" in a slightly Ziggyish voice that makes you want to race your roaches up the wall. Most of their lyrics could pass as the instructions to a game that encourages children to play in the dark.

While there are spots of ho-hum evident in "Deviation" and the pond emanations of the instrumental "Tenant," Japan's second album is nasty fun and a possible meeting point between us normal folks and those Eno supporters.

Insert your own Pearl Harbor joke here.

January 1979

ELVIS COSTELLO
Armed Forces
(Columbia)

Elvis Costello isn't perfect after all.

This comes as something of a shock after two LPs so attuned to pop perfection as to make Cheap Trick sound like a Yes-member solo hog-flay, but it's true. EC's inspired leanness of form has turned to outright carelessness, and it's obvious why this overgrown milkweed has two million songs in the can – he only spends five minutes on each one.

The Number-1 consideration with Elvis is his songwriting ability. His intensely catchy tunes have the same scarecrow-with-bent-thyroid quality as his appearance. Even his plainer melodies have a gem of a twist in them, or at least a nugget of truth. But on *Armed Forces*, many of the songs serve merely as dull frameworks for one Neat Idea and a tiny hook that some of us big fishies can't even see to bite. The man needs a new can of nightcrawlers.

There's still a fair amount of good stuff here, however. A whole side's worth in fact – only it's not all on the same side. "Accidents Will Happen" features a chilling melody borne on a hovering organ that wafts like the dust on my vent. "Senior Service" is another ear grabber, with the keyboards this time alternating between "Sukiyaki" and "Kind Of A Drag," and "Two Little Hitlers" is hard to resist despite a slipshod arrangement.

Trivial arranging is a major problem on *AF*, marring several tunes that might otherwise take off. But nothing short of a tune-change operation could save strictly Piedmont League losers like "Green Shirt," "Busy Bodies" or the ballad "Party Girl," which would nauseate even a pony-queer. Apparently, old stem-head's creative hot streak was really just a backlog of good material.

As for the bonus live EP, we all oughtta know by now that it's free because no one would ever pay for it in the first place. Included are Plaintive versions (I'm trying out for *Cosmo*) of "Accidents" and "Alison" and a take of "Watching The Detectives" that will make EC fans the world over respond with a resounding, "Oh."

At his current rate of deterioration, Elvis' next LP might just be a bonus disc included with the next Nick Lowe album. It's like the fat lady said on *Donahue* a couple days ago: You can't hardly even bake a cake anymore without somebody swiping the ingredients.

January 1979

ELVIS COSTELLO
Get Happy!
(Columbia)

Elvis really means it this time. *Get Happy!* is packed with no fewer than 20 new songs, 18 of which are Costello originals. Talk about getting your money's worth – if Fleetwood Mac had this much material sitting around, they'd come out with a five-elephant set, a feature-length movie and their own mini-series on NBC: *All My Stevies*.

This many cuts on one thin LP record raises a few questions, such as: Does it sound like it was recorded in the kitchen of a bomb shelter? Producer Nick Lowe assures us on the back cover that there is "no loss of sound quality due to groove cramming," and he's right for the most part. Coming through my own high-tech system of Norelco speakers, Kool-Aid amp and a somewhat-worn Gerbiltone turntable, it sounds just fine. Those bass-response fanatics among us who aren't satisfied until the whole block shakes and rattles like Timothy Leary's hand might have to crank it up to Warp Four to get enough thud power, but subhumans have such a *small* say in the marketplace.

An album with this many tracks – none of which are 1:09 throwaways – takes a little time to digest, a fact that puts this reviewer at a severe disadvantage. Not only was I forced to listen to the record more than once, I had to play BOTH SIDES. Next, they'll be asking us to write our reviews in spinal fluid.

The new material is remarkably solid, with only one outright smellbag and a couple of marginal efforts. Of course, the intense cohesiveness of the songs tends to make them all sound alike, a problem which either clears up with repeated play or causes listener O.D. early on. While there are a few standout cuts, Elvis fans will enjoy the majority. Hell, they liked all the other ones!

No complaints about the performance either. The Attractions are as crisp and confident as ever, if maybe a bit subdued. Or maybe they're just plain overpowered by Costello's tendency to cram as much vocal urgency into every track as a herd of neutered buffalo on a hot spring afternoon.

Overkill? Well, let's just say that sitting through both sides of *Get Happy!* can be a lot like eating an entire bag of Double Stuf Oreos. The first couple of handfuls are taste sensations, but by the time you get to the last cookie, the cream filling seems like you're licking a screen door.

If all this sounds BORING to you, then join the club. Personally, I think Costello is a rather whiny, one-dimensional performer who's made a legend out of two riffs. But then I like Moon Martin *and* The Dickies. Big deal – if I had taste, I'd be a decorator. Elvis fans will love this record and, while it's an arguably strong performance, it won't win him any new friends –or enemies.

Or, as Pearl of Pearl Harbor and the Explosions says: "I don't care if your aim is true."

My sentiments exactly.

March 1980

ELVIS COSTELLO
Trust
(Columbia)

Special note to readers: The author wishes to *take back* all the bad things (well, *most* of 'em – at least *two*) he's written about Elvis Costello. Having been recently "enlightened" by a certain well-known abuser of codeine, I can now look back and see that my complaints were due to temporary insanity, listening under duress, shit-for-ears or maybe somebody put drugs in my coffee. Or coffee in my drugs. Anything, except *I was wrong.* C'mon, don't rub it in! I already feel sheepish enough to line your winter jacket.

Trust is yet another amazingly solid effort from Elvis C. Where he comes up with all his material, who knows? He certainly is a dedicated recycler of his own words and music. His trademark melodies share the soar-and-sink properties of rock-skipping, recently shot ducks and airplanes crashing during takeoff. The lyrics all *sound* like they mean something, although in most cases they're just another blast from a mental shotgun loaded with irony, misogyny and paranoia. But, of course, the *sound* is the thing.

This album is a lot speedier than recent efforts. It could be Elvis is getting tired of repeating himself or maybe he's just picking up on this season's dance vibes. *Vibes?*

Top rockers: "Luxembourg," "White Knuckles," "Fish 'N' Chip Paper" and "Strict Time."

Top midtempo melodies: "Clubland," "Watch Your Step" and "You'll Never Be A Man." Plus, there's a superb ballad, "Shot With His Own Gun," and some hi-protein soy filler.

But *only 14 songs?* What a rip-off!

February 1981

BROWNSVILLE
Air Special
(Epic)

After 10 long years of so-so success in spreading their deadly pods of decibel doom, Brownsville's throb is not just still intact, it's stronger. Pretty good record compared to – oh, say, the Stones on their10th birthday. Personally speaking, when I was 10, the thing that impressed me most was that if you turned the year 1961 upside down, it *still read 1961.*

Well, either that or sex.

Despite dropping their last name and the mighty Cub Koda's disposal of the trademark owl specks he once swiped from a *Shindig* dancer, the boys still sound pretty much the same, which is just fine. The Cub's heated guitar fights with Beezer and Slutz are as dirty as ever, and when he unleashes his ultra low buzz-saw voice on amped blues like "Cooda Crawlin'," children melt and grown men shout, "Come on *down!*"

All 10 cuts are solid rockers, from a great version of "Who Do You Love," that'll finally make everybody forget Quicksilver (who?) to the three-chord speeding opener, "Taste of Your Love."

Don't bother, Cub – it tastes like thumbs.

There's also a second update, "Down the Road Apiece," that should once and for all answer the question of who's the world's greatest rock 'n' roll band.

I give up. Is it Poco?

February 1979

NATIONAL LAMPOON
Greatest Hits of the National Lampoon
(Vista)

The *National Lampoon* isn't that funny to start with, much less sick. Like *Saturday Night Live*, you spend most of your time wading through ads and filler to get to a handful of jokes, one or two of which are worth the wait. Their hard-core followers are so programmed to laugh at everything, however, that their selectivity vanishes completely. Maybe it is sick after all.

Some of the bits on this album are well done, but most consist of one good idea stretched beyond the limits of bloato hype. Even the best material ("Deteriorata", "The Immigrants") is only funny once. In fact, it wasn't until our resident Economic Council—who generally amuse themselves by research-ing this mag's budget-applied unit-pricing standards to this record – that the real laughter began.

But the real reason I didn't like it was because there weren't any ads for *Animal House* T-shirts.

February 1979

TONIO K.

Life in the Foodchain

(Full Moon/Epic)

Now here's a *real* character. Wears a moldy BERTHA HAS BALLS T-shirt, sings like he's got the New Jersey Panhandle in his mouth, never got past the *Highway 61 Revisised* stage musically, and backs his hate-filled story/tunes with an attempted kick-ass band that guest stars everybody from Dick Dale to Garth Hudson. (Unfortunately, Sandy Bull and Don Rondo were unavailable.)

And talk about your inspirational verse. How about this heartfelt "A Lover's Plea": "Think about heartbreak, misery/think about all the things that we've been through/ or think about how a cast would look on you." A real toucher, eh? That's nuttin' compared to the end of "H-A-T-R-E-D": "Yes, I wish I was as mellow/ as, for instance, Jackson Browne/ but 'fountain of sorrow' my ass, motherfucker/ I hope you wind up in the ground."

So, obviously, the guy's got a great attitude, but, still – I dunno. The whole first side is a series of heavy-but-funny diatribes on Amerika, Egg McMuffins, Tru Value Hardware and all that stuff, backed with absolutely typical three-chord donkey fear. Which is OK unless you OD'ed on Dylan replication three or four Bruce Springsteens ago.

But, like Tonio himself says after his autobiographical rant-poem on the sleeve, "POLORIS PBEDKE OCEANEIN MECH LUMENSOFF." Which, roughly translated from some Scandinavian or another, means something like, "We drank all the beer on the sub and then sank in the ocean."

Goddam, *more* inspirational verse!

March 1979

JOE JACKSON

Look Sharp

(A&M)

Everybody and his flat-tired wrecker has been calling this guy the "West Coast Elvis Costello," which oughtta make us all prit-tee sick after the last 24 Bruce Springsteens, 16 Beatles and at least 1 "next Chocolate Watchband." But Joe Jackson's good stuff is so good it makes your ears feel like sneakers, and his so-so stuff is pretty good, too. Plus, he's got a fine sense of humor, so who's getting defensive?

The Elvis comparisons are there, but of little importance. He's got a similarly positive attitude (hate everything that don't crawl off the plate), the same kind of edgy voice and a sound that bounced off the same wall. This JJ sound is something else though – extreme, almost reggae-like sparseness on the verse, building into deadly catchy refrains that display superb ear-to-heart coordination. Love that simplicity, though – just the drums and bass with the guitar usually not electrified to the point where, if a rat sneezes in a nearby tunnel, the guitar plays the first eight bars of "Purple Haze" by itself.

It's somewhat reminiscent of Chicago's WGN-TV's *Bozo's Circus* house band, with its enduring organ, trumpet and drums lineup.

Lots of highlights on this one, with the Rick Spotlight falling on "Is She Really Going Out With Him?" – a tune that's fast sweeping my block (which is a pretty big deal, I think, when a bunch of us dumb shoehorns all pick up on one thing other than dinner). The title alone has been a popular question around everybody since forever and still nobody's got an answer except, "Yeah, but *why?*"

Joe sings about the "pretty women out walkin' with gorillas on my street" in his usual cut-and-cut manner and then hits the hook line with a tune that aches like a dejected blue-veiner on its way to the showers, as our hero adds, "If my eyes don't deceive me, there's something goin' wrong around here."

Tell me about it! Great song, and women can turn it around because pretty men walk around with prospective T-bones all the time. Isn't romance cute?

Running out of time here before *Family Feud* ... other high spots include, "One More Time," "Baby Stick Around" (a near-exact remake of "California Sun"), "Throw it Away" (could almost be Ron Nagle or the first Little Feat) and the busted rewiring of "Instant Mash," which contains the greatest line of this week: "heat it, beat it, eat it, turn around!"

Sentiments we can all agree on, I'm sure.

Look Sharp sounds sharp and is every bit as cool as the white pointies on the cover. Joe's sharp, too, but he doesn't let it stand in the way of his basic ugliness.
April 1979

GRAHAM PARKER / RUMOUR
Squeezing Out Sparks
(Arista)

If there's one thing you can say about Graham Parker, it's that he's consistent. Not consistently *irritating* like Marshall Tucker or consistently *useless* like the Stones. Just consistently ... *consistent. Per*sistent, some might say, or possibly even BOR-ING.

He's not all *that* dull though. The man's got a great band, he writes excellent lyrics, and he's always been dedicated to applying boot to poot. Parker's the one who broke ground for the like of Elvis Costello, with his straight-ahead back-up, outstandingly rotten attitude and a corrugated voice that sounds a little like Van Morrison in the grips of Lumberjack Fever.

But the whole U-Haul is starting to get old. Parker doesn't share Costello's composing talent, and appears to be stuck in a rut of look-alike songs with progressively more pessimistic outlooks. Even pessimism – the lifeblood of '70s rock – gets tired after awhile, and as much as I agree, I'm getting sick of songs like "Don't Get Excited," "Love Gets You Twisted" and "Saturday Nite Is Dead."

Especially when they all sound alike. Three-chord verse, then pound the title into the ground for a chorus, over and over. Now, I like repetition as much as any carbon-brain who's sat through the same episode of *Dick Van Dyke* 200 times, but when you start to Z on the very first spin, you know you're in trouble.

There's some good stuff though, and all at once. The record kicks off like an Ex telling you that Things Will Be Different This Time with "Discovering Japan," a smooth rocker that's not the joke tune the title suggests. Then some nasty stuff about "Local Girls" ("don't ever leave your footprints on the phone") and it's into the highlight of the album, "Nobody Hurts You," a Buddy Holly-ish snapper that hits the clown right on the beak ("nobody hurts you harder than yourself").

That's it, though. The next cut is an acoustic ballad about abortion (get them razor blades out, everybody) and the rest are just standard GP depression pedestals (OK, now: *Slit!*). Good background music for casually bemoaning your fate, or just plain bemoaning.

If Parker could start delivering songs like the first three on *Sparks* regularly, we'd have something to look forward to. *Look Forward to???!* Sorry, forgot myself. Keep cranking out the old Z-bop, Graham, we all have some heavy moping to do.

April 1979

GRAHAM PARKER
Another Grey Area
(Arista)

It's been two years since Graham Parker delivered his last new album, and the eight consecutive summer vacations apparently haven't hurt him.

It improved his songwriting, for one thing. Once a notorious formula composer, he's widened his strategic range and added protective coloring where needed. Hard-core GP fans may be disappointed at the slight rounding of edges. Unfixated citizens, however, can take 'em as they is.

What I'm trying to say is he's "mellowed" a bit more without using the awful word itself. Brings on smoked-out visions of dummies sitting around spool tables in condemned farm buildings attempting to discuss their diminishment of brain function. Who, *me*? No way – my spool table is out on the *porch*.

The first cut, "Temporary Beauty," tips Parker's pitches. The near-ballad features a likeable melody that could stomp the Adult Contemporary (AC) charts without delay. Three other mid-tempo tracks are in the right direction, though they won't make anyone forget Cliff Richards. That's like trying to forget World War II.

His rockers haven't suffered in the transition. The top pick here is "You Hit The Spot," where a rogue rhythm section seizes control and just plain rolls the muthuh. Ditto "Can't Waste A Minute," with its undeniably pop melody and hot-footers like "Big Fat Zero" and the title tune.

"Can't" is the only cut where co-producer (with GP) Jack Douglas momentarily gets blatant about his sordid past. About midway through the song, he gleefully throws in about five seconds' worth of expanding producer-gum learned about at the knee of Bob Ezrin. You find yourself suddenly disoriented, expecting Alice Cooper to come on and holler *"school's out forever!"* then fire a brick eraser at your ear.

It's only a few seconds, though. Don't panic. You can tough it out.

Another Grey Area otherwise presents a smoother, more subtle Graham Parker who's very … 1982. It's a good record to start on for the brand-new GP fan. And it's a logical continuation for the already Parkerized.
February 1982

GIZMOS
Never Mind The Sex Pistols, Here's The Gizmos!
(Gulcher)

NOT INCOMPETENT! That's what strikes you about the "new" Gizmos right off. The power chords have a real buzz factor, the drummer and the band generally play the same song, and some of the vocals will not make you want to go grab a wet electrical line for relief. But now that they possess a certain "quality," have Indiana's Finest lost their sick charm?

Not a chance – let's have a little faith in our trash for once, huh? Head stinks Eddie Flowers and Ted Niemiec got these new Gizmos from respectable places like classified ads in comic books, supermarket checkout lines (EXPRESS *only*), and even found one pawing through the remains of a torn-down gas station. All class guys.

Plus, they actually *kick ass*, especially on the studio side of the new EP. "Tie Me Up" has four great chords plus their trademark shouted-through-a-broken-window backup sounds, not to mention Ted's de-wormed lead vocal. "1978" demonstrates actual Band Dynamics instead of pushing each other out of mike range, and "Just A Little Insane" is a genuine re-destruction of a Sex Pistols B-side delivered in a genuine fake English accent. Ted Niemiec – the next *Saint*?

The live side, from Max's K.C., is full speed as well. The sound quality (they recorded on old fishing line) is everything it's cracked up to be. They recommend that you full blast it and go stand in the next room, but I achieved the best results by going outside and cowering by the railroad tracks. A freight car carrying a shipment of Disco Jeans derailed on that spot the next day.

The band once again punts rumps throughout, particularly on "American Dream," with Billy Nightshade's attack of vocal water croup, and "Cry Real Tears," which has a melody *and* the most directionless guitar solo since Capt. Peachfuzz. Best of all – no annoying applause to interrupt the proceedings. How'd ya manage that, guys?

YOU TOO can own this outstanding debut by the new, improved Gizmos. Not only will you play this EP when you're sick – you might even catch something from it!
April 1979

GIZMOS / DOW JONES AND THE INDUSTRIALS
Hoosier Hysteria
(Gulcher)

From scenic Bloomington, Ind., "the vegetable everyone likes," as it says on the cover, comes a ferocious battle of the bands where it makes no difference whose side you're on.

The Gizmos have been around in various configurations for several years now. Cagey old vets that they are, they can still spontaneously detune or drop a beat with the best of 'em. Not only are they "the stupidest looking band in this orbit," as their bio explains, but they play *stupid* songs *stupidly*. In short, they have everything a great band needs except money.

Musically, the 'Mos sound something like the Shadows of Knight piped through a distant fusebox. They attack their instruments with thumbs and humor, ignoring such outdated concepts as "musicianship" and "talent."

Spewing forth from a fairly traditional rock/punk power base, they waste no time in going completely nuts. The opener, "Progressive Rock," should be required spinning on all AOR radio stations like the national anthem is on TV. "Progressive rock, progressive rock," it goes, "it really sucks, don't it/don't it really suck."

They just don't write lyrics like that anymore.

Other hit tracks include the dubiously catchy "Bible Belt Baby," a version of "Take Me To The River" that – with any luck – could shatter David Byrne's eyeballs and the touching "Dead Astronauts," featuring some inspired guitar rips and lovely, indeed *poignant* lyrics: "I wanna be a dead astronaut/it's a really good way to get talked about." Guaranteed to suck the cockles of your heart.

On the flip side are Dow Jones and the Industrials, a Purdue-based fighter escort with broken radar that dabbles in electronic noise.

Dabbles?

Equal in speed to the Gizmos, the Industrials' sound is … well, *industrial*. Using a complex basement system consisting of Norelco flood alarms, a cracked donkey gauge, a toaster oven, an amped-up Singer Golden Touch 'n' Sew, a little hearing aid feedback, one slightly dim-witted aluminum-can crusher and two packages of Evenflo nursing pads with enclosed transaxle drive, they add numerous weird noises to their music without downgrading the bambam.

Among Dow's biggies are "Rocking Framers," with its likeable big, dog-tongue bass line, a wild MX-80-ish flash fire that reduces "What's The Difference" to ashes and, of course, the beloved "Hold That Coed." (Listen, it beats holding your nose!)

This remarkable 15-song LP (great graphics too) may not be available at your local pharmacy or grain elevator, so ask around. And while you're at it, look for their in-depth band bios, which are packed with such sparkling truisms as "Dale's favorite color is girls," and "Billy is a flashy dresser. Someday he will die."

Okay, the battle of the bands vote count is now complete. Here's the results: Gizmos 13, Industrials 9, REJECT 142. What more do you need to know?

October 1980

JOHN HIATT
Slug Line
(MCA)

Bo Diddley goes Jamaican. Al Kooper arm-wrestles Phil Spector. Van Morrison made obsolete. All this and more on Slug Line.

John Hiatt is another simple-but deadly rocker on the same beat as Elvis "Dukes" Costello and Joe Jackson. He sometimes sounds like either or both of the above, sticks equally nasty lyrics on similarly irresistible tunes and even has that same hit-by-speeding-Spam expression on his pasty puss. He's *modern*.

Hiatt's music is basic New Wave guitar-bass-drum thump with some slightly bent optional equipment. There's lots of reggae influence, including a couple straight reggae tunes complete with fake dialect like, "Hey, mon." But mostly the Jamaican edge is limited to his brakeless guitar while the rest of the band goes Diddley whanking, like in "Radio Girl," which adds the dimensions of a Van Morrison rip while competing as a super single designed for car radio rape.

His rockers are even better, the top stranglers being "(No More) Dancin' In The Street" ("Martha and the Vandellas taught you how to do as you please/ now all you idiots are dancin' with the Bee Gees"), the hook-electrified air of Costello-menace that makes "Sharon 's Got a Drugstore" more than just a great riff, and "You're My Love Interest," where Searchers guitars meet search-and-destroy rhythm's in an impossibly catchy tribute to our hero's girlfriend, whom he looks up to as "the actual size."

For mid-tempo fans there's "Washable Ink," a tune many *already* consider a classic in its earlier incarnation with the Neville Brothers and the title track, the chorus of which sounds something like "Sweet Talkin' Guy" performed by the *Blonde On Blonde* house band.

This is one real tasty LP – a must for Joe Jackson supporters (start with side two!), a solid maybe for the more courageous Costello fans, and an *always* for these poor bored ears. I personally would not trade it for anything except drugs or possibly oral sex. It's that good.
May 1979

JOHN HIATT
All of A Sudden
(Geffen)

John Hiatt is not exactly a big name. His more recent claims to fame include having a song covered by Rick Nelson ("It Hasn't Happened Yet"), contributing to the delinquency of the soundtrack of some film bomb (I think it was *I Shit On Your Grave*) and being great-but-obscure. That's right, about as big a deal as being the world's second most reclusive billionaire.

Not gonna make it on good looks, no sir. With his "inside-I-am-juggling-chain-saws" expression and a wardrobe from the Jack Nicholson Collection, he's not the kinda guy you would invite to one of Thelma Lou's hen parties.

When Hiatt escaped MCA for Geffen this year, I thought *all right!* I mean, MCA is the music biz equivalent of deportation proceedings, but Geffen is hot stuff this week. A hit for Hiatt would be as personally gratifying to me as the brutal and hopefully painful extermination of Lola Falana.

OK, so the guy makes good music, honest. And this being his biggest break yet, he – *naturally* – has turned in a rather so-so effort. Too many of the tunes are just plain not up to his writing talent. They lack his keen edge of hatred for humanoids, not to mention the Female Problem that drives so many male songwriters. Also, they're too putt-putt.

I say we blame it on producer Tony Visconti. John's got enough problems of his own. Whoever it was that thought Tony's brand of mud-whopper gypsy-moth defoliation would enhance Hiatt's music should be sentenced to 20 years' hard labor with Smurf cartoons. Tony, will ya get outta here and go ruin another David Bowie LP, please?

The actual songs contain some fine gems amidst the sandman debris. "I Look for Love" would make a fine radio hit despite Visconti's application of molten killer-bee-progress maps. "Secret Life" ("complete with a secret dog!") is ditto above and "I Could Use An Angel" is everything Squeeze wanted to be on their last album.

Stinkers? None really. Just some fairly listenable mid-tempo selections that sing good and don't contain the sick power of his Slug Line LP or the calm viciousness of *Two Bit Monsters*.

OK. Listen up, porkchops. Skip this one unless you're a Hiatt fanatic. (That would make two of us). Go out *right now* instead and get one of his MCA albums. Probably cutouts by now. Aren't we all?

Don't have time for an ending here, so here's one John Kordosh traded me for a middle: I'd like to say more about this, but a careening motor home driven by an evidently glaucomatized and drunken ex-low-level employee of Chair World whose hobby is memorizing the gestation period of small mammals is headed straight for my typewriter and I've gotta get out the way.

April 1982

JOURNEY
Evolution
(Columbia)

A journey usually means that somebody's going away for a long time. No such luck in this case; these guys don't go away, they *evolve*. It says so right here on the cover.

But did they evolve, or were they pushed? There's definitely a survival advantage in their current catalog of FM-strokers and neon geese, but their material is so drearily tame that you haven't to wonder if the band's brains aren't really vestigial organs.

Vocalist Steve Perry offends my reproductive system the most. To say that he's a whiner does not do the man justice. Perry's a whiner's whiner, squealing away furiously in the implausible air that falls between rarefied and denatured. If they ever create a cartoon character based on snot, Steve will no doubt be called upon to do the voice.

The rest of these dinks just mumble away on their instruments, making huge swamp-footprint sucking sounds that give listeners endless opportunities to reconsider their attitudes toward dim slither. When Columbia runs their ads full of descriptive quotes from reviewers, the best they can come up with on Journey is stuff like "Tolerable," "No children's choirs anywhere," and "Made me temporarily forget my chemo therapy symptoms."

Then to top it off, the liner contains this big suck job about how great AOR radio is (for the dead, maybe), how their roadies all go build hospitals and animal shelters when they're not busy tearing down Gregg Rolie's synthesizer jigsaw, plus the following shining example of lip-to-ass coordination: "Those of you who aspire to a career In music should know that Columbia Records stands alone in the field of developing new artists and seeking out young and gifted talent." Yeah, especially if you used to be in Santana, huh, guys?

Bluesman Zuzu Bollin' summed it all up better than I ever could: WHY DON'T YOU EAT WHERE YOU SLEPT LAST NIGHT?
June 1979

CHEAP TRICK, VARIOUS ARTISTS
Over The Edge
(Warner Bros.)

Great album here, disguised as a soundtrack. And not mixed by beekeepers like the *Rock 'n' Roll High School* LP – just solid blaring sound and lots of good songs that you can use to replace two or 20 dud records in your collection.

The only two good songs on the Cars LP — "Best Friend's Girl" and "Just What I Needed" – are here, so you can unload the rest of that Roy Thomas Baker plug-in crud. Some good-if-not-essential Cheap Trick (Goodbye, *Heaven Tonight*!), Van Halen's "You Really Got Me" (a small fortune on old Kinks albums), plus stuff by Little Feat and Valerie Carter that you'd never have bought in the first place if you had any brains.

The movie itself is one of those road epics where foolish teens discover sex, drugs and rock 'n' roll and proceed to destroy themselves with inventive combinations of the three. You've probably seen 'em all – *Go Ask Alice, The Survival of Dana, The Rick Johnson Story* – they're all the same and they're all great, particularly the preachy parts, where you can sneer, boo, puke and otherwise righteously defend the pathetic fun of your own life.

Another neat aspect of this LP is trying to envision the scenes from the film that the songs are meant to illustrate. "Downed" and "Teenage Lobotomy" are pretty easy to figure, so flush the toilet. "Just What I Needed" brings on a disgusting picture of Melissa Sue and Ronnie Howard running in slow motion through fields of wildflowers normally reserved for disposable douche commercials. And Valerie Carter's "Ooh Child" – nice song and all, especially before she ruined it – you just know it's got to be at the end, with Frigid Marcy reclining on her little suburban bed with posts

131

and stuffed Teddies, soulfully staring into the flame of a solitary, mope-scented candle and mentally muttering about all the disgusting shit she did in the first half of the movie. There's possibly a flashback explaining why she experiences uncontrollable sexual excitement whenever she encounters the smell of bowling alley wax. Ooh child!

This record is about the best bet this summer for blasting out the window while you lay stoned out of your mind on top of a crummy old picnic table, soaking up the sun and providing a blistered heliport for horseflies and brown buzzers. And if the goofy neighbors ask you to change the record after the 39th consecutive spin, tell 'em you can't change it, it's *perfect already.*

So there.

June 1979

CHEAP TRICK
Dream Police
(Epic)

The guys in Cheap Trick currently find themselves in a no-win situation critically. While their fame has reached a level sufficient enough to guarantee them platinum popularity on momentum alone for the next handful of albums, their talent appears to be getting stale beneath the frosting. Cupcakes gone too far.

It can hardly be considered a mistake that Cheap Trick produced a near-perfect LP (*In Color*) early on, one of the great songs of the '70s in "Surrender" and the biggest fluke hit (*Budokan*) since the election of Jimmy Carter. I mean, *nice goin'* and all, but now what? Boss Trick Rick Nielsen's songwriting is showing signs of desperate recycling and the band's playing has never been anything more than crisp, lending further credence to this detractor's feeling that Cheap Trick is the most overrated group of the decade. Well, them and El Chicano.

Dream Police is packed with previously-owned riffing, pasted-on vocals and dead donkeys in general. The title cut, another in a long line of Jeff Lynne tributes penned by Nielsen and parroted by Zander, is a monument to the application of over-ambition to lack of substance. The melody is wrenched from the chord progression like a stuck boxcar, the lyrics are unintentionally laughable and the eruption of strings (or a very stringy synth) halfway through the cut all add up to an amusing novelty tune. It's a wonder to me they didn't use little tin-frog clickers in the rhythm track. Played backward!

Apart from novelty, there's plenty of good, old-fashioned boredom to be found. "Gonna Raise Hell" and "Need Your Love" add up to 15 minutes (nine and six, respectively) of humdrum guitar drone and some of the most unconvincing vocal work put on vinyl since Debbie Boone's version of "Volunteers." Now, if AC/DC or some other slime creature had tackled "Gonna Raise Hell," you could actually picture them humping farm equipment and knocking each other around with old barges. But Cheap Trick's idea of raising hell is probably something like stealing the clock from the Ladies'

Room of a Catholic school because nuns had looked at it after defecating.

Other potential snooze inducers include "The House is Rockin'" and "Writing on the Wall," a couple of mediocre rockers similar to the ones the almost-dead Beatles recorded on that windblown rooftop and never used, and still another pair of scrawled signature tunes ("I'll Be With You Tonight" and "I Know What You Want") that fill in the remaining airspace on side two. It sounds as though they're trying to recapture some of the buzz 'n' thud of their debut album, which was no pretty postcard from Japan itself.

While bright spots like "Way Of The World" and "Voices" – both ballads, interestingly enough – demonstrate that Nielsen is far from cashed in in the material department, you have to wonder if this isn't just another case of a band that peaks early in their career and then hangs on mainly by their reputation, like some marginally-talented utility infielder going for an extra pension year. But what can one really say at this point?

Cheap Trick, cheap dream. Cheap shots.

October 1979

CHEAP TRICK
All Shook Up
(Columbia)

Ain't *nothin'* left to say about Cheap Trick, anymore. Any complaints? I didn't think so. What say we wrap this one up quick-like and get an early start on the cookies.

Okay, 10 songs. That's gonna make the math a lot easier. Instead of wasting time on good vs. bad, let's just stipulate: eight heavy-riff rockers, one ballad and one novelty throwaway. Wait a minute, wise guys, George Martin isn't the novelty, he's the *producer.*

Moving right along, the heavies are the same kind of stuff as the last LP—a further retreat to the English school of hoagey-metal that start the boys on the road to Budokan. So, if you like the direction of *Dream Police,* you should like this one 41percent more.

The ballad isn't bad. It sounds a lot like a Beatles track from the *Let It Be* era. *Era,* that's a good one! Actually, now that I think about it, the Cheapies oughtta be sent on a punishment tour of Australia. Opening for Utopia.

Wake up, we're almost there! George Martin's frostbitten production gives the whole record the feel of an old Move album. Buzzing instruments, tons of layering, and the type of over-powering bass guitar that first led listeners to appreciate the technical term "dinosaur poop."

—The end.

Ricky Johnson, age 4

November 1980

133

CHEAP TRICK
One on One
(Epic)

    Bam bam bam bam bam bam bam bam bam bam bam bam bam bam bam bam bam bam bam bam bam bam bam bam bam bam bam bam bam bam bam bam bam bam bam bam bam bam bam bam bam bam bam bam bam bam bam bam bam bam bam bam bam bam bam bam bam bam bam bam bam bam bam bam bam bam bam bam bam bam bam bam bam.

May 1982

THE KNACK
Get The Knack
(Capitol)

FACE DANCER
This World
(Capitol)

    Got a couple of real fine debut albums here, a phenomenon almost as unheard of as consciousness in this sad disco summer of pointless comebacks and glorified licking noises. Good hot weather music too, especially if you set up your stereo next to a central air vent and crank 'em both to infinity. Take that, Ayatollah!

    The Knack are getting the big company push, but don't let that put you off. Despite the heat, they're just plain good. Tuff singing, tight playing, solid writing and no lamby-fart tenor-sax solos anywhere.

    But most important of all, they're catchy. I keep finding myself singing "My Sharona" when I'm hosing down my apartment, "Your Number or Your Name" while I'm making voodoo dolls of my neighbor's record collection, and "Frustrated" when ... well, never mind. These tunes stick in your head like good pop should – erasing all worries of gas snipers, Anita Ward and the U.S. of Ronco's nifty Skylab falling like flaming metallic puke on your tomato patch.

    The Knack's sound is your basic hot-guitars-and-engaging-vocals, with undertones of early Beatles and Who that surface occasionally as influences completely digested. The "tuneful" cuts – I don't know what to call 'em but they sure ain't ballads – hit you like buzzing melody Jeeps deperately escaping Saigon. Treadmarks never felt so good.

    Here comes the transition. There it went!

    Now, Face Dancer is a D.C. (Dodo Corral) band that sounds a bit like the late great, Stories after a lengthy immersion in an amphetamine steam bath. Some truly good melodies on this one, too, pushed by a high-energy band starring hot dog *excelsior* guitarist Jeff Adams and kiss-your-girlfriend-bye-bye singer Carey Kress.

    The runaway winner on *This World* is "Red Shoes," a hard-charging natural single about the evils of fun that the National Safety Council is lobbying to have banned, fearing what will happen to their precious death stats if this song gets on car radios come Labor Day. Lots of other hot-to-trot rockers too, but always based on deadly hooks that could make 'em heel and shake paws if anybody wanted 'em to.

So ignore all the big-shit LPs coming out now and pick up in these fine new bands. And in case there's still a few of you left with wintery white grub-worm skin, these records are both excellent for those intense speakers-out-the-window, ray-catching sessions. Makes 90-degree heat feel like moonbeams.
July 1979

FOREIGNER
Head Games
(Atlantic)

Head Games isn't half the smellbag I expected it to be. In fact, the only real problem I've encountered with the album is dealing with Lou "Candy" Gramm's vocals. He probably likes to think that his brand of growl 'n' grunt indicates the presence of moose herds cavorting in the tundra of his sexual apparatus. Actually, the nearest equivalent in the animal kingdom to Lou's *grrr* is an enraged three-striped ground squirrel. Hey, why do you think it has *three* stripes?

Other than that, though, Foreigner produces very competent bambam with a platinum consistency. The Foreigner Beat, which sounds like the tails of several hundred dazed and partially frozen St. Bernards thumping their tails in unison, keeps most of the songs on a fairly high slug-level. And, while most of the melodies resemble one of those unfortunate pedestrians that get hit on an expressway and are then run over by an entire rush hour, they do get the job done. The job being Thud.

The only really noticeable stinker, the one that will make listeners with cats wrinkle up their noses and pronounce "littuh oduh" is "Blinded By Science," one of those Turgemobiles ELP specialize in. Molten molt.

So if it's a choice between spending your hard-earned extortion money on *Head Games* or the True Value Tool Value of the Month, well, find out which tool it is *first*.
October 1979

PEARL HARBOR AND THE EXPLOSIONS
Pearl Harbor and the Explosions
(Warner Bros.)

Here's a real good one that officially slipped under the wire 12/31/79, but I say we call it the first and definitely the hottest baby of 1980. At least, until the next one comes along.

PH&E's sound falls on the Wave side, if anybody's still keeping score. A three-piece with a sharp, basic approach, the band is vaguely reminiscent instrumentally of some of the less criminally insane tracks of Talking Heads or the B-52s. It's a lot steadier of a beat though – the rhythm section having already digested disco and eliminated the nasty hulls. If they were ballplayers, commentators would comment on their "poise."

Topped with Pearl's cooly engaging vocals and channeled through a tight, no-frills production that's as slick as the Beat but with tapered edges, PH&E's debut covers all the ground it needs to. The group-composed material ranges from solid to at least one bonified classic, that being "You Got It (Release It)," a truly great single with a melody you can't get off your brain without the use of a concrete David Byrne lyric sheet.

Other clicks to click include "So Much For Love" ("I don't care if you aim is true"), "Up And Over," with its irresistible threading of beat and vocals and a newly recorded version of their independent hit, "Drivin'," a dynamic container for the key phrase, "I'm only drivin'."

Highly recommended as a less-calculated alternative to the odd dance music of the aforementioned bands. Pearl Harbor and the Explosions – despite the crazy name – are so natural, they don't *have* to act weird.

February 1980

LONELY BOYS
The Lonely Boys
(Harvest)

Good name for starters. Implications of too many late nights spent daydreaming, inspecting, that fine collection of bowling ball fingerhole pumice, and checking the palms for signs of new hair. Looking up "sensitive" in the dictionary to see if there's a picture.

No excess sensitivity on *this* disc, thank goodness. No excess anything, for that matter.

The Lonely Boys' sound is a well-thinned cross between the very Englishness of Squeeze and some of the Police's lighter material. Keyboards carry the riff but do not in any way dominate the medium-sparse, reggae-shaded tunes.

"Song-oriented" is the key here – it even says so in the bio, so it must be true. Some good material too, from the catchy little desperation icebergs like "Heartbreaker" to the inspirational verse of "Annoying All the Neighbors": "I like annoying all the neighbors/ I don't see why I should do them any favors."

Can't argue there.

Let's add this up: 12 cuts, half of which are excellent, with the rest ranging from good glove/light bat to acceptable between-cuts that will not make your eardrums feel like hangover trampolines. I'd recommend the majority and keep and eye on this group.

They have a big future if any of us live that long.

March 1980

CRETONES
Thin Red Line
(Planet)

First off, the Cretones don't sound like their name at all. If you're looking for something from the lower L.A. school of primed-out latecomers, you're barking up the wrong gutter. If the Cretones are cretinous, then the Durocs can actually oink.

Secondly, the word is out that Linda Ronstadt — you know, the one who's promised to deliver the Cub Scout vote — recorded three of writer Mark Goldenberg's songs for her new LP. About as good an omen as vultures over McDonalds, right? Well, try not to think about it. She's ruined songs by much lesser songwriters than Mark and guilt by association is out this week anyway.

Beneath the exceptions, the Cretones are basically a very likeable, song-oriented pop/rock group with access to some good hooks and uncommonly intelligent lyrics. The majority of their tunes are well-paced, keyboard-dominated numbers topped with solid vocal work in a dense, no-nonsense production by bassist Peter Bernstein.

The many catchy tunes aside, Goldenberg's lyrics are regular synapse-Milkbones. He keeps the sledge hammer under wraps, setting disarming little picks like "You want a night that won't be traced / Inside a life that can't be erased," and then coming back a few lines later with the tickler, "You never ask yourself where you stand / You just sit there looking at your glands."

Truer words, etc.

A couple of these songs, "Everybody's Mad At Katherine" (but she don't care!) and "Justine," are instant ear-grabbers meaty enough for an all-day hum. A couple more are bubbling under and the rest go fine in between with but one clinker. "Mrs. Peel was probably included here so that at least one cut would really have "a Peel," and there's an occasional drift toward sap.

Still, *Thin Red Line* is an enjoyable record from both sides of the fence, and you'd better pick up on it fast, because all the Ronstadt money will probably be the end of this group. In fact, Mark G. has already collaborated with the meow-dervish himself, Andrew Gold. See what I mean about vultures?
March 1980

GENTLE GIANT
Civilian
(Columbia)

SQUEEZE
Argybargy
(A&M)

Gentle Giant is one of those groups who cleaned up its sound a couple of years ago in order to gain wider commercial acceptance but still don't sell jackshit. They just keep heavin' them LPs into the wind, in hopes that they'll score the big hit – by process of elimination, if nothing else – and proceed to sell out the entire back catalog. This is a great approach. Remember how well it worked for American Tears?

England's Squeeze is getting much the same company treatment – that is, keep the product coming whether it sells or not and catch ya later. The big difference, though, is that Squeeze has talent. They've got a strong songwriting team in Glenn Tilbrook and Chris "What's The" Difford and more importantly, their – while cheerfully derivative – is definitely their own.

Gentle (i.e., Mild, Moderate, Placid, Bland, Benign, Lenient, Meek, Submissive and Outright Wimpy) Giant is merely a generic equivalent of Genesis and/or ELP. With both of those bands pretty much out of order these days, the Blandos want to grab that particular audience, witless or not. *Civilian* will not be the album to do it, however. Even in these sad, if not outright ludicrous days of Fink Ploy dominating the LP and singles charts, they just don't have what it takes. What it takes – at the very least – is novel material, and this echo of log-sawing guitars, keyboard wash and weary, boinging sounds and the vague tinkling of gratuitous studio effects all becomes psychedelic-dotage Muzak at best. They freaketh out, but they know not whereof they freakish.

The Squeezeroos, on the other hand, know pretty much what they're doing. It's just a matter of whether the "Listening Public" (that's a good one!) will go for the rather quaint, overwhelmingly English sound. With the exception of a handful of highly melodic rockers, their material is very reminiscent of Ray Davies during his aren't-we-Limeys-cute phase.

The music is updated, of course, and translated into Squeeze's keyboard-oriented approach. How about the "Lonely Boys" performing "Village Green P.S.," does that help any? (I know, who the heck *are* the Lonely Boys?) Let's just say well-defined melodies with wordy-but-witty lyrics thriving in a pool of tight, well-layered arrangements. Got it, sleepyheads?

If you're not a fan of the type of material Squeeze does so well, it might just sound like novelty music to you, I'm afraid. I suppose it is, in a way, but not like Gentle Giant's leaking cessbarge of dillydrone and dueling engineers. Besides, how can you not love a group like Squeeze when they sing, "Her mother didn't like me/she thought I was on drugs?"
April 1980

TRILLION

Clear Approach

(Epic)

Like dental plaque, Trillion is a powerful enemy. But can mint Dentu-Creme wipe out this group?

I think not. These are *ground-in* days we're living in. Too tough for Spray 'n' Wash. Too deep for Lift 'n' Vac. This is a job for ... Nuke 'n' Hose!

Really now, I hate this group, don't you? Nothing but a bunch of petrified Yes moves, vibrato vocals flopping in fish-like harmony and lyrics full of insightful questions like, "Are we living in a fairy tale?"

Yup. *Spectreman Meets The Five Little Piggies.*

Let's ask the guys in the group; maybe they know what's wrong.

"There's nothing but originality in Trillion," says drummer Bill Wilkins.

Listen, bub, not only is that Rick Wakeman's line, but who cares what drummers think anyway? Nobody but other drummers.

How about the bass player? They always stand in the background, chewing their bass cud and looking bemused.

"We're as sophisticated as Queen or Yes," insists former New Colony Six-oid Ron Anaman, "but we have the appeal of Foreigner or Boston."

Why is that funny? Because he *means* it, that's why.

Okay, cowpokes, this is the final poop: Trillion sounds just like a trillion other artsy-craftsy bands. They can't even redeem themselves with a sense of humour like Russia or the Brady Kids. They make you want to rip your SUPPORT MIDWEST MUSIC bumper sticker off and replace it with something sensible, like CONTAINS ILLEGAL DRUGS, DO NOT SEARCH.

You know, if somebody would give these guys some woodworking tools or a paint-by-number kit, they might just leave us alone.

(P.S. – NEWS FLASH! Just heard on the radio that Trillion are going to play for Teen Night at Comiskey Park. "Prog-Rock Demolition Night!" Can you see it?)
June 1980

NYC ROCKERS
Marty Thau Presents 2 X 5
(Red Star/Jem)

There's been real big ink on this year's NYC scene, and no wonder. Where else do they chop up strippers, screw geese on stage and drive taxis full of Brooklyn Dodgers memorabilia off skyscrapers into waiting traffic cone loudspeakers? I mean besides Sioux Falls.

Under the guiding peep of Marty Thau (more popularly known as "The Fifth Bloodless Pharoah") and Blondie's Jimmy Destri (who produced all 10 cuts), these five new-ish bands present two tracks each of honestly hot, fairly challenging NYC schmooz. They're not so challenging that you want to shoot 'em when their backs are turned, but logical extensions of American punk 'n' pop – not those goofy reggae-fired Ramones chords the Limeys have been bouncing off us, but stuff Sky Saxon could relate to.

Here's a lineup that'll keep Bosox fans in their holes another few years:

"Bloodless Pharoahs" – I've been "dying" to hear these guys ever since I first heard their name, and you know what? They really do sound like bloodless pharoahs. Tomb-Rock could be the next big thing if their intensely original combination of mysteriously horizontal keyboards, drowned surf guitar and, well, bloodless vocals gets some exposure. Also, great lyrics, none of which I can savvy. This group should obviously be locked up now. Is there any higher recommendation?

"Student Teachers" – With a fuller, somewhat more pop-directed sound, this is the most "accessible" group on the set. In fact, they may even have as much commercial potential as those new combination jukebox/fish tanks with the pink flamingo legs. "Looks" is actually catchy, if not Peppy, thank goodness.

"Revelons" – This band is the closest to the B-side revelations of '60s punk. A good hot capture by Destri, if the material is a bit (intentionally) thin.

"Fleshtones" – They're also on the punkoid side, with a lot of megazomb presence, plus they blow-that-harmonica-Steve on both tracks. It's just a crying shame that Keith Relf isn't around to hear this – it'd kill him!

"Comateens" – Another weirdly catchy proposition, they have dry, upfront vocals and keyboards assuming their proper importance: none. Just good ol' fills and new ol' modulations, no herds of wounded Styx anywhere to be found.

But best of all, every one of these groups remind me of the Nightcrawlers.

July 1980

SHIRTS

3rd Album

(Capitol)

The Shirts are a cut above most of the other "new" pop groups when it comes to maturity of material. An attractive package of oddly catchy, angular melodies, energy-efficient hooks, and lyrics having nothing whatsoever to do with high school or having "fun," their tunes stand out that much more in tight, spare arrangements that pledge non-interference with the Sound or with the territorial integrity of Afghanistan.

You don't have to be a sucker for lead singer Annie Golden like I am, but it doesn't hurt. Her strong, well-rounded voice is a real tickler, but it also bears a cutting edge that, when exposed, can kill quickly and accurately – if not callously. None of this vague wailing from the bottom of a flooded elevator shaft – she's an official, registered Real Singer after all, having starred in the film version of *Hair* (not that I ever saw it, which strains my hipster credentials no end).

E-Z facts: This is the band's third album, and since all I've got is a test pressing, I can't tell you the title, the producer or who brought the doughnuts. Oh, well – never stopped me before! You get 11 tracks, two ballads, the rest upbeat wave clickers. Suggested cuts: all.

See? Anybody can write for *Billboard*.

Once again, if you liked their two previous albums, you'll go for this one too. And if you've never "tried 'em on" (Oh, Rick, you're such a Potsy), this is a good place as any to start.

The Shirts: Wear them anywhere!

July 1980

AC/DC
Back in Black
(Atlantic)

The *second* question about the new AC/DC album has to be: how is the new lead singer, Brian Johnson, who stepped in for Bon Scott when the latter bit the bitter mudpie of finality?

He's not bad. Johnson is somewhat screechier than Scott, but at least he's got a pulse. Every now and then, you get the impression that he's scraping his larynx on a blackboard, an occupational hazard, I'm sure. But if you live through Robert Plant, Brian presents no big adjustment.

Back in Black is highly consistent, basic heavy metal. It's not terribly fast, but that's not necessary when you've got the throb down. And this band has it: loud, thumping bass, well-chopped guitars and an occasional gang-chorus. I'd go so far as to say that this record contains all the excitement of death by drowning – without the inconvenience.

There's no problem with the material, either. The new kid surprisingly shares one-third of all composing credits with the Youngs. Top cuts include "Hell's Bells," a refreshingly threatening opener, the slightly melodic "You Shook Me All Night Long," "Let Me Fuck Your Brains Out," "Lookit My Big One," etc., etc. They've got the formula down so pat, they even saved the clinker for the last cut. All you need do is scan the title, "Rock and Roll Ain't Noise Pollution," and remember to Reject early. Is there such a thing as a remote control Reject switch? If not, I'll gladly split the patent with whoever wants to invent it: 60/40

Okay, a moment of seriousness before we unlock the toys. *Black* is one of the best HM LPs released this season, recommended both to fans of the group and the casual seeker of brain debris. Now we can get on with the interesting stuff, like when is BJ going to come up with a satisfactory explanation of how his fingerprints got all over Bon Scott's neck?

Almost forgot! The first question is *why?*
August 1980

MARK ANDREWS AND THE GENTS
Big Boy
(A&M)

At a glance, one could easily mistake Mark Andrews debut as the long-awaited second Lenny and the Squigtones album (where they do "Stairway to Heaven") or as another sterile Revivalist snoozer.

Instead of the next Andrew Squiggman, what we have here is a highly talented singer/songwriter in the Joe Jackson vein. Andrews comes through with uncomplicated rockers featuring catchy melodies and strong refrains, packaged in no-nonsense arrangements that are the product of tightly regulated band dynamics.

The obligatory reggae influence is smoothly built into the overall sound, not unlike John Hiatt's tunes. The one straight reggae cut is a breakthrough rendition of "Born to be Wild" that even Mars Bonfire himself would agree is natty. It's no novelty throwaway, though – the way Mark and his Gents put it together sounds so natural that they make the other 10 million remakes sound like the novelties. But if Mark Andrews is gonna be the next John Kay, who's gonna be the next Goldy McJohn?

Top cuts include "Say It's All Right," "Don't Let Go" and "Show Me" – all from the previously mentioned Jackson/Hiatt school of powerhouse lyricism – and full speed donkey whippers like "(I Want Love) Laid on A Plate" (awright!) or the officially designated Killer Cut, "In A Jam," with its epic Music Machine keyboard moves.

Big Boy's low dog content (0.5 clinkers per side, scientifically speaking) and variety of solid tunes provide more than enough good music to chew on while we wait with "baited breath" (again, nightcrawlers) for that Lenny & Squiggy LP.

I think they're going to include "The Pusher," too.

September 1980

TALKING HEADS
Remain In Light
(Sire)

The main thing that people and Talking Heads fans alike want to know about the new, improved lineup is: What does it sound like? Well, either that or, can it get those stubborn plutonium stains out of Junior's bib?

The Heads' sound *has* been altered somewhat, but it's not drastically different. If you likes "I Zimbra" on their previous LP, you're all set because that approach has been colored in and filled out here. Guitars riffing and figuring and chick-chicking, little jabs of keyboard, extended rhythm section, group vocals and *lots of percussion*, that's the story.

The "disco" allegations are already starting to fly, but forget it. There hardly even *is* such a thing as Disco nowadays, anymore that there are "official" packages of Soul or New Wave. Everything's all mooshed together now (you can quote me), and just because something's got a good beat doesn't mean it leads directly to the hard stuff.

The band's latest twist is carried off successfully, for the most part. Side one features three longish doses of the new beat and the old paranoia. I think I'll just pass on the lyrics this time, except to ensure that at no time does anyone scream out "Papa's got a brand new bag!" (Even though it sounds like someone *should*.)

Side two – the "B" side going by today's conservation of talent – contains more variety and fewer guitars going deedle-deedle. "Houses in Motion" is the standout, as Byrne kicks it off with some trademark numb mumblings and then everybody jumps in on vocals. It has the kind of melody that leaves one expecting the group to break into Swahili at any moment, but they resist. In fact, all of this music has more to do with Africa that it does with disco.

That about covers it. Remember the key: If you like "I Zimbra" you'll like *Remain in Light*. If you hate it, or never heard it, then try to picture

David Byrne suddenly reaching sexual maturity in the middle of singing a
James Brown song.

The Talking Heads are *bad*, man.

October 1980

UNITS

Digital Stimulation

(415 Records)

Most all synthesizer bands sound like a slightly warped copy of *Who's
Next* played on a bargain-basement cardboard hi-fi with one broken speaker. Tweets and buzzes, icy tapping, keyboards on Rinse – you get the picture. For the most part, there's little progress since Silver Apples – the
most notorious unlistenable electronic band in the history of the Why-
Did-They-Record-This? School of Thought – started all this nonsense back
in the Golden Age of Cutouts.

San Francisco's Units avoid many of the pitfalls of beep-beep by not
taking it all too seriously. Or rather, they mean it but they don't shove it
done listeners' throats through their ears. You might say they're even fun.

A three-piece setup consisting of two synthesizers and a drummer
(they've since added a vibes player), the Units keep things moving by
using the electronics more for percussion than as coloring agents. They
have a stronger bottom than one expects from this type of group,
although not really enough for these depraved ears. A keyboard bass
would fit in nicely, though I'm probably missing the point.

The Units most likeable aspect is their song-oriented approach. No
wandering around on green keys for these folks. They deliver 11 compact
tunes, some of which are even catchy.

In fact, "Mission" is Top 10 in this household, with its very entertaining mixture of direct keyboard riffing, deadly rhythms, good melody and
novelty effects. Several other cuts also fall into the easily accessible category. The one longish (5:17) instrumental, "Cowboy," is another highlight,
slipping from an atmospheric base of hovering keyboards into a vaguely
B-52-ish jumper.

The lyrics suck Gary Numan's diddling diode, so tear up the lyric
sheet immediately after cracking the wrap. And if you can't easily find a
copy to open, search for it. But if you make contact, don't forget to ask
'em if they have any tickets left over to the Summer of Love.

November 1980

MOTORHEAD

Ace of Spades

(Mercury)

Motorhead is not exactly Steely Dan. You want bambam, they got bambam. You want hollering, they got hollering. Not to mention thuds, crashes,

143

burps, total blooey and at least one miked fart. Thank you, 20th century!

They're not trying to *trick* anybody, that's for sure. One look at the front (the guys dressed in leather and fringe like a spaghetti western posse) tells you this is not the Little River Band. The back is even better – "Thanks to anyone who helped, got drunk, humped gear, girls, etc. Have a long squawk ..."

Have a long squawk! All right! Mohead deadheads are not looking for socio-political enlightenment, and a big, long squawk is a perfect description of *Ace of Spades:* all-out, top-speed, strap-down-that-baby Heavy Metal bamshalam.

The typical Mohead tune features relentlessly relentless riffing and shouting not dissimilar to earlier AC/DC, back before they learned how to make records for radio. As a bonus, all 12 cuts are typical if not actually fatal.

"Motorhead's existence is pure excess," goes the unusually accurate bio. What makes them such a big act in European headbanging circles? Uh ... "Mohead and their fans' ideas, wants and inspirations converge at a perfect tangent."

A perfect tangent! Why didn't I think of that? 'Course, I dunno what a tangent is, do you? Can you wear it or do you eat it?

What I do know is that their "ideas" (*hey, let's rip off a gas station!*), "wants" (*hey, let's rip off somebody's clothes!*), and inspirations (*hey, let's rip off the Scorpions!*) add up to something other than Paul Williams.

Great names too! Lemmie, Philthy Animal, and Fast "Relief" Eddie. They don't sound like a power trio, though. They sound like six power trios.

This here is the "real stuff," metal maniacs. All fast, all hard and more engagingly primitive than outfits like REO or Judas Priest, who turn it down on vinyl.

So keep them perfect tangents rollin', Mohead, and don't forget: LEM-MIE RULES!

February 1981

EDGAR WINTER

Standing On Rock

(Blue Sky)

Oh, boy, Edgar Winter is in love. Hallelujah, have a cigar, unbag that rice, you sure caught a fine one this time, Dad hasn't lost a daughter, he's gained albino chromosomes for the family gene pool.

And, of course, will Edgar wear white to the wedding?

Has it affected his music, asks NATO? I dunno, how can you tell? He's still making the same decent-if-uninspired boogie noise that he started out with, although the ballad content is nearing 50 percent. Fair enough.

You can hear AM soul, Doobie-tinkle, things-that-bark and other recent influences that prove he's been alive all this time, but it's marred by the usual farting around and the all-new, overwhelming sappiness of a performer hopelessly caught up in the Old-Lady's-Picture-On-The-Sleeve Syndrome. Lotta good that did John Sebastion, Van Morrison, Sly Stone and Stevie Wonder, right?

Since the Prosecution has established that the music bears a common, Biclike dispensability, let's hear it for the lyrics. The biggest laughs occur when Ed describes himself as a "punishment without a crime." Now *that's* insight. Many music fans have wondered what they did to deserve Edgar Winter.

Insult To Injury Dept.: Everybody's third favorite Caucasian, Jerry La Croix (rhymes with La Choy), somehow got into the lyrics jar again. Isn't this stupe ever gonna leave us alone?

Anyhow, this year he's preaching "Let rock 'n' roll and disco soul unite?" Hey — right on, daddio! Tear down the walls! Free Joe Jackson! All power to the Village People! 1-2-3-4, we don't want your — *(author kneecapped)*.

Could we get serious for a moment, fellow worshippers? You know, there aren't that many good love songs to kick around anymore, and Boss Winter has turned his googoo-eyed moronic infatuation into what are probably the two best lines of the '80s. Nah, in rock 'n' roll *history!* Actually, *in the entire development of romantic music since at least the Inquisition:*

"We sip champagne to set the mood,
"We go out for Italian food."

We go out for Italian food. Did I mention the guy's the most important poet of the 20th Century?
March 1981

BRAINS
Electronic Eden
(Mercury)

The Brains are another group of model citizens you don't want to turn your back on. According to their possibly apocryphal bio, leader Tom Gray's previous day job was machine-gun factory foreman. Rick Price is a reformed hog chopper/pool hall manager. Bassist Bryan Smithwick claims to have been a "military adviser" (i.e., blood-happy mercenary) in the Ethiopian civil war and drummer Charles Worth ... well, Charlie's just a down-home guy who's looking for a new pet wolf spider because his old one croaked.

Charm School City, as you can plainly see. Slightly more important is the fact that they've developed their own sound in these days of a new Raspberries every five minutes. A veritable Iron Butterfly for the '80s, the Brains are hot 'n' heavy but a lot smarter (and not nearly as boring) as the famed gadda-geeks who, you'll recall, turned a drunken slobber-coinage into the record industry's first platinum LP.

The Brainbeat is rooted solidly in a no-nonsense rhythm section that combines all the best features of tractors plowing concrete fields, coal barges scraping the hoods of submerged autos and overpopulated bleachers collapsing in mid-*mighty mighty*. Brains' brain and vocalist Gray fills things out with surprisingly full-synth keyboards that often sound like a real organ instead of rioting geese. Plus, there's the required angular strips and punctures from guitarist Price.

The material is even stronger than that of the first album, from which came the remarkable "Money Changes Everything," the big noise (if not big seller) of '79. The Brains draw much of their inspirations from classic American punk-rock of the '60s, with muscle supplanting the decade's notoriously tinny rhythms.

Producer Steve Lillywhite pretty much kept his educated paws off the *artistes*, defining the elements and secretly disconnecting the brake lights. While the first LP was stunning mud, Electronic Eden allows separation without diluting the effect. The effect being massive *thud*.

Don't Miss: "Eyes Of Ice," a dominating pounder bearing the most overpowering baseline since "Hungry"; "Little Girl Gone," a dynamic flashback to the days of Ed Cobb and the Chocolate Watchband; and "Asphalt Wonderland," a tune that the Ramones oughtta cover fast if they ever want a hit.

Let the Brains stomp yours today.

April 1981

RAINBOW
Difficult to Cure
(Polydor)

It's "new Rainbow album time" (Number 6) – and you know what that means. That's right, new bodies because – in the words of Mr. Witch Hat himself, "I get very bored with people."

Join the club, daddio. This time, the new employees are singer Joe Lynn Turner (ex-Fandango) and New York state drummer Bob Rondinelli. The drums could be a bit heavier, but the vocalist is a real improvement. He screecheth not and can even hit the low notes. He will never be mistaken for Lou Christie.

Difficult To Cure is just what fans have come to expect from these guys. Blackmore's trademark riffing, solid rhythms and High Speed. Not only is Ritchie the patron eel of metal guitarists, but he's also still one of the three or four hottest. When he steps up to solo, local weather officials declare a Severe Blammo Watch. That is, conditions are right for ear surgery without the scalpel.

You want names and places? We got names and places.

"Magic" and Russ Ballard's "I Surrender" are top-grade stompers with actual evidence of melody. "Spotlights" and "Freedom Fighter" go fast 'n' hard enough to have just got off the boat from Deep Purple's *Machine Head*. The colorful gents even toss in Beethoven's Ninth disguised as the title cut. It says so on the cover.

"Can't Happen Here" is the officially designated Killer Cut, with Blacky tying riffs into knots and then hacking them off at the break. Neato lyrics too: "Contaminated fish and micro chips / huge super tankers on Arabian trips / oily propaganda from the leaders' lips." *I got it* – the winning entry in the "Write A Song For Ritchie" competition? Close, but no pen-and-pencil set. Besides, what's most "important" is that the tune is such a hard driver, *you don't even notice the lyrics*. Is there any higher compliment?

Now for the biggie: why the letter "t" in Ritchie? Seems that his name was misspelled that way on the cover of the first DP album. Numerologically speaking, that made him a "six" instead of a "nine" (whatever that means) so he kept the Ritchie spelling.

Big deal!
May 1981

VAN HALEN
Fair Warning
(Warner Bros.)

Another hot one from Van Halen.

Evidentally, they weren't satisfied with mere slash attacks on the national ear, because this one will have fans everywhere mailing their brains to Shriner Burn Treatment Centers. Special delivery.

Nine cuts, eight killers, for a stomping percentage of look-it-up-yourself. There's lotsa three-four note riffs, two chord riffs, and the rare rhythm that makes "Sinner's Swing!" swing them sinners. Of course, if you have a musical sensitivity rating higher than a toolkit (i.e., sissy), *Fair Warning* might not be your cup of nitro. But if you're looking for top-of-the-line fast 'n' hard blamola that you can hear three area codes away, this is it.

A very special explosives team is assigned to Eddie V.H., whose completely insane ripping and jamming further cements his rep as Number-1 Heavy Metal guitar strangler. I counted 17 orgasms on side one alone, more than most folks could handle, uh, *One Day at a Time*. Ah, shit, Val, I thought you were saving yourself for me!

Roth is in fine form as well, the highlight being this campfire chat from the middle of "Unchained": "Hey man! That suit is you! Wooo-ee, you'll get some leg tonight for sure!" Then producer Ted Templeman's voice comes on the moniter and says, "C'mon David, gimme a break!" And they do.

Speaking of Ted, he gets platinum earplugs for an excellent job of clout-separation. His production is reminiscent of platters like Aerosmith's Toys In The Attic from the good old days of hyper-electric lip chatter.

Get it now, 'cause *Warning* has already copped Best Summer LP honors on my block. Bees sting walls, birds fly upside down, and butterflies dart off in terror when you crank it up. It may even mow your lawn.
May 1981

DEAD KENNEDYS
Fresh Fruit for Rotting Vegetables
(IRS)

CAROL HENSEL
Dancercize
(Vintage)

Everything but everything in this mad, mod world of ours is changing at a break-neck pace. Wristwatches calculate everything from slugging percentage to ovulation. Eggs can be scrambled without cracking the shell. And in what can only be called the Eighth Wonder of today's world, modern man can now answer his telephone through his TV set.

Is it any wonder, then, that the Pop Pscene is advancing even faster than Billy Altman with a new pair of scissors? After all, music comes from the soul (I think, or maybe the left elbow) and in these days of long yellow lights and the seedless cupcake, we all need *fast souls*.

Which brings us to one of the most advanced combos extant, the Dead Kennedys. With a sly ambiguity bordering on futuristic, these daddio cats have altered the very *form* of the long-playing record. That's right, they've ash-canned the traditional side one/side two approach in favor of a brilliant "face up"/"face down" format. Then, taking it all yet another great leap forward, the DKs perform tunes so proudly equal that even the most gifted listener *cannot tell which side is playing*! How novel, how daringly 1984!

The single most impressive track is definitely either "Kill the Poor" or "California Uber Alles." With an anguished vocal performance bordering on bedwetting, singer Jello Biafra recklessly rhymes neutron bomb with Jane Fonda and sportingly invites his audience to "jog for the master race." This is not mere *music*, this is climate control!

Other nest stains on the tree of enlightenment: a sterling tin updating of the Blues Magoos legend singularly titled "Let's Lynch the Landlord" or "Stealing People's Mail"; the waves of haunting cupid traffic hinted at in the unique "Drug Me" or "Ill In The Head"; and the one-in-a-million, never to be duplicated "Forward To Death" or "Kill the Children." A true dawg trash exorcism.

Speaking of exercising, newcomer Carol Hensel's *Dancersize* LP touches on a minimalist approach that can rightfully be called Wimp Dub. As her rhythm-heavy band bravely takes a conceptual walk off a short pier with a long pole, Carol –in a sing/talk style not unlike early Jim Stafford–recites her opaque lyrics ("touch left/touch right/lunge to the floor") in a detached manner similar to Blondie's "Rapture."

Having anticipated the current dance-rock modernism of such acts as the Talking Heads, Spandau Ballet and the Mandrell Sisters, Hensel's aerobic rhumbas virtually *define* the genre. "I Go To Rio," for example, builds gradually on a jetstream meow factor of the Big Beats until the musicians suddenly drop out, leaving Carol alone in the mix wailing, "snap your fingers/keep it loose/slap your knees/ready—hip twist/jump/hop/continue!" *Continue...* Eat your heart out, Bruce.

Ms. "Pre" Hensel is no elitist either. Amazing as it may seem, every song on this album sounds like a potential hit. From the heartrending *dooby doos* of "What A Fool Believes" to the lovely, if *greasy*, ballad "Summer Nights", all her tunes feature big mahooga hooks and an irresistible beat. It's no exaggeration when I say she could be the next Sugarhill Gang.

Although it seems unlikely that the Cleveland Songbird could top herself, she does just that in the final cut. Joined by second vocalist Tommy Chris, she slips easily into the currently popular Duet Syndrome to deliver a tune she calls "Just The Way You Are":

She: Let's cool it down

He: Don't go changing …

She: Get ready with the right leg

He: To try to please me …

She: Turn it over/legs apart!

With unforgettable material like that, is it any wonder that *Dancersize* is No. 72 with a white cross on the *Billboard* chart? Lyrics enclosed in both albums.
June 1981

GO-GO'S
Beauty and the Beat
(IRS/A&M)

I've gone googoo for the Go-Go's.

You will too, but you should probably play the record first: 11 neat little packages of irresistible hooks with a touch of '60s "girl group" action in the writing and singing. Not nearly as far gone as the B-52's, but in that direction.

I don't know much about these five women, who've outslitted the Slits in the ugly-LP cover sweepstakes. Big deal: Why bother knowing anything when the music is this good?

A typical Go-Go's cut features a melody that grabs your ears like the title beast in *Alien* grabs your face. The delivery is outstanding, whether individually wrapped sighs or ultra-smooth group vocals. Plus there's a fine beat, silky playing and all-white production from Richard Gottehrer and his pal Rob Freeman.

Another plus is the enigmatic, two-ply teen lyrics with a sly sense of humor. Stuff like "I need promises/You want *Motor Trend*" or the frankly epic "You can't walk in your sleep if you can't sleep."

This typewriter wants to type "smooth" every third word and it's right. There's an antsy-sexy muscle tone to the music that allows the album to stand as a whole, or in bite-sized snacks.

There's no dud tracks either, a regular in the filler world of normal album packaging. In fact, the closest near-dud ("Automatic") is 47.3 percent better than the best cut on any recent LP.

Got it? Get down and go gaga for the Go-Go's.
August 1981

QUEEN
Queen's Greatest Hits
(Elektra)

Queen's Greatest Pix
(Quartet Books)

There are two good things about greatest-hits collections. One is that when you get it, you can ignore all the act's other records. You've got the greatest – it says so right on the cover – so forget the others. Number 2 is that you don't have to actually *play* the thing because you already know all the songs.

So I was pretty damned pissed off when I found that the "nasty Queenies" (their words, not mine) had tagged "Under Pressure" – their recent collaboration with David Bowie – onto the LP, figuring it their next bigaroonie.

Personally, I hope it bombs. Mess around with my conveniences and you're toddlin' on my turf, daddio. I mean, would you buy individually wrapped cheese product slices if they were packed in chains? Or safe?

Of course not, except for you thumbbrains. It was bummer city, man! I had to dig my turntable out of the mountain of empty ZigZag and M&M packages, disconnect my speakers from the space heater, etc., etc. Any dope but me could have predicted the result: large quantities of Z. If you buy this record for "Under Pressure," I have some rotten boards with bent rusty nails sticking out for sale that I'd like you to take a look at.

Anyway, all the hits are here. The gum card opera. The American Nazi Party's cheer rip-off. The cute little ditty that makes best friends hate each other. Naturally, they left out the one Queen tune that I like, "Death Spins The Platter."

Meanwhile, *Queen's Greatest Pix* is a medium-sized trade paperback that's out in England and I think here soon. It costs four pounds sterling over there, which is equivalent to about $1.38 and a Goldblatt's rain check in U.S. funds.

What you get is 95 pages (27 American pages) of real good color stage snaps and B&W candids. All the pix are here. Freddie as angel in chinos. Brian trying to decide which bathroom to use. Big ugly security cops wielding iron yardsticks. And several faceless audiences waving their fists at the band. (I think they want to beat them up!)

Plus there's a brief text ("The first time I attended a Queen concert I fled in pain!" – Paul Gambaccini) and a good discography. In all, a beautiful gift item that you will want to spend countless seconds skimming.

Woof-woof! Uh-oh, here's Bernice the Research Dept. dog with a note saying there's no such Queen song as "Death Spins The Platter." Am I every silly! That's the title of an Ellery Queen mystery. You remember. The one where he tries to discover why all the people buy Queen records.
December 1981

ALICE COOPER

Special Forces

(Warner Brothers)

It's Halloween time again and you know what that means. Best Costume contests interrupting your serious drinking. Little kids writing "soap" on your windshield with candles. More screenings of the most over-rated horror movie of all time.

And, of course, Alice. He's been cranking 'em out every autumn longer than anybody can remember—if they *wanted* to—establishing his own standard of consistency. Besides, anybody who says their favorite color is money is OK with me.

Coop's tackled a couple of oldies here, one a tuffy, one not. The tuffy is Love's epic '60s smash, "Seven and Seven Is." If you're familiar with the original, the treatment here sounds like someone whipping a kiddie-size swimming pool with an artificial flower. If not, it's a pretty likeable cut, and Alice can *"oom-bip bip-yeah!"* with the best of them.

The E-Z one is his own "Generation Landslide," this time performed fairly hot in concert. That's right, this is the tune that contains flashes of lyrical genius such as the immortal "see ya/Korea" and "boyzees/toyzees" couplets.

Alice apparently can still recall his *Love It To Death* period, resulting in several highly reminiscent tracks. "Who Do You Think We Are" and "You Want It" are standard examples of his how-bad-am-I approach, while "Skeletons" is a bit meatier and features an actual *harpsichord*. Walk away, Renee!

"Don't Talk Old To Me" is new poop from the Coop, with catchy shadings of radio pop coloring the eat-me chorus. Also yummy is "You Look Good In Rags," which goes from a slightly Aerosmithish lipwalk into an *a capella* workout at the end that snuck away from the Beach Boys while they were arguing about the effects of birth order.

Minus a couple of supposed-to-be funny throwaways, *Special Forces* is as well-presented as any recent Cooper effort. And for you troublemakers that keep asking "*Why?*", don't bother me with it.

Go ask Alice!

September 1981

GARRISON

Garrison

(Spirit Records)

The word on Garrison is that they're some sort of all-star collection of ex-members of various OK Midwest groups none of which I've ever heard of. Let me try the names on you: Garrison Yerkins, Steve Frarey, Jim DeMonte, Keith Robbins and Earthquake Drake. Does that help any? Don't ask *me*. I'm the guy who thought Joe Jackson was from California, remember?

Garrison is fairly likeable in a fairly likeable way. Their more successful material is based on interacting riffs and low-key vocals, both of which Yerkins is responsible for. Oh, wait, *Ferguson* Yerkins; that's who I was thinking of before.

First thing you do if this LP comes into your possession is to tear up the lyric sheet as fast as you can and drop it from a small plane circling your neighborhood strip mine. The words sound pretty good as *sounds*, but as lyrics, they just don't hang together. Guess that means they'll have to hang separately.

Did I mention Elvis Costello? *Big* influence on Yerkins, particularly on vocals. Plus the aforementioned Joe J., whose "Happy Loving Couples" obviously served as the blueprint for the lead cut on side two, "Unwed Lovers." Better watch it, guys. Our good pal George "He's So Fine" Harrison didn't exactly get his wrist slapped in his plagiarism trial. And contrary to the popular belief, he *does have wrists*, not fins or tassles.

Did anyone come up with something on these guy's names? No? Well, send postcards. All contestants will receive a tiny portion of the Garrison lyric sheet, suitable for ignoring.

September 1981

LESTER BANGS & THE DELINQUENTS
Jook Savages On The Brazos
(Live Wire)

It must be the future already, because a comedy record worth playing more than once has arrived on the scene.

I think *three* spins oughta do it.

Lester Bangs — pivotal rock writer, dunce, Antichrist and Troggs fan extraordinaire — demonstrates once again that critics are just failed performers in their own particular field of *espertissimo*. Film critics want to be directors. *Smart* film critics want to be producers. Architecture critics, who really do exist, play with blocks at home. Except in Kansas City, where they get to play with real buildings. *Wheee!*

And rock critics…well, hold the phone! Lester's music falls (or was it pushed?) into the usual spray-on *avant* dada chatter data of musicians who can't really play or sing or any of that stuff. Over the Delinquents' bare-bulb attack of rat guitars and shopping carts in heat, Bangs combines the raw vocal elements of Lou Reed, Jim Morrison, Porky Pig, Kurtis Blow, Bob Dylan, the Godz and Iggy into one big calico beanbag from the dark side of "catchy."

The 10 originals here demonstrate a style of songwriting that, if it were a nuthouse or prison, would be described as "seriously understaffed." Top cut is "Accident of God," a likeable torment featuring some great Disney-influenced "Sister Ray" psychobabble. Another hot one is "Fade Away", which is slightly reminiscent of the Thirteenth Floor Elevators during there where's-the-stage? period. The surprise cut is "Life Is Not Worth Living (But Suicide's a Waste of Time)", a cagey country-punk tune featuring an actual *banjo* that they were too embarrassed to mention on the cover.

The one time I'd like to see a lyric sheet it's no dice, little campers. Foghat, Krokus and even REO Speedwagon give you their horrible lyrics, but Lester's horrible lyrics have to be guessed at, which is probably the manner in which they were written in the first place. Other than the sly pairing-up of "slime" and "time" in "Suicide," most of the words vanish in the hurricane curtains of Bangs' unique sing/talk/whimper/stutter style.

Do *you*, the listener, want to own this record? Only if your sense of humor is functioning at the grate/puree level of conceptual arf-arf. *You*, the collector, might be interested, or even *you*, the dogcatcher. But not *you*, the Sheena Easton fan.

In case they aren't stocking this at your local Jaycees pancake breakfast, Live Wire Records (and tapes!) can be obtained directly from them in Austin, Texas.

But, Lester, don't quit your day job.

September 1981

JACK LEE
Greatest Hits, Vol. 1
(Maiden America Records)

Technically speaking, Jack Lee doesn't have any greatest hits of his own, but he *should*. Blondie had a big English smash with his "Hanging On The Telephone" (the first song Lee ever wrote), and included his "Will Anything Happen" on an LP. Plus, he's penned tunes for Rachel Sweet and Frankie Miller.

I know—*big deal*—let's try this approach. Jack Lee was one-third of The Nerves, who were the ultimate progenitors of the entire L.A. scene. His teammates were Paul Collins, now head of The Beat (Yanks, not to be confused with the English Beat) and Peter Case, now with the Plimsouls. So there you have two the very finest contemporary recording rock groups. If you like either of their records, you should also like *Greatest Hits*. This is *not* a request.

Jack's composing chops evolved as a kid in Sitka, Alaska, where he apparently spent all this time listening to '60s Beatles and Stones records. Maybe go watch a walrus, polish the igloo real quick, and then back to the juke.

The material here is uniformly solid. His sound—built around a basic if not stark guitar attack—leaves lots of room for deadly hooks and ladders. There's strong vocals too, sounding like the aforementioned Collins tackling some John Hiatt tunes.

Hits' hooks to click include the inevitable favorites "Good Times" and "Give Me Some Time," as well as "Come Back and Stay," where our hero rips off George Harrison, of all people. (If Georgie ever notices his own "Don't Bother Me" enclosed within "Come Back," he's going to sue for bloody murder even in his wilted state. After all, he's got to try to make back of the cash he's blowing as a film producer).

Hard-edged tracks like "It's Hot Outside" and the true-but-so-what "Crime Doesn't Pay" keep the LP strictly out of Cutesville, not that the more melody-pronged cuts are in any way soft. His own version of "Hanging On The Telephone" far surpasses Blondie's, containing as its does actual desperation.

If you can't find this record at your local razorblade sharpening stand or pacemaker factory outlet store, try Maiden America Records (and Films!) in Los Angeles, Calif. It's Lee's own label and he only pressed 10,000 copies.

The Maiden America label has to go anyway, because it's a shameless steal from Slick 'Em and Kitchen Magician's own Maiden Macomb undistributed one-copy-only reel-to-reel tape with genuine tinfoil on the box. If *those* characters decide to sue, poor Jack may well be *cheeseless for life.*
October 1981

VARIOUS UK ARTISTS
Apprentice Dance
(Sounds Interesting)

The *Apprentice Dance*, go the credits, is a collection of debut recordings from the musicians of Poole Dorset, UK. Wherever that is (by Dakota, I think).

The artists can be protestingly dragged and forcibly squeezed into three categories. Hell, *anything* can be shoved into three categories. Pringles, religions, left-handed pitchers, birds of prey, Kellogg's Nutra-Grain cereals, bamboo, life itself. Three categories. Nice and neat.

Group One consists of wacky British turf groups Da Biz and Surfin' Dave. Da Biz hit hard with "On The Beach" (a grows-on-you representative of the "can't wait 'til summer comes" school of PARTY!), plus the highly singalong-able "This Is No Audition."

Surfin' Dave, on the other hand, display a neat sense of humor on their very stripped-down cuts. It's not unlike a drunk DJ playing early Beach Boys through a conch woofer.

All of side two falls (or was it tripped?) into the second category, which is a bit of a catch-all. Executive producer Charles P. Lamey calls it "a bit more experimental, but it still has melodies." Couldn'ta said it better myself, Chipper.

Paul Chambers is the real stand-out performer of the album, demonstrating able musicianship and, above all, good material on his two tracks. Both are very vaguely in the New Romatics direction, but are far too likeable for that genre, particularly "Steering Solo."

The Hollows provide two interesting folk-rockish tunes, with the required bossy bass player but featuring more thump. Ditto Ca Va Ca Va on "Man In Sorrow."

The final washload is raw-but-enthusiastic pop units Tours and Contacts. The Tours' "Language School" is a hot one, reminiscent of the first Sorrows LP. Contacts are OK, but they lost me during "Young Girls" when they say they want 'em 16 years old. C'mon guys, you can do better than that! Play your cards right and I'll show you my *Guide to Midwest Nursery Academies* map, color-coded as to severity of local statutory rape ordinances.

All right, we got 14 cuts in all with only one major stink spill (Ca Va Ca Va's skin-crawling "Chinese Voices"). Give it a spin and keep an ear peeled for more Paul Chambers.
January 1982

154

MONDO ROCK

Mondo Rock Chemistry

(Atlantic)

I had to give this one a spin because it reminded me of a "Mondo Rock" record column for a local rag, which had this total no-talent who'd scribble it out in five minutes every other week, viciously attacking LPs unfortunate enough to be released that month.

Great attitude, but no commercial potential.

That particular hackster (ahem) went on to udder things, but speaking of no commercial potential – meet Mondo Rock the GROUP. From Australia (strike one), they have bassist with two first names (Paul Christie: strike two) and a cover with a lotta pink (strike three).

Their music (strike four) is conventional mainstream diddle that falls somewhere between AC/DC and Split Enz. Really narrows it down, right? How about lightweight AC/DC with a few melodies that go right to work? Close enough.

I'm not one to kick a good melody out of bed, though. The unlikely-to-be-a-smash "Step Up Step Out" is frankly unthreatening and the other good-ie, "Cool World," grows on you at least as fast as guilt.

Cuts range from medium rockers (the aforementioned "Step Up ... ") and horrid ballads ("We're No Angels") to useless-in-any-context splat (such as "Mondo Sexo").

Adam Ant died for this?

A handy lyric sheet is included should you want to memorize a few grease spots like the refrain from "Mondo Sexo":

"Oh oh
Mondo sexo
Oh oh oh
Sexy nudo
Ooh-ah Ooh-ah
Ooh-ah ooh-ah
That's Mondo
That's Sexo
It makes you want to go
'AAARRRGGGHHH!!!' "

The *self-criticizing record*!
What'll they think of next?
February 1982

XTC

English Settlement

(Virgin/Epic)

I got dem lowdown good side/bad side blues again, mama.

This time it's the new XTC. Upfront, I think it's great for artists to put all the yummy tracks on one side and the undercooked brain niblets on the other. Saves people a lot of time at the PAUSE button.

So let's go with the good side. Number-1, of course. Why the record biz doesn't go with single-sided LPs (a la *Second Winter*, record two), I'll never know. It'd certainly put a dent in everybody's new material problems (I'm talking to you, Steve Miller). Not to mention the artists' fees and royalties saved.

Anyway, the first half of *EngSet* is very close to the group's previous effort, Black Sea, which is far and away their best set ever. The somehow precise mixture of post-WW4 jungle boogie, brainy lyrics and highly contagious hooks proved mucho accessible both ear and chart-wise.

Colin Moulding's new comps, in fact, sound like he's been listening to his old Genesis and Stackridge records again. That's not a complaint. His two cuts on side one are remarkably catchy, especially the keyboard figures in "Ball and Chain." *Not* the Janis Joplin biggie incidentally.

The second side is for fans who really like XTC's chant-and-destroy numbers. On these, it sounds like bossman Andy "Keith" Partridge decided to throw out their last album and be a Talking Heads with a singer instead of a highly mobile optometrist's kids-to-college fund.

Lots of percussion again – drumbo Terry has the most extensive drum kit in the history of bambam, including a stuffed trampoline, a junior weightlifter's outfit, a scale model of downtown Poughkeepsie, some cheap aluminum siding with hail damage, a partially frozen sand dune, several dozen tintype cookies and all the meat mallets east of Belgium.

The beat is overlaid by too much Asteroid Belt for this meat 'n' potatoes listener. Worse is the inclusion of some of the most laughable lyrics since the Swingin' `60s. "Melt The Guns" is anti-TV violence (snore), "No Thugs" charmingly compares housewives to insects, and the biggie, "It's Nearly Africa," is – well … see for yourself: "Go tell your stale friends/go tell false prophets and drug traffickers/not to try to push our bodies any faster." Just so happens that some of my stale friends are here right now, so I'm gonna try it on `em.

HEY! *You stale friends over there! Go hump a prophet, man!*

No reply – guess I got `em that time!

One more thing, XTC: Will you lay off the understated avocado album covers? This place is starting to look like a showroom for appliance dustcovers.
April 1982

"Only 67¢" & other capsules

Not too many years ago, when the music biz wasn't as intense as it is today, records that didn't sell generally went the route of scrap paper. (In fact, there is a housing project in easy New Jersey constructed almost entirely from the ground-up remains of leftover copies of *The Singing Nun*.)

One day, however, some bright retailer found that by reducing the price of dud LPs by a dollar or two, he could breathe new commercial life into them and avoid writing them off as a complete loss. All it took was a sticker that said, "WAS $5.98—OSCO PRICE $1.97" so that people would know what a good deal they were supposed to be getting.

Besides being the final resting place for several thousand Lovin' Spoonful albums, the bins abound with obscure taste threats that – considering the current glut of low-grade hot dogs – are frequently more interesting than the higher-priced spread.

PROCESSION (Smash): Procession has a commercial-progressive sound similar to early Traffic or maybe the Moody Blues minus pretension that should have gored the charts but now goes for 87 cents in the bin by the Excedrin PMs.

HERD/ *Lookin' Thru You* (Fontana): Fronted by Peter Frampton and Andy Brown, the Herd shared top cream dream honors with the Small Faces, leaving a mass of slippery seats whenever they stopped to sing their hits.
August 1973

∎

13th Floor Elevators/ *Live* (IA): Yer not gonna hear any twaddle about washed-out smellbags blowing bubbles on their Mood synthesizers from us – at least not when you can still dig in to a bargain bin right net to the Fasteeth display and pick up on a band who did up all their sound effects on an electric jug – a band whose lead singer was so flaked out that he had to be led *on*stage by the hand – who put out a fake live album that used the exact same canned applause after every song — and whose record label was responsible for coating all their covers with the most vomit-inducing acid grotesqueries this side of strychnine. The 13th Floor Elevators are the world's greatest unappreciated psychotic rock band, who terrorized their fellow Texans with some of the most controlled manic hostility known to rock music outside of the Velvet Underground and Syd Barrett's Pink Floyd. In the background of almost every 'Vators song is an overdubbed dubdub that's about halfway between TV's *Sea Hunt* scuba bubbles and an astronaut farting in zero gravity. Their "She Lives in a Time of Her Own" is a chiller that puts the entire folk-rock genre to shame, with its rarefied harmonies working off a bass line that's in an awful hurry to get somewhere, preferably between your legs.
November 1973

∎

The McCoys/ *Human Ball* (Mercury): The recent ascension of ex-McCoy and present All-American Boy Rick Derringer is a bonus for budget-bin-busters, since some good early work exists for as low as 22 cents at discriminating Monolith Marts throughout the Midwest. This finds the McCoys live in New York City, waiting around to give Johnny Winter the best band he's ever had. The songs are cynical, self-consciously shocking, pretty lame stuff. But the band pulls it together very now and again, and Derringer always was pretty good.

The Everly Brothers/ *Roots* (Collectors Choice): Old Everly Brothers albums are now turning up for the discerning cutout inspector willing to spend $2 to hear the sweetest, best pair of singers rock will ever breed. This, their best album, can be had for $1.69. It is beyond price. Of a level of *Sgt. Pepper* and *Buffalo Springfield Again*, this record truly captures the Everlys at the last of many peaks. "Illinois," the first Randy Newman song I can remember, is here; so is "Shady Grove," maybe the best version ever done by anyone anywhere ever period.

January 1974

■

Wimpy music's been with us a long time. In fact, it's been an integral patina on pop music ever since "Toot Toot Tootsie" and "An Angel Peed on Me Last Night." It's the staple of AM radio, the tinkling consumer hook of TV commercials, and the eerie tin violins that cover up the cash register dings at Kmart. Studies by creepy psychologists show that all you need in your store is some wimply canned Muzak and a Coke machine in the corner by the drinking fountain, and people will trance out and buy useless plastic things to hang on their walls, stick on their refrigerators or leave in a convenient place in the kitchen.

Wimp's main selling point is its total accessibility.

What we wanna do here is just take a very quick look at some of the superb wimp that's been surfacing in the 67-cent bins lately.

INNOCENCE (Kama Sutra): Led by the sorta famous songwriting team of Anders-Poncia, Innocence gained a bit of cash with a dipped-up version of "Mairzy Doats," then promptly vanished behind a film of beautiful melodies and cute diedeez, Most of their album is superb NYC-oriented vocal stuff, all very catchy but dangerous to play near easily influenced child molesters.

EVERY MOTHER'S SON (MGM): Most everybody remembers these puds from "Come on Down to My Boat," and rightfully so – it was a perfect summer song and both of their albums (especially their first) are great for making pigeon-mouth on the beach. If you want credentials, one of 'em is now leading Rick Nelson's Stone Canyon Band, but if you *really* want credentials, it sez on the cover of the first album that "Chris believes in the Easter Bunny."

MAGIC LANTERNS/ *Shame Shame* (Atlantic): Here's where we gotta draw the line 'tween wimps and twerps. Twerps are the kinda guys that sniff little girls' bicycle seats. They pee their pants during reruns of *Circus Boy*. The Magic Lantern are twerps. "Shame Shame" was a smasheroo and the rest is of equal neatness – the kinda stuff that would make Karen Carpenter see paisley Tinkerbells.

HARPER & ROWE (World Pacific): Every cheapo bin in the Midwest contains at least 25 copies of this, so one day I bought one just so the next guy wouldn't have so many to look at. Turns out it's a real fine wimpy frosting wipe.

SAGITTARIUS/ *Present Tense* (Columbia): One of the most outstandingly dippy wimp artists of all time, Sag was mainly the brainchild of Gary Usher (producer of such fave raves as the Byrds, Chad & Jeremy, the Wackers, and the Peanut Butter Conspiracy) and Curt Boetcher (who produced the Association's "Cherish"). They had their hit single with "My World Fell Down," a piece of Beach Boys sheep fluff, and their LP features tones of memorable melodies and ice cream harmonies. These same two were also the mainmen (along with Crabby Appleton's Mike Fennelly) behind Millennium, whose *Begin* LP (also on Columbia) out-pussied even this.

So anyway, this wasn't meant to be an authoritative rim job on wimp pimpery, just a glance at some of the stuff that's more likely to turn up along with all the overstocked David Crosby albums at your local plastic

store. There's tone of other prize poodles, like the Turtles, the Clique, Heard, Lemon Pipers, Kitchen Magician, Merry Go Round, Emmit Rhodes, etc. – all very digestible stuff. Try it at yer next Tupperware party.
May 1974

■

"Mondo Rock"

DAN FOGELBERG/ *Captured Angel* (Epic): Dan didn't just leave Peoria; he was pushed. He's one of those guys who drag a stool and a guitar to every party and sing Joni Mitchell songs until everyone gets bed spins. Now that he writes his own Joni Mitchell songs, he's big time. Just keep this album away from the fridge or the cheese will spoil.

FOCUS/ *Mother* (Atlantic): You have to give these clowns a couple of points for recording a song called "I Need A Bathroom," but it still all sounds like snails menstruating to me.

NEIL SEDAKA/ *The Hungry Years* (Rocket): Neil's first all-new American album in years is packed with enough class pop poop to make terminal wimps see cupcake mirages. Lots of great radio music, including "Bad Blood" and a new version of "Breaking Up is Hard to Do." You too can be a sissy.

BLACK OAK ARKANSAS/ *X-Rated* (MCA): There weren't any good heavy metal albums released last week, so this will have to do. Jim Dandy has toned down his gobble a bit and the production is tighter than ever, making for some good thud music to drain kegs by.

RUSH/ *Caress of Steel* (Elektra): Anemic Led Zep with rats sneezing in the background.

ABBA (Atlantic): The "Waterloo" folks are back. Lots of stupid titles and pleasantly dumb music.

AMON DUUL II/ *Made in Germany* (Atlantic): More Nazi-go-lucky from the original space drones. Great titles like "Loosey Girls" and "Top of the Mud," but the music suffers from the same zero-zone syndrome that afflicts all the post-*Cabaret* German dope bands. Like watching *Hogan's Heroes* on acid.
September 1975

■

AMERICA/ *America's Greatest Hits* (Warners): All their good ones, like "Sister Goldenhair," plus others that can melt ice cream at 50 yards.

Kiss/ *Kiss Alive!* (Casablanca): Not technically a hits job, but it does have their best antipersonnel tunes.

JIM CROCE/ *The Faces I've Been* (Lifesong): That guy was so dormant when he was alive that his death was redundant.

LITTLE FEAT/ *The Last Record Album* (Warners): A once great band now pawing through the kitty litter.

LUCIFER'S FRIEND/ *Banquet* (Passout): Suggest an Axis Powers revival as these dizzy Krauts invent space-wop-rock that sounds like the Buckinghams playing Pink Floyd.
December 1975

■

LOGGINS & MESSINA/ *Native Son* (Columbia): The highlight – the disco-styled Chipmunks-meet-Sly-Stone number, "Sweet Marie." Although "Pretty Princess" nearly outdips "Wildfire" for wimpy tear-slag, the only complete tidal smell is "When I Was A Child," based as it is on Messina whimpering, "Time gas no mercy." Right, Jim, and snake have no elbows!

BAD COMPANY/ *Run with the Pack* (Swan Song): Bad Company really should be a great band – what with Paul Rodgers' woke-up-with-an-itchy-crotch growl and Mick Ralph's hot punk guitar – but somehow they just don't make it. Their main problem is a near total absence of songwriting ability. Ralph's songs are all standard Maytag progressions that run off into plant-life choruses, and Rodger's one-chord acoustic-guitar-dominated ballads are even duller.

GRAND FUNK RAILROAD/ *Born to Die* (Capitol): This is one of their best, the doom-content of the title cut alone whipping the nihil-input of the Doors and Black Sabbath combined.
March 1976

∎

BILL WYMAN/ *Stone Alone* (Rolling Stones Records): Wyman's second solo LP, this is worse than anyone could reasonably expect, with his "voice" taking on new levels of sub-Ringo dog pain.
April 1976

∎

CRAWLER/ *Snake, Rattle & Roll* (Columbia): Mainstream shotgun effort that should appeal to folks who *love* FM radio. I bet these guys wouldn't drink a glass of water without first adding some Water Helper.
October 1978

∎

HUEY LEWIS & THE NEWS (Chrysalis): Sounds like the Sanford/Townshend band performing the best of Elvis Costello.
February 1981

∎

The '60s were just like the '70s — only they came sooner

Lawrence Welk's eat-it-right-out-of-the-pan approach to the Nothing World of television stuck with me, and helped me through the years to understand such diverse cultural phenomenon as *Real People*, Cher's tits, the Gerald Ford administration, and commercials suggesting that you redecorate your home with attractive mirrors. A game-show host without a game, Welkie was one of the first to condense Low Budget into an art form – on the tube, at least.

Brief B-movies for viewers with brief B-expectations.
March 1981

160

Norelco fear: TV

Summer Reruns

Summer's back and you know what that means. Right – heat, sweat, sweat-eating bugs, broken glass, inhaling beach-ball fumes, all that good stuff. The whole world turns into a Nat King Cole song.

But another thing you can always count on come June is the prime time of re-runs. The only new shows on TV are rejected pilots starring Mary Ann Mobley and variety hours hosted by Peggy Cass or Paul Lynde, And would you believe some jukebox-brains actually watch that stuff? Hell, how do you think Tony Orlando and Dawn made it? People look at *TV Guide* and say, "Nothing but repeats. I'll watch anything else!" A star is born.

Well, if you don't like reruns, you're missing the whole point of successful tube abuse, slowpoke. When a show is removed from the context of prime time, all kinds of yuk pointers begin to stand out. Already knowing the story, you can concentrate on Jaclyn Smith's tireless delayed-action approach to "acting" or Edward Asner keeping an audience on the edge of their shoes using only his forehead. Secret continuing jokes become apparent and there's time to figure out important items like the layout of Felix and Oscar's apartment. Besides, you can never really understand a show until you've watched it regularly in your underwear

Wiener Wrap

Of course, the real action is in daytime television, that great bargain bin of the airwaves. If a show can survive five days a week of desperate-straits afternoon-fear, it has to be good. In fact, some shows have achieved cult status mainly through their continued exposure via repeats. Forget *Star Trek* – legions of *Dick Van Dyke Show* fanatics argue about the exact pointy-ness of Laura's bras in seedy, late-night bars. The entire hierarchy of *Leave it to Beaver* is available on T-shirts, even Larry Mondello. There are guys who will slit your throat over the names of obscure character actors on Hazel.

Reflecting the wiener-wrap quality of recent programming, the last few years of prime-time product has fared pretty poorly in the grim light between disembodied *Rocky & Bullwinkle* episodes. While some goodies like *The Partridge Family* are starting to look like neglected gems, *Room 222* and *Brady Bunch* will always leave appalled viewers throwing their baby food at the screen

More recent winners like *All in the Family* and *Sanford and Son* are still too new to tell. Old hippie and hardhat jokes that currently induce stomach reprisals might be really funny again by 1984, and maybe kids that didn't grow up on Jethro and Granny can take Redd Foxx at 9 a.m. without muttering into their cereal.

Chihuahua Tongues

The real test, however, will come later this year when *The Mary Tyler Moore Show* hits the grainy daytime screen. While the best '60s sitcoms indulged in fairly subtle (for TV) characterizations, MTM is the most finely tuned example of the best '70s programs' approach: Hit the audience over the head with a baseball bat while simultaneously tickling their pickle.

If you don't buy that, sports fans, we'll rub *MTM* up against *Dick Van Dyke* (the author is harping) and see if we can roast some weenies. Want to show that Lou Grant is tuff-with-a-heart-of-Twinkies? Just have him weep profusely for three straight shows and the summies'll get it. On DVD, the best you ever got out of Allen Brady is an off-note swivel of his chair, but one gets the idea. It only took bald lackey Mel 10 minutes in six seasons to establish his underdog respect on Van Dyke, but Mary (or Murray) had to quit every third show and nearly pout to death before us morons in antenna-land caught on. She's mad, I get it, huh-huh-huh. Gimme back my crayons, Doc.

Based as they are on the premise that TV fans have a collective brain the size of a Chihuahua tongue, the '70s-spawned re-runs are going to have a tough time diverting viewer attention away from their stamp collections. Really now, can you see Millie and Jerry Halper living next door to Rhoda?

Quit Your Job

But enough of this griping, there's too much great stuff on the tube right this very minute to waste any time thinking. What you should immediately do, right now, is quit your job, turn on the set and *start absorbing*.

Based on a comprehensive poll of national media critics on my block, we now exclusively reveal the five shows worth missing a food-stamp interview for:

McHale's Navy – the crew is captured by natives but they escape when Tim Conway dons witch doctor garb and darkly chants, "In-A-Gadda-Da-Vidda."

Andy Griffith – Opie accidentally discovers that Aunt Bea is actually his mother. Fun and laughter ensue.

The Honeymooners – Ralph and Norton go into the potato-lure business and do a TV commercial. Ralph freezes, his eyeballs turning into Easter eggs, and Norton Nortons their way out of it. An early double fake-out.

The Adventures of Superman – You pick the episode, This is the only double fake-out drama left on television. It's so intentionally dumdum that it's not, but now that even that angle no longer holds, it's dumdum again (but everyone thinks they know, so it's still not, therefore it must be). Yes, it's Superman, strange visitor from another planet.

Dick Van Dyke – Rob has one of his dreams-within-a-dream where Kolak (Danny Thomas) of the planet Twylo leaves Absorbitron-filled walnuts everywhere; the nuts make humans breathe water and lose their thumbs and imaginations. You haven't lived until you've seen Mary Tyler Moore (c. 1964) come rolling out of the living room closet on a wave of walnuts.

Dirty Water

Another pointless treat to look forward to is rock groups on sitcoms.

Not that long ago, rockers were small enough draws to make all kinds of cameos. During Beatles '65, producers were slipping on each other's jelly-beans trying to lure any Limey on their show, and even the Flower Power days attracted their share of "these kids are weird, but they're real Charlies" efforts as well. The Number-1 classic in this category goes to the Standells' shot on *The Munsters*. After a weekend house party at Fred and Lily's – complete with beatniks and bongo-bongo – all Fred can say is "I'm going to sleep a lot better tonight knowing that the future of America is in the hands of boys like the Standells."

Another good one is Chad & Jeremy as the "Rockin' Redcoats" on *Van Dyke*. They use the Petries' home as a hideaway before their appearance on *Allen Brady*, but the kids find out anyway and have orgasm workshops on their New Rochelle front lawn. Besides other highlights including Phil Spector playing himself on *I Dream of Jeannie*, there was Commander Cody & His Lost Planet Airmen dancing it up and staring at Angie's bod on an episode of *Police Woman* (which of course hasn't gone into syndication yet, but nevertheless will turn up somewhere in this summer's wasteland of current shows' re-runs), Little Feat's Lowell George as a drunken pony gynecologist on *F Troop*, and, of course, the classic Rolling Stones appearance on *Bewitched*, where Keith playfully rips off Samantha's dress before they discretely cut to a Kitchen Magician commercial. Next scene is Sam dreamily brushing her hair and softly humming "Satisfaction" while Darrin fumes in the background.
June 1977

The Teevee Jee Bees

Blame it on the PTA. Blame it on the Baptist/Catholic Church conspiracy. Blame it on the voodoo psychologists. Blame it on the bossa nova. But most of all, blame it on that stupid kid in Florida who let the air out of some old ladies and then said he learned it all on *Kojak*.

The fall TV schedule is their fault. Too much violence, they said. Soon, everyone old enough to pull a trigger will be out in the streets gunning down patrol boys, raping baby carriages and stealing embossed bookmarks from Jesus creeps. Then, after the last supermarket is pillaged for its cat-food, the Commies will move in and make us turn in our comic books and wear gray jammies.

So the chief network quiverwrists, fearful that the government – or worse yet, Proctor & Gamble – would step in and put clothespins on their dinky you-know-whats, erased every last sign of mayhem, replacing good clean death with strained apricots. *Starsky & Hutch* will now sing their villains into submission. *Police Woman* will plea-bargain with self-snapped Polaroids and Kojak punishes the bad guy (who read magazines at a drugstore without buying them!) in his season opener by putting a sucker stick in his mouth and making him run down a treacherously steep hill.

But as Sparks once said: "Ha ha on the girls now." All the chop-chop has been replaced with the one thing that bothers these stiff-necks the most

– SEX! Little did they know, instead of shooting robbers, they'll be shooting beavers, and the church-lurches have only themselves to blame. That oughta teach 'em to mess with the sensory bombers of TV land.

Tube sex mainly boils down to winks, leers and tits, just like real life. The first televised donkey-hump may still be a way off, but if you use your imagination (look it up) you can find all kinds of video whoa-whoa in the new season. The one everybody's got their bloodshots on is *Charlie's Angels*. The new breast in town, Cheryl Ladd, has already created a booming business for TV repairmen called in to clean tongue stains from sullied screens, and even Kate Jackson's school-teacher bod looks a bit chummier. She has a neck! Now if they can just thaw out that old Wella-Wella somehow, hormones nationwide can end their hunger strike!

The other big sex bulletin of the year is the blooming of Marie Osmond. While the very idea of doing *anything* to a young Mormon may be palatable only to true deserters from adult sexuality, you have to give ABC credit. They gave her a Little Richard hairdo and makeup job, dressed her in boots and rags, and removed the steel rod from her spine. This is supposed to make five-year-old boys everywhere stop mentally undressing grasshoppers and start yearning for an invite to the ongoing pajama party in her bomb shelter. Can a Runaways cartoon hour be far behind?

Several of the "new" shows are also taking the gland-hand approach. *Soap* is bound to be an instant smash on the order of *The Johnny Carson Show*, It does contain lots of genuine humor amidst the secretion though, which is more than can be said for some of the others. *Love Boat*, with Gavin MacLeod of MTM fame, is merely *Love American Style* interjected with sardine wit. Hopefully, they'll take after *LAS* and have Carol Wayne guest star every other show. No chance of her drowning with those water wings! *Operation Petticoat* is another wet one, as Five Shapely Nurses join Mr. Patty Duke on a leaky sub, leading to more periscope jokes than anyone could possibly find useful. On dry land in *On Our Own* (who else would want 'em?) and the return of *Three's Company*, featuring four boobs and a dummy.

But who cares about sex anyway? What this country needs is more *action*. There won't be any kids killing junkie milkmen this year, so get ready for lots of *nice* action. The big hit looks like *ChiPs*, which is not about Pringle banditos but about the California Highway Patrol. In what may be the first example of the access-ramp genre in which the white line has more personality than the stars, two clean-but-dumb *Rookies*-types use spatulas to rescue hapless drivers pinned under girder trucks and give bad guys wrong directions. *Man From Atlantis* may also make it with Patrick Duffy's superhuman kelp-breath and several multi-talented squid. Best of the losers are *Big Hawaii*, kind of a *Bonanza* in grass skirts with Cliff Potts as the wise guy with the lawn mower, and *Logan's Run*, which continues the cardboard futurity of the film.

If those aren't funny enough for you, there are 10 million new comedies to choose from. One catch, though: Comedies, with few exceptions, are no longer funny. They're heart-warming. So is puke and that's what these are. Thanks to our much-beloved pressure groups, family shows are all over the place, and not Manson family either. These all have at least 14 kids of every possible age and a dog. Mom is a cookie engineer for the PTA, Dad sells plant insurance and they all live happily in a big house on Moo Avenue. In short, *Father Knows Best*. All is not lost, though, because they always have a daughter or three with big 'uns, like *The Fitzpatricks*. Better yet, it takes place in Flint, Mich., home of Grand Funk, and one of the kids is always going around shirtless with a bicep bracelet yelling "People let's stop the war!" Can't miss.

A handful of sitcoms and comedy-cum-dramas (but no plain cum dramas) look promising. Betty White has an entire show to her apron-like self, but they missed a golden opportunity by not casting real-life hubby Allen Ludden as her blank spouse. Fortunately, the non-personality gap is filled by my personal hero, Tom Posten, in *We've Got Each Other*, a klutz glorification project also starring one of Bob Newhart's patients and Nancy Walker's post-*Rhoda* TV daughter, old test-tube nose Beverly Archer. Whether Ed Asner's *Lou Grant* spin-off will be more ha-ha or more boo-hoo remains to be seen, and *Rosetti and Ryan*, this season's lawyers show, faces the same rubber see-saw.

Variety shows make their last gasp this fall. Redd Foxx is going to give it a try (goodbye, Redd!), as is Richard Pryor — although Pryor is already trying to fink out on his contract before his career vanishes into the game show void. Sha Na Na and Wolfman Jack also have syndicated shows that will undoubtedly be wiped out by *The Muppets*. Variety nothing. The papers called it suicide.

To keep viewers off-balance so they won't realize how zero the new shows are, the networks have all kinds of specials and mini-series coming up. The blockbuster that wasn't, *Washington Behind Closed Doors*, wasn't bad, but they couldn't get Andy Griffith to play LBJ, sp why couldn't they have Don Knotts as Hubert Humphrey? What they should do is make a mini-series of R. Meltzer's *Gulcher*. Can you see a two-hour dramatization of "Surefire Methods for Lunkers" or "Grappling's Cascade of Blood?" No such luck. What we get is stuff like *Loose Change* (four women learning how to string beads in the '60s), *Aspen* (opens with a slight, dark-haired girl zooming down a ski slope, smoking revolver in hand, humming "Moon River"), *Brave New World* (more cut-on-dotted-lines future muck) and *Boys and Girls Together*, which isn't so hump-filled as it sounds. Also, there are specials on teenage alcoholism (not a how-to guide, unfortunately), the Beatles, Doonesbury, Vietnam, the Kennedy assassination, and the little-reported Ford assassination. For this they pre-empt *Laverne & Shirley*?

There is one major development of cosmic importance: *The Mary Tyler Moore Show* finally hits the rerun circuit. Now you can watch the putty fall off her face every single day! No sense re-wiring those boredom circuits all the way. *September 1977*

165

Blue Jammies & Kitten Lips

Talk about your strange visitors from another planet – George Reeves was one of the strangest. Although various George-watchers insist that the actor had no difficulties distinguishing between himself and the Man of Steel in real life, you have to wonder. He did, after all, regularly trot around in costume, soliciting funds for kids with legs like pliers and other worthy charities, even going door-to-door on some occasions. Did Jimmy Olsen ever do that?

Reeves also made appearances on *I Love Lucy* and other shows, which was odd for an actor who was supposedly trying to shed that image. It's not like Desi Arnaz had guested on *Superman*, leading an army of deadly conga pods or anything. No, Reeves just couldn't turn down an opportunity to flash his cape on screen. (Of course, he did manage to pick up one of Little Ricky's drumsticks.)

Then there was his bizarre appearance on *Our Miss Brooks* as Mr. Boynton's brother Bill. Bill is one of those deadbeats with a heart of gold who fixes stuff around the house while eating everything in sight. Really sickening, in short, and his remarkable resemblance to tube-brain Boynton doesn't help any. It's a long story, but Walter Denton ends up with a mouthful of some weird laboratory slime, enabling Reeves to get off the best line of his career: "Don't come any closer, Walter, I can smell your teeth from here."

But George's brief spell of devil tongue doesn't make up for the ending, where – you guessed it – Superman appears to give the students a cornball speech about finishing high school. Connie notices Bill is missing, but Boynton takes the air out of her suspicions with some stupid story about nightspins and bunkbed fear. When somebody invents canned vomit, I want to be a stockholder.

Another thing to consider is howcum they picked a guy who looks like somebody's dad to play the strongest man in the universe? You could hit that tinsel jaw of his with a wet pretzel and knock him through a wall! And who could resist when faced with George's perpetual wise-guy expression, a sickly cross between Tony Randall and Sid Vicious at his most pimped-out. It's no wonder Superman was always getting attacked – the crooks really didn't care about the money, they just wanted to wipe that goddamn look off his face.

It was the sick-but-true personality split between Superman as hero and Superman as total puss that finally did in George Reeves. He wanted his character to protect all the macho hoodoo inherent in such a role, but came off as old picklepuss George in blue jammies. You can see it in his other roles too, especially the westerns where he tried so fervently to be a villain that he actually grew a moustache and learned how to pronounce "hombre" phonetically. It was no use, though. He'd ride up on a half-dead horse, waving a shotgun and clutching his Chuck Connors baseball cards in his vest, and the first thing you say is, "There's old kitten lips trying to act hard!"

It didn't take long for it to dawn on Reeves that he was doomed to a bit role lifetime of cameos and high camp. It's too bad he didn't commit suicide with a symbolic flourish, like hanging himself with his cape. After a short and confusing career, he deserved one big last laugh.

George, wherever you are now don't feel too bad. If you were still around today, you'd probably be the host of *Family Feud*.

January 1979

Death, Cod & Houseplants: TV's 2nd Season

It's television's Second Season time again, when the networks try to make winter doom passable by burning a heap of new shows in our cabin-fevered living rooms. While certain detractors claim that it's called the Second Season because it's only half as good as the first one, that's not altogether true. Following that reductive formula, they'd have to call this the Hundredth Season. And it sure does *feel* like it.

Sour grapes aside, the net-wits are apparently trying to give us wieners what we want. The only trouble is that some want more almost-sex, some want more dead shoplifters, some more adventures with shiny helicopters, and some even want more shows about houseplants. At least *that* group got what they wanted – just give *Makin' It* or *Hello Larry* a try.

Enough complaints; CBS did bring back *WKRP* after all, and *Sword of Justice* is nowhere to be found. Now if they could just kill *Love Boat* somehow … if something terrible happens to Lauren Tews, I'd certainly like to have a finger in it. But all pleasantries aside, here's a quick scope at some of the best and all of the worst.

NBC

Supertrain – This may be the first program ever in which railroad crossing lights steal the show. NBC is mighty disturbed by their overall ratings – which place them substantially behind the Rex 'n' God Network – so they decided to sink big bucks in this *Love Boat* on wheels. Result: a nationwide epidemic of train-pulling jokes.

Brothers And Sisters – With the exception of great newcomer Jon Cutler, this college number has all the humor of a dormitory john after Beaver Week.

Turnabout – Neat premise: a sportswriter and his wife swap identities. Would have been funnier if they'd exchanged identities with people instead of fish.

Hello Larry – McLean Stevenson's punishment for leaving *M*A*S*H* isn't over yet. Watch for his guest appearance on *Turnabout*, where he exchanges identities with Margaret Trudeau.

Cliffhangers – A special self-help show for people who live in cave dwellings and can't figure out how to hang up their clothes.

BJ & The Bear – A spinoff of the last eight Burt Reynolds movies, this program is Claude Akins' last chance to earn enough money for an operation to restore movement to his face.

Sweepstakes – Ed "Kookie" Byrnes is back as the emcee of a million-dollar lottery. This is another of those three-plots-in-one grab-bags, a must for channel flippers who never know what's going on anyway.

CBS

Mary Tyler Moore Hour – Coming up soon, Mary's completely rebuilt show is supposed to be funny-on-purpose, instead of the unintentional hilarity of her theme dance numbers like the quaintly-regarded "Salute To Boards." It sounds like another bomb, though – MTM's an excellent supporting actress, but as a live host she's got all the stage presence of clean sheets.

Flatbush – Inspirational verse: "That's not crabgrass, that's a flat bush!" – Mr. Wilson.

Married: The First Year – Anybody that's smart tries to avoid Boring Young Couples in real life, so why put this kiss & sniff stuff on TV? Coming soon, *Death: The First Year.*

Dukes Of Hazzard – Here's my candidate for the Emmy in Children's Programming, Tits Division. The real question, though, is: Will Waylon Jennings now do the music for *Yogi's Space Race?*

Stockard Channing Show – they've been threatening us with this one for months now, but it still hasn't turned up. Fine with me – it's about Stockard taking a job in a west coast natural food store, complete with a cast of supporting vegetables.

ABC

Delta House – This legit rip-off of *Animal House* isn't too bad if you like the Little Rascals and/or the Three Stooges. Josh Mostel as Blotto is destined to be a superstar, or at least several appearances in Ugly Panty Breath commercials.

Angie – Another halfway decent show from ABC, which continues to violate the new cardinal rule of network programming: Befuddle The Viewer. Angie is little more than a stripped-down *Rhoda*, but there's nothing to switch to after *Mork and Mindy* anyway except PBS' fascinating *Canoe Waxing Tips.*

Makin' It – It had to happen: a disco-comedy that's just as stimulating as your standard disco conversation. Every other line is, "Huh?"

Salvage One – Another fun kiddie show, with Andy Griffith and a couple new Barneys setting forth on various Fantastic Missions, like the one where they try to salvage the mentality of our readership. Don't bother, Andy – they look pretty happy, but I with they wouldn't moo so loud.
March 1979

Wasteland's New Season

"Sickness is the newest trend on prime-time television," goes the *TV Guide* commercial, and this time they're even more on target than the time they predicted handy, rechargeable wristwatch televisions by 1964 at the *latest*. In a new season where the biggest event is a tossup between Charlie hiring a new Angel with Nerf breasts and Meadowlark Lemon slow-breaking into the cast of the biggest airball in TV history, *Hello, Larry*, there's definitely nothing happening on the ween-screen that you'd want to tattoo on the underside of your penis as a memory aid. Yes, this sickness is like love: too many stiffs and not enough punch lines.

"Modern viewers," one top network laff-fascist explained, "just don't want reality to intrude on their entertainment." No *contrito*, Benito – they don't want *reality* to intrude on their reality either. But watching Jimmy McNichol trying to differentiate between himself and sneezing piglet is not my idea of escaping reality. Now, shoving that oinky little nose of his some roller-coaster gears – why, *that's* entertainment!

But as the saying goes, you can't have the milk and the pail too. (Not only that, but you can't get to squeeze the udders, either.) The network programmers have nailed the barn door shut, but they can't stop the smell. ABC is "Still the One" (demonstrating the need for more severe punishment of repeat offenders). CBS is "Looking Good" (as compared to a freight train/Bloodmobile collision) and NBC is "Proud as a Dodobird." But can it quack?

You bet your Motorola, Ayatollah. The '79 season can make every noise in the zoo except for the fatalistic sigh of the shit shoveler. So let's check out our annual hit-and-rundown of the new shows while we try and keep in mind the essential differences between sick and sickening: none whatsoever!

Sick

Trapper John, M.D. – Wayne Rogers' *M*A*S*H* character grows up to become ... Pernell Roberts? Come on, even if he did grow up, he wouldn't be played by a guy whose first name sounds like a shampoo for cows. Extra Credit: the nurse in this show is nicknamed "Ripples" because (A) her enormous breasts create ripples in her uniform, (B) her ponderous bosoms cause ripples of excitement in the staff, (C) her gigantic, bowling-ball-sized boobs are the subject of ripples of laughter, (D) because "Ripples" rhymes with "nipples."

Sloane – And now, one of America's most common mistakes about dog food, Robert Conrad, caught in the act of being himself again, portrays the ace super spy of UNIT (Unite Norma's Intricate Tights), a secret government organization that's locked in a never-ending (for at least eight weeks) struggle with the nefarious KARTEL (Karen and Ralph Traded Expensive Linens). It co-stars Ji-Tu Cumbuka (pronounced Villechaize) as Sloane's sidekick Torque, a 6'5" goon cadet with a stainless-steel fist. Hairy palms were bad enough!

Lazarus Syndrome – This will be remembered as the year that TV's Black people were permitted to stop running around in their jimmies and us two-syllable words like doctor, "Doc! Doc!" and "Oh, nurse?" As racial spokesman Jack Brickhouse has pointed out, "The only good thing about this game is that it was played in a hurry."

Shirley – Criswell Predicts: When this show about a widow and her kids roughing it at Lake Tahoe proves to be a ratings disaster, the family will form a band (The Lips of Susan Dey) and have smash hits with "Theme from Man Undercover" and "It Ain't Necessarily Tahoe."

The Baxters – TV fans have learned to dread the words "innovative new

169

show" just as they dread certain phrases like "substantial penalty for early withdrawal," "armed and extremely dangerous" and "no apparent leak of radioactive materials." And for no small reason – in this innovative New Show from Norman "I Give Up" Lear, actors wade through some heavy topics like death, sex or the morality of kittensicles during the first 15 minutes, and then real people – although not real enough to be on *Real People* – spend the next quarter hour discussing the first half. I think it should be the other way around.

Eischied – Joe Don Baker plays a cop who's tougher than landlady sweat but has the body of Mattel's Suckerman. Watch him track down psychotic killers, killers who only murder psychotics and From Here to Eternity: The War Years - William Devane, Roy Thinnes, Kim Basinger, Barbara "Tweet Tweet" Hershey … I think Lou Grant summed it up best: "Sounds like a Who's Who of suckers to me."

Sicker

Buck Rogers in the 25th Century – Ex-soaper Gil Gerard still acts with all the mobility of a Fotomat, but as Brent Musberger once said, "His head looks normal, so I guess he's okay." Only bright hope in this mental stun gun is watching Pam Hensley – one of my own objects of slobber – try to break up a career spent portraying long-estranged and-bitter-daughters.

240-Robert – Now that the longevity of *ChiPs* has been endangered by Erik Estrada's enrollment in the Duane Allman School of Motorcycle Safety, ABC has unleashed the crew of Trap, Thib and Morgy-Morgy (one for each Morgy) to carry on the time-honored ridiculous-rescue genre. With the combined intelligence of a bookshelf, they buzz around in flying dune buggies assisting itinerant vacationers, backpacking paramedics and, in one episode, surfers trapped in a burning oil spill. It should be fun watching them try to put out the ocean.

Paris – James Earl Jones, who many consider the greatest living Black actor after Jimmie Walker, portrays a police detective whose idea of off-job recreation is pound on a body bag stuffed with drugged hamsters. Hey, at $50,000 per, it pays a lot more than Darth Vader voiceovers.

Hart to Hart – Robert Wagner is back as a glossy male rich bitch who, along with writer-wife Stephanie Powers (author of *Carpet Commercials: Candygrams From the Dead?*) jets around the world solving murders and grinning that where'd-my-other-lip-go? grin of his. This is an Aaron Spelling production of a Sidney Shelton script, a new height in cosmic redundancy.

Benson – Robert Guillaume extends his character from *Soap* with the personality of a magnetic window cleaner. This show is presented courtesy of the FCC's Equal Time Provision to counteract the effects of *Lazarus Syndrome* and *Paris*.

The Associates – Hot off their success with *Taxi*, the folks at MTM have used the same casting method (dragging a magnet through the Camp for Icky People) to come up with this wacky-lawyers show loosely based on a novel by the author of *The Paper Chase*. Toss in an old guy who likes like a shriveled-up sex organ of indeterminate gender to cancel out Shelley Smith (an Ozone Advisory has just been issued for my underpants) and you have an apparent winner, Of course you could run 30 minutes of Denture Odor commercials in this time slot (right after *Mork & Mindy*) and still have a smash.

New Kind of Family – Here's that half hour of Denture odor blurbs I was talking about. The only new thing about this family is that they're all named Eileen. The twist: none of them knows how to spell it!

Sickest

The Misadventures of Sheriff Lobo – More stereotyped Southern pork and jeans, this time starring Claude Akins, whose face looks more than ever like two pies in an overturned hubcap.

Struck By Lightning – A takeoff on the Two-Mints-in-One commercial, with Ted Stein as a spooky caretaker with the eyes of a sadistic optician and Jack Elam as his monstrous alter ego who's so mean that when he looks at you, your internal organs feel like your skin is being sandblasted.

Out of the Blue – Jimmy Brogan as a combination angel/babysitter/high school science teacher whose first science project is to demonstrate that, due to their unique ability to fix nitrogen from the air, turtles actually function as walking beans. Ditto for Brogan, who you may remember from the last time you caught your reflection in the toilet bowl.

Big Shamus, Little Shamus – This disgustingly kissable detective series features Brian Keith during his Hawaiian phase, even though it takes place in Atlantic City, that hotbed of danger where crazed tourists use too many hotel towels, lock themselves out of their rooms and leave their TV sets on all night with the sound off! But why didn't they call it Big Dick, Little Dick?

California Fever – (Science Note: "Under steadily increasing heat, devolutionary processes accelerate.") Thus, this cartoonoid about the perfumed lives of SoCal teens who spend all their time disco surfing, sharpening their skate keys and pressing their budding pudenda against sputtering Camaros. Starring Jimmy McNichols, who's often referred to as two cheeks in search of a face or a butt, whichever comes first. California Fever – cure it!

Last Resort – Just when it looked like we'd never have to see another froth-brained college kid on television ever again, along comes this group of summering collegians with the collective personality of a silent alarm system. If good lines were correct answers, this show would need 25 more to score an Incomplete.

Working Stiffs – Jim Belushi – who looks exactly like his famous brother except for the huge tooth in the middle of his forehead – stars in this cast-of-janitors comedy that's so low brow its toenails have eyelashes. Plus the entire show takes place in the basement.

Hey daddio, I don't wanna go...
October 1979

Make Room for Doody

The 1981-82 television season may well be remembered for decades to come as the year the networks dumped all the gimmicks, bucked all the trends, and opted for the Total Desperation method of programming. Here are a few of the viewing highlights you can expect this fall:

• Lots more people get shot!
• Two former football stars get their own shows!
• An epidemic of widowed fathers with 10-year-old sons!
• Tony Randall confirms that Felix was gay!
• A possible use for Elaine Joyce!
• Still no Chipmunks tour!
• The triumphant return of Tom Ewell!

You get all the above, the world's greatest little combination baby food warmer/chainsaw, two free spatulas and enough bankable names to stuff Montana. Any moderately successful male lead of the past 15 years is fair game in '81. Apparently, somebody hollered, "Haul in them tuna, matey" and sooner than you can say sooner, everybody from James Arness to Yoshio Yoda was back on the screen.

The network dodobrains are calling this a New Era, which is about as funny as a privately catered Emergency Room visit. You should can any expectations you may have right now, and get set to forget. As influential media critic Buckwheat once said, "We don't expect it, we just want it!"

As far as prognostication goes, any worm could simply predict that *all* the Fall Crawl debuts will bomb. Since 80-90 percent of the new shows can be expected to achieve cancellation by the second commercial in any given season, said worm would rack up a smart .850 batting average. Hello, Atlanta!

By the way, this worm predicts that all the new shows will bomb. Now me real big smart! But please use the award money on a gift sub to HBO, okay?

Code Red – This one's about as easy to take seriously as Libyan airspace. Lorne Greene is a burned-out Los Angeles fire chief with a pair of paranoid sons who spend most of their time trying to get L.A.'s first female firefighter to uncross their hoses.

Father Murphy – A gnaw-inspiring creation of Michael "I'm not insane!" Landon, this show's got everything: a "rugged-but-warmhearted" cowboy who impersonates a priest, a Black soot prospector, a little brat, a dog named Drugs and the mandatory "feisty-but-pretty" schoolmarm. Punch line: "So *all* the boys stayed after school to clean her erasers."

Simon and Simon – Youngish brothers run "freewheeling" detective agency in San Diego (?) Deciding which dick is most offensive is almost as hard as figuring out which way to open a hot dog bun.

Powers of Matthew Star – Peter Barton plays a super-powered alien who can read minds like menus, give good telekinesis and disappear after a couple of weeks up against *60 Minutes*.

Strike Force – Robert Stack is commander of an L.A. police squad of itchy trigger fingers. A must for all you morgue-teases out there.

Maggie – Erma Bombeck created this bizarre combination of *Please Don't Eat the Daisies* and the never-aired sequel to *Shampoo: Snip*. Punchline: Your mother sweeps dust bunnies in Hell.

Maverick – James Garner as you-know-who from you-know-what show. The co-star is a female journalist/photog stolen from you-know-where. The only question is: Do you know why?

Fall Guy – This storyline is almost as bizarre as a "perfect day." Lee Majors is an unsuccessful stuntman turned part-time bounty hunter. I believe this is what Archie Bunker would call an eager bleeder.

Love, Sidney – In scenic Macomb, Ill., the token duck pond is located next to a cemetery. A couple weeks ago, a friend of mine took a loaf of used bread down to feed the ducks – a popular local activity. Unfortunately, the quackies were nowhere to be found. So she thought, "What the heck" and fed the graves instead. From NBC's own What-the-heck Dept. comes this sitcom with Tony Randall as a gay artist who takes in an unwed mother and becomes part-time daddy to the illegitimate spawn. Punchline: "So the guy said. 'What the Hell, let's all take the morning train!' "

Nashville Palace – Here's the one program that's almost as bad as having someone take away your Clorox for a month. The 'pone-brains behind *Hee-Haw* launch this guaranteed bomb that'll probably be cancelled after the first song. This week's host is Roy Clark, who will re-enact his monumental appearance on *The Odd Couple*.

Shannon – *Kojak's* ex-puppetwipe Kevin Dobson is one of the many widowed fathers with 10-year-old sons this season. Not to miss a trick, they've given him a zany housekeeper and have already filmed the obligatory impotence episode.

Jessica Novak – Now *here's* a novelty. An actual, grown-up woman gets the lead in a TV drama and it's not strictly for aureola addicts. Helen Shaver portrays a TV reporter who keeps getting stuck with adorable human-interest stories when she'd rather tackle important issues like the scandal of incomplete doorknob checking or the need for warning lights on lawn chairs.

Best of the West – Tom Ewell is back! Yes, the demands of the Tom Ewell Protection Agency have been silenced by casting him as the alcoholic veternarian in this western sitcom. That's Tom Ewell, the thinking man's Tom Poston.

Today's FBI – Mike "Mannix" Connors is a 20-year vet in this series "as boring and predictable as today's headlines," as it's said. He bosses the usual heap of violence-crazed hotshots, including a woman agent who makes rude jokes about the pistol range.

Open All Night – Beer blurb star Bubba Smith is a night manager of a 7/11 type grape Slurpee stand. I wonder if it'll be like the local all-nighter here, where – when the food gets old and moldy – they simply mark down the price.

King's Crossing – Just what the world needs: another soap from the Lorimar (*Dallas*) detergent dispenser. Bradford Dillman, owner of the face that most looks like it belongs under a condom, stars along with the usual jockey-screwing heiresses and amnesia salesmen.

The Angie Dickinson Show – In Angela Lansbury's public-service spot about battered wives, she says that "Every 18 minutes a woman is physically abused by someone she loves." In this reheated version of *Police Woman*, Angie Dickinson is that woman.

Mr. Merlin – Oh boy, here's the same boy-meets-reincarnated-magician, boy-receives- magic-powers, boy-tries-to-make-Elaine-Joyce-vanish story line.

Devlin Connection – Rock Hudson (whose chief claim to fame was getting to drop depth charges on Susan Saint James' torpedo tubes back before she became a complete idiot) returns to the tube as a widowed private detective! The twist – his son is more than 10 years old!

And just in case you're wondering why we skipped a few of the new shows, it was to leave room for the following announcement: This is the season that CBS has chosen to broadcast *The Return of the Beverly Hillbillies*! Who needs Gabe Kaplan, right?

September 1981

The Golden Age of Trash Video is Now!

August burns like an overheated television set. It makes summer seem as endless as a network anchorperson's biography. But it also means opportunities for prolonged TV viewing in the shade, if not the cool.

The 1980s have been good for at least one thing. ("New Liquid Dentrol?") No, I'm talking about the dribble-down of inexpensive video technology to people who take out their own garbage. It used to be that incredibly lousy movies made an appearance or two on network television's Dummy Hour and then vanished into a secret subhuman society: fanatics devoted to incredibly lousy movies.

What a loss that was! Junk masterpieces like *Plan 9 From Outer Space*, *Hot Rod Hullabaloo* and any number of films whose titles started with the word *Don't* were lost due to program executives who failed to appreciate the fearlessly crummy. Yes, fellow video-philes, we once faced a world without *Mars Needs Women*.

But no more. Now many of these … unique films are available on video for rent or sale –not to mention as home recordings of the hopelessly (maybe deservedly) obscure late-night presentations. Yes, the Golden Age of Trash Video is truly here!

In fact, guides to the unabashedly stinky movies have become a publishing fad. Danny Peary's *Cult Movie* books – while shamelessly overwritten – still come up with good selections. The Medved Brothers' *Golden Turkeys* first applied the proper attitude to cinematic debris: Eat it before it crawls off the plate. Now we even have the *Psychotronic Encyclopedia of Film* (by Michael Weldon), an entire reference source of movie muck.

Everyone east of Indianapolis seems to own one of these books, so we'll avoid titles that have been covered to death (not that they were ever very lively). In my two-protractor household, where trash is science, my poor VCR has had to submit to endless hours of early-morning timer abuse in pursuit of enlightened waste so that you – who may still possess shreds of dignity and good taste – can catch up with the latest in uselessness.

I have to admit, I had to floor my search button on a couple of these (You will too after about 20 minutes of *The Creeping Terror*). But a few nuggets of greatness here and there more than make up for the lingering minutes of badness. These flicks are, after all, art. (OK, it's art with a character that defines its own category – Great Trash – but each one of these is guaranteed to be a "good see").

No Survivors, Please — This 1963 German production is so legendary one local TV horror host introduced it with this stunning praise: "All I can tell you is it's in black and white." He was too kind. Another entry in the old aliens-take-over-bodies-of-Earth-peeps genre, *No Survivors* is one of those rare works that's so boring, it's interesting! After a spoken prologue which compares the human race to flies - always a catchy analogy - viewers observe various scientists, doctors, diplomats and military men disappearing in novel ways, like being thrown from airplanes and falling off ocean liners, When they reappear elsewhere unharmed (but with aliens "inside"), nobody catches on except the inevitable crusading reporter. His sets up lots of exciting visual possibilities, like about 30 minutes of airplane interiors. Apparently edited by a bobbing pigeon, the story jumps around so witlessly that when the *Time/Life Home Repair and Improvements* book commercial comes on, you want to run out and build a deck - on anything! Eventually, one of the space guys "remembers" what love is, and another invasion is down the drain. Shucks.

The Creeping Terror — Amid a fleet of indistinguishable blobs of light, a UFO lands in Angel County, Calif. (The landing scene is just a NASA rocket launch film run backward. Another $1.97 saved!) Once grounded, the craft resembles an air conditioner with a bad reputation. Oh, wait, there's some smoke! It's *really* getting good now. The National Guard arrives in a pickup truck, followed by a squad car that rear-ends it. The no-expense-spared sets include a gymnasium, various kitchens and dens, and a vacant lot. The monster – who looks like a Chinese New Year parade dragon in the form of a giant Aztec turkey – goes around eating fishermen, kids with crew-cuts doing the Twist and just about anything with a pulse. The beloved Vic Savage stars.

So Young, So Bad – This features Anne Francis' debut – as Loretta, teenage moll-ette, incarcerated in an unnamed penal institution for wayward starlets. Fellow juve inmates include Rita (then named Rosita) Moreno and a very young Anne Jackson. Francis, as Cool Hand Loretta, is nasty and massively sexy, too – even in her iron nightie. After a bit of arson and hosing, nice-guy shrink Paul Henreid takes her case: *Lolita*-city, molestation amnesty fans. "I like a lotta guys for a little while," she tells the doc. (I think I love her.) Meanwhile, Rita gets depressed and hangs herself. Enreid "cures" Loretta, of course, making the world safe for Sheepskin underwear once again.

Champagne for Caesar – Thought I'd include a respectable one to check attention spans. Intellectual giant Beauregard Bottomley (Ronald Colman) is standing in a crowd watching a then-new television through a store window. On comes *Masquerade for Money*, a popular game show sponsored by Milady, "the soap that sanctifies." Host Happy Hogan – introduced as "that merry, mad, mirthy minstrel of magpie" – turns out to be none other than Art Linkletter before his "career" got underway. The unknowingly prophetic B.B says Hogan's "the forerunner of intellectual destruction in America," and Bottomley decides to do something about it. ("Get Linkletter before he reproduces?" No such luck.) Beauregard goes on the show as "The Encyclopedia" and immediately runs off an unstoppable winning streak. This makes for tons of shots of tube-tied Americans falling in love with his brainy abandon. Vincent Price, as Milady's president, is superb throughout, displaying more range than the inside of a horse ambulance. During Mouli ("with five different blades") commercials, Price tries to co-opt B.B. with a job offer, but no go. Next he tries the impossible question route. "How does Einstein regard the space-time continuum?" Happy asks him. (With *affection*, right?) Bottomley's lengthy answer is ruled incorrect – until Einstein himself calls in to say B.B. was right! Fun and laughter ensue, as Happy falls in love with Bottomley's sister (Barbara Britton) and the answer man himself goes for Flame, a temptress Price has set on him. The whole nation tunes in for a final question, with the entire Milady soap empire as the grand prize. I don't want to spoil the ending for you, so let's just say that the soundstage bubble machine works overtime.

Murder is My Business – Ward Cleaver, tough guy! That's right, Beaver's small-screen dad, Hugh Beaumont, appears as private eye Mike Shayne, a p.i. with a heart of putty. When he delivers lines like "Murder is always serious," he could just as well be saying, "Beaver, what's that rock doing in the den?" Plus: He smokes cigarettes! He roughs up butlers!! And, best of all, he chases "dames" with genuine sex appeal!!! Is June going to be *mad*.

The Centerfold Girls – His odious psycho-killer chase picture is strictly an extended excuse for displaying Jaime Lyn Bauer (of TV's *The Young and the Restless* fame) in various states –countries, even – of undress. Some slashing fool stalks models from his favorite skin mags, murders them, and mutilates their bodies - skinning them for his collection, Not only horrible and despicable, but as bizarre a concept as referring to *anything* as "one of Clint Eastwood's greatest roles." So sleazy and badly done, it's funny.

The Love-Ins – A priceless artifact from 1967, this one tackles the Hippie Era head-on - but brings it down in the wrong end zone! Richard Todd is a college professor (manipulated by hip capitalism) who advocates "free LSD" as the solution to everything. He makes adorable speeches about "hypocrisy" and "the straight world." He steals Susan Oliver away from her good-guy boyfriend and rots her mind in no time, sending her off on an unforgettable Alice in Wonderland acid trip during which she rips off all her clothes at a

UFO concert. "Pat, you took too much LSD last night," he helpfully reminds her the next day. "I know," she confesses. "I was so ... *aware*." Look for actual Haight-Asbury shots and appearances by the Chocolate Watchband and Joe Pyne. Wigged-out, man!

Secret File: Hollywood – A new record for microphone boom sightings is set in this fearlessly trite late-'50s detective flick. The title is also the name of a slimy scandal rag that's really a front for blackmailers. Max Carter (Robin Clark) is the most ridiculously hard-boiled dick in film history. He's usually hung-over and always slurry-lipped – perhaps from banging his head on all those dangling microphones. Great dialogue throughout. Everybody's either a "kook" or a "doll-face," just like real life. There's an inventive use of interiors, too, as the same enormous, tail-finned furniture keeps turning up in different scenes. Blackmail turns to murder, and boredom turns to giddiness. Unfortunately, the blackmail ring is busted up right before they go after Zippy Daniels, "the rock and roll kid." I'm still waiting on the sequel.

Warlords of the 21st Century – *Road Warrior* fans must see this New Zealand *Mad Max* rip-off. Set "after the Oil Wars," the plot concerns Annie McEnroe (the next Jamie Lee Curtis) and her adventures while fleeing some baaaad 21st Century dudes. Led by a masterful creep called Straker (James Wainwright), these guys buzz around the shattered countryside cruising for diesel fuel in a neat truck/car/tank that's the real star. Its front end looks like a cross between a locomotive and a Brinks' truck; it's attached to a box-car-like mobile headquarters in the rear by an accordian-esque device resembling those extendo-buses in Nowsville, USA. Annie gets rescued by Hunter, a character on a futuristic motorcycle who's waging a one-man battle against the fuel suckers. Straker is my own new personal hero, spitting out lines like, "Wars are not won by men of political ambitions - there's too much lipstick and not enough napalm." What a guy!

Satan's Cheerleaders – This one received some praise for its mischievous banality. Featuring the most obnoxious surf-disco soundtrack ever performed in the line of doodee, it's the tale of a small herd of cheerleaders whose car breaks down in Nether, Calif. (pop. 360). Uh-oh, the sheriff's name is Bill Z. Bubb! All the townspeople turn out to be Satanists who were probably kicked off pom-pon squads in their youth. (Frankly, this has some of the sexiest teens seen since the version of *Little Darlings* my imagination cooked up when I dozed off in an M&M trance in the front row of a mall theater). The whole thing is basically tongue-in-oral-cavity, particularly the end, where boss rah-rah Patti (Kerry Sherman) turns out to be a witch and wrecks the town!

Flight to Mars – "It's like closing your eyes in the dark. Suddenly, there you are – alone with your soul!" At least, that's what one guy claims in this jumble of '50s sci-fi clichés that resembles a garage-sale *Forbidden Planet*. The usual gaggle of Earthlings – you know, an ornery pilot, a couple of scientists, a token female and a stunt baby or two – crash-land on Mars and discover civilization. Instead of space suits, the crewmembers wear brown leather jackets and World War I-styled gas masks. The Martians wear the space suits! Epic thrills like the guys playing cards and the Mars men lusting after guess who (not the stunt baby) make this one a forgettable film to remember.

The College Girl Murders – Many of these titles run like the reels aren't just in the wrong order, but in the wrong solar system. This one's no exception, stringing together more unrelated undressing sequences than a documentary on the evolution of the locker room. The villain, a mad scientist in a red, pointy-hatted KKK outfit, goes around killing coeds with a poison-shooting gizmo hidden inside a hollowed-out hymnal. Honest! The girls who catch glimpses of this joker dub him the Red Mask. I swear! The authorities, as usual, think they're all hallucinating (and, for once, maybe they're right).

Initiation of Sarah – This '78 TV-movie stars Kay Lenz as a Carrie clone named Sarah, Morgan Fairchild as a lean, mean sorority queen, and Shelley Winters as the housemother of the mysterious rival sorority, PED (or Pigs, Elephants and Dogs, as Morgan calls them). You'll probably want to catch the infamous sneaky-peek shower scene which Fairchild later complained almost spoiled her skin-premiere in *The Seduction*. No matter what you think of her, she's always a great snot, and when she plays a particularly vicious prank on Sarah, you really want to see her get what's coming to her. After almost spilling a piano on her fair-weather sis (Morgan Brittany), Sarah realizes the full extent of her powers. With a little help from Shelley, she fries Morgan's face and then proceeds to burn down the whole campus – and herself with it. Sorry, Kay - that's what you get for marrying David Cassidy!

August 1984

A lot about nothing:
SLEAZEDOWN STORIES

Sin City Social '75

Welcome to Budweiser Woodstock, or The Juicing of America

ALCOHOL!

Yep, booze. It's always been around, but the doper's disdain for *spiritus fermenti* is no longer fashionable among the young and hip. Tequila is fashionable. Puking is fashionable. Bloody Marys and bloody noses. (Peace and love was for *sissies!*) EVERYTHING YOUR OLD MAN DRINKS IS HIP. But you know that already – that's why he's put a lock on his liquor cabinet. Because your destructo culture has caught up with his.

Ain't it fun, being reunited at last in the same gutter?

The Sin City Social was billed by word of mouth as something of a Budweiser Woodstock, with more kegs of the stuff than five Evil Kneivels could shake a cast at. An annual brown-out staged near the unlikely town of Virginia, Ill., it brings all the area basket brains tumbling out of the woodwork to out-drink, out-puke and out-boogie-down one another while local bands grind out some of the most hope-deadening power drool ever to fall off a stage.

Only a couple of years ago, the SCS was just another small town acid quiz similar to the ones that sprang up all over the Midwest during the late '60s and early '70s. The usual yellow-eyed pot grins and tripped-out zeroes were to be found spread over the field like quivering ironing boards, everyone content in his or her own personal dimwit heaven. People sat around thinking up new ways to give the peace sign and toyed with the dull Sony introspection that was typical of the time.

Not this year. A few diehards still dropped acid, but mainly as a kicker in two-quart Kool-Aid jugs of gin and Squirt. Of course, there were enough joints going around to reconstruct the stage at Altamont 10 times over, but the hoarse giggling and mind games were replaced by a canine aggressiveness that resulted in several gory stretchers stacked outside the first-aid tent. Kids that used to get stitches for stepping on broken glass were now having Ripple shards removed from their foreheads. And the real action was the continuous brawl at the flat-bed truck covered with kegs that were being drained so rapidly that SOS helicopters were being considered.

Whatever happened, anyway? How did this coarse new willingness to deal in the aesthetics of destructo impulses and world-gloom in such a party-fied way come about? Said one old timer, a 24-year-old with waist-length grease, an Art degree and a Phillips 66 jar consisting of 1/2 bourbon and 1/2 Diet Shasta raspberry soda:

"Oh yeah, I remember what it was like back then," he said. "I used to do tons of acid but it gave me such a Swiss-cheese memory that I switched over to booze so I could *feel* like something.

"We went through all that cosmosis crap ... talking to windows, making faces at each other, the whole number. But a man can only go so far and then he's there, right? Now we just get a couple cases of beer and maybe a fifth of Jack for a rush and don't think about anything but the way to the john."

Quite a few people, mainly in their mid-to-late twenties, expressed similar sentiments. What's ironic is that creepy psychologists once had their eyes on LSD as the perfect cure for alcoholism, the idea being that the alcoholic would have great revelations and clean up his act. Now a growing number of ex-acidheads are using alcohol to burn out the very insights they were cruising for in the first place.

Drowning out acid paranoia is hardly the major preoccupation of your average teen rock 'n' roller, as anyone who's roller-skated over the empty bottles at any concert can tell you. Even the weekend downer duds and reds-and-wine geniuses that are still kicking are making the grand crawl over to swill.

The reasons for the switch may be no more complicated than survival of the fittest: How much Sopers and Southern can you load and still make it to the emergency room in time?

A few actual converts do exist however. A character who calls himself Lump dredged up at a recent Kiss concert is the classic product of the Juicing of America. Two hundred pounds of fat jaws, muscled eyebrows and damp-rat hair on a frame like a sagging coffin, he was on his second fifth of some cretinous whiskey with a name like Old Dogfood when he drooled out this explanation of his move from down to drown: "I did enough Thorazine last year to flatten a dinosaur. Had this buddy who used to swipe 'em from his crazy old lady and we'd take it and grind it up and smoke the shit! That way, it only takes about 15 minutes and you turn all cold and start to feel like some asshole's got your head in a tin can. Then we'd head out." After a few months of that, Lump couldn't wake up at all and started on the ever-popular wake-up shots technique – "two shots of whiskey for every time the pipe went out."

When the hooch warm began to be more fun than the down cool, he gradually switched over, not so much in a conscious plan as a logical progression like a chimp who finds the pleasure button some mad scientist has just planted in his brain. At any rate, Lump's now knocking off almost a case of Old Squidbarf a week with his friend, and he's starting to gag on blood every now and again.

"Tastes like dead rubber."

Although mixing downs and booze is gradually fading out along with its more ardent admirers, it's still a favorite pastime among some of the less functional specimens one can still find sludging along at Uriah Heep shows. With Black Sabbath touring again, they should be rolling 'em out in wheelchairs and iron lungs.

While they still create pretty much the same old pukeslides and bruise jockeys as heavy soakers, a mixer subwit with a broken bottle creates a bit more tension than a typical drunk or pre-sponge, 'lude dude would on his own. There was something almost *comforting* in the knowledge that the urge to kill was generally the last symptom before trank thud. Double dosers just get stronger, more belligerent and less predictable as the night wears on. Face pulping, tooth shoveling and pole vaulting on unsuspecting women are just meat under the bridge to these jags, who – while possessing a certain malignant charm – can still get their last laugh out of separating you from your face while still barely able to distinguish between themselves and the upholstery.

"I use anything I can find to get fucked on," said one upstanding young retardo called Dommy (for Dominance, most likely) "I drink, drop, shoot, smoke, anything. Nothin' replaces nothin' for me – I just keep adding shit."

Everyday high-school hardcores are about the only group of nouveau alkies getting any press these days, favorable or otherwise. They pee in their sneaks, get locked in their own lockers, and pile up the highest number of car wrecks of any age bracket. Nothing to wet your pillow over: They're just as bad as the rest of us, only they get caught more.

It's the *reasons* that are so weird. Said one teen sighsucker with a two-ply voice soft enough for a snake to snooze on and budding tumescent pastries poking through her silk halter: "I don't think you really know someone until you find out what they're drinking. *Really* ..." Her boyfriend, kind of turtle-toed but retaining a genuine pimp factor, explained further: "You ain't got what they don't want anyway, so who gives a fuck?"

Mostly, it just seems like the thing to do, as it always was and probably always will be. Suburban flash tonnage, as one smartass put it.

Back at Sin City, the last band is wrapping it up. The field looks like a tuna farm, with bodies in various degrees of slow motion flapping about here and there. Anybody with higher metabolism than a snail has crawled off into the bar, the car or the pond.

It sure beats sensory deprivation.

October 1975

Household Hints for Dolts

LAWNMOWER REPAIR: mowing the lawn is strictly for peons. Suit yourself.

E-Z TV REPAIR: Outsmarting the tube is not as difficult as it sometimes seems! The old "stir yerself out of fetal position and walk to the set, thus making it start to work again the second you touch it" trick is generally effective, but requires too much effort. FEIGNING getting up sometimes works, too – but TVs are pretty smart animals. They watch you when yer asleep. You think when you turn it off it still isn't doing electronic surveillance on your lack of brain function? Ha ha, foolish you. Now, you can get a midget guillotine and place the plughead in it, leave a tiny cup of water and a crumb of bread by it, and tell it it's gonna die at sunrise, but this is rather drastic.

I've always found the old SHOE METHOD most effective. Obtain a nuclear power plant worker's lead-lined boot and keep it within reach. Then, when those disgusting yellow lines that look like Opie start to appear during *Happy Days*, throw it on the TV. Gently, the first time. If the beast tries it again during a thrilling Cubs-Montreal game, throw it again, only this time with FEELING.

After that, send $1.25 for the handy pamphlet HOW TO REMOVE GLASS SHARDS FROM ARMS & WOODWORK.

Dear Rick:

I recently spilled gravy on my albino Chihuahua and the stains just will not come out! What can I do?
WORRIED RUNT

Dear Worried:

Simple. Get him a little stool and mate him with a Dachshund, and keep the resulting pups! They're charming, and best of all, rarely live long.

Dear Rick:

Some jerk at a party left my best coloring book on the toaster and now my best pictures of Lassie befriending squirrels and skunks are all runny and wrinkly! If I can't fix them, I will commit hari-kari with my tuning fork. Pleeze help.
ANXIOUS CRAYOLA FAN

Dear Anxious:

Put away that tuning fork, the answer is E-Z. Just throw away your coloring book in the washer (preferably a Norge model), remove the lint from the remaining pieces, and spend the rest of your life reassembling it! This is termed "creativity."
October 1976

College Bars: From Frats to Freeks

Back in the old days before the climate changed, fall used to be fun. "Crisp," they called it. The whole place looked like a Hamms commercial, and the kids, all wearing orange-and-red-checked scarves, roared back into town in their Mustangs, gleefully firing footballs at nearby infirms. Trees did Pete Seeger imitations.

It was nice while it lasted. Now, fall is a season truly befitting its name. Leaves fall early from water bloat, hitting the spongy ground like overpowered Kleenex. What corn hasn't already succumbed to "The Rot" has become condos for black buzzers. The kids, all decked out in their new Diver Dan suits, roar back into town in their speedboats and stripped down ocean liners, wearily playing ring toss with passing periscopes.

With all this worm weather going down, this year is going to be better than most for hitting the bars. The meteorologists are already there. Lift a few with your fellow frogmen and compare flippers while watching *Jacques Cousteau* and *Sea Hunt* on the tube. Sex in diving bells will create scandals and tiny home mildew farms will be all the rage.

Perhaps I'm slightly exaggerating with all this, since it really is hard to picture bars changing at all. They better not, either, because bars are a demilitarized zone for the brain. Us slurpers need reassuring surroundings to put the gas in our pass-outs.

And the best way to hit the right bars (where you won't feel stranded on Mars) is to watch for the ever-present "types." All bars fit some type, and college bars are exceptionally typecast by the remarkable herding instincts of students. Marks all. Who else wears lighted beanies and walks around carrying armloads of Econ books? Ironworkers?

Anyway, we have sorted out these types so that you, the dummy with the wrong room key, can get in the right place to do the wrong things. And ain't that what life is all about?

THE FRAT BAR – Everybody picks on frat slats, but if you ask me, they're pretty damn courageous for adopting total phoniness as a way of life. So does everyone, but who's counting?

Before you even get into the FB, you have to make a living I.D. out of yourself besides the requisite 40 you'll need to get stamped at the entrance with some word like "OK" or "PLACEBO." This means: cool clothes, a pyramid haircut, and a Patronizing Manner. Sharp threads this year (other than fishing gear) include stained bellbottoms with pictures of mustachioed-men playing ukuleles on them, Saran Wrap shirts with lemon-yellow Dago-T's underneath, a tweed jacket that comes to the knees, and rainbow shoes. (Hey, I read it in *Esquire*).

Once in, all you have to do is laugh a lot, insincerely if possible, and always meet people's eyes, especially when lying. How to laugh insincerely: Don't go "Haw, haw, haw," like usual. When the punch line arrives, skip a beat, then start out slow and build ... "ahuh, ahuh-huh, aahhuh, huh, huh; ahuh, aHUH, aHUH, aHUH, HUH, ahhhhh ... man."

Do that, avoid pointy questions and above all, don't puke on the silver wallpaper with pictures of mustachioed-men playing cornet, and you're in.

REGULAR NOBODY BARS – This covers a lot of territory, but RNBs make up nearly half of all drinking establishments while at the same time making up none of the good ones. You probably frequent one yourself. Danger signals here are school T-shirts, shop talk, fervent nodding as if to say YES regardless of the conversation, lots of looking over shoulders every time the door opens, and a general air of uneasiness.

Nobody bars can be used as hideaways or as picking grounds for insecure "Major League" scouts. You figure that anybody that has to hang around here would drop dead at the mere opportunity to speak to a whiz like you. Dream on. However, one thing these places are great for is playing pinball in private. Then strut back to your regular bar, win a couple of million and everybody will say, "God, you must play a lot!" What a feeling.

HIPPIE BARS – Talk about characters, Hippies are twice as funny as they are pathetic. While some of their numbers have defected to Punk (safety-pins through the eyes and sewing machines worn on chains around the neck) you still find plenty around. They grow 'em somewhere.

Your standard HB will always be dark enough to make a coal bin look like a drugstore, so don't forget your infra-red specs. Other necessities: an old Dago-T some frat guy threw out years ago, jeans encrusted with runny jean encrustations, sneakers that show seven toes (not six and not eight – very important for counting purposes), and a cap from some obscure baseball team like the "Mud Hens"). This is called the just-got-struck-by-a-steaming-tractor look.

Behavior is simple. Just remember that you're dealing with children. Talk slower than even you can understand. Get lots of beer foam on your mustache (women can get it on the ends of their hair, if they can reach that far). Hobble to the john like a wheezing country preacher, and then pee your sneaks anyway. And don't forget the Number-1 pick-up line on the Hippie circuit this season: "Hey, ya wanna come out to my farm and see my collection of antique drugs?"

PHILOSOPHER BARS – These are always off in the corner of the town square somewhere and possess unsuspecting names like "The Nud" or "Hankie's." Everybody wears baggy clothes and mumbles a lot. The dead giveaway, though, is that *I Dream of Jeannie* is always on the bar tube. The way to do these places is to sit in a corner, guzzle a few Zombies and get the bleak-but-thoughtful look on your face. Remember, these wits do everything backward, so the more dunce-like you appear, the deeper you actually are. Soon, some washed up Soc/Anthro prof will mistake you for one of their own, and, after a couple of innocent baseball questions, will say, … "Y'know … baseball is kinda like death, isn't it?" (Say no).

There are plenty of other bar types, of course: Jock bars (numbered gym shorts and much pounding on the back tables); Ick bars (so-called because everyone looks like a Virginia Slims ad and says, "Oh, ick!," all the time; Oink bars (where the Guys on the Floor go and eat 100 sausage things and throw up all over their own boots); and the ever-present, ever-popular, Tattoo bars (bruisers within, cement mixers and garbage trucks double-parked outside). You can even invent your own types and then go to them. No one else will.

Have a nice fall, and don't forget your snorkel, yokel.

September 1977

The Death of Punk
Rusty Razors in Drain City

It was fun while it lasted.

Rat Scabies of the Damned answering Paul Kantner's backstage congratulations after their L.A. debut with a hearty "Fuck you, rich boy" and an unceremonious boot out the dressing-room door.

The Dead Boys' Stiv Bators climbing out from behind the wheel and onto the roof of the car going 70 mph in order to dramatically moon members of the Dictators in the heap behind him.

A thoroughly befuddled NBC-TV reporter in London telling the audience, "Something definitely seems to be going on over here in Merry Olde England" while punks and Teddy boys go after each others' eyes with tent stakes not 20 yards behind her.

Sears selling "Get Punk" T-shirts complete with off-color bloodstains; K-tel gearing up for a *Punk Power* oldies LP.

The Stranglers' tremendous single "Peaches," being denounced as "beyond sexism … a true hatred of women" while it zoomed up the UK charts.

The Ramones' single "Sheena Is A Punk Rocker," backed by their triumphant tour of Midwest plankton staging areas, setting a new record by staying in the *Billboard* charts 10 weeks without ever going higher than Number 90.

And, of course, fashion designer Zandra Rhodes – old humidifier-charm herself – putting on a "chic punk" fashion show featuring porcine NY models who rented body hair for the occasion, strutting around in ripped-up pajama tops held together by 14-karat gold safety pins.

It was fun all right, but now it's all headed for Drain City.

The British punk scene – overcrowded with new bands and weekend fans who dressed up in elevator cables and sewer grids on Saturday night and built supersonic ashtrays during the week – is collapsing under its own pale weight. Here in the States, where the tall dollars lie, punk rock appears increasingly unlikely to generate the wallet-playing power necessary to maintain anything more than a hair-palmed handful of local scenes.

The commercial failure of punk, however, is actually its biggest victory – not that it was ever intended to succeed on a big scale in the first place. Dodo fad status is now guaranteed, and the danger of punk being taken seriously is past. Now the true subversion of Sneak-Impact can begin.

DEAD ZOMBIES

When the big media first started coming onto punk rock – a good five years *after* rockers did – it was met with a hateful curiosity usually reserved for Idi Amin stories and tank truck/school bus collisions. The English had the first round with this "new" phenom, and they went after it like a full-moon cheetah with a sticky membrane.

"It's true that these youths have little or no future, economically speaking, other than the dole," wrote one London observer as he waited for an operation on his impacted colon, "but that hardly serves as an excuse for the aggressive attitudes and mindless violence these so-called 'punks' glorify in. No matter what their claims, it is most decidedly *not* our fault."

Thank you, observer. A press agent couldn't have said it better. "Mindless Violence" (M.V. … I think that's when a dead zombie hits you over the head with a frozen carpenter) is everybody's favorite daydream pastime, but despite its attractiveness, it doesn't have any real staying power. It's that us-against-them mentality that made punk appear *real*, a genuine threat to everybody's underpants. Here's this Limey limp-lip steaming up his monocle in fear of crazed hordes of 18 year olds wielding razor-implanted chew-sticks breaking down his door and dropping Fizzies in his fish tank, when the worst thing most of them would even consider doing is giving him the finger behind his back. Tremble, tremble.

Honky-baiting was punk's first big breakthrough. A bunch of jerks who communicated strictly by rumor suddenly became a Movement, or, as those tea-brains over there like to call it, a New Wave. Community councils throughout England, fearing M.V. and upside-down haircuts, cancelled all punk shows at public venues, thereby creating a Cause, and the ever-astute BBC banned the Sex Pistols' first single, neatly falling into the band's plan and creating a Number-1 smash with no airplay.

FORKLIFTS

Things rapidly got out of hand. The Pistols, premier bad boys around town, went on a rampage. They were dropped from their first record label – which paid a small fortune and piles of comic books to get them – for molesting company secretaries and pissing in the boardroom. Not satisfied, they signed with another company for a huge advance and were immediately dumped there, too, mainly on reputation and repercussions from the previous incidents, although singer Johnny Rotten's well-publicized description of the company's president as "a shiny-faced piglet stuffed with old shoes" may have had something to do with it.

Other bands immediately tried to out-punk them. The Vibrators planted roadies in the audience to throw bottles at them. This backfired when the lead guitarist caught one in the forehead and, instead of casually muttering "things go better with Coke," leaped into the crowd, swinging his guitar like harvest time in Bulgaria. The Clash arrived at one gig on a forklift and promptly ran over a cop's foot. Best of all was the Stranglers, whose gimmick is simply RATS, tossing a few dead ones (complete with little collars inscribed with the title of their LP to the fans. All very cute until bassist J.J. (Jean-Jacques) Burnel reached into the box and got one that wasn't quite dead yet. Surprise! That's one finger he won't be sticking in his nose for a while.

The publicity blitz resulting from all this craziness swept the country, and in the ensuing Hula Hoop fever, the early polarization was cast aside. Members of Parliament began showing up wearing Buzzcocks decoder rings, and Princess Fatso revealed a secret longing to have Johnny Rotten sniff her saddle

PINBALL MONEY FOR LIFE

American punks aren't nearly as demonstrative as the Limey slimes. They don't need to be, having *invented* the whole shit-fling back in the '60s. Besides, look what happened to Iggy. From the Stooges' phalanx grunge to Bowie's pop kitty-cat. Grrr, purr, yuck.

While their philosophy of life was once described as "somewhere to the left of whoopee!" by renowned punk thinker Jason Robards, Yankee punkers

– having to deal as they do with a monolithic recording industry that's nearly impossible to manipulate from the outside – have pretty much played it straight. Straight into oblivion, because they ain't got a chance.

It's one thing to freak out a dipshit little country like England, but it takes a mighty big safety pin to stick it to the USA. Local scenes are little more than rusty flashes in the pan of obsolescence, and nationally, don't expect to see the Heartbreakers playing Yankee Stadium real soon.

But that's okay. As much as I'd like to see the Ramones make enough pinball money for life, mass acceptance of punk rock would immediately consign the whole idea to Lake Erie silt status. If this anti-chord alley slop becomes commercialized and competent musicians start to tinker with it, it'll become just another boring toy. Barbra Streisand reading dupa poetry at CBGB's, Paul Lynde performing pinhead take-offs on *Donny & Marie*, Poco adding steel guitar to "Beat on the Brat" and scoring their first hit.

Nope, the only real success punk rock ever had was as a reaction-inspiring fad, a Commie pet rock, and as a fad it's already over the hill. None of the 10 million punk records that come out in the next few months are likely to make it, and in a year the whole public drool will be forgotten.

And that's as it *should* be, because the above-the-boards death of punk is the only thing that will keep it alive. The true hardcore punks, the moron saints who would still pour Mad Dog on their french fries even if nobody was watching, will become even more embittered, inventing even more disgusting insults to the music biz. The next generation of punk rock will probably be a little-known Japanese band, Mass for Amputees, pushing a garbage truck full of M&M's over a cliff and recording the impact for their debut album, *Eat Around The Bad Spots*.

Like the Stranglers say, "It's better than being down on the streets/or down in the sewer/or maybe on the end of a skewer."
October 1977

Rot Your Teeth, Not Your Mind

Life is just a big restaurant of cruelty, and every day they change the menu. One never knows what to expect from the crumbs of life, and that goes double with the stuff we so love to pack our greasy faces with. The only sure thing is that if you like it, it's bound to be bad for you.

The question is, is junk food really all that bad? Shit, yeah, why do you think they call it dope? The only real identifying characteristic all these goodies have is their promise of Nutritional Doom. If the grease and sugar don't get you, the preservatives will.

But there are worse things in life than mere doom and there are definitely two sides to the issue. Let's take a look at the plus and minuses of junk food:

DISADVANTAGES	ADVANTAGES
1. Teeth like Keith Richards	1. Ladies like Anita Pallenberg
2. Udder-chin	2. A more complete understanding of the cow mind.

3. Diabetes	3. Shoot up whenever you want
4. "Empty Calories"	4. Ideal for empty minds
5. Invisible plaque	5. Better than visible plaque

The Dog Ate It

Junk food is like everything else: The only way to find anything out is to eat it. Eat it raw. All of it, fast, under sedation if possible.

You may or may not already be familiar with some of this lovely crap-eat. Due to the bizarre marketing procedures followed by the major food fascists, in which the eighteen residents of Porkyville or Togotown decide what the rest of the country will swallow, products appear in different areas at different times. Also, I was curious (bloato) about some of the more baroque Taste Sensations unknown to my buds, and figured this was as good an excuse as any to give 'em a try. My digestive tract begs to differ.

The one thing the scientific eater must be forewarned about is: *Don't try all of these at once* like the foolish author. As I recline here on my little platform, the bottom half of my body replaced by a tube leading to a sewer, there's only one thing I can say: IT WAS WORTH IT!

Biohazard: Eat At Own Risk

PIZZARIA: Typical of the time-honored Blender Approach are these profane crackers that are supposed to duplicate the flavor of pizza. While Too-Much-All-At-Once is a proven junk-food ideal, you can only take it so far. At this rate, we'll soon be seeing Three-Course Meal Chips, Entire Cow Mix, and New Car Smell Twirls.

DIXIES: Right after Nabisco released these adorable drumstick-shaped crackers, there was a reported epidemic of legless pigeons in Atlanta. If they come out with something called Wingies, I'm leaving the country.

POPT SNAX: Voted the Most Devo Food of the year, these X-ray flavored bits are supposed to be a sort of artificial popcorn. While the makers brag "no nasty hulls," I say "insult to injury." Bring some along to your next artificial movie.

STARBURST: These are the fruit chews that squirt berry slime down your throat when you bite 'em. A woman friend of mine told me to try chomping down a pack of these before I ever asked her to do "that" again. *Now* I understand.

CORN KORKERS: Recommended only if you have some leaky corn.

CASA PUERTO PORK RINDS: Declared a cruel and unusual snack food in 17 states, these taco-flavored slips of I'm-afraid-to-guess are at best a firing squad for the taste buds. Blindfolds, please.

HOSTESS KRUNCH BAR: Big chocolate wafers in a cute plastic wrapper that strongly resembles the straw in a bear wallow.

DISCO'S: Blaring from the shelves like some unspeakable Japanese junk food, these dancefloor-flavored chips do not have a good beat. You *can* boogie to them, but I prefer reliable Mexican bottled water for that particular step.

FREEZER PLEEZER MINT ICE CREAM SANDWICH: Show *yer* pink! A new low for the food coloring industry, the first pink ice cream

188

sandwich looks like a particularly bad reproduction from *Hustler*. So sissy-looking you want to challenge them to a duel.

LITTLE DEBBIE "ZEBRA CAKES": Little Debbie, a Shirley Temple-styled snout-with-eyes, whose picture appears on all her fearful products, is the Bad Seed of junk food. Her only appeal is to those poor unfortunates who can't afford Hostess. These mongoloid cake-things use the type of grade-Z chocolate that tastes like essence of paneling and a truly pornographic filling. Here's my vote for childhood diseases.

COOKIE CRISP: Better you should feed your kid a snowmobile than such a ridiculously sweet cereal. Give 'em this and next they'll want Birthday Cake cereal.

LIGHT DAY PANTY LINERS: These dainty wafers are so thin, you could stick them on our face for a razor cut. Awfully weird flavor though; I can't quite put a finger on it.

SHIVER: A totally flat chocolate mix you add to ice water; the only shiver you'll get from this is a shiver of recognition when you see something floating in a canal.

PENGUIN FARM CHOCOLATE CHEESE: Once a dormitory specialty at various PCB-infected schools in Michigan, this crud is now becoming available to non-captive consumers as well. With the consistency of the bottom of a compost heap, it should only be served on strawberry hamburgers.

SKINNY MUNCHIES: Diet-minded fools might like these crouton-flavored crunchies that contain only 59 calories a bag. Only thing is, the *bag* itself counts for 50 of the calories.

Edible But Forgettable

SWISS WEDGIES: With a vague taste ranking right up there with Prevailing Winds, it was necessary to hire a psychic to find out the true flavor of these sporty triangles. Although she solved a handful of murders and predicted two assassinations, the best she could do on these was "fragments of JFK's skull."

FIDDLE FADDLE: "Clusters of popcorn with peanuts in a *delightful glaze*." Well, it's cheaper than a Funkadelic concert.

MUNCHY MONSTER LEMON CRUNCH: Ugly witches, scary goblins, mean devils and lifelike Debby Boones are included in these animal crackers sprayed with Lemon Pledge. Not bad if you can think of your teeth as tiny end tables.

COSMIC CANDY: AKA Space Dust, Pop Rocks, *et. al.*, this is the stuff that shimmies and shakes when dumped on the tongue. Real nutritious too – the first three ingredients are just different names for sugar, which is like brushing your teeth with bacteria paste. Great fun though – three licks and you're guaranteed to see Foghat.

MRS. GOODCOOKIE: One look at the sugar content of these and your pancreas will hop a freight. So fool your body. Put carrot or celery masks on 'em.

BLAMMO SOFT 'N SUGARFREE GUM: Speaking of artificial sweeteners, further studies at the Guy Lafleur Medical Center in Montreal have established that saccharin is harmful only to people with rat bladders. All of the Stones and Elvis Costello swore off Tab on the spot.

PRINGLES: When they first came out, Pringles were unfairly discriminated against as the most artificial food ever invented, so now they have a big sign on the can that says MADE FROM REAL POTATOES, YOU ASS-HOLES. What they don't mention is that these potatoes are imported from Saturn. Now available in three styles: *Hearty* (in the denim-look can, good for patching jeans), *Light* (same calories, but they float) and *Ripple*. Fake Ripples, what next?

APPLE JACKS: Only if you have a flat apple.

CRAZY COW: If you can believe the stupid cow with the porkpie hat on the box, you can believe a cereal that "makes it's own chocolate milk." But can it balance a checking account?

GO AHEAD BAR: A tasty glob of peanut butter, nuts and chocolate that's supposedly "packed with nutrition." Right, and so are window frames.

RAID ROACH HOTELS: These tangy little cakes are obviously designed for the doper market. You have to admit that a hotel for "roaches" is a pretty funny idea, but watch it with these. Drop one on the floor and it attracts all kinds of bugs.

True Taste Treats

LIFE SAVER LOLLIPOPS: Definitely an idea whose time has come and also useful for rescuing drowning flies. "Here little fella, grab a hold of this! Uh-oh, got your little wings stuck. Damn, now I'll have to lick 'em off!"

TOFFIFAY: A truly excellent new candy with caramel, nougat and a hazel nut that's sweeter than Shirley Booth's pecan. More fun than torturing Bobby Buntrock.

CHIPPERS: A yummy potato and cheese combo from Nabisco that actually succeeds in making pseudo-taters taste like something other than bed worms.

PECAN SANDIES: It's hard not to hate Keebler products, what with those hamster-faced elves sticking God-knows-what into their cookies. Sandies are just too crisp and tasty to hate though, unless you had bad experiences with your grandmother.

OREO DOUBLE STUFF: Tampering with a classic is dangerous business, but these are dee-licious without being too drastic. The only drawback is their tendency to crumble when pulled apart to get at the marrow or when questioned by police. I recommend sucking the whole goddamn thing. They melt great and it sounds just like fish sex.

NATURAL PLASTIC WOOD: A novel cellulose fiber filler that looks a lot like donkey wax. Plastic Wood adds a mischievous tang to your favorite cracker. Eat too many though, and you start to get this funny, dizzy feeling. Maybe I shouldn't have finished the whole bucket. Wait a minute, what's this on the label – "Extremely flammable. Harmful or fatal if swallowed!!"

Oh, they *all* say that.

April 1979

New Load of Metal Pounds Out Heavyweight

I really thought I'd permanently OD'd on Heavy Metal about 10 Aerosmiths ago. The thud element still had its appeal, but the bloato pomposity, overproduction and incurable solo neuroses that most of the early metal pinheads had drifted into was worse than merely boring. It was at odds with what the spirit of HM was supposed to be about in the first place. The spirit being: (*author imitates sound of radioactive eggbeater cloudburst striking a rusty John Deere thresher graveyard*).

While the BOCs and the Lizzies and the Led Squeezos were so busy going down the drain and taking all the press coverage with them, a practically unknown generation of heavyweight thrashers was staring to mature into pesthood. A Heavy Metal Revival swept England like a granite broom, and before long, they were calling it the New Wave of HM.

New Wave? Well, yeah, that's fair enough. While not as drastic departure from its secret origin as, say, the Flying Lizards are from "Hound Dog," the new stuff *is* different. These new groups let some of the hot air out of the music, keeping the songs more in the three-to-five-minute range instead of 18:32 worth of solos unraveling like tapeworms. The overall sound is thus denser and more blitzful to the ears. Best of all, though – these guys are *fast*. You can tell that they picked up on the early junk by Deep Purple, Queen, Led Zzzzz, et. al., and possibly a *little* Sex Pistols and Ramones.

The best of the lot has to be Def Leppard and their high-speed iron pepperoni sticks of bambam. Some of the other top acts: Krokus are really *something else*. How they digested blatant metal garbology so thoroughly in their Swiss home base is a mystery, especially considering the ludicrous efforts of other Eurodopes like Lucifer's Friend and the Scorpions. However it was they did it, it came out fine. Powerful riffing, a standard vocalist, and an LP cover so brilliant in its trashiness that you'd think this was a local release on some speed-freak label out of St. Louis (Grungotone). What more could anyone ask for?

Well, if you're one of those picky griddlebrains that demand actual songwriting ability, Girl is what you're looking for. Vaguely reminiscent of the two or three good cuts that the early Free somehow backed into but with more variety, their occasional swagger or pose comes off because they've still got a sense of humor about themselves. Are these guys cocky? Check out the album dedication: "To the girl that has everything, wants more ... and knows how to get it."

Ah, the joys of brute victimization!

New York maniacs Riot have been around for a while, and they're already top attractions in the UK and in Pink Ladyland. The absolute fastest of the lot, they follow in the great tradition of Northeast dizbusters like Dust, Bull Angus and Sir Lord Baltimore. Plus, their bass player's name is Jimmy Iommi, so there should be speculation as to their parentage. This band is *hot*.

Similarly heated by crazed velocity is Iron Maiden, another group making big waves in England. Their tunes come tearing out of Deep Purple's "Highway Star" era into future-now doom-throttle. They feature another

191

great LP cover, and besides, how can you not like a group with song titles like "Transylvania" and "Charlotte the Harlot"?

Last but not least is Saxon, another Limey outfit that's been kicking around for some time. They hardened their iron-wedge thongs of snap brutality with a couple of years on an English club circuit that didn't want to hear anything but punk, and it paid off. Stronger and heavier than most of the other units cited, they're on their way to superstardom overseas and will make a big dent in the U.S. charts if there's any justice.

(Uh-oh, here comes Dr. Joyce Brothers again: "Did he say justice? The author is obviously suffering from severe riff fatigue.")

It looks like this Heavy Metal Revival is going to be the Next Big Thing. Well, either that or wicker hamper surfing. Headbangers and other cool toddlers should pick up on these groups *now*, because I'll bet a million smackers and all my duct tape that these bands are going to go arty, pretentious and *bor-ing* themselves by the time they get to their third album, if any of 'em even get that far. Who wants to sit down with headphones, logarithm charts and rock encyclopedias, trying to decipher epic, triple-length studio masterworks by something as ridiculous as Krokus?

August 1980

I Call on Hoot 'n' Annie

MACOMB, IL – The Twentieth Century ground to a thoroughly embarrassed halt as I entered the home of my neighborhood hipsters, Hoot and Annie. They reside in a *déshabillé* hovel furnished in a hit-and-miss style that decorators sometimes refer to as "of uncertain parentage." Loom debris battled warped dulcimers for wall space, while child goners with names that sound like different brands of cough syrup were scattered across the floor, observing rug wildlife.

Hoot wears a cowturd hat, as is the nature of all hoots. He *means* well, but so did Jerry Lewis. Aye, he doth hoot, but he knoweth not whereof he hooteth.

Annie likes to throw on three or four long dresses and picture herself the Stevie Nicks type. Either that, or a tent city in a typhoon.

A visit to Hoot and Annie's is generally one of those Magic Moments in a person's life, like borrowing your dad's level or being presumed dead. These little gatherings, which the local *garfunken* had dubbed "hootenannies" for some arcane, small town reason, featured fools with beards and cropduster goggles honking on mandolins and paint-can bass, singing, "Whoa." The other beardlings sat on the cat hair in various postures of soulful monotony, humming along like the Limelighters in an ice shed. Someone was actually heard to mention "civil rights."

If I had a hammer ...

At the kitchen table, the hosts and two or three budding cheese representatives were smoking something that smelled like a burning heap of synthetic wigs from a hookah-style water pipe. Hoot pointed a hookah at me.

"Wanna toke, cowpoke?" he hooted.

"Hey man," I quickly retorted, "Is that thing loaded?" That one gets 'em every time. They cackled like snapping turtles in pain for a while, then forgot what they were laughing about as I quickly slipped out of the room.

When I find myself on the ice amongst this dizzy hockey team with no goalie, I start to feel like I'm the only human being presen't in a school of particularly loathsome, possibly alien fishies. And to think I laughed when my agen't tried to sell me some bluegill insurance.

You know how, on TV, whenever you see a group of airline passengers, at least one of them is a nun? Well, here I was playing Sister Morphine in the Wicker Ward and beginning to panic. In threatening situations like this, I always stop and ask myself, what would the Beaver do?

In this mess, he'd hang back and *observe*. This group con'tained more varieties of flakes than a year's worth of itchy scalp ads.

Among the more unusual species and their strange and frightening characteristics:

Farmhand — He looks like somebody dropped him and a bale of alfalfa off the top of a silo to see which would hit the ground first ... always scratching at long-term case of now-sightless crabs ... makes Eb Dawson look like Ric Ocasek.

Woman's Woman — She's the contemporary equivalent of the "man's man" ... voice quality of tape hiss ... T-shirt motto: "The More I Know About Men, The More I Want To Stab Pitchforks In Their Stupid Ugly Faces" ... enjoys untying knots.

Hep Capitalist — He's got the personality of un-gummed rolling papers ... turquoise imagination ... alleged owner of a beret.

Drug Casualty —With a ravaged face resembling an abandoned go-kart track, he'd be typecast as an amnesiac if he were an actor ... if you've got a couple hours to kill, ask him his name.

Musician — A continuous harmonica-of-the-brain ... he always has some sticky, milk-related substance on his beard, a regular facial tinkle-tail ... spends most of his time playing the world's saddest song on the world's smallest violin.

Mixed Veggies —They're the standard assortment of gutter balls and dimmer switches ... like the Mom on TV says, "These kids aren't happy unless they're murdering their clothes!" ... being virtual prisoners would be an *improvement* ... group photo caption: "Suffered only bruises and mild shock in the collision."

Bro — He's looked like a washed-up biker since he was 10 years old ... should be required to wear a "Do Not Feed The Vicious Reptile" sign around his neck at all times ... everybody thinks his name is a diminutive of "Brother," but it's really just short for "broken."

The "entertainment" continued to spill out like a bladder disorder. One of the musicians had brought along his Mr. Microphone, making him lead guitarist by default. The sound of dirty fingernails on catgut filled the air, resembling a sadistic tape loop of the opening of the Mamas and Papas' "Dedicated To The One I Love": "Before you go to bed (SCREEEECH) my baby/whisper a little (SCREEEECH) prayer for me ..."

While morbid tunes about eagles, trains and mountains turned the air

193

in the room to moosh, I tuned out the musicians and tuned in the various wined and twined conversations.

"Doesn't this town seem like a concentration camp for corn?" one hoopster asked another.

"Well, they have to grow it somewhere!" came the well thought-out reply. (It was getting hard to tell the *non sequiturs* from the wrong answers.)

". . . are you sure they were *real* robins?"

"She said she was the *original* 'Jackie Blue'."

". . . but only *six million* Americans are into ginseng."

"Sea legs?"

". . . and so he got to the top of the ladder and found out it was leaning against the *wrong* wall!"

"Well, a *floor* can be a *place*, ya know?"

"Yeah, yeah, well my favorite ball player is Burt Hooten."

That had to be our host.

As the hooting subsided and slow songs concerning pasture love and coal miners unraveled like waterlogged yarn, I recalled my original reason for coming. Simple lust. These flop parties may not be good for much, but they're always good for a couple of fiddle-dazed members of the opposite sex who, like many Major League pitchers, often found themselves in trouble early.

I tried to strike up a conversation with an overripe Mary Travers nod-alike who I had once described as "a fun couple," but she indicated that she was "really into the music." So, *squat* on *a tuning peg*, Toots. I'd hooted enough for one night anyway and besides, I think coal miners are plain stupid.

Wouldn't you know it — the next day I heard that, just after I'd left, somebody sat down right on a tambourine.

I always miss the good parts.

February 1981

Loverboy: Because They're There

Part 1: Testing

"Test, test, test ... testing, 1-2-3-4-test ... testes, testes ... hog balls!"

We're at the Office on a typical afternoon, performing sophisticated tests on the little, teeny tape recorder of possible Sears derivation that we'll be needing to capture every syllable of today's interviewee, Paul Dean of Loverboy. It turns out the little machine is good for capturing lotsa stuff – like every sound in the room magnified to car bomb proportions.

What you mean "we," Kemo Sabe? Well, you know, we being us: Editorial Assistant Kim Green (since deposed) – the brains of the operation – and over-aged Cub Reporter Rick J.

While it's true that this particular Cub Reporter has been "around" a while, he's been *off* the interview beat longer than many young crydicks have been *on* anything, except drugs.

Seems the ol' boy had a couple … bad experiences interviewing victims in the past. How bad? Well, there was the infamous cowpoke Mascara Massacree with ZZ Top, for one. This was way back in the days of the glam-rock fad – you remember, when all your favorite groups were trying to out-gay-stereotype each other.

As the talk got around to the dreaded but inevitable Image Questions, Cubby kept asking the by-then-annoyed-beyond-amusement Dusty Hill why he didn't wear eye shadow and frilly underpants onstage. It was just sup-posed to be a damn *example*, but Dusty started turning purple all over (pre-sumably) until finally, he jumped up on his hotel bed and hollered, "If we wore any of that shit back home, we'd get FUCKIN' KILLED!"

Hey Yogi, wait for meeeeee!

Then there was the now-standardized Phoner with Geddy Lee, during which the much-maligned Rush bassist saved the extremely drunk Cub's butt by giving him the poop on their *2112* album months before it was released. Ya know, we make fun of the guy (with that nose … aw, never mind), but here he was, nice enough to sit still through several Severe Beer Pee breaks and even patiently spell stuff out for the dupe with no taper. (We will not discuss the hangover.)

Or how about the even-drunker little talk with the Sweet? ("C'mon, Brian – hic! – how cum all dem little gurls wanna cop yer wieners?"). Or the Cubboid's own personal favorite, the trip to colorful Seymour, Ind., to see John Mellencamp when he went by the moniker Johnny Cougar? The crack journalist combined too many writer's-helpers and wound up passed out on the floor of his Holiday Inn room, missing the interview, the show, and the official meeting of Coug's parents. To this day, all he remembers is that it was the year Bill Madlock stole the NL batting title from Ken Griffey on the last day of the season, a bigger disgrace than even the recent Reek for Possum Queen smear campaign.

So anyhoo, here we are, years later, and Cubbis is more terrified than ever. Worse yet, he's since quit drinking and other nervousness cures make him either too stupid or scared *worse!*

'Course, this time he's cajoled/threatened/intimidated Kim, who used to have her own TV show where she routinely interviewed celebs almost daily. But little does Cubbo know that in her past, she shares a DEEP DARK THROBBING SECRET with the band. More on that later.

Part 2: First Grimace

As Ace and Cub wander into the hotel, they're met by Marlene P, of Loverboy PR, who's mucho nice but admits early on to being a Canuck her-self. As she leads us into the hotel restaurant to meet Paul, Cubaroo's anten-nae begin to peep. Something about the way she *talks*, or else he's got his undies on backward again.

Paul himself looks a lot like his pictures: tall and lean, healthy, and rather athletic looking. Got quite a jawbone – you could say he has a lantern jaw, if only lanterns had … aw, never mind.

It's not a big fancy restaurant we're parked in, but it's not exactly a dump. Only a handful of tables are occupied, mostly by soft-spoken business types who are undoubtedly buying and selling us 10 times over before the Tab even arrives.

Cubbub – who's making the *Tab* nervous by this point – starts to "set up" as kool, kool Kim makes casual chatter with Paul and Marlene. After dropping the cassette only four times (a new Cub record), he gets his machine ready and glances around at businessmen and ferns, avoiding all eye contact, except with the plants. Some things *never* change.

"All set?" asks Paul.

What a cool guy!

"R-r-ready, I think," croaks Cubly, pressing a button on the taper.

"HOG BALLS!" hollers a recorded voice loud enough to rattle the silverware in the kitchen.

Great start. Kim finds this slightly hilarious, but the mortified Cubbit needs something to cover up his blunder, *pronto*.

"How about the Letter!" *Gimme a ticket to an air-o-plane...*

The Letter is a short, nasty note from a reader in Minot, N.D., that Cubmo thought would get things rolling.

Mike Reno of Loverboy is the most conceited fag I have ever met ... it begins.

Bad idea. Dean grimaces and glares across the table accusingly at Marlene.

"Doncha think this is kinda funny?" sputters Cubbinski. "Doncha wanna show it to Mike? I thought you'd crack up! Does it aggravate you sorta?"

"I guess the brighter the light, the better the target," replies Paul ominously.

Part 3: Time Warp

Much later, as Cubbity tries to write up the interview, he has a sudden, brilliant realization.

This is boring, he thinks. What the hell am I gonna do with this? Being a cub and a moron besides, he tries the time-spit-on Q&A approach.

Rick: Reno doesn't strike you as that kinda guy.

Paul: No, he doesn't.

Marlene: No.

Kim: Uh-uh.

Paul: He was just totally bummed-out for months, you know what I mean?

Rick: Oh yeah.

Kim: Yeah.

Marlene: Like you wanna call home but there's nobody there.

Kim: Yeah.

Paul: Yeah

Rick: Uh-huh.

So much for the Q&A approach.

Part 4: The Story (First Version)

OK, back to the "present."

After a few more questions about Fans Around The World, Cubaroo has warmed up to the point where he wants to get snotty (again).

196

"Did you by any chance catch *PM Magazine* last night?" he asks Paul.

"Uh, no." (*PM what?* he's thinking)

And so it came to pass that the Cubesque One relates the following story: "There was this Canadian kid, see, who lost an arm and a leg in a farm machine. Only reason he didn't bleed to death right away was the arteries were mangled shut. So the poor kid somehow crawls onto the tractor, drives it to the house, crawls into his pickup and drives three miles to the hospital. OK? Later, they ask the kid, 'How'd you do it?' and he says, 'I didn't want my mom and dad to come home and find me that way.' Then the nurse next to him goes, 'That's what the Canadian Spirit is all about!' "

Silence. More grimaces.

"Is this true?" asks Paul.

"Oh, yeah," Cubba-hubba assures. "Is this, indeed, the Canadian Spirit?" *Indeed* – what a cool guy!

"Sounds like the Australian Spirit," he mutters. "Or the Chilean Spirit … I dunno, I can't put a finger on a Canadian spirit anymore than I can … it's like say, 'Are you proud to be a Canadian?' Well, no, not particularly. What's that got to do with anything?"

Paul Dean hates his homeland! You read it here first!

Part 5: Shot By Both Sides

Maybe we should examine this Canadian issue more thoroughly.

Why do you think Canadians get typecast as dumbos?

"Haw, haw – they do?" laughs Mr. Dean. "I'm sure the Bob and Doug thing has a lot to do with it. It's the only reference I can think of that's blatantly Canadian that's dumb and humorous."

"Yeah, I always got teased in school, just because I'm part Canadian!" adds Kim. Part Canadian? *Now she tells me!* It means Cubadub is sitting there with three actual Canucks! Well, that explains why all three of 'em missed the point of the Story. The point being not that the kid actually demonstrated a lot of spirit and gumption and all that. The point is, the kid went through all that pain and misery just to spare his parents the gruesome *untidiness* of it all, not to save his own crummy life. Now, *that's* the Canadian Spirit.

This leads into dangerous territory.

Paul: "Your mag is the king of putdowns. You're always making snide remarks and I think it's funny. You always see people writing in and saying, 'Howcum yer always pickin' on us?' I just laugh. You guys ain't exactly polite."

Cubface (disbelieving): *"Not polite?"*

"No," emits PD. "You're very opinionated. You're bound to get mad reactions and that's what you're looking for, basically. It's not a factual thing like 'Loverboy played in town tonight and everybody had a good time and now they're going to Chicago.' "

Loverboy played in town tonight, the Cubcake wrote later, and everybody had a good time …

Part 6: The Story (Second Version)

What's kinda funny (now), is that Cubarooni caught the same *PM*

197

Magazine segment again after the interview on an out-of-town station. Turns out the whole thing took place in *Ohio*, and the nurse said *Buckeye* Spirit, not Canadian.

Part 7: Paul Confesses

When it comes to listening preferences, musicians have the most hopelessly banal tastes of all. You ask your typical Limey-flash-superstar-guitar-player what he actually likes, and 9 times out of 10, it'll be Lonnie Donegan.

So what does Paul Dean like?

"Well, when I put on Billy Squier's *Don't Say No*, I thought, 'Every song's a monster! It's great! This album is huge!'*Foreigner 4* was another one."

See?

Asks Kim, *What do you think of synth-pop?*

"I like it. I really do. I wouldn't want to get stuck performing it 'cause I'm a guitar player and like to play Heavy Metal. Loud. Distorted. Overdriven Noise!

"(Synth-pop) is the kinda music I'd buy to listen to myself. I don't really listen to Heavy Metal. I *hate* Metal to listen to, but I love to play it."

Paul Dean hates Heavy Metal! You read it here first! But shee-it, then he has to go and *qualify* it.

"There are some Heavy Metal bands I like. Def Leppard, they have melodies and production. AC/DC – actually, I wrote 'Teenage Overdose' after listening to both sides of *Highway To Hell* ...

"Joan Jett I like in a really kinky kinda way, but I'm not sure what her appeal is. Her punk appeal, her curled lip appeal. I think. I don't find her sexy but she really strikes that punk chord in me."

Part 8: Dirty Tricks

"Marshall, your material sounds fresher every time I hear it."
—Teacher Rob to obnoxious student on TV's *Square Pegs*.

"OK Paul," sneers the emboldened Cubthroat, "this letter comes from Kansas City. It says, 'Loverboy's material sounds fresher every time I hear it.' What d'ya think?"

"That's great!" replies Paul.

Part 9: Inevitable Questions

What kind of image do you think you've established?

"Long pause," says Dean, after a long pause. "That's a good 'un. Let's see – fun-lovin', clean-cut, hard working, honest, responsible, reliable."

The kinda guy you take home to Mom? asks Kim.

"Exactly. We're not too crazy about that image sometimes, because we don't want to be known as the Osmonds of Heavy Metal. I think a lot of people miss the darker side of the band. We want people to know we think about more than just girls and parties."

There's more? thinks His Cubness in genuine wonderment.

Kim then asks, "What's something about Loverboy that never comes up?"

Cubford thinks – *never comes up?* Haw, haw, haw ...

Paul: "It's true that we're nice guys, but we're more than that. Some of us would like to be taken a little more seriously. We've been written off as just being nobodies. That's a little disturbing. Nice is better than not nice, but we're not just *sops*."

Part 10: The Story (Third Version)

What's really, really, *really* funny is that Cubfoot knew all along the kid wasn't from Canada. He only thought the poor guy was from Ohio. And there *was no nurse!*
[Kim Green also contributed to this article]
December 1983

One Times One Equals Some Pair!
Duets from hell!

It was another typical afternoon at CREEM's posh eddytorial digs in luverly downtown Birmingham, Mich.

Einsturzende Neubauten tapes blare, almost drowning out Bill Ho'ship, who is alternately hallering "He'p!" and "Yoohoo!" out the window at pedestrians below. Dave DiMartino has his face buried in the glacial wastleland of his desk, softly whimpering a sad song, the lyrics to which sound something very much like, " ... drummm ... supplement ... " Eddytorial Assistant Ann Marie is up on her seat, screaming "NO MO' AD COPY! NO! I REFUSE! I WILL NOT WRITE THE WORDS 'WIN BIG' EVER AGAIN!'"

Meanwhile, the author is slyly writing all this down between trips to his "private" office. Being a deranged Tab Addict-especially when the idea flow is down-and never being one to let a sleeping bladder lie, the author misses many of his fellow eddytors witticisms. He hopes.

Yes, these are desperate times. Deadline approacheth, as deadlines are wont, from "around the corner," to "almost there," way past "about that time, kiddies," right up to smack dab in the middle of DOOM DOOM DOOM. The only thing that elicits a smile from the misbegotten eddies at this point is the occasional hateful in-joke about "paying" the writers.

Suddenly, the sound of the eddytorial hatch being unbolted from the outside fills their hole with metallic scraping sounds not unlike what's playing in the tape deck, only much more melodic. The door swings open eerily, and several Mr. T-sized uniformed men rush in. After a quick sweep with metal detectors and a sawed off-staple remover, CREEM's Fearless Leader herself strolls in, views the slimy premises, somehow keeps her lunch down at the sight of what appears to be a cross between an Alien Sex Fiend dressing room and a maximum security Roach Motel, and snaps, "attenshun!"

"Whudduh concept," mumbles the author as the motley eddy crew fumbles to their very best approximation of "attention." Looks like they're gonna need some pipe cleaners.

"I heard that new Michael Jackson/Mick Jagger record on the way in today," Fearless Leader begins (amidst barely audible groans of "Not again" and

199

"Fluffo alert!", and "That's gonna be our next cover! What d'ya think, kids?"

"Wonderful," says Dave.

"Excellent," says Bill.

"Quite excellent," says Ann Marie.

"Best idea I've ever heard," adds the ever brown-snouted author.

"OK, then do it – A.S.A.P.!" FL suggests in a somewhat forceful manner, pounding her fist on the author's head. Kronk, it goes, emptily. The bodyguards form a phalanx around Fearless and negotiate her through the free-fire saccharin zone safely.

"Guess that means we'll have to scrap that Butthole Surfers cover," complains Dave bitterly.

"May be we can get Kordosh to interview the Jacksons' dog," suggests Ann Marie.

"What does A.S.A.P. mean?" wonders the author.

Meanwhile, Ho'ship is gingerly unwrapping a new razor blade. "Who wants first slit?" he asks.

The eddies, however, are silently grateful for the inspiration, which does not naturally occur in their environment. The author, in fact, is as grateful as a murder victim whose killer was caught from the skin found beneath the deceased's fingernails.

His fun reverie is shattered by the sound of his phone buzzing like a particularly objectionable answer on a game show. It's Fearless Leader again.

"And kids,' she suggests sweetly, "don't make it all filler this time, K-O?"

* * *

... don't make it all filler this time, the author writes.

Now, there are many ways of interpreting the concept of "filler." Does she mean *substance added to a product as to increase bulk, weight, viscosity, opacity, or strength?* Or perhaps *a composition used to fill in the pores and grain of wood or other surface before painting or varnishing?* Or how about *a piece or slice of boneless meat of fish?* Oh, sorry! That's *fillet!*

Just as author-face is thinking of different ways to express fillerous filler, bloated bloating, fluffy fluff, and/or megamung, the phone screeches again. Gotta oil that thing someday.

"Listen, kiddo," uh-oh, it's FL's voice. "I have changed my mind," she announces, exactly like Jethro Bodine in the famous Jethro's Magic Act episode of TV's *Beverly Hillbillies*. "That Jagger and Jackson record's a *bomb!* I have a better idea: Let's make it a Michael Jackson and David Lee Roth cover instead!"

"In a word, brilliant!" says the author, clutching at his throat as though a noose was being tightened around it.

"And I want it today, or else I'll cancel your dry cleaning allowance!"

"You got it, boss!" sez me, ruminating on the unpredictable mechanics of genius. Either that or senility – he often confuses the two these days.

(TIME WARP: At this very moment in "real" time, one of CREEM's art jammers tiptoes up to the author's desk with this actual story in one hand and a bloodstained sledgehammer in the other.)

"Hey, dirtball," she squeaks politely, " We need another 14 lines in the basket case of an intro."

"14 *lines*?!" wails Tabman with mock interest. "Haven't the readers already suffered enough?"

"Fergit those knuckleheads!" she announces with a wink, not knowing her every word s being added to the article. "We got *priorities*!" (GAME OVER)

Hmm, now that we've got that settled, let's see ... Sonny & Cher, Jan & Dean, the Righteous Brothers, the Eurythmics, Dale & Grace, Friend & Lover, the Captain & Tennile, Chad & Jeremy, Hall & Oates, Bachman-Turner Overdrive ...

I dunno about you, but this author does not want to even *think* about these people, much less write about them.

October 1984

Bambam: SPORTS

'Real life would be a lot more fun
if you could hit a foul ball and still be up'

Baseball '77: Foul Tips

It looks like another comic-book year for Major League Baseball, and the season's hardly begun. While there still hasn't been anything to compare to last year's hijinx (Astrodome rained out, Monday rescuing the flag from the Symbionese Liberation Army, Wilbur "No-Knee" Wood lending new meaning to the word "grimace"), there have still been some great moments. The power failure in Anaheim that plunged the stadium into total darkness after the White Sox had sent one batter to the plate was like a ghostly preview of the Sox' future. Bill Veeck said later that his life passed before his eyes.

Another aesthetic triumph was the Yankees' new method for choosing a starting lineup: Drop the players' names in a hat and pick the order blind-folded. Chris Chambliss may set a new record for RBIs by the eighth batter.

But all this hilarity aside, the top story of the new season was Lenny "Don't Call Me Punk" Randle's dugout KO of Texas manager Frank Lucchesi. Not only does he leave Lucchesi stunned and bleeding profusely all over Bert Blyleven's batting gloves, but then he runs out to center field and starts doing wind sprints like nothing happened. Who needs Mark Fidrych?

At any rate, it looks like we're in for another interesting season. Listen, if they can sell World Series tickets in Toronto ("Rose hurt sliding on tun-dra"), then *anything* can happen. Including these predictions, painstakingly researched by the author, using his 1974 copy of *Who's Who in Baseball* and a table of random numbers. (You got a better way?)

NL West

1. Cincinnati: This could be the last big year for the Reds, and it's going to be a tough one at that. Another series of unnerving trades has brought them three questionable pitchers at the expense of dependable players like Perez and McEnaney, but even considering that and the fact that Rose and Bench are hurting, the Reds are *still* better man-for-man than anybody anywhere.

2. Los Angeles: With the best pitching in the West and Rock Monday now on full-time flag duty in center, the Dodgers could win it except for one thing: They always choke. With half the team recovering from injuries or L.A. Schlock, they'll always have one foot in the second division.

3. Sam Diego: Ray Kroc, Padres owner and McDonalds kingpin, went after new players like they were so many cheeseburgers and put together a nice team. In a year or two, they're going to be World Series material, but not this season.

4. Atlanta: The Braves finally have some muscle with the addition of

Burroughs, Matthews and Montanez, but even with Messersmith, their pitching is suspect.

5. Houston: It looks like rain in the Astrodome again. Houston has everything balanced on last year's crop of amazing rookies. At least half of them will bomb out.

6. San Francisco: ABC-TV's cancellation of The Streets of San Francisco earlier this month was the final blow. What a waste of chrome hot dog Count Montefusco.

NL East

1. Pittsburgh: The Pirates can back in to first place this year, as the Phillies gradually disintegrate. They have no problems with their hitting, and their newly acquired bullpen should keep the pitching at least so-so enough to pull it off. No chance against the reds or Dodgers, though.

2. Philadelphia: Injuries and defections among key players have left last year's quiz-kids full of holes. Look for the Phils to do a Boston and disappear early.

3. Chicago: Wishful thinking aside, the Cubs' bizarre pre-season trades may have somehow cancelled out each other to produce a fairly interesting team. Murcer is having a field day in Wrigley Field, and if what little good pitching they have comes through, Chicago could again top the .500 mark in baseball's worst division.

4. St. Louis: While one barstool-brain I know thinks the Cards are going to win as some sort of collective last gasp, I don't know. They do have the great Al Hrabosky, but one hot dog does not a weenie-roast make.

5. New York: With their all-star pitching developing snags and Kingman still mad at the world, the brightest development on the Mets is the acquisition of Lenny Randle, who may add some belligerence to these weak sisters.

6. Montreal: despite the addition of Cash and Perez, the only things Canada's good for are hockey and mooses

AL East

1. New York: Even if the Yankees spend the entire season bickering with each other about who has the biggest paycheck, size just doesn't matter. Who's gonna beat 'em? Their only competition will come from K.C. or California in the playoffs, and their oppressive pitching advantage should get them past that. The Series, however, will demonstrate the weaknesses of patchwork teams like the Yanks.

2. Boston: When you're in the same division as the Yankees, it's like the next best thing to being there. Bill Campbell might push the Red Sox past Cleveland, but don't watch too closely.

3. Cleveland: The Indians' pitching staff can match N.Y.'s on a good day, but their bats produce too many zeroes. A run-producing trade with someone like Minnesota could make all the difference.

4. Milwaukee: The most improved team in the East, they have a classic collection of great sports names – Jamie Quirk, Sixto Lezcano, Robin Yount – *this* is the stuff that baseball cards are made of.

5. Baltimore: The Orioles are fast becoming the Kansas City A's of the '70s. (Sell 'em to Charlie Finley.)

6. Detroit: The Tigers could move up a couple of slots if Fidrych heals and they keep hitting. Watch out for Dave Rozema, who's being groomed to be the next Bird.

7. Toronto: Not that bad for an expansion club, they could become the real thing in a couple of years.

AL West

1. Kansas City: Despite all the millionaires humming "Happy Trails" in the background, the Royals have more than enough to repeat this season. Some better hurlers are going to put K.C. in the Series one of these years.

2. California: The Angels used their dollars much more wisely than the Yanks and they're going to be a constant threat. With Joe Rudi fronting a booby-trapped offense behind two of the best pitchers in the world, anything could happen.

3. Texas: The addition of Campaneris brightens up a basically ho-hum team. Far too boring to win.

4. Minnesota: The Twins may have had the highest batting average in the league, but the loss of Mary Tyler Moore is going to hurt. Another case of questionable pitching makes all the difference.

5. Oakland: With new players being added every day, the A's just might end up with a pretty good team this year. Then again, they might stink. Who cares?

6. Chicago: The Sox don't look half bad right now, but when your big bats include guys like Eric Soderholm – the only player to *foul* into a triple play last year – you have to wonder.

7. Seattle: If there was no such thing as the Mariners, Bill Veeck would have to invent them to keep the Sox out of the cellar.
April 1977

'77 Season Redux: The Golden Fungo

As Joe Garagiola once said while sitting on Yogi Berra's face mask, "Baseball is a funny game!" Yogi was laughing too hard to reply, having just removed the Wet Paint sign from that very mask. Watta prankster!

The real question though, is funny-strange or funny ha-ha? When we took our last look at the bat-brows and mitt-mouths a few months back, who would have expected the strange events of this season? Two Chicago teams in first place. The Reds kidnapping helpless vets from the Old Pitchers Home. Reggie Jackson getting a candy bar named after him (Butterfinger). Gene Autry issuing regular leaky basement reports. And of course, the whole world demanding to be traded.

With all this weird stuff going on, it was time to Assemble The Experts and let them figure out what's going to happen. So with promises of hot nights and ballerina tights in East Moline, we tediously spell out for you, the stupid idiot, just what the diamond dunces have in store for the rest of the season. Yogi would *love* that.

NL West

There ain't much to say about Major League Baseball's worst division at this point. Anybody with half a walnut can see that Houston – with its quiver-inspiring gang of sluggers like Roger "And Out" Metzger, "Dead" Ed Herrmann and Wallopin' Wilber Howard – making the lofty Astrodome look like just another dingy Shell restroom, are bound to overtake the pitching-depleted Dodgers. That is, if the Padres and iron-armed Randy Jones don't take it all.

So with the race pretty much wrapped up, all that's left to decide are the recipients of the much-coveted Golden Fungo award. According to Wilber Wood, winner of last year's Fungo for Fattest Pitcher With A Shattered Kneecap, the award "changed my entire life. I bludgeoned Ron LeFlore's mother with it." That's the spirit, Wilby!

Following are this year's NL West nominees:

BRUTE SPEED: Gene Tenace (S.D.) for his inside-the-park single against the Braves.

BEST NICKNAMES: Doug "Eat It" Rau (L.A.), Enos "Transatlantic" Cabell (Hous.), Rowland "Principal's" Office (Atl.), and Elias Sosa "What" (L.A.).

BEST NAME NEEDING NO NICKNAME: Biff Pocoroba (Atl.) – It sounds like somebody who throws anvils at speedboats.

WORST TASTING SURNAME: Mark Lemongello (Hous.)

UGLIEST HR HITTER: George Foster (Cin.) Looks like somebody put a crawdad in his jock while he was balancing a lathe on the bridge of his nose.

ERIC SODERHOLM MEMORIAL FREE-AGENT AWARD: to Reds' Prez Bob Howsam for trading his entire "pitching" staff away for some outstanding WHA? draft picks.

ME TOUCH GUY: Reggie Smith (L.A.), who punched out Muhammed Rick Reuschel for beaning him on the leg.

MILLION DOLLAR ARM: Pete Rose (Cin.), for his spectacular throw from third base into the stands during a Reds-Giants game at Riverfront, which his son caught with a minnow net.

RIPLEY'S BELIEVE IT OR NOT: Don Sutton (L.A.), for carving the entire Old Testament into one side of a baseball using only his belt buckle.

FANS WITH MOST ADVANCED SENSE OF THE GROTESQUE: to the Dodgers' fans for giving Boog Powell a standing ovation whenever he draws a walk.

BEST QUOTE OF THE YEAR: Mario Soto (Cin.): "Not much money, but I no want to work so I play baseball."
August 1977

Baseball '78: There Goes the Shutout

Dave Kingman will hit an entire ball-bag out of Wrigley Field, tipping the senility scales at last on Jack Brickhouse, who, instead of croaking his usual "Hey HEY!" will flip out and start screaming HOLY TITS!

Charley Finley will sell the A's at the last minute to a group of soybean tamers in Disco, Ill. The team will be renamed the Disco Mofos.

Los Angeles will perform like complete shit and Manager Tommy La "Kinda" Sorda will start babbling about Dodger Poo.

Cardinals owner/boner Augie Busch, envisioning himself the Liberal Hero for rescinding his player grooming edict, will decriminalize marijuana in the Redbird dugout, provided it's kept out of sight in club-provided "Augie bags."

These are just a few of the startling predictions that our expert baseball panel (a sofa mechanic, a studio audience applause-meter technician and an official Topps baseball card smeller) has made for the 1978 season. Sparing no expense once again this year, we brought in diamond dopes from as far away as Peoria Zeller and the Galesburg Research Center to spell out for you, the dummy eating Muke Chex out of your batting helmet, the how's and why's of the game of glorified foul pops.

Seeing how last season these very same cleat-clowns picked the White Sox to play Hank's Moped of Moline in the World Series, there's no sense steaming up you face mask over our genius selections. As Jim Wohlford once said, "Ninety percent of this game is half mental." And the other half is 150-proof.

National League

The sound of the Dodgers choking will be the loudest noise in the NL West this year. Burt Hooten's permanent pucker will get so pinched that he'll make only small sucking sounds for words, and Rick Monday himself will have to be snatched from irate fans trying to burn *him* in protest.

Nothing will help, though, because L.A. is due to be punished for crimes against the laws of averages. Nearly all of their regulars played way over their heads early in the '77 season, and that fact, combined with the Reds' collective impersonation of little Artis Gilmore in Dreamland, gave them the flag despite their post-June convalescence. The addition of questionable reliever Terry Forster isn't going to make much difference if certain key players don't repeat their super seasons. Look for half of the 30-homer club (Baker and Garvey are my bets) and half of the starters (Tommy John and Bert the Twert) to slip this time out.

Having been a Cincinnati fan prenatally (if not sooner) may cause some slight prejudice for this writer, but I believe the Reds are ready to stomp all pindicks once again. This season may be their swan song, what with several of their stars inching over the hill, but a full year of Tom Seaver carving out new insults to the strike zone and the team's renewed determination to make the Dodgers lick the bitter basepath should be enough to take it.

Nobody else in the West appears to have a shot at the title. You can cite Houston and San Francisco's soon-to-be-traded pitching and the Padres' over-rated burger patrol, but all three are a year or two away from serious consideration. Probably, Atlanta will win it on the strength of Biff Pocoraba's name. Candy dealers everywhere will be deluged with requests for Biffy-pop popcorn and Almond Pocorobas.

In the NL East, this could finally be the year that *nobody* wins in baseball's most snore-provoking division.

There's no reason why Philadelphia shouldn't repeat. Although they haven't improved any, none of their competitors' additions are anything to throw monsters at. But if Steve Carlton falls off any or Greg Luzinski's beef farm stops producing, the Phils could finish as low as fourth with their highly suspect pitching and mostly mediocre infield attack.

There's never been any reason why Pittsburgh shouldn't knock off the Phils, but something always crops up. This year it looks like the bullpen, which can't possibly overcome the loss of Rich Gossage. The addition of Bert Blyleven and another good season from John Candelaria should help that situation some, but Candelaria in particular looks like a huge, overcooked broccoli sprig in the late innings.

There's no reason the Cubs shouldn't embark on their perennial fourth-to-first-to-fourth tour of the division again this year. Manager Herman Franks still seems like the kind of guy who would plant a minefield in hope it would grow into a gold mine. The presence of Dave Kingman should add 20 points to Bobby Mercer's average and Bill Buckner is off of his pogo stick. But Chicago's pitching staff is as predictable as a hogtoad on Beaver Day. If Ray Burris had a consistent season, one other starter besides Rick Reuschel came through and Bruce Sutter stays healthy and doesn't put on any more weight, who knows what might happen?

Speaking of who knows, St. Louis is another team ready to move up at the first sign of Philly-nillies. Like everybody else in the East (except Montreal, of all things) the Cardinals are all set but for pitching. The acquisition of All-Star clutch hitter Jerry Morales in a great trade highly uncharacteristic of St. Louis should really help run production, and if the youngsters live up to their potential the Cards might have better things to do come October than to throw out their Trac II's.

With the strongest starting rotation in the division and the best young outfield in world, the Expos should not only top the .500 mark but could easily move into the first division. The muttering Mets, Met-like as ever, have a few more years of relaxation before anybody has to take them seriously again. The again, maybe *Nino* will have a big *April.*

Ha ha ha, isn't baseball cute?

April 1978

Baseball '79: Best Position — Prone

Maybe 1978 wasn't exactly the most arresting baseball season ever played, but it did have its moments. After all, anything would have looked slow after '77, what with Chicago experiencing temporary world domination and everybody and his den mother socking 32 homers because they were using hot dog ends for baseball cores.

But '78 did bring Rose's Streak, the Yankees/Bosox playoff, the amazin' A's (for a while), and a two-team winning binge early in the season that saw the Sox and Cubs combine for 28 victories in 30 games. The Cards we will not mention. Also, there were the usual unforgettable sights like Bobby Murcer arguing about a call after he was the fourth out in a weird, pointless double play.

Speaking of pointless, our expert panel bit the bitter shin guard again last season, giving us a .300 percentage over the last two years. Listen, that's better than Jean Dixon's been doing lately (Zapruder assassinated?), and besides, we really thought Toronto would turn it around. So here they are: faultless, thoroughly researched and based-on-hallucinations picks for 1979:

NL East

1. I'm only picking the Phils by about one booger, and it's more like to come from the face of Steve Carlton than the Rose Nose. Far and away the best hitting and fielding team in the division, Philadelphia has practically no starting pitching and an iffy bullpen. Plus, Something Is Going To Go Wrong with these guys because teams that look good on paper inevitably start to *fold* like paper after a while.

2. Pittsburgh: The question here is not whether Prker will have a great year (he will) or whether Rennie Stennett is healthy (who cares?). The Pirates have to get better pitching to edge the Phils, meaning a comeback by John Candelaria and continued good work from Blyleven and Robinson. Add a revival by one of their dribble-ball throwers (Reuss, Rooker, Bibby) and they might just make it.

3. Montreal: The addition of starter Bill Lee and reliever Elias Sosa probably aren't enough to push the Expos past the Big Two, but stranger things have happened. As the great baseball philosopher Jim Wohlford has often noted, "Ninety percent of this game is half-mental." If the Expo starting eight can forget Canada (sounds easy) and play like a team, be one the lookout for pennant-crazed mooses.

4. Chicago: Ah, the Cubs finally – (author is struck with brick and awakened).

Barry-fucking-Foote? Whoopee shit. The Cubs don't look any better and with Sutter having reached the on-again/off-again point in his career, there's nobody to carry the team over the rough spots except Sluggin' Sammy Mejias. Third base is shaky with Ontiveras coming off surgery, and Scott and Putman gone; right field could be a joke is Murcer can't overcome his fear of white flying objects; newcomers Jerry Martin and Ted Sizemore might hit .240 between 'em. Personally, I'm going to ignore all this and groove on Kingman.

5. St. Louis: The Crumblin' Cards have a good chance to pass the Collapsin' Cubs this year, but mainly by default. They can't hit, they only occasionally catch a moving ball, and their left-handed pitchers accounted for a spectacular four wins last year. Hey're not quite as bad as they look,

but don't unplug the respirator just yet.

6. New York: Sure is nice to have the Mets to kick around again. Wotta buncha spitmarks.

NL West

1. Los Angeles: What's fast becoming baseball's most hated team can't help but back in to the flag again this year. Losing Tommy John will hurt some, but they had more starters than they knew what to do with anyway. With Terry Forster coming off tough surgery, the bullpen appears doomed, but that juts puts them on the same *Jaws*-endangered rubber rafts as the Reds and Giants. At least they'll get *dirty* this year.

2. San Francisco: Almost, but not enough. That's the Giants' story again this year. The best starting pitchers in the league, but there's not way Jack Clark and Vida Blue can goose them team the whole first half like they did last year. Good enough to scare the Dodgers, though, and A Scared Dodger Pouts.

3. Cincinnati: The incredible stupidity of the Red's front office has finally run this team into the ground. No Pete, next-to-no pitching, and a starting lineup full of questionable attitudes all should leave Cincy fighting it out with the Padres for a first-division finish. I still love the Reds almost as much as the Sox and Cubs, but I just can't play third or pitch for them. My best position is prone.

4. San Diego: These guys look a little bit better every season, and this might be the year they make their move into actual contention. Tremendous pitching, but that essential sound of ball striking bat is heard in San Diego about as often as snowplows striking roller skaters.

5. Houston: The return of superstar Cesar Cedeno will help the Astros some, but not enough to make them any more than J.R. Richards' backup band. That's okee-doke with me – I think they deserve eternal last place for their part in the invention of Astroturf.

6. Atlanta: The Braves weren't going anywhere anyway, but if they don't sign Rookie of the Year Bob Horner, Ted Turner's cable-TV system may as well show *Rick's Boxing Buff Show* as this hopeless squad. Of course, when nothing else is on, reruns of dropped pop flies, botched double plays, and multiple relievers in the first inning do have a certain Wrigley Field sort of charm – especially at 3 a.m. on drugs.

Post-season Poop

If the series is a snooze, there'll be new episodes of *Mork & Mindy* on by then and if that won't do ya, then you can got out and stand under a leaf all week.

April 1979

Baseball 1980: No Balls, One Strike

It's that time of year again, sports fans. No more wondering who a point guard is supposed to point at. No more trying to figure out what happens if the blue line melts. No more Indoor Soccer. No more Iowa AA Girls Flyweight Swim Meets. No more Celebrity Tennis Tournaments. *Ice fishing?* Never happened.

Best of all, it'll be months before anybody again has to a make a Sunday afternoon disappear by pretending to watch the New Zealand Junior Luge Qualifying Runs. Now we can all sit back in our favorite wallow, snap open a cool one, light up a hot one and spend this weekend as God and Abner originally intended: zonked deep into the Baseball Zone, beyond boredom and oblivious of anything that takes place outside those long white lines. You know, real life would be lot more fun if you could hit a foul ball and still be up.

Speaking of foul balls, the 1980 season stumbles underway with the threat of a May players strike hanging over it. This hovering anxiety of incompleteness somewhat queers one's initial enthusiasm (not unlike certain no-fun methods of birth-control: The Bitter Squeeze Method, The Aim-It-At-The-Wall Method). In either case, you just have to get down and *not think about it.*

Since not thinking is our calling card, it's time for our Fourth Annual / Totally Accurate / Can't Miss / Based on Duck Migration Patterns Major League Baseball Predictions. Once again, we've tirelessly scoured the area's Skid Rows, clown schools, chemical-dump souvenir shops, and drug-rehabilitation agencies' list of hopeless cases to put together our Panel of Experts (an easy out, an easy lay, a one-man team error, and a permanent case of On Deck) to assist you, the hit batsman, advance around the choppy infield of life itself.

Will our Expert Panel – which now has a resounding cumulative batting average of .063 for correct predictions (not including a devastating .000 in post-season play) – take the third strike looking again this year? Hard to say, fans. But to play it safe, don't go betting all the money your local utility is paying you for your excess windmill power on any of these picks. Save those pennies, and in about 15 years you'll have enough for a brand new lightbulb!

NL West

1. Houston: This team makes me puke, but I'm picking them just to get all you Red-haters off my case. Ryan, Richard and Niekro are too inconsistent for the Astros to put together a convincing Murderer's Row of a starting rotation, and those fastball pitchers have a way of getting drilled by good hitters. Even though the entire *team* barely edged Dave Kingman in the HR race (49-48) several players were hitting way over their heads. Besides, *Houston?* I say move 'em to Dallas – they've already got a J.R.!

2. Cincinnati: The Reds appear to be making a remarkable transition from the Big Red Machine of the '70s to the Young, Fast & Scientific Red Machine of the '80s. The fine mixture of contact, speed and power in the lineup – not to mention George Foster, the dominant bat in the NL – will have to try to offset some liabilities in the field and a pitching staff reminiscent of the White Sox for its youth, potential and clumsiness.

3. Los Angeles: My total hatred of the Dodgers and everything they rep-

resent has been well documented in these pages (not that I ever read about it or anything). The pitching staff is still iffy despite some excellent free-agent additions, and the rest of the team has definitely lost that lovin' feelin'. "...And it's gone, gone, gone, whooooa whoa." What this squad really needs is a *new producer*. Let's get Mikey to try it!

4. San Diego: The Pods, the *Pods*, the PODS!! Can you believe it? I can see the headlines now: *Pod Fear Sweeps West*! Whether or not they're going to be lifeless Pods again this is season is *anybody's* cheeseburger. An entertaining new infield of Willie Montanez, Dave Cash and Aurelio "Alrighteo" Rodriguez join ace shortstop Ozzie Smith, Dave Winfield (himself) and a couple more pitchers on a tear that will surprise no matter what they do. Hey, did you hear that Winfield wanted a McDonald's franchise as part of his dryly humorous new contract? The Catch: Dave's a vegetarian! Ha ha, Ronald, the cat's out of the bag. Or is it a horse?

5. San Francisco: Gimmie babies! The Giants management is bragging about the addition of Rennie Stennet and Jim "90 percent of This Game Is Half-Mental" Wohlford to a club that dissolved into teardrops in late '78 and never recovered. Just off the record, I *dreamed* the Giants were gonna win it this year and want it in print just in case. That was the same night I dreamed Kristy McNichol gave me a million dollars. Hey, I was *worth* it!

6. Atlanta: Relief pooch Gene Garber said it best: "What this club needs is a little sickness." The addition of The Mad Hungarian – my personal hero – to a ravaged bullpen adds a little positive sickness, and Chris Chambliss is a nice guy and hit that one homer and everything. But *really*, when you see the higher-up dumdums continually squabbling with budding superstar Bob Horner and nonsense like that, you can see this team is going nowhere. Next Week: Van Halen!

May 1980

Baseball '81: High and Inside

Here we go again. It says here on the map it's Spring. Tweeting and pussywillows, big deal. Sap and hornets, oh boy. Kites. Floods. Baby spider invasions. *Easter Bonnets*? Wake me when it's over.

It's also the time when baseball players emerge from their winter moo-state and start saying goofy things like "Play me or trade me!" "Trade me or play me!" and "Thanks a million, Claudell!"

The zany (some say wacky) club owners are back with their annual compensation plan, which I refuse to discuss any longer because it's *stupid*. If you feel sorry for those crybabies, why not throw a party for your landlord tonight?

The *real* moment amidst all this wabbit zooting and vernal yahoo is – as every schoolchild knows – our absolutely fearless, darkly prophetic (rhymes with pathetic), based-on-trout-fat-and-squirrel-pregnancies Third (or Fourth) Annual Baseball Picks. This time for 1981, although we seriously considered predicting 1962 Twister results.

Once again, the sports staff here (staff?) (sports?) has combed the area's detox parties, worm-obedience schools, Bobby Troup fan clubs, and potters fields to assemble our famous Panel of Experts (a day sleeper, a night beeper, a bad excuse and a scarlet ruse) to help you, the stupid sissy, separate the missed bunts from the foul tips.

You want facts and figures? We got facts and figures. Although last season's prediction were all wrong again (Dottie's Knit Shop whips the Hiroshima Carp in five-game World Series), we did manage to keep our guessing percentage below .100 (.050 to be brutally exact) – which would be some kind of E.R.A., huh?

As us diamond gumshoes send out our reputations to be dry-sullied, please remember that baseball guessing, like saber-rattling, is just a silly game!

NL West

1. Houston: Last season's most exciting team should be tops again this year, although several Potential Dooms lurk. Biggest kitchen disasters are injuries to Cruz and Cedeno and the absence of Joe Morgan and traded third baseman Enos Cabell. Don't look for J.R. Richard this season, but consider the addition of Don Sutton and Bob Knepper to an already-strong staff. That's not to mention the West's best bullpen.

2. Los Angeles: Can the continued influx of hot young trotters like Howe, Valenzuela, Guerrero, Rudy Law and friends keep the old timers awake? The Dodgers' starters aren't helped any by a questionable bullpen. But more importantly, can Lopes and Garvey be arranged to die? It would mess up Steve's consecutive game streak but who cares?

3. Cincinnati: This could finally be the year that the future catches up to the Reds. A likeable team except for the front office, Cincy is reminiscent of the White Sox, with a similar group of young pitchers and plenty of room for competition at most positions. Comebacks by Concepcion, Foster and Seaver are needed and Bench *has* to play whether he catches or not. A dark horse for first ... or last.

4. Atlanta: The Braves have an excellent group of young players who finished red-hot last season, but they'll need some breaks to repeat in that fashion. Anybody who's seen Claudell Washington's stunning delayed reactions in the outfield at Comiskey Park has to laugh at the big bucks dumped on him by owner/clown Ted Turner. I don't think The Mouth knows two shits about baseball, and the dreaded Turner factor is a bigger problem than any on the field. If there aren't too many sophomore slump-outs, the Braves are strong contenders.

5. San Francisco: Hiring Frank Robinson as manager was a sign that the Giants may yet stoop to contend one of these years. Newly added vets Cabell, Jerry Martin and Doyle Alexander are as big a plus as the newly departed problem players (Knepper and The Count), but there are just too many mystery positions to expect much. Top notch 'pen (Holland, Minton, Lavelle) is a big help to questionable rotation.

6. San Diego: You have to applaud a team that unloads most of its boring vets like the Pods did. Adios Tenace, Montanez, Rodriguez, Dade, Fingers, R. Jones, Shirley, et. al. Ditto Dave Winfield (Zzzz). San Diego is starting over this year (and without Jill Clayburgh!) and prospects like Terry Kennedy, Randy Bass and the four young pitcher they got from the Cardinals make for a much more lively team. It won't keep 'em out of the cellar, though.

April 1981

Baseball '82: Trapped Balls or Dugout Itch

Looks like it's that time of year again. Says right here in *TV Guide* it's Spring. April Showers. May Showers. Raisinet showers. Icing the puck? Never happened.

Spring's also the time when baseball players emerge from reliving 1957 (or whatever they think they do off-season) and start saying unquotable things like "Don't quote me" or "George Foster … you *dog*!"

We all remember the strike, but let's not cry about it any more 'cause we're watering down our Hawkeye Gold. What we oughtta be doing is thanking that big pitching machine in the sky for removing Jack Brickhouse, Bob Kennedy and Gumhead Jr. from Chicago sports in one dramatic, unassisted triple play.

Of course, the *real* moment amidst all this pussywillow zooting and vernal quim is – as any schoolchild knows – our absolutely fearless, darkly prophetic, based on fingernail half-moon cycles and calorie guides Fifth Annual Baseball Picks. This time for 1982, although we seriously considered predicting Henry Fonda would win an Oscar, then die.

Once again, the sport spurts here have combed the area's organ-donor directories, opium/poker cults, sewage treatment plants and Salvation Army death rows to assemble our famous Panel of Experts (an apprentice manual scoreboard balk tabulator, a low-level employee of a Tater Tots testing lab, an embryonic carpet magnate, and the inventor of the test-tube doggy bag) to help enable you, the basepath face, to separate the trapped balls from the dugout itch.

You want facts and figures? We got facts and figures. Although last year's picks were all wrong again (Memphis Police SWAT team over Gary Coleman in one), we did manage to keep our guessing percentage under .100. It's now .050 (down from .063 in '81), which would be some kind of hanging-in-effigy percentage, right?

So as us slaphappy hitters prepare to "pass guess" on the upcoming baseball season, remember that hardball prognostication, like working for a living, is just a silly game!

NL West

1. Los Angeles: I sure do hate to pick the Dudgers, but what can you do? Fernando won't have as great a season as in '81, but with Hooten, Reuss and Welch right behind him, L.A. has a starting rotation second only to

Houston. Bullpen is iffy again, but full of live young arms (have you ever heard of a *dead* young arm?). Power, defense, hot prospects – they've got 'em all. They've even got Jorge Orta! But if the starters falter – and they *can't* be as awesome as last year – it's goodbye Dodger blue.

2. Houston: OK, here's the best pitching staff in the NL. Ryan, J. Niekro, Ruhle, Sutton and Knepper. Sutton is pouting again, but why worry? They've also got a superb bullpen. Only problem with the Astros is that if anything goes wrong, they're in trouble.

3. Cincinnati: The Reds have drastically altered their lineup. Their '81 outfield moved to New York for almost $29 million (!!!!!) and all they really got out of it was a new catcher and a Number-3 man for the pen. Bench has moved to third, where he's laughable at best and the new outfield (Clint Hurdle, Cesar Cedeno and rookie Householder) has to learn to play together. Very strong pitching, but this isn't the young staff's love-it-or-leave-it year any more than it is for the White Sox hurlers.

4. San Francisco: The Giants were my dark horse team until they unloaded Vida Blue last night. Without him, they go into the season with three AL castoffs in the starting rotation. OK, Renie Martin isn't a reject, but can he start? Fine bullpen, though, plus some new power, including Champ Summers, one of my faves. New arms will tell the story.

5. Atlanta: The Brave pretty much stunk last year and owner/liability Gums Turner added nothing for manager Joe Torre to play with . They do have a promising prospect in Brett Butler, and the power boys (Horner and Murphy) will make everybody forget their '81 off-season. But who's gonna *throw* the goddam ball at the plate?

6. San Diego: The Pods should enjoy another season as laughing stock of the West. Not just the NL West, but The West, *period*. New offensive acquisitions Gary "Can Count To At Least One" Templeton and…yes *Sixto Lezcano* will help some, but the only improvement on their awful pitching staff is Eric Rasmussen's new mandibular orthopedic repositioning appliance. Now he can chew gum and squeeze the bitter resin bag at the same time. *Devastating* is the only word.

April 1982

Baseball '83: Obstructed View

Looks like it's that time of year again. Says right here in the Christy Lane Appreciation Society Newsletter it's Spring. In like an amoeba, out like paramecium – all that good stuff. *North Dakota?* Never happened.

Spring's also the time when it starts to dawn on baseball players that they must soon renounce the cosmic pleasure of lump sensations and begin to face the great Ho-Ho-Kam Park of Reality.

We all remember last season: some guy named after a bird in one league and a couple of real Birds named Smith in the other. Hint: we're not talking about Sixto Lezcano, Jose Cardenal or Brad "The Animal" Lesley.

Of course, the *real* moment amidst all this egg-squatting worm yank is our absolutely fearless, darkly prophetic, based-on-soil-erosion-patterns and the results of Jack Brickhouse deprivation experiments, Sixth Annual Baseball Picks. This time for 1983, although we seriously considered predicting the emergence of sugar, caffeine and water-free soft drinks or the *eventual* death of Arthur Godfrey.

Once again, the seam-suckers here have combed the area's collision shops, Anti-Smurf terrorist organizations, creosote pole-treating plants, and Boat Cushion Inspector Academy honor rolls to assemble our famous Panel of Experts (a bad excuse, a sly papoose, a ludicrous example of abuse, and a budding Toulouse) to help enable you, the obstructed-view seat occupant, separate the designated hitters from the desecrated Hottentots.

You want facts and figures? We got facts and figures. Although last year we missed three out of four, it was enough to send our right-pick batting average soaring near the .100 mark. Next year – who knows? – .112!

So as us hide-swatters prepare to "pass guess" on the upcoming Major League Baseball season, please remember that diamond prognostication, like "writing" itself, is just a silly game!

National League-West

1. Atlanta: Process of elimination, that's all this racket is about. It's taken only three seasons for the NL-W to go from the best division in baseball to the worst. So there's no real reason why the Braves should win it. They plainly played over their heads last season and would never have gotten off the ground without The Streak. But you can take Atlanta and L.A. and throw out the rest when it comes to serious pennant contention. The Braves still have a laughable starting rotation, but it didn't stop 'em last year. A bullpen of Garber, Bedrosian and newly acquired and oft-injured Terry Forster should help on that account. The infield and outfield are pretty much set, and that's where the Braves surpass the Dodgers. Nobody else has a pair of killers like MVP Dale Murphy and "Large" Bob Horner, with consistent bods like Chambliss and Washington to keep the opposition hurlers honest. Depth is certainly a question here, but – I dunno – I'd call it an absolute toss-up 'twixt these guys and L.A.

2. Los Angeles: The Dodgers have the starting pitching to go all the way – *if* everything works out. Valenzuela, Reuss, Welch and Hooten, plus several strong young arms and the talented but soft-headed Pat Zachary (ex-Mets) look real good from here. The Bullpen is more of a Question. Steve Howe's personal problems and the relative newness of people like Niedenfeur and Pena are big iffies. As for the everyday players, the Blue Boys plan to start rookies Brock at first and Marshall in the outfield, not to mention moving sore-armed slugger Guerrero to third. If these guys don't work out, L.A. does have depth – Landreaux, Roenike and Monday, among others. Catching is less than sensational, but the whole division is like that. Like I said above, it's L.A. and Atlanta and forget the rest.

3. San Francisco: Third place (who cares?). If the top two teams look like a toss-up, the bottom four could just as well play from a table of random numbers. It's process-of-elimination time again here. The Giants picked

215

up promo starter Mike Krukow, but gave up superb reliever Al Holland in the trade. The best of the rest are Laskey and Hammaker, two former American Leaguers who probably benefited from freshness as much as superior talent in '82. There's still quality in the 'pen: Minton, Lavelle and youngun Mike Chris. The chief trouble with S.F. is trying to replace the punch of Reggie Smith and Joe Morgan, who accounted for 32 HR and 117 RBIs last year. The Giants haven't done anything about this situation, which means that Jack Clark won't see many good pitches despite the talents of Chili Davis.

4. Houston: The Astros aren't as bad as they looked last year, but, hey – neither am I! Top four starters Niekro, Ryan, Ruhle and Knepper have hot arms despite the latter two's failure in '82. Big problem in the bullpen though – as we go to press, ace reliever Sambito may be out for the century with another elbow operation. D. Smith and LaCorte are, uh … often promising. The addition of free-agent Omar Moreno will really help the offense, though with the Astros' peep-peep attack, they have to get almost *all* the breaks to win.

5. San Diego: The Pods still have my favorite team nickname, but that's about it. It's hard to believe in this squad, no matter what you feelings are toward manager Dick Williams. Way too many of the regulars are first- and second-year players – the kinda guys whose consistency is suspect. Starting pitchers Lollar and Show were epic last season, ditto relievers Welsh, Chiffer and DeLeon. But young pitchers are notoriously uneven, so figure half of these guys to stink in '83. The everyday player picture is a bit brighter. Terry Kennedy has proven himself dependable and the addition of Steve Garvey is a major team plus. Injuries are troubling infielders Bonilla and Templeton, and the outfield is somewhat doubtful after Lezcano and Gene Richards.

6. Cincinnati: This may be the last time in print I ever admit that this pathetic team is one of my all-time faves. A shining example of what an inept front office can do, the Reds have lots of "interesting" youngsters and … uh … heard any good knock-knock jokes lately? Strong points are Mario Soto – one of the finest starters in the Bigs – and a rather talented bullpen of Tom Hume (coming off '82 surgery) and tender sprouts Price and Lesley. Good infield – featuring the great Dave Concepcion – if you can forget Johnny Bench's incredibly lousy attempts at "playing" third base. After that, we'll see how well young guys like Milner, Walker, Redus, Esasky and Householder can perform. Even though they're calling the new Phillies infield of Rose, Morgan and Tony Perez the Big Dead Machine, I think Cincy is more deserving of the honor.

April 1983

Hot Poop on Hoop Dupes

All you ever hear about in the NBA these days is Dr. J's latest insult to gravity or how neat & swell Portland's championship teamwork is. You'd think nothing else was going on besides Erving putting one in from 20,000 leagues beneath the sea while juggling living ant farms with one hand and tap-dancing in Morse code. As for the Trailblazers, if they want to be the L.A. Dodgers of basketball, boring the entire league into submission with back pats and glad hands, let 'em. It's in the script that Reggie Jackson in the form of David Thompson or Darryl Dawkins will clutch-slam them into hamburger sooner or later (or Hamburger Helper in Bill Walton's case).

In order to get some recognition for the vast majority of non-champeens in the NBA, our expert panel of sports authorities and raccoon trainers has been called to hand out awards for bad acts, crass flash and outright cases of slobbering dunk-lust. Not just anybody can grab these honors, by the way. Dave Twardzik, for example, never will because of his Tward-like name. So what if he shoots two-hundred proof from the field – a jerk is a jerk and a Tward is a Tward, as it's said. So without further blabla, we present the Silver Sweat Smear Awards ...

IT'S NOT SLEEP, IT'S REST: the Bull's Artis Gilmore, who – except on those occasions when he's motivated by a toe in the poot – looks like the ghost of a hammock.

WHO NEEDS PUMICE: Kermit Washington, after his one-punch demolition of Rudy Tomjanovich's face, casually wiped the spinal fluid off his fist with his jersey and remarked "greasy knuckles are so *déclassé!*"

MIRACLE METS MEMORIAL AWARD: The New Jersey Nets, who have racked up half of their 10 big victories when opponents were unable to find the seedy college gym they call home and were replaced by the All-Jersey City Church Organist team.

LEAST APPROPRIATE NAME: Chicago's premier hoop dupe, Tate "which way did they go?" Armstrong. Not even a potato could look as rimmed-out on the floor as he does.

CUTEST INJURY CURE: Tom Burleson (K.C.) wrapped a cut-up truck inner-tube around his twisted knee. Too bad he didn't injure his face.

BEST DICK VAN DYKE IMPRESSION: Houston's Mike Newlin, who can create outstanding floor-burn opportunities from any position.

SPECIAL AIRBALL CITATION: To the Chicago high school player who, thinking time was out, playfully duked the ball at his opponents' basket. Noting that the buzzer had not yet sounded, a humorless ref counted the basket, giving our hero's opponents a 67-66 victory.

MOST CHARMING LINE: Philadelphia's Darryl Dawkins, Dawdative center and former roadie for Funkadelic, on why he tries to smash glass backboards with his nuclear slam-dunks: "When that glass hits the floor, it sounds like the Abominable Snowman goin' to the bathroom."

BEST ARGUMENT AGAINST PAROLE: Marvin Barnes, who refused to report when traded to Buffalo until the management got his recently purchased F-16 out of hock so he could strafe Detroit.

SUPERIOR EXPLANATION OF COMPLICATED BASKETBALL STRATEGY FOR THE LAYMAN: "We've been losing primarily because we haven't been playing winning basketball," former Boston coach Tom Heinsohn.

February 1978

Weenie Earthlings, cranium pivots & the U.S. of Rick: BOOKS

HARRY HARRISON
Mechanismo
(Reed Books)

In case you've been staying up nights trying to figure out how light sabers and time machines work or the real difference between cyborgs, bots, androids and Bert Convy, *Mechanismo* is here to straighten it all out. And if you're really susceptible, it might just make you believe in this stuff too. (Except for Bert).

A well-designed effort compiled by SF whiz Harry Harrison, *Mechanismo* is inspiring. It makes you want to build a model car, if they'd only decriminalize glue. While some of the artwork is a bit on the sketchy side, most of the pics are vivid, almost believable portrayals of bizarre objects seen only in space operas or the dreams of pepperoni-addled ad managers.

Harrison's compendium is divided into sections on Starships, Mechanical Men, Weapons, Space Cities, and Fantastic Machines such as the electronic raccoon dispenser. Each chapter includes: a Plan Printout, like the schematic drawing of the *Star Wars* light saber with a corresponding list of parts that includes everything but the lightning bug on a treadmill; a File Printout of the history and development of said object; numerous color prints of the various varieties and a brief summary of the topic by Harrison.

Hardware and jargon fans will flip their cranium pivots over the abundance of freshly coined words used to describe never-invented machines, while us regular old Visual Slobs can eat up on the pictures. Several are suitable for framing and a couple even look like Jimmy Page.

The only thing I can't figure out is why Macomb, Ill., wasn't included among the Space Cities. Oh, I see, it's with the time machines.
January 1978

RICHARD SIEGAL AND JEAN-CLAUDE SUARES
Alien Creatures'
(Reed Books)

The Xenomorphs, the Metalunans, the Hydrocephalonic horrors, the Jello Curtain Rods, the crab monsters, the green slime, and, of course, the beloved It! are all here and boy are we ever invaded. Blew up Chicago, dumped sticky yellow stuff in S.F. Bay, converted Peoria to Endust, and – worst of all – turned New York into L.A.!

Luckily for us weenie Earthlings that they're all just in this here book and it's a real beaut too. *Alien Creatures* covers all the x-terrestials, monsters and fungo-creatures that have been menacing us all these years, and in fun form too. Packed with definitive pictures from all the classics (Gort emerging, Robbie the Robot meeting Earl Holliman), several lesser crawls (*Dish Drainers from Mars*) and ugly things that bite all the way up to *Star Trek* and *Wars*, any respectable Teenager from Outer Space will eat this stuff up, rediscovering weird oldies like *The Twonky* (Hans Conried's TV is possessed by aliens) and remembering great lines of dialogue past, like this chestnut from *This Island Earth*: "Our vast educational system ... now rubble."

Besides the fantastic pic, authors Siegel and Suares have provided a witty, fact-filled text plus fantastic extras like original posters and stills (many in color), and the actual page from the script of *The Day The Earth Stood Still* where Klaatu bites the dust. (Ha ha, dumb alien!)

These guys write outstanding captions to their millions of pix, too, like "upon his return to their hiding place, McCarthy kisses Wynter only to discover that now she too is an emotionless pod," or the real showstopper: "The Hydrocephalonic horrors from Mars face death at the hand of irresponsible teenagers and their car headlights." And if today's nuclear protestors really want to make 'em stop it, they oughta get smart like some of these spacers and simply turn the Capitol Dome into puppy-poop shampoo.

I'd rave this book forever, but right now I have to get to work on a low-budget project of my own I'm working on: *It Came from The Dead Laundry Pile. July 1978*

MIKE OEHLER
The $50-and-Up Underground House Book
(Mole Publishing)

Building an underground house was always one of my top childhood fantasies. (That, and somehow slipping into *The Real McCoys* episode where Little Luke ties his sister Hassie to a chair, locking them in the chicken coop, and then slowly unbuttoning Hassie's red-checkered shirt).

Even though the most complicated thing I've ever built was a grudge, Mike Oehler's fascinating new book shows that the construction of an underground abode needn't be just a daydream. Oehler, who has built several such structures and lives in one himself, provides a comprehensive text with numerous detailed illustrations that're not only easy to read and understand, but sprinkled with yukyuks as well.

There are numerous advantages to building underground other than spying on worms. This type of dwelling is much easier to heat and cool and far less expensive. It needs no foundation and little building materials and can be built by *anyone*.

Subterranean housing is ecologically sound, weatherproof, and definitely nicer to look at than crayon-box apartments and – best of all – it makes you that much less dependent on Consumer Nation.

As built according to Oehler's various general designs, an underground house is not a gloomy, airless pit. Located on a slope or on flat land, there are endless possibilities for windows, skylights and cross-ventilation, Mike shows how to go about the entire job step-by-step, right down to milling your own lumber if you're so inclined. Also included are numerous tips on drainage, coolers, greenhouses, building codes and locating the proper materials cheaply.

Almost every question except how to add a bowling alley is anticipated and answered thoroughly in this excellent, self-published book. And needless to say, there's plenty of room for improvisation on these basic plans. Tell some bookstores clerk you want to special-order it. Tell 'em Hassie sent you.
November 1978

BERT RANDOLPH SUGAR
Classic Baseball Cards
(Dover)

Hall Of Fame Baseball Cards
(Dover)

Great Baseball Players of the Past
(Dover)

Baseball cards are definitely one of the Great American Inventions, right up there with light bulbs, Coke and *The Mod Squad*. On one little piece of cardboard, you get not only an often-hilarious color picture of the player, but his vital statistics from birthdate to RBI and usually a little trivia quiz or some useful-only-to-fanatics baseball fact as well. That's not to mention the many other uses for BB cards, such as attaching them with clothespins to your bicycle so that they flap in the spokes and make it sound like Hell's Angels in a mailing tube when you ride down the block.

Bert Sugar is one of the country's top Joe's on baseball memorabilia – and is sometimes referred to as "the guru of sports collectors." You know, guys sit around at his feet while he delivers Earth-shattering gems of wisdom about Chuck Connors' great triple of '51 and such. Sugar not only knows his stuff, but he's got an eye for interesting *looking* cards besides the mere dribble of historical importance.

And there sure are some visual treats here: the skinny young Ernie Banks (who needs *Good Times'* J.J.?), Warren Spahn with a beat-up Milwaukee cap and the glazed expression of a pitcher who has just walked in the lead run, the mouth-watering deco cards of the '30s (with their colorfully shaded and contoured backgrounds of stadium walls and nearby skyscrapers), and the pop stoicism of the early cigarette and Cracker Jack cards.

The all-important backside of the card is also reproduced, so you can check out Great Stats of the Past or bone up on playing tips like the oft-quoted flip of the 1933 Left O'Doul card: "Strong Wrists Are Necessary."

In a similar vein, Sugar has just released a book of 32 postcards, each featuring a superb photo of old-timers like the Babe, the Goose, the Rabbit or the Big Train. These are great for just plain looking at or better yet, for sending cryptic baseball messages to fellow Diamond Dopes.

But the *real* fun with these books, if you ask me, is tearing out the cards on the dotted lines. It's therapeutic as all hell and when you're done, you've got all these neat baseball cards to amaze your friends and generally fool around with.

Excuse me while I go look for some clothespins.
April 1979

LOOMPANICS, UNLTD.

One is always hearing about books on fake IDs, tax avoidance, self-sufficiency sills, space colonization, tapping the black market and other fun subjects that aren't generally covered by your local Book Nook, but *finding* them can be next to impossible. These books aren't exactly as commercial as this month's Harlequin Romances, and some of them almost guarantee harassment from local authorities and nose-cases.

The solution to getting your hands on this straight-forward, exceptionally useful and sometimes illicit information is Loompanics Unlimited Book Catalog. As the introduction proclaims, here are more than 500 of the "most controversial and unusual books ever printed."

The ultimate source for "anarchists, survivalists, mercenaries, drop-outs, black marketers," and who knows, maybe even rock critics.

Some of the subjects covered include Survival, Privacy, Police Science, Computer Crimes, Retreating, Paralegal Skills, Booze, Drugs and you name it. Well, okay, there's nothing on buffing Venetian tiles, but that's about it.

A random sampling of some of the books available includes: *How To Make Your Own Professional Lock Tools*, *How To Steal A Job Stopping Power Meters* (with a special section on Meter Creep), *The Self-Publishing Catalog*, *Uninhabited Pacific Islands*, *Principia Discordia* (of *Illuminatus* fame), *Detective's Private Investigation Training Manual*, *Nuclear Survival*, *Wood Energy*, *How Drivers Licenses Are Made With The Polaroid Camera* and *How To Hide Almost Anything* (sorry, no chapters on pride or erections).

Besides containing do-it-yourself manuals on almost anything anyone would *want* to do themselves, there are a few more esoteric numbers as well. There's *The Health Hazards Of Not Going Nuclear* (a stumper, that), *Why Has America No Rigid Airships?*, *Just Add Water* (on dehydrated bread, cookies, soap, Jeeps, televisions, Fire Departments), *Techniques Of*

Harrassment (excellent revenge on "Big Brother types) and the one *I'm* sending for today, *How To Start Your Own Country.*

The U.S. of Rick — I can see it now.

The 150-page, illustrated catalog sells for only $2, and it's highly recommended for tolling up to ignore our government, culture, etc. — particularly during the National Dreamland of this revolting disco election year.

September 1980

JANE ROCHESTER

Dream Weaver

(Valueback)

I was waiting, as usual, in the remedial checkout lane around the corner from the non-toxic section at my local supermarket when this oversized Valentine caught my eye. It appeared to be an entire romantic novel in the slash 'n' paste tabloid style we've all grown accustomed to: big color pictures, little red hearts, mucky angelwipe and even advertisements – all for only 99 cents.

This 70-page tearsucker turns out to be the second in a hoped-for series from Rhapsody Romances. It must've been a major production, judging from the tons of credits within: Set Designer, Graphics and Location Consultants, Vice-Presidents of marketing, and – most of all – Fashions by J.C. Penney. (How did we already know that?)

The story concerns Halley Beaumont (daughter of Hugh?), a fashion weaver, new chump in town, and "the only girl named for a shooting star." I'd estimate her slurpy count at 94.612 – the kind of gull I'd like to sit on a lot and listen to croon "I love you, Ranger dearest" all night long.

Anyway, she's lurking around the museum one afternoon, looking for ideas to rip off, when she spots a potential Mr. Right, male model Gabriel. If he was on TV's *Ed Sullivan*, they would only show him from the kneecaps down.

Stupid comet-face decides to follow him around the museum.

(Hey! Dumbshit! Remember what happened to Angie Dickinson in *Dressed to Kill?*!)

At any rate, they get to chatting and he invites her to a soiree to be attended by the Big Cheeses of Fashiondom. (I bet she goes!)

Sure enough, at the party she meets Isabella, "the Ruler of High Fashion." Take it, Jane!

"Gabriel and Isabella talked about Halley as if she were a store mannequin, but their manner was impersonal. They did not mean to insult her."

Oh, sure, just because they say our heroine has the charm of a shoe caddy and the intelligence of a butane curling wand, it's *no big deal*, right?

A couple of martoonies later, Gabe and Halley sneak off to fool around on the staircase. They assume the popular "migrating waterfowl" position, which goes great until Gabe calls out, "That's not me, that's the banister!"

Time out for a full-page blurb from Zsa Zsa Gabor: "I used Zsa Zsa's Beauty Cream Z-II religiously. It actually removes those fine lines and wrinkles that crop up after you're 28."

Yeah, right, the dread Age 28 Skin Collapse.

(What kind of a name is Zsa Zsa, anyway?)

Play ball! Uh-oh, "smooth-talking" photog Ty has her pinned between the warp and the woof of her loom! They're entering the last lap of the Powder Puff Deviant Sexual Acts Derby when Ty cries out, "That's not me, that's your loom shuttle!"

The smooth talker limps off disgustedly, looking for another garage.

Blah blah blah blah blah blah. The final scene finds H. and G. getting in to some heavy numnum on her bed.

"Let me make it clear," groans Gabe, "that I am offering once more to relieve you of the heavy burden of virginity before the wedding."

What a sweet guy!

But no dice.

"I think, Gabe, that I will be perverse and wait until after the ceremony," she sez.

Perverse, nothing! I bet she makes it with drive-in movie sneakers when nobody's around.

So much for the happy ending. There's one thing Halley said that stuck with me, though. Right after the aborted loom attempt, she thinks to herself in real big letters: "I DON'T FEEL COMPETENT TO PASS JUDGMENT ON ANYONE WHO ACTED FROM DESPERATION."

Great! Then she'll understand this review!

January 1982

More fun than a bakeoff and a bloodbath combined: VIDEO GAMES

BEANY BOPPER
20th Century
(Atari)

No trouble here. Just plug in the cart and there it is: flying Beanies and a Bopper to bop them with. No maps of the universe, no lady computer saying she wants to lick your retina, just Beanies.

Despite the beauty of simplicity, you're going to need some live eyes and angel fingers. These are *flying* Beanies, remember. They sound like a herd of commuter helicopters trying to pollinate a microwave dish. They've got great personalities and they're really fun to kill as they zoom around the screen, bouncing randomly off an ever-changing landscape of computer-nerf threats.

The object of the game is to earn points by stunning and devouring Beanies and other flying objects with your Bopper. This can be a problem, because the Big Bop can fire its stun gun only in the direction it's facing. That makes for a lot of mad activity as you work them Beanies for a seeing-eye hit.

Once you get the hang of boppin', there ain't no stoppin'.

You get to wipe out frog-bombs, tweety-planes, parachuting Drano personnel and "Faces." It's a riot, a "trendy atrocity" as some might would say.

The top bops are the benign-looking Bouncing Orange Eyes, which dance all over the screen like a follow-the-dot cartoon of "Send In The Clowns." There are great sound effects too, particularly the stunning of a Beanie: *Hum-splat.*
February 1983

What's Round & Yellow & Laughs All the Way to the Bank?

How much do you love Pac-Man? I mean *love*, like you want to have his baby or something. Enough to wear his face all over your clothes? Enough to wash your actual private body with his gnawing yaw? Have you even considered cosmetic surgery?

Avoiding the omnipresent eye of Pac Brother is like trying to go through an entire day without being exposed to a Dick Van Patten commercial on TV. You see him stuck all over traffic signs, bus windows, aircraft carriers, passing street gangs – you name it. Coming soon, the P.M. model kit, made with the Canadian in mind. It's only got one piece!

Us stick-wits certainly don't object. Of course, somebody shot out our collective porch light years ago. P.M.'s bit-eating grin is plastered all over the office, from floor to crawlspace. We consider him as big a star as Treat Williams.

It could be worse. The selling of Pac-Man kinda/sorta generated *itself* from unending waves of popularity, racking up $10 million this year from licensing alone. Of course, this was calculated before the U.S. switched from the gold standard to the Rip Repulski baseball-card standard, but that's still a lot of Repulskis one way or the other.

Concerned consumer advocates that we are, the time seemed right for the thoughtful examination of America's electronic best friend. After all, if *people* were as interesting as P.M., we'd all have people plugged into the back of our TV sets, right?

That's not to mention the human animal's crucial lack of coin slot.

CHALKBOARD (Manton): The sticker on the package screams BUY ME! I'M A CHALKBOARD! If this works, we'll soon be seeing these stickers on day-old bakery products, new brands of gum and American cars. Seriously, though, would you buy a Nazi riding outfit if it said it was a chalkboard?

TUB PET (Playskool): Did you by any chance catch TV's *People's Court* case concerning the Negligent Use of a Hose? Just imagine how you can adapt it to the wiggly Tub Pet. Court's adjourned!

FRUIT SCENTED ERASERS (Empire): All you favorite flavors are represented in these non-food items. Chili, lard, snake cud and even mung-stained tonette. The unspoken question: Who wants to erase fruit?

BALL DARTS (Synergistics Research): "They're safe! They're fun!" says the package and who can argue? Nasty, pointy darts have been replaced with Velcro-covered balls that are to Nurf what surgical cotton is to stove panels. You also get a poster-sized target to whip 'em at, free game ideas and "Bonus Fruit!" What game idea does that give you?

REAR VIEW MIRROR HANG-UP (Kent): Modeled after our ghostly pals Inky, Dinky, Mojo and Clyde, this is the '80s answer to fuzzy dice. Hang 'em up and pretend that other vehicles are cute but-vicious monsters that want to eat your auto. Alternate use: dreadnought beanbags.

FUN PAD (Prestige): I just don't get this one. What exactly is fun? And why does it need padding?

AUTOMATIC BUBBLE PIPE (Chemtoy): It's doubtful whether items this questionable should be covered by an All-American, Sugar-Free Dr. Pepper-drinking critic like me. Read the instructions and decide for yourself: "Blow on pipe, Pac-Man rises and pours out thousands of bubbles." Feeling his Cheerio's, I guess.

PUNCH BALL (National Latex): Now here's something I can relate to. When those unmerciful attacks of Nervous Vowel Syndrome strike, I take this nitrous birthday cake and pound th' muthuh. Beats the scorched-Earth policy, doncha think?

CRIB AND PLAYPEN ANIMAL GRABBER (Fisher-Price): Although these "soft handfuls of fun" bring up frightening anatomical possibilities, they're great for assigning your pet iguana as Animal Grabee. "Perfect for play," indeed.

SHOWER CURTAIN (Hygiene): This is really getting out of hand, but how can you pass up a wrapper that promises "fiber content: 100-percent vinyl?" Plunk it on your turntable and it makes great music, as long as you like "skrreeddddmmmmnnntktkchss."

THINGS YOU STICK ON THE END OF A PEN (Empire): I'm consumer testing the timeless obsolescence of this unnamed product as I write. Guaranteed by the author to be more fun than a bake-off and a blood-bath combined!

MAGIC SLATE PAPER SAVER (Whitman): KID TESTED, the package claims. Bull! Us kids have been performing tests of our own. So far, we've established it cannot 1) swim, 2) stifle yawns, or 3) reduce speed to avoid an accident.

ACTIVITY BOOK (Whitman): The single most useful invention since gyroscopic hubcaps, this 50-page collection is ideal for rainy days or just decomposing. Includes Tic Pac Toe, ghost bow ties to make, humor (Q: Why is Blinky so blue? A: He's just a shadow of his former self!), blank joysticks to color and even the recipe for an Energy Shake. Orange juice, eggs, honey and milk buds … *mmmmmm!*

BUMPER STICKERS (Video Babies): Just what you'd expect — "I brake for Pac-man," "Have you hugged your left controller jack today?" and the inevitable "If power pills are outlawed, only outlaws will show up at IHOP."

BALL POINT PEN (Empire): Sorry, not cost effective. Price is $1.50 and — no matter how you hold it — it won't point at even one ball.

PILLOW (Orton House): Almost the size of a sofa cushion, this makes excellent knee padding for vid-dickers and can also be used to feign pregnancy!

THEME BOOK (Plymouth): There's a real, licensed theme book and a fake one with pseudo-ghosts, pseudo-Space Invaders and pseudo-Italian carpenters. The punishment for such trademark infringement? Life imprisonment in the supermarket Jello aisle.

VIDEO CHAMP SWITCHBOARD (Transcriber): Not an actual P.M. item, but definitely a must. Hang it on your wall "to record names, dates and high scores. Establish the champion of your family or neighborhood!" Champion of what, lack of sales resistance?

HALLOWEEN OUTFIT (Ben Cooper): A little late for this, I know, but honestly—how can you pass up *anything* with "extra-large eyeholes?"

BOARD GAME (Milton Bradley): It says on the box this is as much fun as the arcade game. Sure. You dump a couple thousand white marbles on the board and your cardboard Pac-Man "gobbles" them. About as big a deal as the second worst helicopter crash in West German history, I'd say.

THERMAL UNDERWEAR (Union): Despite the heat-resistant waistband, this item still is not mentioned in "Fun, Fun, Fun."

GUMBALL MACHINE COIN BANK (Superior): Who needs a cure for cancer when you've got a technological development like this? 100 Pac-Man gumballs your for mere pennies, nickels and dimes! I couldn't locate any gumball refills, though, so *chew slowly.*

CANDY (Ragnar): Currently available only in sucker form.

LUNCHBOX (Kedco): Between the paint and the metal, this is a real toxic chemical waste dump of a container. Looks cute, but makes your food taste like the sweatband in an old motorcycle helmet.

PORTABLE RADIO (Norelco): Looks like a hollow-bodied bathroom scale –and sounds like it too.

CLOTHES (Various Brands): Every possible item of clothing can now be purchased with our little buddy's snoot on it. Shoes, socks, ties, T-shirts, undies, bathrobes, sweatpants, gloves, etc. That's democracy, I 'spose, but if you wear too many of these you'll look like a waterbed with a dead horse in it.

JEWELRY (Josten): For the sophisticated set, these adorable 14K gold-filled (i.e. worthless) charms, earrings and pendants are easily the next best thing to canoe practice in the rain.

COLORING BOOK (Whitman): For that special brat with the room-temperature creativity, these pix require a yellow crayon and a flexible sense of the absurd.

STICKERS (Fleer): Unlike their baseball cards, which are so fuzzy you can't tell John Stupor from his mitt, these have been a frankly unbearable success for Fleer. I keep seeing 'em stuck on everything from mirrors to fishballs. In fact, I'm gonna start wearing 'em to the office instead of a garbage bag.

TV BED 'N' PLAY TRAY (Marsh Allan): From the blip-eating fool to the folding legs, this is just what the world needed. That doesn't, however, clear up the controversy of whether this is for bed or play or both? And what do folding legs imply to you?

SOAP (Exclusive): The carcinogenicity of this electronic byproduct has yet to be determined, so don't wash everywhere!

PUPPET (Meco): Real hi-tech manufacturing job here. Take one of your old socks, sew a toothless smile to it then use it to gum the Theragran delivery boy to death for me. Pleez!

CARD GAME (Milton Bradley): Fun level of this creation? Well, it's like what the guy on *Joker's Wild* said about skydiving: "It's a lot like falling."

SHOELACES (Kenco): *Shoelaces!* That's what was missing.

DISPOSABLE BUTANE LIGHTER (Scripto): Here's my own personal recommendation. Take all the Pac-Man merchandise you can find, arrange it neatly in a heap and apply this product. Pretend they're books or records!

THE PAC-MAN CARTOON SHOW
(Hanna-Barbera Productions/ABC)

This is the first new cartoon show I've gotten any enjoyment out of since the last Presidential election. After all, considering the way cartoons are cranked-out these das, a combination of the worst aspects of *Gilligan's Space Doggies* and *Grady Kids meet and Ridicule Yogi Show* seemed the most likely product.

The sight of decent visuals was as shocking to me as the free pantyhose offer on my last box of plastic forks. Not full animation, of course, but truly interesting backgrounds that look something like the Bizarro World (in *Superman* comics) redrawn by the old crew at Warner Bros. Fine color, too – none of these flat turquoise backdrops and leaden lips.

Marty Ingels, the voice of Pac-Man, is a veteran mouthpiece of such cartoon characters as Auto Cat of *Cattanooga Cats* and good ol' Beagle from *The Tom & Jerry/Grape Ape Show*. As if I've really seen them! Yellowlips is a big wimp, naturally, but at least he's got a vague sense of humor. Top chuckle on the first show was dot-face busting somebody for "chomping without a license."

Bad guys are played by the usual ghosts — including a female sheet! — who wear derbies, porkpie belts and motorcycle gear to denote badness. Then there was the evil Pacula, a predictably dumdum take off on Dracula. This was the morning after I'd caught Jack Palance as that wacky historical bloodsucker, making the whole idea that much funnier. I mean Jack Palance? What next, George Kennedy as Bride of Frankenstein?

It wouldn't be that surprising, considering the rest of the cast. Ms. Pac is twice as ridiculous as P.M. himself, and Baby Pac must be considered a serious evolutionary mistake. They're just plain boring, and magnify Pac Daddy's twerp-factor tenfold.

Like Pacula said just before his incarceration, "Nothing worse than a dull chomp!"

February 1983

THRESHOLD

Tigervision

(Atari)

Here's a new game that's even more fun than luring E.T. into the Eat Candy Zone and then melting his crummy Reese's Pieces with rocket exhaust.

For starters, it's an E-Z Learn. There you sit in the usual partially mobile spaceship, blasting waves of missile-spitting aliens that can attack from three directions. You get six baddies per attack and 11 waves altogether, which repeat with increasing difficulty as you plug along.

Only these are not your ordinary space villains. In no particular order, you can expect to encounter barking earmuffs, rubber gulls, nuclear cooling towers, pulsating lamb hearts, dough ponies, razorblade box kites, tap dancing Chevy insignias, seeded-out grain dealer's lips, somewhat retiring carwash brushes, frozen smiles of Country & Western entertainers and topographical maps of dry counties in Western Illinois.

A particularly winning point is that the actual surface area of the targets changes as they tumble toward you, the Chevy insignias being especially hard to nail. It's almost hypnotic at first, helped along by the multicolored, ever-changing bars that border the screen to the left and right.

The only apparent drawback is that "expert" players might find too little change of difficulty between rounds. That can be remedied by switching over to skill B, where the aliens shoot *guided* missiles at your face instead of regular stooped ones.

Now if only they could add a twelfth wave of plummeting Surgeon Generals for the player to — in Mr. S.G.'s words—*police!*

April 1983

G.I. JOE COBRA STRIKE
(Parker Bros.)

OK, here's the picture: We're doing time at the G.I. Joe training camp. Not such a bad place, kinda small, maybe. Gang showers. The view stinks. But you don't have to get your skull shaved, so how bad can it be?

It can be pretty bad. An "evil" organization called Cobra (Crawl Over Barren Rocky Anthills? Call Off Big Ronnie's Attitude?) have attacked the camp in order to facilitate their planned world takeover.

They can have it, right?

Aw, c'mon, that's not the G.I. Joe spirit, little comrades! We gotta take it to these bad guys, whose assault force has arrived "in the form" of a gigantic Cobra snake! Pretty symbolic, if you ask me. I'm surprised there aren't any smokestacks or train tunnels.

This bad Cobra is squirting venom from its fangs and laser beams from its nasty black eyes in a very Kaboom-ish manner. If any of this icky stuff hits one of the recruits, he's either vaporized or beamed up to the snake, *Star Trek*-style. Being up in the slither king is *no fun*. There's nothing to do up there except scrub fangs and tell venomous knock-knock jokes.

Are you, G.I. Joe, gonna let this happen to your poor little soldier guys? Of course not! You're a commando! A lean, mean, fightin' machine! And it just so happens you've got a gun that fires missiles. What else ya gonna do, hit the Cobra with your hoe? Hoe, hoe, hoe – that's the morale we've got here!

Seriously speaking, though, do you *want* to be the good guys all the time? Rescuing Smurfette, saving Earth from total destruction or playing usher for lady frogs? *Noooooooooo way!* That's what's so great about Cobra Strike – you can be the meanies instead.

You've probably seen the TV commercial for this. You know, the one with the Jekyll/Hyde, John McEnroe/Brooke Shields announcer? Well, he's right! We all have an evil side! We *like* to stomp centipedes, break out of prison, and alienate the affections of that poor dumb ape's dream girl.

In this game, all you have to do is kick the game select switch and you, the paddle-wagger, become the Cobra! Let me tell ya' – if you think roasting recruits with your laser eyeballs is fun, wait'll you cop the sensation of spitting venom on the suckers! It's just too bad they don't shrivel up and die like Spider-Man does when he hits the pavement in *his* game.

Overall, the variety available in *Cobra Strike* is a big plus. Your precious little humanitarian side might get torn between the satisfaction of protecting your troops and the pure joy of blasting them into Endust, but hey—what are feelings when you can get points?!

If only there were a mercenary level where you'd get paid for it!

August 1983

STRAWBERRY SHORTCAKE MUSICAL MATCH-UPS

(Parker Bros.)

Here it is. The one we've all been waiting for. Uncontested game of the year. No ... let's say greatest game in the videogame history. No, no ... this is surely the most fascinating entertainment device of the 20th century. Ah, why mince words? *Strawberry Shortcake Musical Match-Ups* is obviously the single most important event in human history.

And yet ... it's a game! Many-leveled, certainly, but still an alleged source of fun. And to further throw serious scientific researchers off the track, the package says *S'berry S'cake* is for ages four to seven! Maybe future historians unearthing the remains of our primitive rec rooms will be better equipped to interpret the scope and impact of this so-called toy.

Some specifics. On your screen, you'll see a member of the *S'berry* cast standing in a perilously cute gazebo. Glenn Ford is nowhere in sight.

After a brief musical intro, you'll see one of the gang, say the impish Blueberry Muffin, all happy and smiling. Only, their bodily parts have been mixed up with those of the others. There stands little Booberry (a mite nervous, but that's understandable), only she's got Lukeberry's demin legs and the Purple Pieman's ... uh, *torso* shall we say?

This confused anatomy – symbolic of American youth? – doesn't just stand there. Oh no, it *dances* to its own personal theme song. Or it *would*, but (pleez sit down) the song is all mixed, just like the character!

Hold on a minute! We still haven't introduced the entire cast! Rude City!

First and foremost is S'cake herself, who looks a little like Shirley Temple in a snake-charmer's hat and soccer sox. Her tune is the probable theme song of the Tilt-A-Whirl in a seedy Tuscaloosa amusement park.

Huckleberry Pie wears a straw hat and coveralls. You've seen him everywhere in Collegetown, USA. His name should be Luke. "Satisfaction" in some odd minor key is his number.

Lime Chiffon wears an apparent birthday cake on her head. The life of the party, I'm sure. The rest of her is ... *lime*. Quick, the Lime Away! Her Parisian ditty would sound best as background music in a *Breakfast at Tiffany's* terrace scene.

Blueberry Muffin is highly reminiscent of Annie Oakley in her "blue" period. Her song is "On Wisconsin" done oom-pa-pa style.

The bad guy, Purple Pieman, looks like a cross between Evil McGreedy and Famous Amos, with a violet New Wave handlebar mustache. He has the best song, a Cossack hopper that makes you want to shout "Hey!" a lot and jump over fires.

Five of the swellest youngsters around, don't you think? The kids from *Fame* got nothin' on this group.

The graphics are real sharp – especially for a VCS cartridge. They're very simple, of course, but definitely edible.

Ditto all the music. This is the first cart where I've voluntarily enjoyed the tunes. They're real crisp, even – dare I say – *sprightly?* My always-mischievous fingers had trouble staying at the controls. They wanted to slam dance from the start.

Speaking of fingers, the game action is just right for the age group it's designed for. Match the bods, match the tunes, match the nose; all that good stuff. It only took me two plays to master, but – of course – *I cheated.* Shame, degradation. Just compared the on-screen tangle to the actual portraits in the directions. C'mon – I know when I'm whipped.

Plus ... the big extra: a free "Thank You" postcard featuring the whole smiling cast with little baby animals. You just fill it out and send it straight to Aunt Bernice.

She'll be tickled.

August 1983

A peek at Reek: RANGER PROFILE

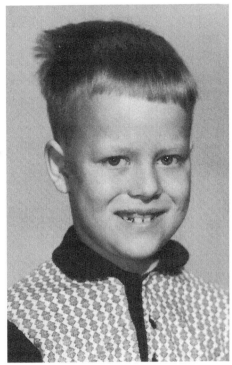

HELLO MY NAME IS
Rick Johnson
HT: six one
WT: 155
FOOD: M&Ms
COLOR: sleep
DON'T ASK ME: where the
new vacuum cleaner bags are
EPISODE OF *BEVERLY HILLBILLIES*: Jethro's magic act
HOBBIES: looking up different things in *TV Guide*
SODA: Sugar-free Dr. Pepper
QUOTE: "Two accidents in one day is no accident" – Millie Helper
AMBITION: to make people laugh wickedly at things they're too
decent to even think of.

March 1981

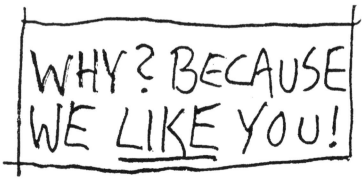

"This is my room" — LYRICS

ROCK 'N' ROLL WRITER

You didn't never want me around
so when you come lookin' for me babe I won't be found.
You didn't ever love me an' it's true,
so doncha come lookin' for me 'cos I won't see you.

But you can call me on the phone,
call me on the phone,
try to make it better,
you can call me on the phone,
baby, but I won't see you.

So now yer playin', baby, in a big rock band,
telling all the little honeys: wanna hold your hand.
You even got your record on the charts
an now you're forgettin' baby where you got your start

I hear you on the radio,
on the radio,
playin' for me baby.
I hear you on the radio,
Baby, but I won't see you.

I'm just a rock, a rock 'n' roll writer writin' reviews,
but everything I write these days is about old you.
But later maybe everything'll be all right
'cos I got your record and baby gonna play it tonight.

I hear you on my stereo,
on my stereo,
singin' to me baby.
I hear you on my stereo,
baby, and I still want you

July 1971

VANITY

Slightly shy and
not so wise,
I'm pleased
by her disguise.

Her mother
calls her Emily,
but we just call her …

Vanity.
Vanity, you surely
made a man of me.
Vanity, Vanity,
you surely made
a fool of me.

Not so young and
not so old,
she's weak
as she is bold,

and when the day
is perilous
it's she who will
take care of us.

(chorus)

Tiffany and
Ivory,
lace and
colored glass,

so slowly I surround
her with,
but still she
thinks me fast.

(chorus)

Spring 1971

CARNIVAL WIND

It's a separate world apart
at the carnival,
but the folks have left it there to rust
and it's all dark now.
Tattered strings of rebel flags,
corners where my friends would brag
how they pick up girls
and let them go.
Yes, I know.

It's a carnival wind,
blow 'til the end,
then we will see
what we used to be,
just you and me.

Old Ferris wheel only turns
in a thunderstorm,
just a creaky reminder that soon I
should be headin' home.
Something in the air is right –
brings to me a summer night
talking until dawn,
telling what we used to be like,
then we lied.

It's a carnival wind,
blowin' 'round in corners again.
Dust devils can
come to look like a man,
yes, they can.

The funhouse never seemed so dark
'til the fun was gone.
Now fears and broken mirrors a feelin'
that something's wrong.
Old tickets are no good, it seems –
only remind me of my favorite dreams,
the hours when …
Oh, to be together again
in the wind.

(repeat both choruses)

Spring 1972

SHILOH

Shiloh sky, low
clouds are gonna touch the water.
Sunrise goodbye,
shine a light upon my daughter.

Hear the sound of feet –
could it be me
that they're lookin' for?
Pass me as I die,
just some more boys
marchin' off to war.

Shiloh, Shiloh,
can't you hear the armies bleedin'?
Grant's answer has come at last,
when it's just a little time we're needin'.

On the Tennessee
a man shot me
'cause I wore the gray.
I'd've shot him, too,
'cause he wore blue,
but he'll fight again today.

I don't know why, but I know why
this boy is gonna die –
everybody runnin' so hard,
they can't seem to agree
and it's killin' me
in old Shiloh.

Shiloh, Shiloh,
I can't forgive the bloody water.
Shiloh, let me die
just so none alive forget the slaughter.

If the wind is good
then all the blood
washes out to sea,
and when I die
ten thousand twice
will be followin' me.

(repeat chorus

Spring 1971

FIRE IN THE WEST

Beatin on a tin can,
Makin' all the bambam,
Blinkin' on the way out of touch.
Daddy's in the carport
Thinkin' 'bout an airport,
Dreamin' of an empty black box.
Last night was like a flipbook,
dawn was just a fishhook,
fire in the West.

California cuckoo
Lookin' for a new shoe,
Walkin' on a big white line.
Something's gonna go wrong,
call her on the telephone –
909-9909 –
just about to scream,
tears in the museum,
fire in the West.

I know you been a long, long way,
but you ain't even near the end.
Revealin, you feelin, me,
Let's hear about yer big bad friend.
Surf across the Mersey and stop there,
let it ride, let it ride.
You can sleep on the stairs –
no one will know yer there.

Residue of impact
shattered on yer Cadillac.
SOS won't get you nowhere,
bompbompbomp yer gonna get a stompstomp –
better stay away from there.
Jumpin to conclusions
Causin' you confusion,
fire in the West

March 1972

PRAIRIE SUNSET
[*title stolen from Walt Whitman*]

Look out my window at the prairie sunset –
every color I see reminds me of you.
How can you be blind
when you know I'm lookin' for you?
You don't look at me, you look right through.

No, there ain't nobody playin' outta tune no more,
and no one's writin' songs to sing.
Just hearin' you laughin'
is like music, and I dream
of harmony that I could bring.

BRIDGE   I know that you
                    didn't wanna do
                    didn't wanna do the things I planned.
                    but when it came to me
                    know all I was ready to see,
                    all that I could see, was a thought I had.

Clouds are rollin' over past the hillside
but I feel your presence like the sun.
How can you laugh
when you know I'm wailin' for you –
your laughter is the footsteps in the dawn.

(repeat bridge)

February 1971

HIGHWAY IN THE SKY

Been ridin' on this highway now
for nearly twenty years,
and I believe I'm comin' closer
to the answer for my fears.
Just like a clean restroom,
in the trouble of these times,
the Lord has paved these roads
and so I'm followin' His signs

> Gonna ride ride ride
> on the rocky mountainside,
> ain't no blessin' upon my weary soul.
> Gonna ride gonna ride
> on this highway in the sky
> and I know that I won't get there 'til I die.

Oh, the weather has been rainin'
and the highways getting' slick,
but we're ridin' with a driver
who knows each and every trick.
The coins I bought my ticket with
Said, "In God We Trust,"
and though I change my destination
I'm still ridin' on His bus.

> (chorus)

Well, the wheels keep on turnin',
and the headlights burnin' bright
are enough to bring some Heaven
in to anybody's night.
So if you hear that horn a honkin'
out in front o' yer home
ya know you better get on board
cause tomorrow we'll be gone.

> (repeat chorus)

May 1972

Mondo, modo, dodo & doo-doo: Q&A

By Andrew Lapointe

for rockcritics.com,

Explain growing up and how you gained an interest in writing about rock music.

I was a big music fan from about 1962 onward, when I was introduced to Top 40 radio. I had my ear glued to the radio every year after that. I mean, I was a heavy-duty fan—it was like I was training to be a rock critic or something. I started seeing actual rock magazines with writing in them in the late '60s and thought, "Hey, I'd like to do that!" And I started working on that kind of stuff, but I didn't have any success with it until 72' or 73'.

What other magazines did you write for? Did you write for anything before **CREEM?**

Yeah, quite a few, actually. The one that printed the first thing was *Fusion* out of Boston. And I don't know, that was in the early '70s. And the men's magazine, *Oui*, I used to write little bits for them, because they paid really good, you could get $50 for 10 minutes work. And just a bunch of different music magazines – *Phonograph Record Magazine*, a whole bunch of local music things too.

Describe your writing. Where did you get that kind of humorous style and all those ideas?

Well, the main place I copied my writing style from was *Catcher In The Rye.* J.D. Salinger. I adopted that first-person kind of style in high school in the '60s.

I read all the early rock magazines like *Crawdaddy, Mojo-Navigator,* early *Rolling Stone,* and so that had a certain amount of influence on me, especially *Crawdaddy,* because that's where Richard Meltzer wrote, and he's kind of my hero.

You also wrote a lot about junk culture, like TV, and you would review toys and candy and beer and stuff like that. How did you come up with writing about those kinds of things?

Well, I just thought they were funny subjects that I could write really good stuff about. I loved to write about TV, so I did a lot of that.

Was TV a lot quirkier in the '80s, and a lot easier to make fun of, than something today?

Well, that's the way I was thinking. It seemed all the rock magazines were starting to become like corporate magazines, and still are. But some of these "for young men" magazines they have now, like *Stuff* and *Maxim,* I've seen writing in those that remind me of the *CREEM* writing—pretty off the wall and profane. They're almost having a revival [of that style] in those "for young men" mags.

But did the writing change at all?
Well, you can see it getting more – I don't know what word to use – less completely insane as time goes by. There was a lot less of totally making fun of everything and a lot more taking things seriously. Not nearly as much fun, I think.

When I'm reading your stuff, I sometimes get lost.
Yeah, me too!

Like, "What the hell are you talking about?"
Yeah. I would do anything to get a good line into the piece. You can tell that after a while, like, "How desperate is this guy to get that one stupid line in there?" You know? Like just write a whole big long paragraph about all kinds of unknown things just to get the phrase "Rodeo Blooper Tape" in there somewhere. That sums up a lot of that stuff actually.

You mentioned Richard Meltzer as being an idol. What was it about his writing that you liked a lot?
The idea that I got from him was that you don't take anything seriously and you make fun of everything, including the stuff that you really, really like. Once I adopted that point of view, that changed everything. So, that was very crucial for me. And when I was teenager, I had read all his stuff in the old *Crawdaddy* magazine, and it was really kind of intellectual and stuff, but then he changed dramatically. His humor is great; I think he's one of the finest rock writers ever.

Who else influenced you?
Well, Lester Bangs, of course. But, boy, a lot of people and stuff, say *Mad* magazine, too – Oh, God ... the rock magazines that were popular then, like the old *Hit Parader*, and I mentioned *Catcher In the Rye*. But let's see, besides Lester and Meltzer, a lot of John Mendelssohn. Oh, you know something that I talked about with Lester once was a couple of influences that we shared, which were Beatnik writers like Allen Ginsberg and Ed Sanders. Those were other big influences on me. See, I was already writing in a style not totally dissimilar from Lester's before I was even published. And he and I had these same influences, so that affected us both in the same way to churn out these three- and four-word phrases that just bounce off each other and try to stand alone without punctuation. That's what Lester in particular got from Ginsberg.

Ranger Rick's Final Ride:
LAST REVIEWS

STEVE KILPATRICK
Westside Crop Circles
(Expeditious Production)

So, this one morning I'm lounging around in my usual frenzy of pro-crastination wondering if I can get away with calling into work *flora* again when the mail carrier drops off a package. My long-awaited Rodeo Blooper Tape, I wonder, or maybe that oxycontin poultice from the AARP Pharmacy By Mail? Too small to be the re-engineered CPR mannequin I'd ordered from *Taboo*, damn it!

After checking to make sure the return address isn't the Al Aksa Martyrs Brigade, I open it to find a CD, of all things. A *CD* – how playfully decadent! Included inside was a letter, the usual Xeroxed bio crap and – get this – a check made out to me! Now this is what I really call a message, Bullwinkle!

Little did I suspect it would, after a token five-minute skip-listen, turn out to be this really cool album from a Michigan singer/guitarist charmingly naive enough to pre-pay an out-of-state writer. I was very moved. I think I felt something like a deaf man hearing a busy signal for the first time.

Steve "the K" (as he joshingly calls himself) makes truly rootsy, free-ranging music with lyrics that vary from suicidal ideation to a cry for help. From what I hear, Steve's not really your typical good field/no hit musician with smoke in the cockpit and a corn appliance up his butt. After a check-ered employment history that's included everything from narco-urologist to maverick worm-bed attendant, he's wound up pushing tote for the Teamsters by day and blasting through the local bar circuit by night, playing every three-chord classic in the four-chord songbook.

Though the K's idea of a big night is coming in third in a wet beret contest, the years of rock 'n' roll slavery have paid off big-time in a major heap of melodies and vocal/guitar stylings that attempt to insult every genre out there, from rockabilly to country porn to angelic harmonizing from a guy old enough to own an inert complexion.

What I'm trying to say here is that *Westside Crop Circles* is one hell of an album, maybe even two hells. But don't just take my word for it, listen to what the critics have to say. After on-target comparisons to Roy Orbison, Tom Waits, The Residents, Brian Wilson, Chris Isaak, John Fahey and Andy Partridge (of the Partridge Family, I think) Jim Santo of *Outersound.com* tags Steve as "an artist who clearly doesn't give a fuck about commercial success." *Cosmik Debris*'s Shaun Dale raves that our hero's "capabilities obviously exceed his judgment," while internationally acclaimed rock critic "GPR" of *Ear Candy* calls it "coherent."

So while you're ponying up a few bucks to send Steve the aforementioned K, let's take a quick cut-by-cut look at some killer sounds while I'm applying for the Disabled List retroactive to forever.

1. "Brothers-In-Law" kicks things off in a cool, mid-tempo style that boasts the closest thing to a professional drum kit you'll hear, percussionwise. Steve's groovy first brother-in-law gets traded in for a humorless new model creepo who would rather live in a cat privacy tent and gets upset if our musical host crashes on his couch longer than 48 hours. The vocal moans like Roy Orbison locked in the trunk of the Batmobile, but he lets his guitar do most of the complaining.

2: "Bruno." This EPA-registered clog-whomper features a sampled pit bull in the rhythm section and a vocal straight out of the itch-care aisle of your supermarket. Deftly avoiding a sing-songy approach, S.K. basically *pronounces* the crazy lyrics. Good idea, because trying to sing words like "Something maybe a little more appropriate to the situation but nonetheless along the same line" could eventually lead to stress fractures of the larynx. And next time, dude, try sampling the other end of the dog.

3: "Bigplan." My fave rave and the most instantly loveable number, this has an innocent-enough sounding acoustic guitar bit growing into an Amber Alert waiting to happen. The plan is to ladder-abduct a brain-damaged woman from her parents' house and hide out in the Arctic teaching her to read and write and count to 10. I am *SO* sure. The deadly/catchy "Car-o-line" chorus has been stuck in my brain for days, thankfully supplanting the dreaded "jaunty" version of "Five Weeks In A Balloon." Semi-true story! Then, stuck to the song's butt is this beautiful x-part harmony coda about the content's of his refrigerator. While the *artiste* himself insists there's "no sexual content, honest," you may want to catch him on his upcoming Unlawful Flight To Avoid Prosecution tour soon.

4: "Multi-Generational." What begins as a fairly clinical sociological rant winds up a potential end-credit track for this season's *Pimp My Improvised Explosive Device*. Steve's lyrics contend he can maintain his cool (or his lukewarm, really) in a five-generation household of *Surreal Life* rejects, while his strange psychic-ventriloquist vocal approach suggests a bad week in the Day Room.

5: "Adjustments." I hate to just come right out and describe a melody as "really pretty" without voluntarily applying for chemical castration, but "Adjustments" is that: an almost impossibly sweet tune the composer himself describes as a "lullaby about plastic titty nipples." Imagine a *Smiley Smile*-era Brian Wilson crooning about "phony nips" over a stack-o-track of TV epiphany tinkles and acoustic guitar and you've got it.

6: "Conjugal Visit." This is one of K-boy's songs with a surprise ending: Not a *Twilight Zone* flying-saucer-to-the-dinner-table kind of deal, but still. He's all "gotta perm this nose hair" and prep bribes for the guards in a very snappy post-Surfabilly kind of way for a babe with "lips like jelly donuts" when you suddenly realize *she's* the prisoner and *he's* the conjugee! Gasp! Yeah, right – we'll see what tune he's singing when Caroline's folks press charges.

7: "Worried Mind." It opens as a likely Beach Boys acid-period outtake, but grows into a stark examination of the ultimate human tragedy. That's right: God has ripped off Steve's television because, "He says I watch too much HBO." That Kilpatrick can turn such primordial misery into a holiday ranking right up there with Towel Amnesty Day should leave us all praying that Steve's talent can someday be harnessed for peaceful purposes.

8: "Smell That Rainbow." A nice, minute-long instrumental that's a cross between lyrical guitar flourish and museum-quality Hendrix nitrogen waterfall rumble, this track should carry a May Poison Livestock sticker instead of a theft surveillance tag.

9: "Me & Oprah, My Pajamas and The Pain." This wacky, slightly sprung waltz came closest to generating airplay on *Westside*'s first pressing. Critics were alternately baffled and corn-fused. While the previously quoted J. Santos dismissed it as a mere "country music parody," widely admired *BEA Entertainment* correspondent J.D. Philyaw termed it the work of "an anti-social couch potato with an Oprah fetish." Even R. Christgau's *Consumers Guide* gave it an Incomplete. Back in his surprise mode, Steverino catalogs his various sufferings and his "search for ways to try to block the pain" (the usual booze-dope-Jesus progression) when from out of nowhere comes a throaty recitation that sounds like a near-death blues singer with a dugout towel in his mouth. Eat your heart out, Rod Serling!

10: "Rough & Tough." Here's yet another late-coming shocker. You think at first it's in the mom-and-poppy vein of that other song about plastic nips (look it up yourself – I've got credit for time served). Then it turns out she's an 80-year-old captive in a hospice. So where's your ladder *now*, big guy?

11: "Me & The Bank." The most inescapable hook of the disc belongs to this airy-dairy peek at things grown-ups reportedly think about. Too bad the term "wistful" has been trashed by entire generations of singer-songwriters who think they're the pooparoo because they can whine for the cycle. But hey – we've still got pensive, doleful, disconsolate and woebegone! *Forget* all that. Me like song, you like song, too.

12: "Old-People Hours." It starts off with a niblet of Brill Building melody that I can't quite remember without sending chagrin-sniffing dogs off to uncover my *Spector Box* from the piles of *Bose Wave Thermometers*, hardcover dinghy tow ratings and parakeet training records in my junk room. It quickly develops into a fingerlickin' good fingerlicker, espousing good old bathroom humor. As if there were another kind!

13: "The Lonely Tonight." Deceptive Motown chords open a frankly happy-sounding Caribbean tweeter about, oh, you know, doom 'n' stuff. When you realize the guy's singing, "I couldn't gun down, outrun or rubdown a broken soul" over the mondo-pinata music, you'll want to speed dial the National Strategic Medicine Stockpile. The poor guy tries everything, including dynamite, Spanish Fly, a fifth of Old Spitoon, "small game full of holes" and – this is almost too cruel – *professional wrestling*. The police report will still read "failure to increase speed to avoid a ballad."

Well, there you have it folks. Please believe me when I tell you sincerely from the bottom of my heart that *Westside Crop Circles* is my absolute, all-time fave (*ring, ring* – Oh, sorry Steve, the bank says your check bounced).

Steve Kilpatrick deserves life imprisonment as roadie for a party-boat DJ. And you can *keep* your Mardi Gras tickets, wise guy.

November 2005

EMINEM
Curtain Call
(UMG)

It isn't every day that a hugely successful artiste like Eminem makes as daring a statement as *Curtain Call*, an affectionate salute to great novelty songs of the past 50 years. Excluding everything in this week's Top 10, there really hasn't been a major novelty hit by anyone other than Mr. Mathers since Weird Al Yankovic's kooky classic, "Smells Like Nirvana," in 1992. *Curtain Call*, however, could re-ignite a genre that's been on paid administrative leave since then.

Every single one of Eminem's wacky hits we all know (and love!) is included here as well as three new potential chart-ticklers. From his earliest songs like "My Name Is" (a zany mixture of vocal tomfoolery that obviously owes a debt to Charle Drake's irrepressible '62 hit, "My Boomerang Won't Come Back") right on up to his more recent smash "Mockingbird" (a sophisticated answer song to the great Mike Douglas tune "The Men In My Little Girl's Life") and beyond, Mathers doesn't need to hide behind the mask of mere parody because he's a veritable Tomahawk chipper-shredder of pop history.

When every track's a classic, it's hard to know where to begin, so I'll start off with my favorite Eminem song, "Stan," a witty celebration of great letter songs of the past. These musical missives, once the province of such minor madcaps as Every Father's Son ("A Letter To Dad," 1967) and the Four Preps ("A Letter To The Beatles," 1964), take a want-'em leap to 21st century poignancy in the hands of Detroit's merriest prankster. A somewhat melancholy reading of a letter from a fan who was an early candidate for the Olympic downhill-cutting team, "Stan" captures all of Eminem's sensitivity while avoiding excess sentiment. Also featured here is a "live" duet of the tune with Sir Elton John, the supreme novelty artist of the '80s. Though best known for his take on "Lucy In The Sky With Diamonds" (from the Beatles' comedic opus *Sgt. Pepper's Lonely Hearts Club Band*), Sir John handles the vocals originally recorded by the optilicious Dido with style and panache. E.J. isn't nearly as pretty as her, but hey – you can't tell on a CD!

Piquancy is never far off the table in the paws of a singer as delicate as Mr. M. His Top 10 smash "Cleanin' Out My Closet" is a touching-yet-zany reworking of Allan Sherman's famous 1963 hit "Hello Mudduh, Hello Fadduh! (A Letter From Camp)." With the tender portrayal of his own parents here and elsewhere on the disc, Eminem truly has acquired the type of endearing fame normally spread only by migratory birds.

"Like Toy Soldiers" is another gimcrackin' souvenir for the listener's heart. Emmy-boy takes his Wayback Machine way back to draw inspiration from Frank Sinatra's hilarious '59 gem "High Hopes." Where Sinatra is backed by "A Bunch of Kids" from the distinguished film *A Hole In The Head*, Mathers employs an in-studio Kiddy Khorus to drive his droll take on militarization in our society. But it's no comparison to his masterful "Sing For The Moment," where he borrows a trick from the collective sleeve of Buchanan and Goodman's "The Flying Saucer (Parts 1 & 2)." If you can't recall that 1956 epic, it was one of a throng of songs featuring an amusing narrative interspersed with punchlines taken directly out of other recordings. In this case, Eminem honors acclaimed '70s novelty kings Aerosmith by appropriating wiggy bits from their '73 chartbuster "Dream On" throughout. The result is so heart-rending it would make any listener want to dunk themselves in a tub of kiwi-flavored Valtrex.

If you don't care as much for Eminem's slightly serious side, fret not! Our Michigan Mirthmaker's tunes inevitably lead to an increasingly jocular frame of mind, as in "Without Me." Here, the rapster speeds up some of his vocals in the studio not unlike the unforgettable Chipmunks with David Seville celebrated #1 single "The Chipmunk Song (Christmas Don't Be Late)" from 1958. But the real laff-riot on this album is the sonically daring "Just Lose It," where M.M. throws caution to the wind by capturing some actual flatulence for the rhythm section. Talk about intelligent design!

Three brand-spanking-new tracks continue Eminem's more-recent tradition of flat-out facetious wackiness. "Fack" is a very catchy, totally rearranged take on Chuck Berry's delightful 1972 barn-burner "My Ding-A-Ling." Mathers' innate sense of dignity, however, takes the subject of human reproduction out of the gutter to a place where tiny angels cough up pixie dirt. My only quibble with the track is his slightly irresponsible suggestion of a new all-organic dwelling place for pet gerbils. Don't try this at home, kids!

The other two virgin songs are equally funtabulous! "Shake That" is a laugh-fest delivered by a treasure chest of silly voices, including wildly popular cartoon character Nate Dogg from *The Magic Bartender Show*. Plus "When I'm Gone," a doting accolade to Napoleon XIV's '66 #3 hit, "They're Coming To Take Me Away, Ha-Haaa!," the song that likely first inspired Mathers to employ humorous vocals over a primitive Casio beat.

Where does a comic genius like Marshall Mathers go from here? Well, this novelty aficionado would love to see him take it to the limit and tackle some *really* challenging influence like Sheb Wooley's stupendous "The Purple People Eater" from 1958 or maybe the great Ray Stevens' ethnically perceptive '62 track, "Ahab, the Arab." But whatever Eminem decides to put down on wax, we can be sure it will be a glorious grab-bag of inspired lunacy.

Darn him!

December 2005

About those who helped out

Like any self-respecting "staff" of alternative, music or underground publications in the '70s and '80s, contributors to the (mostly) monthly **SunRise** *magazine and the weekly* **Prairie SUN** *couldn't agree on lunch, much less music, a Movement or a mission.*

But dozens of former writers agreed to lend a hand to help resurrect early writings published there by Rick Johnson, and returned to the keyboards to type in decades-old text.

Most of the folks below had fallen out of contact in the intervening years, but volunteering to re-read, re-type and re-live some classic bits of commentary seemed like the least we could do.

Silly, snotty or both, Johnson's writing deserves to be enjoyed.

CARY BAKER is chief czar of conqueroo [www.conqueroo.com], an independent music PR firm in Los Angeles representing edgy singer/songwriters, indie rock and roots music. Prior to that, he worked as head of publicity at Capitol, I.R.S., Enigma, Discovery (later Sire) and Morgan Creek Records. The Chi-Town native also journaled all through his teens and 20s in such pubs as the Chicago *Reader, CREEM, Trouser Press, Record, Bomp, Prairie SUN* and a litany of fanzines that have long since fallen off the map. While in college at NIU in DeKalb, Ill., Baker drove to Macomb to lay eyes on Rick J., and sampled Macomb's widespread rep for being a primo party town. His wife, Sharon Bell, a former *L.A. Weekly* editor and *CREEM* subscriber/letter writer now a co-conspirator at conqueroo, assisted with the transcriptions.

Recently retired after 21 years on the executive staff of the PGA Tour, GARY BECKA is currently "basking in the sun in Florida," living off his (not dad's) financial holdings. Several future opportunities are being contemplated, but all things golf are – thankfully – a thing of the past.

MIKE "BECKOLA" BECK lives in the fetid swamps of Northeast Florida, commonly known in the area as "Georgia's asshole," and spend his time trying to download the Internet. He has not yet succeeded.

Twenty-five years past the *Prairie SUN*, RICH BORGERSON mans a cubicle at MultiAd, Inc., in Peoria, where he does electronic art quality control and archiving of product images. Married to Debbie Sue for 20 years and the father of Erik (in his last year of high school), Rich sees a glimmer of retirement in Minnesota coming into view. Then "I can finally record the one album in me and go on a tour of rest homes. If only Rick was still around to slice-and-dice it with his famed arsenal of hyphenated adjectives."

RICK CLEMONS helped run *SunRise* magazine and its assorted ventures, like Morning Star Record Service. In recent years – when he wasn't teaching writing, film and journalism at Western Illinois University – Clemons could often be found at Cady's Smokeshop in Macomb·discussing music, politics and our beloved Cubs with Rick Johnson.

STACEY CREASY, 47, was a correspondent for the *Prairie SUN* in the early '80s, after which he became an entertainment writer for the *Macomb Journal* and other Park Communications newspapers from 1982-85 and 1990-93, a reporter for the *South Bend Tribune* and *Indianapolis Star*, an editor, regional news director and publisher in Indiana, and a radio newsman and talk-show host – all before returning to Macomb in 2004 as *Macomb Journal* editor. Before moving to Monmouth, Ill., to become GateHouse Media's Regional News Director in 2006, he visited with Johnson a few times a week thanks to a smoking habit.

MIKE FOSTER is retired from teaching journalism at Illinois Central College in East Peoria and for more than 10 years has been the North American representative of the Tolkien Society. He was assisted by his daughter MARTHA FOSTER, herself a scholar and collector of '60s pop music.

Former *Prairie SUN* Champaign correspondent JON GINOLI lives in San Francisco and plays in the band Pansy Division. He met Rick Johnson face-to-face only once, by chance sitting behind him at a Kinks concert in Macomb.

One-time *Prairie SUN* record reviewer BOB GORDON has run Acme Comics, Music & Movies in Peoria, Ill., for 15 years. Bob used to write for various Central Illinois newspapers and magazines, but now spends more time with Danielle, his wife of 10 years and their three daughters.

"The Rev." KEITH GORDON for 33 years, day and night, has walked the pop culture beat, writing about albums that few hear and hyping bands that nobody cares about. It's a lonely chore, but a fate he was destined to follow from the day when Rick Johnson first sent him a Hello People LP to review. The Reverend's disembodied literary presence can be found online at [www.mondogordo.com].

KEVIN HAY worked with Rick in Macomb, Ill., as a member of the *SunRise* Collective and spent many a drooling night listening with him to various tunes of terror. Presently living in Wayzata, Minn., Hay is convinced that the government is run by the descendants of Cthulhu.

Artist and designer ROBERT JOHNSON is an accomplished illustrator whose work has appeared in *Discover* magazine and other publications. Johnson (no relation to Rick) does the graphics and layout for *Focus* magazine, published by the College of Arts and Sciences at Western Illinois University, where he also is curator of WIU's Geology Museum.

BILL KNIGHT was a co-founder of *SunRise* with Mike Mooney and George Taft in 1972, and edited the *Prairie SUN* from 1977-83, after which he was an editor at the *Washington* (D.C.) *Weekly*, then a reporter at the Peoria (Ill.) *Journal Star*. Husband to journalist Terry Bibo and dad to college student Rusty Baker, he's been a journalism professor at Western Illinois University in Macomb since 1991. Knight's books include *Video Almanac* and *Fair Comment: Essays on The Air*, plus nonfiction anthologies such as *R.F.D. Journal*. He also wrote the audiotape collection *The Edge of Knight*, edited the trade paperbacks *Midwestern Gothic* and *Peoria People*, coordinated the round-robin murder mystery *Naked Came The Farmer*, and co-authored *The Eye of the Reporter* with Deckle McLean and *The Cub*

Fan's Christmas Wish with Mike Foster. Honored by the Illinois Associated Press (Best Commentary), the Illinois Press Association (Business Reporting), the International Labor Communications Association (Best Column), and the Suburban Newspapers Association of America (Best Sports Writing), Knight freelances for publications such as *The Labor Paper* in Peoria, *Heartland Journal* in Chicago, and *Illinois Issues* in Springfield, plus WIUM public radio in Macomb. Despite editing Johnson for decades, they still got along.

TRACY KNIGHT used to contribute record reviews and short stories to *SunRise*, and is now a clinical psychologist teaching at Western Illinois University. He's also a novelist whose books include *The Astonished Eye* and *Beneath a Whiskey Sky*.

Former *Prairie SUN* publisher BILL LOVE is owner and editor of *Heartland Outdoors*, a fishing and hunting magazine he's published with his wife Linda for 20 years.

Co-creator of the *Prairie SUN* humor column penned by the Luchs Brothers, KURT LUCHS is now vice president/general manager of American Comedy Network.com, a multimedia comedy company, and editor of TheBigJewel.com, a literary humor site. The author of *Leave the Gun, Take the Cannoli: A Wiseguy's Guide to the Workplace*, he is often described as "a little bit country, a little bit rock 'n' roll, and a little bit unsuspected serial killer."

MOIRA McCORMICK is a Chicago-based freelancer and regular contributor to the Chicago *Tribune*, for whom she primarily covers underground hip-hop. Other credits include the *New York Times*, *Rolling Stone*, *Billboard*, *Vogue*, *CREEM* and *Musician*. She wrote for the *Prairie SUN* through the early '80s, and has fond memories of beer and volleyball games with Rick Johnson at the periodic *Prairie SUN* retreats in downstate Illinois. She is married and has an absolute peach of a teenage daughter (really).

SunRise co-founder MICHAEL G. MOONEY (AKA Gary Michaels) has spent the last 24 years covering a variety of news for the *Modesto* (Calif.) *Bee*. He's looking forward to the day when he can re-grow his hair, climb a tree and learn to play the flute.

CRAIG MOORE has an ongoing legend that will last a lunchtime. He's covered many bases in the music business, from AM and FM DJ, performer, recording artist, reviewer, retailer, producer and more. A contributor to *SunRise*, the *Prairie Sun*, *Goldmine*, and *Discoveries* magazines, his numerous reviews and interviews – with everyone from Carlos Santana and Steve Marriot to Judas Priest and a gleeful John Mayall (showing off his nude *Hustler* spread while a coked-out Joe Cocker tugged Moore's pant leg to tell jokes) – are the stuff of *Almost Famous* one-liners. He's also been the *subject* of stories, too, with a 40-year career as a rock singer/songwriter/bassist whose recordings have ended up on the Rhino *Nuggets* boxed set and numerous other group and solo albums on major and indie labels. As bassist with his first group, GONN, from 1966-67, Moore is also an inductee to the Iowa Rock 'n' Roll Hall of Fame, alongside Buddy Holly, the Everly Brothers, the Trashmen, DJ & The Runaways, Bobby Vee, and many more known and unknown. He owns and operates a collectible records and memorabilia shop in Peoria, Younger Than Yesterday, and continues to write, record and perform, touring semi-annually through Europe and Russia as well as appearing regularly with several local group projects.

One-time newspaper/magazine production and graphics guru STEVE O'NEILL is now a slumlord in Portland, Ore. He pines for the days of all-nighters laying out the *Western Courier* and *SunRise* magazine and listening to "Sweet Home Alabama" over and over.

Chicago's BILL PAIGE started writing about music and pop culture in 1975. Following a decade-long career as a journalist for United Press International and numerous entertainment publications (including *Billboard, Performance, Chicago Sun-Times, CREEM, VIDIOT, Illinois Entertainer, Heartland Journal*, and the *Prairie SUN*), he has spent decades in "media relations" (not to be confused with "journalism") for *Playboy* magazine, Platinum Entertainment, Legacy.com, and Mancow Muller, among many clients. He currently is manager of communications for Oakton Community College in Des Plaines, Ill.

BOB PATON, like many of his friends, has a lapsed journalism degree (Southern Illinois University) and currently works at a Peoria hospital, writing "blood" and words even more complex than that.

Ex-record reviewer STEVE RAGER gave up on a career in journalism when the *Prairie SUN* folded, thus losing the lone outlet he had for his opinions, and *Rolling Stone* or *CREEM* didn't exactly come knocking at his door. He moved from Peoria, Ill., to Columbia, Mo., in 1989 to join a surf band. The Untamed Youth released eight albums, appeared on 20 or more compilation CDs and toured the United States, Canada and even Europe. But mass stardom eluded them, leading Rager to a career as a Project Manager at FedEx Kinko's.

RICHARD RIEGEL became a lasting pen pal of Rick Johnson while both essayed "rock criticism" for *CREEM* magazine in the 1970s and '80s. Riegel is the only fellow *CREEM* writer known to have ventured out to deepest Macomb to pay his respects to the shy Swede, who eschewed the use of automobiles throughout his life.

Former *Prairie SUN* cartoonist BILL SHERMAN works in social services by day and freelances reviews and pop culture commentary – along with fiction under the name of Wilson Barbers. For the last five years he also has web-logged about pop culture "plus the occasional egocentric socio/political commentary" as the Pop Culture Gadabout online at [http://oakhaus.blogspot.com].

After years of freelancing for *SunRise* and the *Prairie SUN* before working as a weekly newspaper editor (and one stint in public relations), STEVE TARTER is now a reporter and media critic for the *Journal Star* daily newspaper in Peoria, where he also helps stage classic films at the Apollo Theater with ex-editor Bill Knight.

7668973R0